INTERNATIONAL POLITICAL ECONOMY
AND SOCIALISM

INTERNATIONAL POLITICAL ECONOMY AND SOCIALISM

MARIE LAVIGNE
Université de Paris 1

TRANSLATED BY DAVID LAMBERT

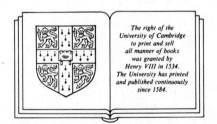

The right of the
University of Cambridge
to print and sell
all manner of books
was granted by
Henry VIII in 1534.
The University has printed
and published continuously
since 1584.

CAMBRIDGE UNIVERSITY PRESS

CAMBRIDGE

NEW YORK   PORT CHESTER   MELBOURNE   SYDNEY

Published by the Press Syndicate of the University of Cambridge
The Pitt Building, Trumpington Street, Cambridge CB2 1RP
40 West 20th Street, New York, NY 10011–4211, USA
10 Stamford Road, Oakleigh, Melbourne 3166, Australia
and Editions de la Maison des Sciences de l'Homme
54 Boulevard Raspail, 75270 Paris Cedex 06

This is a revised and expanded version of *Economie internationale des pays socialistes*
originally published in French
by Armand Colin 1985
and © Armand Colin Éditeur, Paris, 1985

First published in English by Editions de la Maison des Sciences de
l'Homme and Cambridge University Press 1991 as *International political
economy and socialism*

English translation © Maison des Sciences de l'Homme and Cambridge
University Press 1991

Printed in Great Britain at the University Press, Cambridge

British Library cataloguing in publication data
Lavigne, Marie
International political economy and socialism. – Rev.
ed.
1. Socialism. International economic aspects
I. Title   II. Economie internationale des pays
socialistes. *English*
335

Library of Congress cataloguing in publication data
Lavigne, Marie, 1935–
[Economie internationale des pays socialistes. English]
International political economy and socialism/Marie Lavigne
translated by David Lambert.
p.   cm.
Translation of: Economie internationale des pays socialistes.
Includes bibliographical references.
ISBN 0-521-33427-6. – ISBN 0-521-33663-5 (pbk.)
1. Communist countries – Foreign economic relations. 2. Council
for Mutual Economic Assistance.   I. Title.
HF1411.L364713   1990
337′.09 171′7 – dc20 89-22289 CIP

ISBN 0 521 33427 6 hard covers
ISBN 0 521 33663 5 paperback
ISBN 2 7351 00000 0 hard covers (France only)
ISBN 2 7351 00000 0 paperback (France only)

WT

CONTENTS

TABLES

Appendix: Domestic growth and foreign trade of the USSR and Eastern Europe

PREFACE

This book was written and processed through the usual editorial procedures in 1988–9, at a time of unprecedented change in the USSR and Eastern Europe. As is well known, in usual practice, the author tries to present the most up-to-date view of his or her subject, generally to the dismay of the publisher who is confronted with numerous proof corrections. I had the feeling that such a practice was no longer appropriate here. I would probably now write another book, whose title would not contain the word *socialism*, and whose content and structure would be different. However, this does not mean that by now this book is to be classified in the history section of libraries. True, most of Eastern Europe, and perhaps (probably?) soon the USSR as well, are turning away from socialism, and are eager to enter the world of the market economy. But one cannot make a clean slate of the past. For quite a long time this past will cling to the international behaviour of these countries, of their enterprises, of their people, now matter how violently it is rejected. In dealing with these countries, in helping them through the transition, the West will have to cope with this legacy as well, and to begin with, will have to know about the complex set of institutions, attitudes and mechanisms, inherited from what was called real socialism. Here, I believe, is the usefulness of this book.

This is why I have not changed the text as it was written in 1989 (the present tense in the book referring to a pre-November 1989 situation), including the wrong forecasts I made then – I was not the only one who was mistaken. I am grateful to my publishers for allowing me to add a few pages at the end of this book. There I include the most necessary update, referring to the relevant pages and sections of the main text. The most significant changes are signalled, in the text, by asterisks indicating that the reader is referred to the Postscript. I would like to add that in these reflections on the nature of the transition in the East, I greatly benefited from the intellectual environment I had in New York, during a research stay first at the Harriman Institute for the advanced study of the Soviet Union (Columbia University), and then at the Institute for East–West Security Studies, during the first months of 1990.

Marie Lavigne
May 1990

ACKNOWLEDGEMENTS

This book is a revised and updated translation of *Economie internationale des pays socialistes*, published in 1985 by Editions Armand Colin in Paris. Most of this work was done during my sabbatical year 1988–89, which I spent as Visiting Professor at the European University Institute in Florence (Italy) and as Volkswagen Foundation Research Fellow at the Federal Institute for International and East European Studies (BIOST) in Cologne, Federal Republic of Germany. The support provided by these institutions is gratefully acknowledged. I have also been very lucky to work with Sheila McEnery, whose professionalism and kindness I have greatly appreciated.

INTRODUCTION

The European socialist countries account for less than 8 per cent of world trade. However, the position they hold in international economics is much more important politically. The influence of the USSR, the second world power, its relations with the six small European countries of Comecon and the converging or diverging strategies of the members of this group towards the rest of the world, all arouse interest which goes beyond the relatively limited economic impact of their trade.

There is a wealth of information on this subject but it is still incomplete and scattered. A particular event or situation may be thrown violently into the limelight. In 1981 the Polish crisis illustrated the vulnerability of the socialist system to external disturbances supplemented by internal economic problems and social conflict unprecedented in scale and intensity. In 1982 the 'gas pipeline affair' brought to light a complex network of political and economic interdependence in East–West relations. The 'reverse oil shock' and the fall of world oil prices in 1986 suddenly shook the creditworthiness of the USSR. And, since 1986, the international impact of Soviet *perestroika* is felt in almost any field or area of Eastern international trade and finance. Thus, almost anything one states today is bound to be obsolete tomorrow, including the fact that past events are reassessed or past figures are (sometimes dramatically) corrected. With all these caveats, this book aims to present a comprehensive view of the strategies and achievements of the socialist countries in international trade. We are using the word 'socialist' to encompass what the English language literature usually calls the 'communist', or 'centrally planned', or 'Soviet-type' economies, i.e., we retain the wording used by the countries concerned themselves.

The socialist world is not included here in its totality. The socialist countries under review are the USSR and the 'Six', i.e., the smaller countries of Eastern Europe (Bulgaria, Czechoslovakia, the GDR, Hungary, Poland, and Romania, in other words, the European members of the grouping called Comecon (Council for Mutual Economic Assistance). We sometimes use the words 'the East' or 'the Eastern countries' to define this group, which is presented in its present-day reality and its recent history, that is, since the start of the economic crisis of the seventies. The 1973 oil price boom and its consequences deeply altered the nature and trends of international trade and were also to affect the European socialist countries.

The first question is: are these countries autarkical? It is often claimed that they are, especially when they are treated as a bloc following in the wake of the USSR. However, their development since the Second World War shows a growing opening up to international trade. Like market economies, they have been subject to external constraints in the seventies and eighties, at the same time, but not in the same way. The mechanisms peculiar to centrally planned economies have determined the way in which they have opened up to the outside world, and transmission of external disturbances and the methods of adjustment. A general incursion into these internal mechanisms using a theoretical framework is therefore indispensable (chapter 1).

The world as seen by the socialist countries is extremely polarised. This polarisation is governed by political criteria according to which 'the East' (the countries belonging to the socialist system) is a privileged trading group followed by 'the South' and then 'the West'. Systemic preference seems to win out over any idea of international specialisation based on comparative advantage which (at least in theory) is the rationale behind trade between market economies. Fundamental economic interests peculiar to the national economies are then superimposed onto this three-way polarisation. This has the effect of compartmentalising trade as well as of turning it in a certain direction. In each trading area, each Eastern European country has its particular balance of trading gains and losses. The priority given to the various interests as a result of this, does not always match up with the order of preference for one ideological system or another (chapter 2).

Within an institutionalised framework divided up into these three trading areas, Eastern European countries have developed with the outside world what they call international co-operation governed by the 'mutual advantage' of the parties. What is this advantage which each country seeks to make the most of? In relations with 'fraternal' countries, mutual advantage stems from prearranged specialisation negotiated through plan co-ordination. This specialisation proves to be less efficient than specialisations born of the market in capitalist countries. Why is this? Is it due to plan rigidity? To conflicts of national interest? To the imbalance which pits a large country well endowed in resources against six dependent partners? These various reasons all come together to ensure that the fields of specialisation remain at a level which alienates the national sovereignties as little as possible, even if the economic cost of doing so is not negligible. In trade with capitalist countries, cooperation becomes an exercise in seeking the most advantageous position since any markets offered to the capitalists must pay off. So, a dialogue of the deaf ensues in which the East talks of industrial cooperation while its Western partner takes this to mean compensation. Compensated trade (or counter trade) accounts only for a small fraction of East–West trade and to some extent involves the goods most difficult to sell off among those offered by the Eastern countries (manufactures and semi-finished goods already saturating Western markets). It therefore becomes a perfect example of East–West constraints. With Third World countries, cooperation means aid and assistance, yet here the principle of mutual advantage is still upheld as in the other types of trade relations. Is it possible to give one's partner real aid while benefiting from it oneself? The socialist countries usually justify themselves by mentioning the qualitative characteristics of their economic cooperation with the developing world. For more than a decade now, their Southern partners have been increasingly reluctant to take that at face value and they want to know what this cooperation is costing them in quantitative terms using the Western methods of compu-tation. Explanations have been provided, but have not laid the matter to rest (chapter 3).

For Eastern European countries international trade is an affair of state. This is why in the West they are referred to as *state trading countries* as opposed to those countries where in principle commercial trade is decided within the firm (even though state intervention can be strong here). State monopoly of foreign trade has altered considerably, especi-ally in the smaller Eastern European countries and, since 1986, in the USSR as well. It is probably the area in which the way these countries see themselves and the way they are seen by market economy countries differs most. The image of the USSR, where state monopoly has long been organised in the most traditional way, is to a large extent account-able for this. Due to characteristics inherent in state monopoly and planning, the socialist countries are not considered 'normal' countries in world trade where the obvious 'norm' is for firms to play the market and face each other armed with their competitiveness. The traditional plan-versus-market opposition here becomes the opposition between protected economies and free trade. Are the socialist countries protectionist 'by nature'? Are the obstacles which block their access to the capitalist markets a justifiable defence or a set of discriminatory restrictions? The question was again raised in 1986, in the framework of the multilateral trade negotiations which opened in Punta del Este between the members of Gatt (chapter 4).

How are we to qualify the role played by the socialist countries in international trade? The industrialised market economies are exporters of manufactured products while the Third World offers raw materials. Where then should one place the socialist countries? The most usual approach is to say that their foreign trade structure resembles a North–South trade structure in which they would be seen as the North by the South and as the South by the West, while among the socialist countries themselves the North–South relationship would be reproduced between the six Central European countries and the USSR.

This presentation, which throws into relief the trading area polarisations of the socialist countries, unfortunately ignores their major trading patterns. In fact, to the triangle of the geo-political trade poles we should add another triangle constituted by the broad categories of products which are fuelling this trade: technology, energy and food. *Technology* comes first, being the key to the internal modernisation process and as such represents the key to the advancement of the entire socialist system to a superior stage according to the most fundamental tenets of Marxist theory. Compared to industrialised capitalist countries, do the socialist countries have a structural technological backwardness which it is impossible to overcome? Should we refuse them access to Western technology or measure it out sparingly? Could they, through cooperation within Comecon, develop efficient techniques? Could they compete with the West (the North) in the transfer of technology to the South? (chapter 5).

The *energy trade* is no less important. It is shaped by the difference in natural energy resources between the USSR and Eastern Europe and by the consequences of the fluctuations on the world energy market which started in 1973. The internal developments within Comecon have been determined largely by the conditions enabling the USSR to continue supplying Eastern Europe with oil and gas. The dynamics of East–West trade have been dependent on the ability of the USSR to pay for its purchases through energy sales. Since 1986 the USSR also, like its East European partners, has had to find goods other than fuels which would be saleable in the West. Finally, over the decade starting in 1973, the oil-exporting countries have become Eastern Europe's principal partners in the South. But here too, this position has been shaken by the 'reverse oil shock' of 1986 (chapter 6).

Agriculture is the third trading area in this trinity. Here, once again, we must start by looking at the various domestic situations. The basic feature is the poor state of socialist agriculture as a whole. Yet, there is a gap between the USSR, very much dependent on grain imports, and the smaller Eastern European countries, some of which are net exporters of agricultural products (chapter 7).

Grain, oil and technology – these are the *real* motors of the international trading strategies of the Eastern bloc. Along with the flow of products comes the *flow of finance*. The socialist economies are not by nature monetary economies. The Eastern bloc countries have had to accustom themselves to the financial instruments of international capitalist economics while maintaining among themselves a trading system in which the importance of money is reduced. The golden age of East–West trade in 1970–5 coincided with an unprecedented expansion of commercial export credits to these countries, followed by financial credits. Recession in the West, born of the crisis, jeopardised the East's chances of paying these off through exports. The East's indebtedness peaked at the beginning of the eighties. In spite of the rescheduling of debt payments, a measure to which some socialist countries have had to resort, can they still be considered reasonably good risks? What specific financial restraints could affect their trade? Can they play a role in the international monetary system and institutions? (chapters 8 and 9).

The future of the East in world trade and finance depends on these various elements. By the end of the eighties, the new wave of reforms encouraged by Soviet *perestroika* added domestic constraints to external contingencies such as the international financial situation, world energy requirements, political relations between the USSR and the United States, the strengthening of the European Communities, and prospects for world economic growth. Is trade within Comecon to expand or to wither? Has East–West trade a future based upon sound economic interests, or is it just a political challenge? Have East–South relations any specificity? The socialist countries can only partly influence the answers to these questions. The magnitude and the nature of their involvement in the international trade and financial systems depend on Western strategies as well as on their own design.

This book addresses these issues in a political economy approach. It suggests possible answers in a time when developments in the USSR and Eastern Europe are increasingly complex and uncertain. It also aims to provide factual material for the reader's information and understanding. In any case, the future of the socialist economic system on the international scene is an open question – perhaps even to the point when a new system might emerge, with far-reaching consequences for the world economy itself.

September 1989

CHAPTER 1

———————— · ————————

AUTARKY, OPENING UP AND EXTERNAL CONSTRAINT

Autarky is usually seen as a distinctive feature of foreign trade behaviour in the centrally planned economies. The USSR could certainly have been called an autarkical power between the wars. The ratio between export and national product, which in pre-revolutionary Russia was 10–12 per cent, had fallen to 3–4 per cent in 1930 and to 0.5 per cent in 1937. This situation could be explained by specific causes such as international policy towards the USSR and planning conditions at the time of the first year plans. Moreover, the sheer size of the country meant that it could be independent of the outside world whereas, after the war, the European people's democracies were much more open to foreign trade. This opening up was first to the new socialist community and, in particular, to the USSR. The development of trade with other geo-political areas did not come about until the fifties.

It is impossible to understand the rationale behind these international economic relations without first examining the nature of the domestic situation in which they come about.

The type of mandatory planning which was introduced between 1945 and 1955 in the European people's democracies was borrowed from the Stalinist Soviet model. It treated foreign trade as a residual contribution to growth, called upon to produce what the national economy could not. The strategy of economic growth imposed on the smaller Eastern European countries was in its turn derived from the Soviet model. The elements composing it are well known: priority is given to industrialisation by the accelerated development of heavy industry such as the steel industry, machine-building and energy; the shift of manpower from agriculture to industry; and, finally, a large share of investment in national product. This strategy was very energy- and raw material-intensive. It was to bring about the dependence of the smaller Eastern European countries on the USSR and establish an asymmetrical trade between them, the USSR providing raw materials in exchange for manufactured goods.

The rapid growth of the fifties coincided with an increasingly marked opening up to international trade. The twenty years from 1955 to 1975 saw the irreversible inclusion of the socialist countries in the international division of labour. This period also saw profound changes in the domestic economic systems of the Eastern European countries. Economic reforms in the mid-sixties led to greater relative flexibility in planning as greater autonomy was granted to enterprises and this was accompanied by profit-sharing in the results of their activities. Foreign trade, until then seen as the means of providing the country with goods which could not be (or were too expensive to be) manufactured within the country, was now seen as an additional source of economic growth. Outside the socialist camp favourable circumstances accelerated this development: the high growth of the Western economies, political détente in East–West relations from the middle of the sixties onwards and, following decolonisation, links formed with the newly independent countries of the Third World.

The economic crisis which originated in the oil crisis of 1973–75 caused an upheaval in this state of affairs. Having been until then a source of growth, international trade became a source of disturbances. Recession in the West brought in its wake a slow-down of economic growth in the East due in part to the impact of the Western crisis but especially to the fact that the economic reforms had exhausted themselves and internal structural problems in Eastern European countries had worsened as a result of the growth strategy of the fifties. Three questions may therefore be asked:

(1) Do the basic and permanent characteristics of a centrally planned socialist economy lead ineluctably to autarky from which it can only partly free itself?
(2) How are we to interpret gains from international trade in a context of growth?
(3) What is the impact of external disturbances in a context of crisis?

The planned economy and international trade

The idea of a link between planning and the seeking of maximum self-sufficiency is strongly rooted in the West and the existence of this link has been argued by many specialists (for example, Holzman, 1974).

Proof of its existence was first made through reference to the USSR. But in this case, the propensity towards autarky stemming from planning is reinforced by the effect of dimension. Planning in itself predisposes to autarkical behaviour. One of the fundamental objectives of planning is the reduction of uncertainty and risk including those coming from outside. Limiting trade is one means of achieving this. Directive planning from above of the Soviet type tends to isolate the domestic economy and organises international trade on a macro-economic level. Direct inter-firm trade which forms the basis of international trade in market economies has long been impossible in the USSR and Eastern Europe and is still only developing, and then only in certain countries. Competition between direct producers is not an incentive to trade.

One has to add, however, that planning from above came about and was consolidated in the USSR, a vast country which was not very dependent on the outside world and which holds generous supplies of natural resources. These two considerations remain uppermost in the public's mind and even among specialists. No Eastern European country, however, has ever been able to claim self-sufficiency.

The smaller Eastern European countries cannot do without foreign trade to the same extent as the USSR. However, they may not be immune to the 'trade aversion', characteristic of the centrally planned economics (to use the expression of F. Holzman). We should point out that this presentation of the question contains an implicit comparison with the international market economy which is taken as the norm, i.e., planning tends to reduce foreign trade *below* the volume which would come about automatically in a free-trade context. There is a fundamental bias in such an approach which is worth pointing out.

However, this bias is almost inevitable in that the socialist theory of international trade offers few possibilities for the working out of an autonomous concept relating specifically to a planned economy. We will first examine the difficulties which are met with in the construction of such a theory, going on to look at the statistical evaluation of the dependence of the socialist countries *vis-à-vis* international trade. The answer to the question which has been raised in this section will finally be sought through the functional criteria of the autarky of a planned economy.

WHICH THEORY SHOULD BE APPLIED TO THE ANALYSIS OF INTERNATIONAL TRADE UNDER SOCIALISM?

Marx did not fully develop his analysis of the world market. In *Discourse on the Question of Free Trade* (1848), he shows that free trade leads to the exploitation of the proletariat. He also deals with foreign trade in *Capital* (book I, chapter 22; book III) and in *Theories of Surplus Value*. The law of value in international trade undergoes an essential modification; not only comparative advantages but absolute advantages too may be gained from international trade (if we assume the means of production to be immobile). Thus, a poor country can gain some comparative advantage from trade with a rich country and all the same be exploited due to the fact that it must spend more social labour time per item produced than the developed country. There is a transfer to the rich country as there is no standardisation of the unit of labour time which differs in intensity from country to country.

Marx's theses are always applied by him to a capitalist context. *Critique of the Gotha Programme*, the basis of the marxist theory of socialism (communism) contains nothing on the foreign trade of socialist countries.

Subsequent Soviet analyses are characterised by the specific nature of the various periods at which they were carried out. Lenin, in the long term, foresaw one sole world market but in the short term he saw peaceful coexistence as a way of setting up relations between a socialist country and a group of capitalist countries. What exactly relations between socialist countries would be after the triumph of 'the international dictatorship of the proletariat' is not very explicit in Lenin's writings. It is probable that he foresaw the removal of national economic barriers: 'The United States of the world (and not of Europe) is the state form of union and freedom of nations which we associate with socialism until such time as the complete victory of socialism has abolished every state, including the democratic state' (1915, *Complete Works*, 5th edn, vol. 26, p. 354).

For Trotsky, at the start of the Soviet revolution, as long as socialism existed in one country only, one should 'trade with the enemy' and exploit the differences between the developed countries. Trotsky was advocating commerce only in order to import and was hostile to 'concessions' or joint ventures with foreign capital. Later (1925) he defended a very classical view of the international division of labour, and collaboration with the West (including the importation of capital and technology) as well as the need to establish 'comparative coefficients' to evaluate the gap between Soviet and capitalist industry (we can see in this the beginnings of the 'efficiency coefficients of foreign trade' which were later presented in Soviet works).

After the war, in *Economic Problems of Socialism in the USSR* (1952), Stalin developed the thesis of the long-term existence of two parallel and opposed world markets. In this text, the socialist countries are presented as still dependent on imports from capitalist countries but likely soon to feel 'the need to sell their surplus production abroad'. Nothing is said about trade between socialist countries, their relations being based on cooperation and mutual assistance (Comecon had been set up in 1949) in which assistance offered by the USSR has the largest share.

The writings of Marx and Lenin hardly provide an adequate basis for modern authors in socialist countries seeking to work out a complete theory of international trade for relations with the non-socialist world and moreover for relations within the socialist system. Present theory takes as its premise the existence of one sole, though complex and heterogeneous *world* market where two systems, capitalism and socialism trade and interact. Is an overall theory explaining the international division of labour conceivable?

In debates between Eastern bloc economists in the sixties, the question of retaining the classical theory of comparative costs were raised. A Hungarian economist presented this temptation very well by bringing out the points in common between the Ricardo approach and fundamental aspects of international socialist economy (Ausch, 1972). Ricardo takes labour value as a premise (here, one should of course introduce the differences between his theory and Marx's theory). He reasons on the basis of trade between countries not between firms. He takes no account of capital movements and ignores the demand side. On all these points, his theory fits in with the actual situation in socialist countries.

However, despite its 'rational basis' which has been recognised by many economists from socialist countries, Ricardo's theory is not quite appropriate. It would just be admissible as an explanation of an East–West division of labour except for the fact that it presupposes free trade which cannot exist in these relations. If the theory is applied to East–

South trade, one must then acknowledge that this trade is of the same nature as that set up in the capitalist system between rich and poor countries. But it is precisely as a justification of capitalist domination of the Third World that Ricardo's theory has been criticised in the East. If it is applied to trade between the socialist countries, a division of labour which is disadvantageous to some countries seems justifiable with the 'Portugals' of the East (Romania and Bulgaria) destined to specialisation based on agriculture, while the 'Britains' (the GDR and Czechoslovakia) enjoy industrial specialisation. This is, however, more than just a political debate as specialisation based on this model was actually put forward by the USSR in 1962 within Comecon and it came up against very strong opposition from Romania.

Theoretical research is therefore seeking a solution to the contradiction which would still allow a line of reasoning based on comparative advantage to be retained. Certain works (in particular those of the East German economist G. Kohlmey) deal with defining and evaluating international values in the socialist system. Others concentrate on compensatory mechanisms designed to correct the effects of the 'unequal trade' which results from the implementation of the law of value on an international scale. These mechanisms include price corrections and development aid with particular regard to the 'equalising of levels of development', one of the objectives of socialist integration within Comecon.

Beyond Ricardo's theory, a Hungarian economist, T. Kiss (1971), tested the application of the neo-classical theory of specialisation and proved the validity of the Heckscher–Ohlin theorem in the case of Hungary, a small, open economy better endowed with capital than with labour, exporting low capital-intensive goods and importing high capital-intensive goods (especially in its trade with the USSR). The American economist, S. Rosefielde (1973), also tried to demonstrate the theorem in the case of the USSR. According to the hypotheses advanced by the author and bearing in mind imperfections in Soviet statistics, this gave a positive result.

We may wonder if it is right to attempt to transpose constructions as specific as the Heckscher–Ohlin theorem onto the socialist countries, especially when one is working with statistics which are bound to be inadequate (incomplete input–output tables, the absence of links between external and internal prices, especially in the case of the USSR) and in view of the criticism which the application of the theorem raises in the market economy. Moreover, is a theoretical analysis derived from Western theories generally relevant to Eastern Europe?

This question is dealt with by the American economist, F. Holzman, in many articles (see, in particular, *Foreign Trade Under Central Planning*, 1974). His conclusion is as follows: none of the traditional adjustment mechanisms (neo-classical or Keynesian) can be successfully applied to the socialist economies mainly because these mechanisms involve the system reacting automatically through external imbalances (classical theories) or corrective state intervention (Keynesian theory). However, socialist countries with centrally planned economies have internal mechanisms designed especially to prevent any automatic reaction by the system, which gives them a kind of 'functional' autarky.

This stance, which is shared by the British economist, P. Wiles (1968), though he presents it differently, runs counter to that taken by other economists, one of whom is R. Portes (1980, 1983). Portes basically suggests that a macro-economic analysis of the monetarist type is very much in keeping with the characteristics of the planned economies. He considers that an analysis (even one which is formalised and econometric, and despite statistical difficulties) conceived for market economies can quite justifiably be applied to the Eastern bloc.

One can indeed see in the works of Eastern European economists the influence of the theory of comparative costs, especially in calculating the efficiency of foreign trade. Such 'borrowings' from Western economic theory (or its methods) have, moreover, very often been noticed in other fields, for example, in the field of price theory or investment efficiency where, in the Soviet school of mathematical economics, evidence of recourse to neo-classical economic calculation is undeniable. This does not mean that an all-embracing theory can be drawn from this. We are still in need of a basic theory of international trade which takes as much account of a *socialist* international division of labour as of the inclusion of socialist countries in the international division of labour on a world level.

HOW SHOULD THE DEPENDENCE OF THE SOCIALIST COUNTRIES ON FOREIGN TRADE BE MEASURED?

Due to the statistical and accounting particularities of these countries, difficulties arise when one attempts to evaluate the share of foreign trade in the national product of a given country.

The relationship between exports and national income (for 1967, 1980 and 1986) show that no European socialist country can be considered autarkical (except the USSR at the beginning of this period):

	USSR	Bulgaria	Hungary	Poland	GDR	Romania	Czechoslovakia
1967	3.9	28	40	20	22	17	30
1980	8	40	54	31	33	27	29
1986	8	42	58	32	33	20	32

Sources: M. Senin, Socialist Integration, Moscow, 1969, p. 98; O. Bogomolov, The Socialist Countries in the International Division of Labour, Moscow, 1986, pp. 238, 288; data for 1986, O. Bogomolov, Socialisme et compétitivité, les pays socialistes dans l'économie mondiale, translated from the Russian, Paris, Presses de la Fondation Nationale des Sciences Politiques, 1989.

Why are these figures, taken from Soviet sources which themselves make use of Soviet and Eastern European data, calculated as an export /national income ratio and not as an import/national income ratio as is usual when calculating rates of dependence for market economies?

The answer lies in the very concept of dependence in relation to foreign trade. As will be seen, the plan first of all sets out its import needs, exports being designed to cover these needs. Dependence is therefore expressed as the domestic production costs of the goods which must be exported in order to procure the imports the country needs. These costs are themselves divided by the aggregate of net material product, or national income, which is different from the gross national product as we define it in the West. That is to say, it does not include most services, these not being considered 'material product' unless they are directly linked to production (goods transport comes under this definition of net material product, but not passenger transport).

The interpretation of these figures raises another difficulty. Foreign trade and national income statistics are not directly comparable in Eastern bloc countries. At first sight, this raises no problem as the data is expressed in the monetary unit of the country in both cases (roubles, marks, korunas etc.). However, in actual fact, what we have here are two different currencies.

Let us take the case of the USSR. National income figures are published in the Yearbook of the National Economy of the USSR, in current domestic roubles. They are comparable with figures for other macro-economic aggregates including investment, individual, and collective consumption. Foreign trade figures published in the Yearbook of Foreign

Trade are also in roubles. Here, however, we are dealing with 'devisa roubles'. The value of Soviet exports in devisa roubles bears no relation to production costs or the domestic price of the exported goods. The devisa rouble is a unit of measure which allows imports and exports to be aggregated. Foreign currency returns from the export of goods to the various countries of the world as well as foreign currency payments covering imports, are converted into devisa roubles by using the official exchange rate which bears no relation to the actual value of the national currency as far as parity of purchasing power is concerned.

Any meaningful evaluation of the ratio of dependence (based either on exports or imports) should involve the use of input–output tables giving figures for exports, imports, and material product in domestic prices. For most of these countries, the tables published make evaluation impossible. For the USSR, for example, the latest input–output tables published give only the balance for foreign operations and no separate values for imports and exports.

American researchers in 1982 clashed over this question. The political background to this academic debate was the 'gas pipeline affair'. The problem lay in proving the extent to which the USSR was actually dependent on the outside world and deciding what pressure could therefore be brought to bear on it. Two different methodologies were applied to calculate an import/national income ratio with a common unit of evaluation for the nominator and the denominator. Two procedures were possible, one converting the two elements of the formula into domestic prices, the other calculating them as world prices.

The first method was applied by V. Treml and B. Kostinsky (working for the Department of Commerce, i.e., the US government). By reconstructing the domestic prices of imported goods (domestic wholesale prices are never published in the USSR), these researchers showed that in 1980 the import/national income ratio was 20 per cent. Using the second method and recalculating Soviet national income data at world prices, J. Vanous (for the Wharton Econometrics forecasting institute) got an import/gross national product ratio of 4.1 per cent which corresponds to an import/national income ratio of 5.5 per cent.

How is this difference to be interpreted? It could be said that the Soviet Union selectively imports goods which, valued in internal prices, are extremely expensive. If we bear in mind that in both studies the export /national income ratio is about the same (7 per cent in the first study and 8 per cent in the second) this means that the relative domestic prices of imports are much higher than export prices when compared with world prices:

$$\frac{\text{Domestic prices of imports}}{\text{External prices of imports}} > \frac{\text{Domestic prices of exports}}{\text{External prices of exports}}$$

If we suppose that internal domestic prices in all cases adequately express factor costs (and factor scarcities) only one conclusion can be drawn: the USSR benefits greatly from the international division of labour, exporting low production-cost goods and importing high production-cost goods. However, in view of domestic price setting in the USSR, the gap mainly shows up domestic price distortions. Both methods are based on statistical reconstructions which are necessarily arbitrary. The method used by J. Vanous has the advantage of allowing a comparison to be made between the rates of dependence of the USSR and those of market economy countries and would, to our mind, seem preferable.

This statistical development had the particular aim of showing the approximate and relative nature of statistical measurement. For all that, the data given are enough to indicate that the small Eastern European countries are all dependent on foreign trade (though less so than small Western European countries) and that the USSR is much less so (less too than the United States with which it can be compared in this connexion).

Similar conclusions may be drawn from a World Bank report (Marer, 1985) which aimed at determining an acceptable estimate of the GNP in dollars for the centrally planned economies, and deriving foreign trade participation ratios from these estimates. For both sets of data (GNP and foreign trade participation ratio, the latter being the ratio between exports plus imports and the GNP), a whole range of alternative estimates were provided, and discussed in terms of accuracy or plausibility, without any indisputable result emerging.

In fact, when we talk of the 'autarky' of the socialist countries, we are talking more generally of a 'bloc autarky', that is, a concentration of trade within Comecon. This concentration has decreased since the fifties insofar as concerns the share of each country's exports to Comecon as a percentage of its overall total exports as the following table shows:

The general tendency is towards a fall in the share of Comecon in total trade undertaken by the Eastern European countries. The lowest point was reached in 1974–5. Since then, there has been a certain increase in this, due mainly to the slowing down of East–West trade. It would be

	USSR	Bulgaria	Hungary	Poland	GDR	Romania	Czechoslovakia
1952	80	89	71	67	80	85	71
1960	55	80	61	55	68	66	64
1980	49	69	53	53	66	37	65
1987	60	82	51	48	67	48	75

Source: Statistical Yearbook of Comecon Member countries for 1960, 1980 and 1987; for 1952, the proportion of mutual trade in overall trade, in F. Lemoine, C. Seranne, 'L'Intégration économique à l'Est: le Comecon', Notes et Études Documentaires, 1976, no. 4268, p. 33.

going too far to conclude that there has been an increase in the self-sufficiency of the socialist system. We could say though that, for the region as a whole, the proportion of mutual trade has levelled out overall at around 60 per cent of total trade, however with great differences from one country to another. We should none the less not make firm pronouncements on figures here, and this for two reasons.

First, international socialist prices have, since the world crisis, developed at a rate which differs from that of world prices, having increased less than these between 1973 and 1980; since then the situation has been reversed. Percentages calculated from overall values are therefore only approximate.

Second, any calculation of shares implies that total trade is computed in comparable units, while trade between each CMEA country and its CMEA partners is expressed in an accounting unit (the transferable rouble), and trade with the non-socialist world is conducted in convertible currencies. To simplify, we may divide total trade between rouble trade and dollar trade. Both may be converted in national currencies using the exchange rate of each national currency with the dollar and the rouble. We shall see below how these calculations are made (p. 26). Up to 1976, the national exchange rates of all socialist currencies yielded a rouble/dollar rate which was identical, and equal to the official Soviet rouble/dollar rate. For reasons explained below, since 1976 several countries have shifted towards a more 'realistic' calculation of their exchange rate, which yielded different rouble/dollar rates. Let us give an example: in 1986, the average Soviet exchange rate between the rouble and the dollar amounted to \$1=r.0.70; the rate derived from the Hungarian exchange rate between the forint and each of these currencies yielded \$1=r.1.64; according to the Polish rates, we got \$1=r.1.90; according to the Romanian rates, \$1=r.1.04. If we calculate the share of the CMEA in Hungarian foreign trade using the Hungarian exchange rate, we get a share of 53 per cent; if we use the Soviet exchange rate, we get a share of 72 per cent! Of course we may say that it is more appropriate to take the Hungarian rate for computing the distribution of Hungarian trade between socialist and non-socialist trade, but then we must acknowledge the fact that the data are not comparable for different CMEA countries (see Wolf, 1987).

With all these limitations, one can nevertheless state that since 1950 the Comecon countries have opened up considerably to international trade in general and to trade with non-socialist countries in particular. The extent to which they have opened up seems to be holding steady at the level reached towards the middle of the last decade.

Is there any justified reason, then, to suppose that there could have been a greater degree of opening up if centralised planning mechanisms had not restrained the process?

DOES CENTRAL PLANNING GENERATE FUNCTIONAL AUTARKY?

According to a widespread belief, a traditional centrally planned economy is autarkic because, all things being equal, it tends to import and export less than a market economy.

Foreign trade is a state activity and its whole organisation is based on a state monopoly overseen by specialised agencies (often called foreign trade organisations, FTOs) whose job it is to implement the plan for foreign trade. The development of this organisation will be treated in detail in chapter 4. Even if these foreign trade agencies are moving increasingly towards the status of enterprises and even if the enterprises themselves are beginning to obtain some rights in the field of foreign trade, it is no less the case that international trade remains the essential preserve of central planning.

Macro-economic planning considers foreign trade as a residue

Planning is carried out basically by so-called material balances in 'physical' quantities.

These 'balances' are tables identifying sources of supply and uses for individual products or product groups. They show *domestic* internal production on the supply side, and its domestic uses (intermediate inputs, investment, non-productive consumption) on the uses side. The two sides of this balance could only be made equal fortuitously. If they are not equal, the balance may be achieved through internal adjustments (production growth, restrictions on intermediate or final uses) and only then through foreign trade which is therefore a residual instrument for adjusting the balance.

This method, worked out in the USSR and applied to the smaller Eastern European countries, would certainly not suit countries open to the outside world, where foreign trade does not play a 'residual' role for many products. It has been imposed upon these countries, with some adaptations, while the general approach remains identical. It means in particular that priority is given to import demand (which occurs, if there is an excess of planned internal uses over planned resources). Export is seen above all as a method of covering those imports which, it is felt, cannot be reduced. There was a 'dramatic' illustration of this when the USSR had to face the crisis of 1929. As the first Soviet five-year plan provided for the take-off of industry, after the crisis the USSR continued to import Western machinery although the fall in wheat prices made these imports increasingly costly (and one should include the cost in human lives due to famine). In 1931–2 the USSR sold wheat at less than two-fifths of the price it stood at before the depression and bought machinery whose price on world markets had only dropped by 20 per cent – due precisely to the high Russian demand which at the time accounted for 50 per cent of the world machinery market (Holzman, 1974: 101).

This example from history is, of course, rather extreme. None the less, the basic principle of planning remains the same. In the Soviet-type planning system, once import requirements have been defined, the planner turns his attention to finding how to meet them. The procedure followed is to turn first to the Comecon countries (and other socialist countries), and only then, to the non-socialist countries. The nature and the volume of exports is determined according to the buyer country, the aim being to reach a bilateral balance with each partner. This bilateralism is most developed with Comecon members as, in this case, trade is carried out on the basis of five-yearly agreements which are brought up to date by yearly protocols establishing the value and/or the quantity of the goods to be traded. For non-socialist countries, the plan distinguishes between trade with developing countries (with whom there are also, generally, trading agreements) and trade with developed market economies. For the latter, the plan in general lays down overall import and export goals without any strict division of trade between these countries. It is increasingly the case, however, that imports from market economies are required to be strictly compensated by exports for the same amount, hence the pressure for compensation brought to bear in East–West trade when import demands become difficult to contain. Where it has proved impossible to contain this demand and where the foreign debt accrued due to this has become excessive, the planner may introduce severe cutbacks on imports even if this involves creating serious domestic bottlenecks (as was the case in 1981–2 in Eastern Europe).

Are these characteristics of traditional planning (treating foreign trade as a means of adjusting internal balances and giving priority to imports in macro-economic planning) still valid for the USSR and Eastern Europe? First, all these countries uphold the advantages of international speciali- sation (which is institutionally practised and organised within Comecon). Specialisation always takes the form of excess production over the country's requirements in manufactured goods where the country has a comparative advantage; it also means that the country abandons domestic production of goods which are not advantageous to manufac- ture. Second, since 1980 all Eastern European countries have given pri- ority to exports over imports, and the USSR has done the same since 1986.

These developments are actually not in contradiction with the basic principle. Specialisation broadens trade by expanding import demands which must of course be covered by an increase in exports (of specialised products). This does not alter the fundamental attitude to foreign trade. This is particularly applicable to intra-Comecon trade which is carried out in an inconvertible unit of account, the transferable rouble. In all trade through clearing, the debtor is in the most advantageous position; he receives more products than he supplies and clearing rules allow him to postpone the balancing of trade. The very organisation of Comecon, which accounts for the greater part of overall trade, therefore exerts permanent pressure for imports and this is of course counter-balanced for each country by the pressure brought to bear in the opposite direction by its trading partner.

As for the export dynamism which has become the catch phrase first for the smaller socialist countries and then even for the USSR, it is not the same as the pressure put on Western firms to 'export or perish'. It is not the need for competitiveness which spurs *firms* on to conquer foreign markets, but the constraints of foreign financing which mean that *countries* must export first if they are to be in a position to import later, unlike the 'import-led growth' strategy developed in the seventies (which lay in importing machinery in order to export the products manufactured by this machinery) (see Hanson, 1982). A Soviet writer has given an excellent summing up of the apparent contradiction between export and import priorities:

> Import policy takes priority over export policy. The maximalisation of exports has one basic goal only, that is, to increase the volume of resources that a macro-economic whole can devote to the practical realisation of a long-term policy in the field of imports . . . Thus, export policy is a mechanism for the implementation of the import policy; this is why the former has a *provisional* priority over the second. (Shiriaev, 1977: 47–49)

The plan in socialist countries is structurally taut

This means that it assumes the full employment (to use the term coined by F. Holzman: over-full employment planning) of all its material and human resources. The Hungarian economist, J. Kornai, has given an exhaustive analysis of this phenomenon in *Economics of shortage* (1980). In it Kornai explains why, in a centrally planned system, demand always outstrips supply, giving rise to a 'seller's market' and perpetuating chronic shortages. Indeed, in such economies the pressure of demand caused by the market does not exist, or exists only to a small degree. The main pressure brought to bear on enterprises (and the agencies responsible for them) is the fulfilling of the plan. As the plan sets excessively high targets, each enterprise's main concern lies in getting hold of the necessary resources, hence the never-ending 'race' for supplies and the 'insatiable hunger' for investment. This gives rise also to pressure to increase imports. The behaviour of the enterprise on the micro level thus adds to the import priority stemming from macro-economic planning methods.

Could we not say, therefore, that this built-in import drive, far from being a sign of a tendency towards autarky should encourage Eastern European countries to have more developed trade than if they were market economies? No, we could not. First of all, the foreign trade plan is itself the result of a taut macro-economic plan: the need to import is only acknowledged once all internal solutions, including import-substitution, have been exhausted. Secondly, import demand is confronted with monetary constraint for trade settled in hard currency (the means of payment are lacking) and a physical constraint of the same nature when it comes to trade with other socialist countries (the supplier-state also argues its import demands).

The fact that socialist economic units have grown used to a world in which the 'sellers' lay down the law (the 'sellers' are equipment and raw material suppliers as well as investment allocating agencies) explains the well-known attitude of foreign trade agencies. They may be excellent buyers using their monopoly to make their suppliers compete with one another. They are, on the other hand, very bad sellers as they pay scant attention to marketing techniques, after-sales service etc., just like domestic market suppliers.

There is another consequence of plan tautness, and this is the lack of 'room for manoeuvre' once all resources have been allocated. This does not mean that they have all been efficiently allocated. Kornai shows how a state of chronic shortage coexists with surpluses born of ever-increasing bottlenecks. Shortage of a certain resource means that complementary goods may go unused for a time (this is frequently the case in socialist countries where irregular supplies of raw materials lead to machines – and men – standing idle). However, these surpluses cannot be mobilised for other purposes. In the field of foreign trade, this leads to a failure to react rapidly and efficiently to demand from abroad. This is one of the difficulties of compensation trade where the Western exporter is faced with a request for compensation, but, in fact, he can find no products to purchase as supply cannot be increased at short notice.

The foreign trade plan is never published (neither is the macro-economic plan, for that matter) except in very general outline. This irritates Western operators as it provides them with no way of carrying out market studies. But this secrecy may be explained: it effectively increases competition between suppliers and, above all, it conceals shortcomings in the plan which might show up the economy's dependence on foreign markets.

Planning isolates the domestic economy from the foreign economy

It is in this last respect that differences between countries are greatest. The readiness of certain small Eastern European countries to open up (Hungary is a particular example of this) has led them to introduce a closer link between domestic and foreign prices and to establish exchange rates which have some economic significance. What follows therefore applies to the traditional model of central planning, whose features are more or less present in the countries under review.

In this kind of planning domestic prices are not equilibrium prices in so far as they do not equate the supply and demand of goods (nor do they set out to do this, but are established through the calculation of the 'socially necessary labour expenditures'). This means that domestic prices are bound to be separate from world market prices. Likewise, socialist currencies are not convertible, which means that they can neither be bought nor sold against foreign currencies. The domestic currency is therefore isolated from the rest of the world. This does have its effect on international trade, and means that devaluation cannot be used as a regulatory instrument, customs tariffs are artificial, and dumping cannot be controlled.

The fact that socialist currencies are non-convertible and that there is a separation between domestic and foreign prices leads to a two-tier planning of foreign trade, in foreign currency (convertible, or non-convertible as with the transferable rouble) and in domestic prices and currency. Discrepancies between domestic and foreign prices mean that the plan calculated in hard currency may be balanced while the 'domestic' plan may not, and *vice versa*.

The clear-cut division between the outside world and the domestic economy, as far as currency and prices are concerned, is accompanied by a fragmentation within the economy itself. There is a domestic non-convertibility which, in turn, has its repercussions on foreign trade.

Domestic non-convertibility can be defined as follows: the holding of the national currency by resident economic agents does not automatically give them access to goods. In other words, socialist currencies are not generally exchangeable for goods at the discretion of their holders. Another characteristic should be added to this: the national currency is not actually uniform even if it goes by the same name for all transactions within the same country. In fact there are two dividing lines.

The first is between the productive sector and the non-productive (consumer) sector. In the first, trade is conducted according to the plan. This means that enterprises get allocations of raw materials, semi-manufactured goods, equipment etc. Settlements are indeed made in monetary form (exclusively through banks, excluding the use of cash currency). If a firm has extra funds, this in no way means that it can procure more goods if the plan does not authorise it to do so. The currency is therefore not a universal equivalent here. Beyond the allocations laid down by the plan and in conditions of 'taut' planning where in fact there are no goods which have not already been allocated and are therefore available to be traded freely, the only way to obtain more goods is to offer more goods. What we have here is barter or what is known as the 'parallel economy'.

The second division is between wholesale and retail prices. The former are established by reference to production costs, the latter depend upon the overall balance established between supply and demand and upon the objectives of social policy. There is no relationship between these prices. Retail prices are not 'derived' from wholesale prices, as they are in market economies with a VAT tax system. The only country to have introduced such a tax system is Hungary, beginning from 1 January 1988. In most countries, the same national unit of currency has a different value at the retail and wholesale levels. As retail prices are frequently subsidised and lower than costs, a monetary unit therefore 'buys' more goods at retail price than at wholesale price. (It is precisely this which makes a tourist exchange rate necessary.)

The level of domestic non-convertibility (also called real as opposed to financial, as we are dealing here with the conversion of money into goods) varies according to the different sectors and channels. It is greater in the field of trade concerned with production goods allocated by the plan. Even in the field of consumer goods and services, the currency is still non-convertible, at least in part. It is certainly true that a person with roubles can go into any Soviet shop and buy whatever is available, but very often he will not find what he wants and the most sought-after goods may only be obtainable through an 'under-the-table deal' (equivalent to a depreciation of the currency) or in exchange for other goods and services (a situation of real non-convertibility) or else in exchange for convertible hard currency.

These are the fundamental characteristics of the planning mechanisms of socialist economies which in turn influence the operation of their foreign trade.

The term 'functional autarky' used in the title of this section may be questioned. Economic literature in Eastern Europe is actually very critical of this way of presenting things. It underlines the fact that planning allows for considerable expansion of foreign trade once the decision has been taken and quotes the rapid increase of East–West trade between

1966 and 1975 as proof of this. Two points should none the less be made here.

Firstly, when it becomes necessary to introduce macro-economic adjustments (like those which followed the debt crisis of the smaller European socialist countries in 1981–82), planning allows a highly effective and speedy correcting of the situation even in a open economy by *reducing imports*. Hungary and Romania are particularly significant examples of this.

Secondly, the numerous sub-divisions within planned economies put a curb on international trade and add to the direct effects of planning and the state monopoly of foreign trade.

All this corresponds to specific mechanisms which have the effect of *reducing* dependence on foreign trade at will. This can be seen not only in trade with the non-socialist world but in intra-Comecon trade as well. There is no 'bloc autarky' directed towards the non-socialist world as opposed to the full expansion of trade within the socialist community. The socialist international division of labour is affected equally (with specific mechanisms) by the nature of central planning, and the entire history of Comecon can be interpreted as a permanent and largely fruitless search for greater internationalisation.

These features of the system account for the nature of adjustments introduced in socialist countries as they have opened up to international trade. At a time of world crisis, such features have also determined the form which 'foreign constraint' has taken in the domestic economies and the various forms of adaptation to it.

Opening up to the outside world at a time of growth

The intensification of foreign trade by socialist countries, both between themselves and with the non-socialist world, at the beginning of the fifties, coincided with a period of great domestic economic growth (10.7 per cent for the seven countries between 1951 and 1955; 8.3 per cent between 1965 and 1960; 6.1 per cent between 1966 and 1970). From 1955 onwards, domestic economic thinking turned to determining criteria for economic efficiency which was to guide planning in the field of investment as well as in the field of foreign trade. The economic arguments which lay behind the planners' choice developed in several stages.

EVALUATING THE ACCOUNTING PROFITABILITY OF FOREIGN TRADE: THE *PREISAUSGLEICH*

How are we to evaluate just how much revenue foreign trade brings in (or costs) when prices and currency are divorced from those of the outside world? A purely accounting evaluation provides an answer in keeping with the *Preisausgleich* formula ('the equalising of prices'). This German term comes from the fact that the first studies on the subject made public in the West took the GDR as an example (Pryor, 1963). In order to justify advantageous foreign trade activity it is not enough to be able to show foreign currency surplus. One must also be able to determine what this actually means in terms of domestic prices.

To make such an evaluation, the planner may draw on two sets of data. He knows the value of exports and imports in domestic prices. For exported goods, this is the same as current wholesale prices. For imported goods (in the traditional planning system still used for a large share of products in the USSR and in most of Eastern Europe), the value is established in keeping with the wholesale price of similar or comparable goods produced in the country. The planner also knows the value of exports and imports in 'devisa currency'. We already employed the term in evaluating the USSR's level of dependence on foreign trade (p. 15).

In order to establish foreign trade figures, one must convert import and export figures all expressed in foreign currency into a single unit of account or 'devisa currency'. We talk therefore of the devisa rouble, the devisa koruna etc., while in the GDR they refer to it as the valuta mark. The rate of this currency, given the use to which it is put, may be completely arbitrary. It must however be the same for all transactions and must be consistent – this is, the cross-rates of this currency in different foreign currencies must correspond to the current rates of these currencies.

The official rates for the majority of socialist currencies have been determined according to their gold content. This initial definition is, to a large extent, nominal. It was based on a certain purchasing power parity of these currencies and the 'capitalist' currencies (when they were themselves, in particular, the dollar, based on gold) but has been deliberately overestimated. Thus, the value of the Soviet rouble was altered for the last time in 1961, and established at 0.987412g of gold for a rouble, which was slightly more than the dollar (0.888g), so that up to 1971, 1r.=$1.11.

The general flotation of Western currencies and the breaking of their link with gold complicated the evaluation of these official exchange rates for the socialist countries. Rates are now usually calculated every two weeks, based on a 'basket' of currencies (using a method similar to that used in establishing SDR exchange rates. The SDR (special drawing rights) is also a unit of account with an initial reference to gold, based on the gold value of the dollar before 15 August 1971).

Foreign trade figures then, were established in this way in all socialist countries until 1976. At the end of the eighties, the USSR, Bulgaria, and the GDR still presented their foreign trade statistics in this way. Hungary (since 1976), Romania (since 1981), and Poland (since 1982) have abandoned this accounting in devisa currency (see pp. 34–5). Czechoslovakia joined this group in 1989. In the traditional system the planner thus has two sets of data at hand: imports and exports in 'devisa' currency (published in foreign trade yearbooks), and the same aggregates in domestic prices (these, however, are not generally available to foreign researchers as they are not published). In the first set of data, values are proportional to prices in foreign currency. In the second set, values express totally separate domestic prices. From these two sets of data the planner establishes the gains to the nation from foreign trade.

The 'product' of foreign trade could thus be calculated as follows:

$$T = (M_i - M_e) + (X_e - X_i) = M_i - X_i + S_e$$

Where:

T = the product of foreign trade

M_i = imports in domestic prices

X_i = exports in domestic prices

M_e = imports in external prices converted into 'national devisa currency' at the official exchange rate.

S_e = the balance of trade at external prices converted into 'national devisa currency' at the official exchange rate.

Thus, for the USSR for 1959 (a year for which there is an input-output table published showing imports and exports in domestic prices):

	X	M	S	
e	4.9	4.6	0.3	(in thousands of millions of roubles)
i	5.3	9.1	−3.8	

We get $T = 4.1$ thousand million roubles.

One adds the difference between the value of imports and the value of exports (in domestic prices) to the foreign currency balance of trade recalculated in domestic currency at an arbitrary rate of exchange (which is always over-estimated). Obviously, the maximisation of *Preisausgleich* is only rational if domestic prices accurately reflect production costs. The calculation is made from the point of view of the foreign trade organisations and the aggregate *T* expresses a double 'revenue', that is to say, in their dealings with foreign countries $(X_e - M_e = S_e)$ and in their dealings with national enterprises $(M_i - X_i)$ since they 'sell' products imported from abroad for use by national enterprises at internal prices while 'buying' from these same national enterprises the products they intend to export.

It is easy to appreciate the perverse effects that the maximisation of *T* can have in the case of irrational prices.

For all that, in the USSR up to 1988 this was still the method used to calculate the financial result of foreign trade which then was incorporated in the state budget with a difference from the initial formulation which gives:

$$T = M_i - X_i + S_e \ (X_i/X_e) \text{ if } S_e > 0$$

$$T = M_i - X_i + S_e \ (M_i/M_e) \text{ if } S_e < 0$$

The final figure for the balance of trade is weighted by the ratio between domestic and foreign values, calculating it on the basis of exports if the foreign trade balance is positive and on the basis of imports if it is negative. This means adding foreign earnings to the 'internal' revenue of the export-import agencies. Foreign earnings in 'devisa currency' are themselves corrected by a kind of exchange coefficient.

Thus, the budget shows as revenue a foreign trade 'product' which is made all the greater due to the fact that: (a) the *positive* balance of trade in hard currency is itself high, which seems logical; (b) the *negative* balance of trade in domestic prices is high, which is usually the case in the USSR because the domestic prices of manufactured goods imported by the USSR are fixed at a relatively high level compared with the domestic prices of exported goods (where energy products dominate). The traditional structure of Soviet wholesale prices, underestimating raw commodities as they do, thus has the effect of generating an accounting revenue from foreign trade which is incorporated in the state budget. This is an inflationist form of budget financing (see Birman, 1981; acknowledged by the Soviet authorities themselves in 1988).

The Eastern European countries have taken the lead over the USSR in seeking other methods of calculation.

INITIAL CALCULATIONS OF PARTIAL EFFICIENCY

These were to appear in the very early fifties in Hungary, where two economists, T. Liska (who is today very well-known in Hungary for having militated in 1982 for a 'neo-Walrasian' form of socialist capitalism!) and A. Marias, came up with a calculation which could be used by planners ('Optimal Returns and International Division of Labour' in *Economic Survey of Europe in 1954*, UN Economic Commission for Europe, 1955).

These criteria were partial since the general division of trade between areas and goods was carried out by the planners according to general preferences, for example, a preference for Comecon, or the priority granted to production means (or goods) needed for the growth strategy. The criteria of choice therefore applied essentially to exports.

These calculations had several objectives which succeeded each other:

(a) at the outset, they served to allow planners to select, as rationally as possible, the 'basket' of exports which were to cover import requirements;

(b) at a later stage, following the 'waves' of economic reforms introduced in 1965–70, these calculations were used to stimulate exports and allowed the calculation of the revenue which enterprises were to receive by converting hard currency gains into domestic currency at a rate of exchange more advantageous than the official rate;

(c) they subsequently allowed the establishment of a link between domestic and foreign prices in certain countries (e.g. Hungary and to some extent Poland, Bulgaria, and Romania);

(d) finally, it is on the basis of these calculations that the 'commercial' exchange rates were established in Hungary, Romania, and then Poland, thus doing away with the 'official' exchange rates based on an unreal gold content of the national currency.

The formulae

The formula generally used in the smaller socialist countries is as follows:

$$E = \frac{C + rC - D}{P_x - P_m}$$

where E = coefficient of efficiency,

C=the cost of domestic production of imported goods, at domestic prices and in the national currency,

r=the profit margin of the foreign trade organisation and the exporting firm.

D=the cost in domestic prices of imported goods incorporated in exported goods.

P_x=revenue in foreign currency obtained from exports.

P_m=the cost in foreign currency of imported goods incorporated in exported goods.

We can therefore observe that E is the quantity of national currency one must lay out *on average* in order to obtain one unit of foreign currency at export. This therefore constitutes a reference *exchange rate* calculated not on the basis of the overall parity of purchasing power, but relative only to the quantity of goods earmarked for export.

As concerns the small socialist countries, the calculation takes account of the imported content of exported products which may be high when exports are manufactured from imported raw materials and equipment. In the case of the USSR, the calculation does not take this into account and this expresses a lower rate of dependence on imports.

The formula used by the Soviet planners for the sole purpose of determining export efficiency is far simpler (there is no link between domestic and foreign prices, neither was there up to 1987 any incentive to export through the conversion of profits into foreign currency as firms always received payment at the national price).

$$E=\frac{P_x}{C}$$

where

P_x=revenue in foreign currency from exports

C=total domestic cost of production which is equal to: $C=C_i+eK$

C_i=domestic production cost at current wholesale prices

e=normative coefficient of investment profitability

K=investments required for exported production.

Noticeable in the Soviet calculation is the recognition of domestic wholesale price irrationality which reflects capital expenditure very inadequately. Thus, the price of goods for export is 'revalued' in the light of investments in the export branches. Another difference, this time a formal one, is to be found in the inversion of the efficiency coefficient (which therefore corresponds to quotation* of the domestic currency in foreign currencies).

For all countries, the calculation of foreign trade efficiency is divided up into monetary zones, or at least into a 'dollar zone' with payment in convertible currencies and a 'rouble zone' for payment between Comecon countries. Divisions can also be made according to groups of products and here we get a set of multiple exchange rates which is for the sole use of the domestic planner. The *marginal* coefficient which shows the planner the maximum admissible domestic cost for export (to acquire an additional unit of foreign currency) is higher than the *average* efficiency coefficient. Calculations of this kind have been carried out by most socialist countries. Here we present the method worked out in Poland as presented by the economist W. Trzeciakowski (chairman of the Reform Committee in the new Polish government of 1989), and which has been applied in part in that country (see Trzeciakowski, 1978).

First, let us take the case where there is a *sole* foreign market. Poland must purchase on this market certain imports which can be divided into two categories:

1   Indispensable imports must be procured and therefore covered by exports to the same value if there is to be a good balance of payments.

2   'Substitutable' imports are goods which can be produced in Poland but only at high cost, and which it would be more advantageous to buy from abroad, provided the export sought does not require greater expenditure. Figure 1 shows on the Y axis the values of the ratio between domestic prices in zlotys and export (import) profits (or costs) in foreign currency and, on the X axis, foreign currency values for imports and exports. Exportable products are set out in ascending order of value for the coefficient domestic costs/foreign currency profits and imports in descending order of value of the ratio between the domestic cost of import substitution goods and their cost in foreign currency. The dotted part of the imports curve shows imports which are absolutely indispensable, while the solid line shows replaceable imports. We can see from the figure that it would appear to be advantageous to push imports beyond indispensable imports to the point at which the two curves intersect. To the right of point of intersection B, export costs surpass the domestic cost

---

*We refer to the usual quotation in the socialist countries, where the exchange rate is given in domestic currency units per one unit of foreign currency. A 'low' or 'overvalued' exchange rate means *less* domestic currency for one unit of foreign currency than the equilibrium rate, and *vice-versa*.

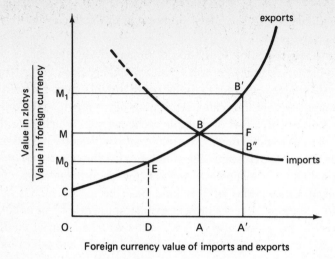

Figure 1   Unit rates for export or import

of manufacturing importable goods. M expresses the marginal expenditure of zlotys on exports in order to obtain an additional unit of foreign currency and also corresponds to B, the point of equilibrium of the balance of payments.

In fact, were one to establish M_1 as a higher rate (equivalent to a devaluation of the zloty), export would be advantageous as far as B', however the cost of supplementary exports in national currency (area $A B B' A'$) would rise above the cost of substitutable imported goods $(B A A' B'')$.

Applications

From the Trzeciakowski figure, we can easily see just how the planner can use this kind of calculation for the four aims mentioned above: i.e., planning of foreign trade, stimulating exports, relating domestic prices to external prices, and setting up a realistic exchange rate.

1   He may simply take into account the marginal coefficient as an 'unofficial' exchange rate and base his choice on this. We should remember, however, that the rationality of his choice is closely linked to that of domestic prices. If exported goods have artificially low prices, it may seem profitable to export them (they would figure on the lower left-hand

side of the export curve), while in actual fact this would be a loss for the economy.

2   He can use this calculation to stimulate exports. Let us suppose that the official rate of exchange (M_o) is over-valued, which is usually the case. If the aim was to encourage export, one would remunerate the exporting firm by converting its revenue expressed in foreign currency by applying not the official rate of exchange but an 'unofficial' rate (M), which would procure for firms additional profit greater than domestic production cost, equal to BMC, for all the products on the export curve *lying to the left of B*. If one especially wants to encourage export activity to the right of B, on the export curve, it is even possible to remunerate the firm, for example, by applying exchange rate M_1 which would be the same as a subsidy equal to BFB'. One can thus obtain a series of different rates of exchange (which in Hungary were called foreign trade multipliers), which allows the revenue of exporting firms to be determined while guaranteeing them special export prices which are higher than domestic prices for the same products (these prices are known in Poland as 'transaction prices').

3   The exchange rate obtained from these calculations can be used to establish domestic *prices* (and not only to determine export *revenue* or import *costs*, domestic prices of products manufactured in the country and sold on the domestic market remaining identical). Here, the foreign price acts as a regulator. If, for example, the foreign market price of the exported product converted into national currency (P_{ec}) is greater than the initial domestic price (P_i) for this same product on the domestic market, the firm will receive authorisation to sell the product at the P_{ec} price, thereby gaining extra profit due to its export competitiveness. If, on the other hand, $P_{ec}<P_i$, then it follows that P_i should be lowered and the firm thus made competitive with the world market. It may be necessary to grant a temporary subsidy to help the firm to adapt while reducing its costs. This is the rationale behind the Hungarian price reform of 1980–81. Experience has shown that where $P_{ec}<P_i$, the economic idea of eliminating non-profitable firms has never been carried to its logical end (although some 'bankruptcies' have been announced since 1984). As concerns the impact of import prices, this hardly ever occurs except for a specific category of goods (non-essential consumer goods). The decision not to let foreign prices have an automatic effect on domestic prices of import goods can be justified by two considerations: first, fear of the

spread of inflation from abroad, especially great since 1973–74, for goods imported from non-socialist countries. Second, as concerns production goods (machinery, semi-finished goods and raw materials), there is the fact that these goods are derived simultaneously from both world markets and socialist markets which have differing prices, and this complicates the problem of the impact of external on domestic prices. Here again, Hungarian practice differs from that of the other countries: unlike the other socialist countries, import prices have indeed affected commodities, energy and raw materials as well as industrial equipment.

4   The logical conclusion from these calculations is to substitute the official exchange rate nominally based on gold values with an exchange rate based on the relationship between costs in domestic currency and export revenue in foreign currency (here one would use the average rate rather than the marginal rate according to Trzeciakowski). This is therefore a kind of 'purchasing parity power' based on the percentage of national production which goes to foreign markets. It follows that the more a country is to open to foreign trade, the more meaningful its exchange rate will be.

These rates are always 'devalued' in relation to the official exchange rate which preceded them. When the Hungarians in 1968 introduced their economic reform, they publicised their 'multipliers of foreign trade' (which other socialist countries usually kept secret): 60 forints to the dollar and 40 forints to the rouble which gives a cross-rate of $1=r. 1.5 while at that time the official exchange rate was 13.04 forints to the rouble and 11.74 forints to the dollar which corresponds to the then official rate of the rouble: $1=r. 0.90. We see here just how much the forint was over-valued – not to mention the rouble! – on the official exchange rate.

Since 1976, the Hungarians have decided to use these rates as official 'commercial' rates, thus dropping the arbitrary reference to the forint's gold value. The official rate of the 'devisa forint' was abandoned in 1976 (not without problems for the conversion of foreign trade statistics). The rate of the forint was then established at 41.3 to the dollar and 35.7 to the rouble. Having been devalued several times against the dollar by 1980 (by 22 per cent altogether), it was again devalued by 40 per cent between 1981 and 1983 and by a further 12 per cent in June 1984. Several devaluations of less magnitude have occurred since 1986.

In 1981, Romania likewise abandoned the official rate based on the gold value of the leu and opted for a commercial rate (established at 15 lei to the dollar instead of the 4.47 lei of the previous exchange rate, and 15 lei for a rouble, instead of 6.7). However, the new evaluation of the leu does remain largely arbitrary. It was more than anything else a symbolic gesture by which Romania was announcing the eventual convertibility of the leu; up to 1984, the leu had been several times devalued (by 40 per cent altogether). Romania, like Hungary, had to abide by suggestions put forward by the International Monetary Fund (IMF) if it was to obtain loans. (see chapter 10). In October 1984, the leu was revalued (at 17.5 lei to $1). The search for international credibility triggered a new devaluation, by 17 per cent, in 1986, followed by a continuing revaluation during the following years.

In 1982 Poland introduced a commercial rate for the zloty which was initially (in January 1982) established at 80 zlotys to the dollar and 68 zlotys to the rouble compared to 3.32 and 4.44 zlotys respectively at the previous rate. Unlike Hungary and Romania, Poland did not avoid huge devaluations of the zloty, the value of which, in dollars, was at the beginning of 1989 14 per cent of its 1982 value. Here the devaluation was at the same time a move aiming to impress the foreign creditors, and a way of keeping in line with the black market rates. During the year 1989, the zloty was devalued eighteen times, and indeed almost reached the level of the black market rate, which itself had been lowered due to the introduction of a parallel legal exchange market for individuals.

Czechoslovakia finally introduced a commercial rate at the beginning of 1989. As for the USSR, the decision was taken in 1988 to establish a new exchange rate by 1991. By 1990, a reduction in the number of the 'differentiated currency coefficients' was to be gradually achieved (see chapter 4).

Due to the fact that these 'commercial' rates are calculated from the wholesale prices of only those goods in the foreign trade circuit, they can be applied only to tourist transactions for consumer goods if the prices of these goods are not excessively out of keeping with wholesale prices. Too high an exchange rate discourages the tourist while too low an exchange rate leads to goods and consumer services being 'sold off' to foreigners.

Following a retail price reform, in 1981, Hungary put the finishing touches to its exchange rate mechanism by doing away with the special rate which had until then existed for tourism. Since January 1982, Poland has in principle been using a unified rate. But, in March 1989, according to a law on the possession and the circulation of foreign currency, the individuals obtained the right to buy and sell foreign currency freely in banks or exchange offices. The resulting free market rate was immediately quite close to the black market rate. The measure aimed precisely at discouraging black market exchange. In Romania, considerable differences between wholesale and retail prices are leading to the maintainance of a 'tourist' rate which serves to attract capitalist tourists.

Countries which keep an over-valued exchange rate are, in their turn, forced either to maintain a tourist exchange rate or find alternative means of attracting tourists (or associate the two). The first solution has been opted for by Bulgaria and Czechoslovakia. In November 1989, the Soviet Union introduced a tourist rate under the pressure of a quick depreciation of the rouble in retail trade transactions. The new rate amounted to ten times the official rate (in roubles per unit of foreign currency). As in Poland, the purpose was to discourage black market exchange, and also to siphon roubles from Soviet citizens willing to travel abroad. The GDR was the last country to impose the official rate on the tourist by the end of 1989.

All countries, with the exception of Hungary, offer tourists (and also residents, except in Romania and in the USSR) the opportunity to purchase goods in 'foreign currency shops' where prices are established below par, which is equal to a discount on the normal price. In Hungary, the current exchange rate is much closer to the black market rate than in any other country, and the normal network of shops offers a great enough quantity of imported goods to both nationals and tourists for the foreign currency shop to be rendered redundant.

The numerous applications of partial efficiency calculations show both the usefulness of such calculations for the rationalisation of economic decisions, and their shortcomings when there exists a separation between the foreign and the domestic sectors, and in addition separations within the domestic economies themselves.

Earlier in this chapter we have already seen an example of these difficulties, i.e. the lack of comparability of national data relating to shares of trade with the CMEA countries in total trade. The issue of devaluation is another case. In principle, the quest for a meaningful, 'realistic' exchange rate should be a precondition for regulating foreign trade through devaluation. In fact, the use of devaluation in such a way implies an automatic link between foreign and domestic prices, and freedom of decision of the economic agents in the field of foreign trade. If such conditions are not met, devaluation remains cosmetic and mainly expresses good will toward the IMF (when its help is needed), or toward Western creditors.*

THE GLOBAL OPTIMISATION OF FOREIGN TRADE

The criteria set out above are partial and static. In order to optimise foreign trade, both exports and imports must be taken into account simultaneously (which was the aim of the Trzeciakowski model which was not in fact used for the import side); and a model which links foreign and domestic activities dynamically must be worked out if we are to bring out clearly the changes in internal restructuring required for specialisation to be efficient.

Such models have been put forward (in particular in Hungary and Poland) but have yet to be actually used in planning. The reasons for this have already been outlined: first, there are no rational domestic prices; second, the planner's preferences ensure the inviolability of the geography of foreign trade (e.g. a preferential orientation towards Comecon), and leave unchanged the industrial structure (the division of production into sectors which give priority to production goods), and final demand (the division between investment and consumption); and third, there is an incompatibility between the objective of internal growth fixed at the discretion of planners (e.g., the maximisation of the growth rate given the resources constraints in a system of taut planning) and the balancing of foreign trade. The Polish crisis was an illustration of this incompatiblity: the Polish 'model' for growth at the beginning of the seventies was based on the premise of sustained development through massive imports of equipment from the West, which would in turn generate exports. As this last condition was not fulfilled, we are left with a debt crisis, which will be studied later.

The nature of the international situation after the world crisis modified one important factor in these calculations, and that is the assumption that there would be infinite elasticity of foreign demand from non-socialist countries for exports from socialist countries. This also involved a series of internal adjustments which were greater for the smaller Eastern European countries than for the USSR.

The socialist countries during the crisis: adjustment mechanisms

From the moment the oil price boom in 1973 triggered off the crisis which dealt the Western economies a heavy blow, the question was raised as to the repercussions it would have on Eastern Europe and the USSR. From this point on, according to most of the comments in the Western press, all the real economic difficulties which the European socialist countries were going through came under the blanket term 'crisis in the East' even when these difficulties were rooted in phenomena which preceded the crisis or stemmed from within the Eastern bloc itself.

Questions may be raised as regards the general theme of 'crisis in the East': Was there a 'crisis' in the socialist countries? In fact, it is not enough to point to the existence of a slow-down in growth (though this is real: see Appendix, Table 1) and the worsening of qualitative malfunctionings (paralysis of economic reforms, inefficiency in the use of capital and labour, shortages, the proliferation of a 'parallel economy', phenomena such as corruption, absenteeism, etc.) to conclude that there is a crisis. Any answer to this question involves: (a) a definition of the concept of 'crisis' itself; and (b) the working out of statistical indicators capable of measuring the crisis (the trends in production, in the factor productivity, prices, foreign trade indicators, etc.).

What are the causes of the situation observed? In other words, if there is a 'crisis', are its origins *internal* or *external*? If we suppose that external perturbations lie partially or principally at the root of the observed difficulties, what are the transmission channels of these perturbations and the corresponding adjustment mechanisms?

These points will not be discussed in depth, as numerous studies have already been devoted to them (these include Portes, 1980; Neuberger and Tyson, 1980; Neuberger, Portes and Tyson, 1981; Vanous, 1985; Balassa and Tyson, 1985). Let us first underline three issues as concerns the questions raised above:

1 Unlike the situation which occurred in the market economies, there was no sudden break-off in the economic development of socialist countries. An obvious decline in growth rates had set in at the beginning of the decade and, one could say, since 1950–1955, with a brief rise during this trend in 1966–70 which reflected the impact of economic reforms. The central problem of all socialist economies is one of shifting from extensive growth based on the use of additional labour and capital to intensive growth based on improved use of those factors incapable of expanding as they had done in the past. It is therefore a problem of increasing the overall productivity of the factors. This increase should go hand in hand with the maintenance of full employment. How is this to be achieved? This is the very crux of the debate over the means of spurring on firms and workers to better performances. Can planning efficiency be improved as in the GDR? Or, should market forces be relied on more, after the Hungarian fashion? The Eastern bloc countries were getting

involved in a change-over to a kind of modern industrialised society whose efficiency they found attractive but for which they were neither prepared to pay the social price nor assume the political risk.

2   The gradual opening up of the socialist countries to the outside world since the fifties has rendered them more susceptible to external influences and it is the precise nature of this susceptibility which we will be examining. However, external influences are not always necessarily negative in result. The USSR has gleaned considerable advantage from the West's crisis at least up to 1985. It affected five Eastern European countries negatively. Poland was initially in a situation basically comparable to that of the USSR; the rise in energy prices should have gone in its favour, yet it suffered the deepest crisis.

3   The Polish crisis polarised world attention and distorted the way in which Eastern Europe was seen abroad. Factors specific to Poland were ignored. The conclusion was drawn that, to all intents, the other Eastern bloc countries were going through the same social crisis, but that in their case it was being suppressed by the ruling authorities and the political weight of the USSR.

In the light of this, I will give particular attention to the Polish question, but first I will make an overall examination of the influence of external disturbances on the domestic economies until 1985.

EXTERNAL DISTURBANCES AND DOMESTIC ADJUSTMENT: A GENERAL VIEW, 1975–1985

The European socialist countries do not make up a homogenous whole. In presenting the fundamental characteristics of the planned system, we underlined the differences between these countries, differences which only increased with the development of the post-1965 domestic economic reforms.

What has emerged is a 'traditional' model (which does draw a distinction, according to size and therefore degree of self-sufficiency, between the USSR and the smaller countries, i.e., the GDR, Czechoslovakia and Romania) and a 'decentralised' model, or at least one with a tendency towards some degree of 'decentralisation' such as Hungary, Poland, or to a lesser extent Bulgaria. In 1974–5, the characteristics common to all these countries were as follows:

(a)   social and political objective of full employment;

(b) central planning which establishes macro-aggregates (in particular the division of national income between investment and consumption);

(c) the absence of a cumulative process of inflation (either because of direct price pegging or centralised regulation of prices and wages);

(d) the absence of speculative monetary movements across frontiers;

(e) even for the USSR, and all the more so for the smaller countries, the absence of influence on foreign prices, the economies in question being price-takers on on world markets.

The following differences help to distinguish between the centralised and (relatively) decentralised models (see Table 1). The transmission of external disturbances will differ according to the size of the country and its dominant functioning model.

1   Transmission channels

Several transmission channels may distinguished:

Pressure on domestic prices resulting from rises in world prices. Foreign import prices did in fact rise. This happened from the outset of the crisis for imports from non-socialist countries and occurred only later for imports from socialist countries owing to intra-Comecon price-fixing rules. This pressure resulted in open but controlled inflation for the countries under model ii (Table 1). As concerns the countries of model i, the ever-widening gap between domestic and world prices in the long run brought about a planned price rise which was often quite a sharp one (thus, the GDR and Czechoslovakia raised their domestic energy and basic raw material prices at the end of the seventies, while the USSR, a net *exporter* – not importer – of raw materials and energy, raised its domestic prices on 1 January 1982). It is worth noting that even where wholesale prices have been seen to go up, there has been no rise in consumer-product prices as a direct result of rises in world prices. In Eastern bloc countries, not only are retail prices unconnected to external prices, but they are also unconnected to domestic wholesale prices. The great retail price rises which were noticed in all the socialist countries at the end of the seventies and the start of the eighties were not the direct result of rises in import prices but were due rather to a policy of 'making the populaion aware' of the world economic situation (in particular, as concerns the prices of imported products such as rice, cocoa, coffee and

Table 1. *Centralised and decentralised models*

	Centralised model (I)		Decentralised model (II)
USSR	GDR, Romania, Czechoslovakia		Bulgaria, Hungary, Poland
Low level of openness to international trade	Average level of openness		Average to high level of openness to international trade
Centralised planning of production and foreign trade			Planning with tendencies towards decentralisation
Weak incentives to maximise profit	Limited incentives to maximise profit		Strong incentives to maximise profit
	(concern management of the basic economic units)		
No link between domestic and foreign prices			More or less limited link between domestic and foreign prices

petrol). Food price rises (in Bulgaria in 1981, Czechoslovakia, Romania and especially Poland in 1982) were also designed to catch up with real prices and thus marked the end of ten years of price stability (twenty years of price stability in some cases for basic foodstuffs!). Hungary is the only country in this group to have organised, since 1974–5, a regular and controlled progression of retail prices linking them to wholesale prices (much less than in market economies but to a far greater extent than in the other Eastern European countries). The annual inflation rate for the country reached over 9 per cent in 1980 but even in this case the effects of 'imported inflation' were minimal when compared to voluntary regulation.

The worsening of terms of trade. Here we must distinguish between the six smaller socialist countries (whose terms of trade with industrialised nations deteriorated betwen 1974 and 1980 by as much as 20–25 per cent, while with the USSR they deteriorated by around 20 per cent) and the Soviet Union which, due to the importance of oil and energy sales to the West, was to see a spectacular improvement in its terms of trade with industrialised countries (by over 100 per cent between 1974 and 1980) which was much faster than in its trade with Comecon countries. This deterioration of terms of trade was not uniform for the Six in their relations with the West; it was considerable for Hungary, the GDR, and Czechoslovakia, while Bulgaria, Romania, and Poland, on the other hand, experienced a slight improvement due to the nature of their sales, over 50 per cent of which were agricultural and energy products.

The increase in foreign debt (see chapter 9). An important distinction must be drawn here between the USSR and the Six. While the USSR (like the Six but less worryingly so, given its potential) saw an increase in its debt in convertible foreign currency after 1975 it did, on the other hand, have a great surplus with the other Eastern European countries due to the change in energy prices (see chapter 6). For the Six, the debt owed to the West is a negative consequence of the crisis, while on the other hand, the debt they owed the USSR was an advantage inasmuch as it was expressed in a non-convertible currency.

The reduction in import growth (and even an absolute reduction in imports in 1981–83 between the Six and the non-socialist countries). It should be noted here that this drop in imports was not due to an automatic reaction to the rise in import prices but rather the result of a deliberate adjustment. We have already seen that import requirements do not rise or fall in keeping with prices. Adjustment is made by means of a planned policy of contraction. This leads to repercussions on production, creating bottlenecks when restrictions are placed on intermediate products or spare parts required by factories previously imported from the West.

The difficulty of increasing exports. Eastern European countries had difficulty in exporting 'sensitive' products (steel, chemicals and textiles) given the crisis in the West.

An analysis of these transmission channels brings out both similarities and differences with market economies. The similarities include the facts that: (a) no economy is protected against the effects of terms of trade deterioration; and (b) the effects of market restriction when there is a general recession are present in both markets and this is also true of foreign debt. As for the differences, the effect of imported inflation is always less, and exchange and interest rate considerations do not arise here. Exchange rate constraint is meaningless when currency is non-convertible and there is absolute exchange control. Hungary may be considered an exception, yet its exchange policy since 1976 has been created by voluntary action and not simply through a passive adjustment to the exchange rates of foreign currencies. Interest constraint, when the currency is isolated from the outside world, only comes into play through foreign debt by increasing debt service.

Given these conditions, it is possible to account for the effect of such disturbances in a theoretical analysis based on those categories found in market economies?

2   Adjustments: theoretical analysis

Here we are using the theoretical framework put forward by R. Portes (1980) which is in line with S. Alexander's theory of absorption (developed in the fifties). Let us remind the reader of the definition of absorption based on macro-economic identities:

$$A \equiv Y + M - X$$

(A=absorption, Y=national product, M=imports, X=exports)

$$A \equiv C + I + G$$

(total of domestic uses; C=consumption; I=investment; G=public spending)

$$Y - A \equiv X - M \equiv B$$

(balance of trade).

Alexander's analysis in the context of a market economy has the objective of pinpointing *domestic* reactions to the forming of an additional trade surplus ΔB (which is needed to reestablish equilibrium in the balance of payments) and determining whether they are compatible with the formation and maintainance of this surplus.

The creation of a surplus implies either that Y must grow (the main solution at a time of under-employment), or that absorption must be cut (the main solution at a time of full employment). In other words, the $Y - A$ gap should increase, which is tantamount to an increase of the $X - M$ gap ($Y + M = A + X$ and so $Y - A = X - M$).

Portes points out that in a planned economy, as in a market economy though for different reasons, there may be an *ex ante* imbalance between $(Y - X)$ and $(X - M)$. Indeed:

either $(Y - A)$ planned $> X - M$ (there is a surplus supply due for example to the fact that the surplus goods are neither exportable nor can they be substituted for M, or a reduction in M would affect Y or A owing to complementarity in production or use);

or $(Y - A)$ planned $< X - M$. This is the more normal hypothesis of excessive domestic demand leading to shortages (and giving rise to queues for consumer goods and delays in investment programmes).

In both cases, the balance will be satisfied *ex post* by failure to meet plans.

It can be demonstrated that in a planned economy any measures taken on *either* of the two gaps (internal and external) will: (a) take the form of *direct* intervention (given that it is impossible to take indirect action, for instance through the exchange rate or interest rate; even if in type II economies the use of indirect instruments is possible, it is very limited); (b) will in principle give priority to measures taken on the *supply* side (i.e. on Y or X) as opposed to measures taken on the *demand* side which in market economies would be given priority.

These corrective measures do however come up against obstacles:

(a) Increasing Y is difficult in case of full employment of *all* resources. This 'full employment' certainly involves a suboptimal and inefficient use of resources. Production could be increased by a rise in productivity of labour ratio P/L or by making savings on resources (raw materials and energy). Indeed, these are the objectives proclaimed by all Eastern European countries and, while saving in material resources have been achieved in certain countries (the GDR particularly), the failure to increase P/L remains obvious.

(b) The planned economies are experiencing a phenomenon which Portes calls the 'supply multiplier' where attempts are made to *reduce the component C in A*, or to *reduce the import M of consumer goods*. Excessive demand for goods (if we suppose real wages to be growing, even if slowly, since there is a tendency to keep retail prices stable and low) cannot be satisfied, which leads to a drop in the *actual* labour supply (due to absenteeism, time wasted at the place of work, slack performance) and a fall in production.

(c) Increasing X meets various obstacles, among them poor flexibility of Western demand, protectionism at a time of crisis and poor adaptation to foreign markets.

(d) Reducing M brings the 'bottleneck multiplier' into play preventing supply from being stepped up wherever domestic production capacity is highly dependent on imports (which is the case of the Six).

Which policies have been effectively followed? R. Portes shows that the six 'small countries' managed neither to increase Y to the extent planned in the five-year plans 1976–80, nor to reduce absorption (whether it be through investment or consumption). As for any adjustment using ΔX or $-\Delta M$, this could not be done despite a *reversal* of the relationship between growth rates of X and M in 1976–80 when compared with 1971–75 (in the period 1971–75 ΔX annually to the West was 20 per cent; ΔM from the West was 28 per cent. For 1976–80, ΔX was 15 per cent and ΔM was 8 per cent. In other words, adjustment during this period was made by relying on foreign finance for the main part, this being supported by the high liquidity of the international money market.

For the USSR, the problem of adjustment presented itself in different terms: (a) because the energy crisis considerably increased the USSR's foreign currency earnings (from the sale of oil, and gold as well as arms) through *the rise in foreign prices*; (b) because its level of dependence on the outside world is low.

After 1980 the situation changed. The adjustments carried out followed a pattern which was much more in keeping with the theory of absorption. First, through action on $X-M$. Given the impossibility of increasing X (in 1981–83 sales by the Six to the West dropped by over 20 per cent), these countries reduced their imports considerably (by almost 40 per cent in three years) as the growing difficulty of gaining access to international loans was making further adjustment through foreign financing impossible.

Second, through action on $Y-A$ by a reduction of A, as any substantial increase in Y was made impossible, this being endorsed in the annual and five-year plans. A *drop* (not only a deceleration) *in investment* and stagnation in consumption was noticed in all these countries.

However, all the Eastern European countries, even in the most difficult phase of adjustment, sought to maintain a positive growth rate. They likewise chose reducing productive investment rather than reducing purchasing power in order to maintain a social policy more in keeping with the overall aim of socialism and this was perhaps also due to political considerations born of the Polish crisis.

Two concluding points must be made on the validity of this *theoretical outline*.

First, it could not be said that the above analysis really transposes the theory of absorption which, first and foremost, is a theory of the exchange rate. If one excludes the effects of exchange and interest rate fluctuations (inconceivable in a planned economy, as we have seen), then one removes the central plank from the theory. It is then no more than a descriptive systematic study of the movement of large real aggregates in Keynesian formulation. Such an analysis leads to advocating deflationist economic policies like those suggested by the IMF for countries with repayment problems (indeed, the IMF did just this for Romania in 1981 and Hungary in 1982).

Secondly, the analysis only actually deals with reactions to disturbances caused by the Western crisis, and adjustments directed towards reestablishing the balance of trade in dealings with Western markets. Adaptation pertaining to East–East trade (intra-Comecon trade) and East–South trade, requires a different analysis.

THE CASE OF POLAND (1980–1985)

Owing to its scale, the Polish crisis requires separate examination (Fallenbuchl, 1986). It can be characterised by the following features:

First, an extremely sharp drop in national income occurred from 1981 onwards (−2 per cent in 1979, −4 per cent in 1980, −12 per cent in 1981 and −8 per cent in 1982) with a worsening of all sectorial production indicators. In 1988, national income still remained below its 1978 level.

Second, social upheaval stemmed from an unprecedented and far-reaching attempt to set up a trade union movement independant of the communist party. The 'Gdansk Agreements' of the end of August 1980 marked the start to official dialogue between the authorities and the trade unions after almost two months of strikes and demonstrations. Martial law declared on 13 December 1981 marked the failure of these attempts. The partial lifting of martial law a year after it was declared did not restore social order. Amnesty granted in 1984 also failed to achieve this as unofficial trade union membership remained outlawed.

Third, total disruption of the economic mechanism was caused by a price rise without precedent in a socialist country (25 per cent in 1981, nearly 100 per cent in 1982) and a drop in the supply of consumer goods in real terms as well as an accumulation of bottlenecks stemming from a dramatic restriction on imports from 1981 onwards.

The principal economic causes of the crisis can be set out as follows:
(a) Long-term stagnation of agriculture, the essentially private status of which has been tolerated since 1956 (80 per cent of cultivated land area is under private exploitation) but which is not provided with the necessary means of modernisation.
(b) A spectacular growth of investment at the start of the decade 1970–80, based on a policy of importing Western equipment (hard currency imports grew by 45 per cent per annum between 1971 and 1975).

(c) The failure to expand exports which should have resulted from these imports, caused as much by the recession in the West post-1975, as by delays in commissioning factories brought from the West as the economy was unable to absorb such massive investments.

(d) A policy of rapidly increasing nominal and real wages in 1971–5 (in order to stimulate expansion) linked with the stabilising of essential consumer goods prices. (The authorities had given in to popular resistance in 1970 and 1976 after attempts to introduce a price rise. This price rise could not be introduced in 1980 either and was finally to be brought into effect in February 1982 and meant the doubling, and even the tripling, and quadrupling of certain food prices.)

(e) The dramatic worsening of the balance of trade with non-socialist countries leading to a foreign debt in the order of $7 billion at the end of 1975 rising to $23 billion at the end of 1980 which accounted for 2/5 of the foreign debt of the Six.

(f) The breakdown of internal economic reform once attempts at management decentralisation and planning flexibility in 1973–4 had given way to recentralisation.

Following 1982, Poland managed to partly overcome the crisis through restoring its external balance and launching a market-oriented reform as from 1982. The Polish economy remained, however, plagued by many problems. Even when the debt was rescheduled (see chapter 9) a significant increase in imports was impossible due to the lack of new money. The bottlenecks thus created in the economy added to the domestic shortages. The political reconciliation between the government and the people was not achieved before 1989, and then through recognition of the trade union Solidarity. This restored the interational political credibility of the country without solving domestic internal problems.

The upheaval experienced by Poland made a deep impression on world public opinion. It was both unique and exemplary. It provided a negative answer to the question as to whether a planned economy can free itself from foreign constraint. It showed at the same time, however, that the internal planning and economic policy conditions, along with specific social factors, determine the way both constraint and adjustment policies are expressed.

In March 1922, in a situation of major crisis, Lenin spelled it out in one of his last important speeches to the Party: 'Imminent financial crisis will put us to a difficult test set by the Russian market and by the international market to which we are linked and from which we cannot

separate ourselves.' At the same time, he continues, the real 'final strug-
gle' is being fought within and it is 'the test of competition between
private capitalism and socialism'. Sixty years on, the conditions have
changed but the basic factors remain: the socialist economies are indeed
part of the world economy and do feel the repercussions of external
disturbances. If adaptation to such disturbances is to be successful,
domestic efficiency must be achieved and here planning has yet to prove
itself.

Over the period from 1975 to 1985, the USSR and the Six were not
subjected to the same constraints. The USSR can soften the blow of
disturbances from abroad by its very size and its economic potential
which means it is less involved in the international division of labour.
The world energy crisis was beneficial to the USSR as it was to OPEC
countries in its initial stages. For all that, its in-built protection against
external shocks and the immediate advantages it drew from the oil price
rises also has the effect of freeing the USSR from implementing radical
economic reform and allowed it to put off the shift to the 'intensive
growth' it none the less recognised as indispensable. The Six felt the full
impact of external shocks resulting in the deterioration of their terms of
trade right across the board and an increase in their foreign deficit.
Planning did not protect them. It could even be said that, essentially, it
was a factor aggravating the effect of external disturbances as an initial
voluntary modernisation policy based on imports rendered them more
vulnerable once markets were closed to their products. Central planning
methods, on the other hand, did allow adjustments after a long reaction
time (until 1980) during which foreign financing continued to support a
sluggish growth rate. The austerity policies implemented (including a
drop in investments and the stagnation of the population's purchasing
power) managed more or less to maintain employment, which only
began to be questioned in some countries such as Hungary.

The USSR was subject to a major external shock as the world price of
oil collapsed in 1986, this depriving it of a large amount of foreign trade
revenues. At the same time, the economic reform (*perestroika*) was initiated both in the domestic and in the foreign trade sector. (The changes in
the foreign trade mechanisms are reviewed in chapter 4.) As for the
domestic reform, should it succeed, the USSR would clearly shift away
from the 'centralised model' towards the 'decentralised model'. In the
short run, the reform is revealing the hidden malfunctionings, fuelling
open inflation and financial imbalances, disrupting the traditional plan-

ned mechanisms. As a result of political liberalisation coupled with economic reform, the Centre had to relax its control over the peripheral (i.e., republican) economies.

The reform movement in the USSR challenged the Eastern European countries both politically and economically. The external constraint which hit the USSR resulted in a hardening in the conditions of trade imposed upon the Soviet partners within the CMEA. The simultaneous occurrence of a change in the world environment, i.e., the collapse of oil prices, and in the socialist system itself, i.e., the new economic policy initiated by the Soviet leadership, opened the way for a new adjustment process. This process is no longer a 'transmission-response' scheme expressing a domestic reaction to external disturbances, but a deeper structural adaptation which requires an efficient industrial policy within each country. Developments in the USSR and most of Eastern Europe (leaving aside Romania) make it clear that such a process may entail a change in the system itself. What should we call the new system? The expressions of 'market socialism', 'reformed economies', 'transition economies' are increasingly used. Poland and Hungary are the first evolve toward a multiparty political system and a market-type, not to speak of capitalist-type, economy. A major component of the transition is openness to the world economy. Openness is required to secure better trade conditions, better access to world markets and to international financial assistance. It requires, in turn, as it is perceived in the East and recommended in the West, a firm commitment to the introduction of a domestic market, hence to the gradual dwindling of planning, and also to non-state forms of ownership. How to get there? How will such trends affect socialist international trade and finance? We shall attempt to provide some answers in the following chapters.*

PART I

———— · ————

POLARISATIONS AND POLICIES

Are the socialist countries engaged in the world division of labour in the same way as market economies? The capitalist system lays down the guidelines for the world division of labour, whether it be the case of North–South interactions or international specialisation linking industrial nations; it does so largely through the network of multi-national companies. How can socialist countries take part in this?

It must be pointed out first that their international economic activity is polarised according to ideological and systemic criteria which divide the world into three zones: East, West, and South. The relations within the first zone are the object of a strong preference which is not without its conflicts. Relations with the non-socialist world were initially based upon quite different principles according to their directions, South or West; they are now following an economic rather than a systemic logic.

To the socialist countries, the principle of mutual advantage is the cement of foreign economic relations as a whole. In its most crudely simplified form, it all boils down to the question of what one can get in return for what one provides. The concept of cooperation conceals the materiality of the *quid pro quo* which includes bargaining among divergent interests within the socialist community, the imposing of countertrade in East–West trade, and assistance which is not quite disinterested in East–South relations.

The trade and cooperation activities are implemented by economic agencies which, initially at least, are bound to the state to an even greater extent than is the case in the domestic economy for state enterprises. State monopoly of foreign trade is however being amended and limited by a series of reforms. The reforms aim at increasing the efficiency of foreign trade by giving more freedom to the enterprise. The socialist enterprises engage in direct trading with their partners, and increasingly take part in joint ventures with equity participation. Does the state monopoly remain an original sin, which confers an inevitably protectionist stamp on the behaviour of the socialist countries? The most open socialist nations complain of not being recognised as 'normal' participants in international trade, accepting the same rules of play and therefore enjoying the same advantages. For these countries, the heavy hand of state trading is only invoked by their partners as an excuse for imposing protectionism which discriminates against them.

In the following three chapters, the reader must not expect to find a review of the postwar or even post-seventies quantitative developments in East–East, East–South, or East–West trade. These developments are summarised in statistical form in the Appendix, Tables 3 to 5. The geographical structure of Comecon Seven's foreign trade is fairly stable since the beginning of the seventies. Trade within the socialist bloc averages 60 per cent of the total trade of the Seven, trade with the West is slightly under 30 per cent, and trade with the South slightly over 10 per cent (see Appendix, Table 4). Trends in the trade values, overall and by areas (Appendix, Table 3), are closely linked with the commodity composition of trade (Appendix, Table 5) which is to be discussed in Part II.

CHAPTER 2

———————— · ————————

THE THREE-WAY POLARISATION OF
INTERNATIONAL ECONOMIC RELATIONS

The world as seen by the socialist countries is divided up on an ideological basis. Socialism is pitted against capitalism, collective ownership against private ownership of means of production, planning against the market.

What are the consequences which such divisions entail for international trade? The increasing internationalisation of the world economy is committing the socialist countries to foreign relations which are essentially heterogeneous. Part of their foreign trade is conducted within the socialist system itself. Another part has been set up with countries belonging to a system which socialism has in principle the ultimate aim of eliminating. Capitalism in itself is not a homogeneous whole as it comprises developed nations whose imperialist domination is said to be imposed on developing nations.

There is therefore an East–West–South polarisation of trade. The political and ideological background of relations within these three poles is significantly different. The economic background is, however, identical: if foreign trade is recognised as beneficial for economic growth, then it follows that the greatest advantage must be drawn from it for the country in question, whoever its partners are. These two rationales are liable to conflict with each other. Which of them is winning? Contrary to a widely held belief, it is in fact economic considerations which in the long run get the better of the political vicissitudes. This is so, in any case, for the East. It is not necessarily true for the countries dealing with the Eastern bloc.

When it comes to the institutional organisation of economic relations, the systemic rationale still dominates. The socialist countries are very keen on the existence of a stable institutionalised framework through which to carry out trade with their partners. The nature of these partners will determine the nature of the framework according to the same three basic polarisations.*

The rationale behind the polarisations

The current geo-political wording of international relations makes use of the cardinal points in a non-neutral way. In East–West relations, the centrally planned economy is confronted by industrialised capitalism. The socialist countries claim to be equal partners with the West. However, they do not admit that they might be taking part in North–South interaction in which they should stand alongside the rich nations of the North; East–South relations are not just a variety of the North–South model. In socialist thinking the South is divided up into two groups of nations. Some have acceded to socialism, and this systemic considera-tion takes precedence over their state of underdevelopment. The socialist Third World is part of the East. The great mass of developing countries is in the capitalist orbit, and it is now acknowledged that they will remain there for some time yet. The classifications used in UN statistical reports reflect the ambiguity of this 'trinity', distinguishing between 'developed market economies', 'developing market economies', and 'centrally plan-ned economies' (this classification, however, does not totally match the socialist one since, for the UN, Yugoslavia (since 1985) and Cuba are both in the second group).

THE EAST

The East – which means here the socialist system – has been formed historically with the Soviet Union at its centre. At the heart of the system is Comecon** set up in January 1949 by Bulgaria, Hungary, Poland, Romania, Czechoslovakia, and the USSR. Albania joined in February 1949 and the GDR in 1950. Between 1956 and 1958, several states received observer status including Yugoslavia, Mongolia, China, the People's Democratic Republic of Korea, and the Democratic Republic of Vietnam. Cuba, which went socialist in 1959, was accepted in 1965 as an observer. Three of the observers became full members: Mongolia in

---

**The official acronym is CMEA, Council for Mutual Economic Assistance. Comecon means exactly the same and sounds more euphonic, however in the Soviet and East European literature the term is considered as politically unfriendly, for reasons difficult to understand. Does it sound too much like 'Cocom', perhaps? According to van Brabant (1988) it is also because the term reminds them of Comintern and Cominform.

1962, Cuba in 1972, and reunified Vietnam in 1978. In 1964, Yugoslavia was granted the special status of associate member. Albania ceased to participate in Comecon meetings in 1961 and as there is no formal expulsion procedure would, strictly speaking, still seem to be a member though to all intents and purposes it no longer belongs to the organisation.

All fourteen states mentioned in the above paragraph are socialist, of which ten are to-day members of Comecon. If the list is to be exhaustive, we should include Laos, a country whose exact date of accession to socialism is difficult to determine but would be between 1976 and 1978 (1978 is the first point at which Laos is seen as socialist by Soviet foreign trade statistics!). As for Cambodia (formerly Kampuchea), its status is left unsettled as long as the country itself remains under *de facto* Vietnamese administration, pending an international agreement which began to be negociated in 1989.

The vagueness over the defining of Laos points to a certain shift in the very notion of socialism. Up to 1976, countries granted the status of observer in Comecon were always 'officially' socialist countries. Since then, countries such as Afghanistan, South Yemen, Ethiopia, Angola, Mozambique, and finally Nicaragua, so-called 'countries with a socialist orientation' have been granted observer status. In 1981 and subsequent to this, Mozambique sought membership and was refused – on economic grounds. It was felt that its membership would have cost the socialist community too much. We can therefore witness the emergence of a set of states on the periphery of East and South, which, while being officially recognised as socialist in orientation, may yet remain outside the socialist community. If they cannot be members they are offered the status of cooperant. The first cooperation agreement was signed in 1973 with Finland – to establish a sort of parallel with the status of the country *vis-à-vis* the EEC; two other agreements followed in 1975, with Iraq and Mexico, without any significant economic consequences. But beginning in 1984 a new round of cooperation agreements were concluded with all the countries with a 'socialist orientation', the last one in October 1987 with Afghanistan, probably both as a compensation for the non-admission to Comecon and as a final settlement of the question. The very notion of 'socialist orientation' is now controversial. Eastern European countries (with the exception of the GDR, which followed the Soviet stance) were never sympathetic to it as it would have meant increased aid from them. Since 1988, there has been much discussion on the matter in the Soviet international literature. This discussion is no longer limited to the issue of the stability of a socialist orientation, as before, but addressed a much more essential question: what is the socialist system towards which the relevant countries are supposed to be oriented?*

Comecon is the privileged area of international trade for its 'Group of Seven' European members. It is an economic integration. May we compare it with the European Economic Community? The issue is not only a point of theory. To understand the exact nature of Comecon is important for clarifying some of the puzzling problems of the organisation, such as that of the 'implicit subsidies' of the USSR to the East European countries. In view of this, it is worth briefly outlining its history which can be broken down into several periods. Comecon appeared as an *ad hoc* politicial move (1949), seemed to move toward a supranational status (1962), then tried to achieve an integration pattern based on plan coordination in a few fields combined with market principles in trade (1971). This plan–market combination proved as little viable as the one which was sought in the domestic reforms. A new round of common structural policies seemed to open in 1984. Since 1988, Comecon is explicitly heading toward an unified market. In fact, the whole organisation has never been shaken so strongly by centrifugal tendencies. This leads to the question of what Comecon really is, i.e., what still holds together the member countries in this common market without market, in this union without any really agreed policy.

The beginnings: 1949–1962

The organisation, set up to counter the launching of the Marshall Plan and reinforce the bonds between the people's democracies and the USSR, had limited competence and activities. The general principles for the organisation of trade were then laid down as were the initial guidelines for concerted specialisation.

The supranational planning dream: 1962–1971

Following the adoption of the 'Basic principles of the socialist international division of labour' and the strengthening of the organisation's institutional structure (1962) the USSR sought to promote genuine multilateral coordination of the national plans. Open opposition (from

Romania) or inertia on the part of the member states brought about the failure of this development.

Combining plan and market integration? 1971–1984

In 1971 a 'Comprehensive Programme for the intensifying of cooperation and the development of integration' was adopted. It brought about a compromise between two very opposed standpoints on integration, through the market or through the plan. Integration achieved through the market is supposed to draw very close to the EEC model. It implies the free circulation of goods within the area, rational market-type prices, and the gradual introduction of convertibility for socialist currencies. Such an integration obviously requires a greater flexibility of domestic planning and enterprise management in each country. Integration through the plan, on the other hand, means more far-reaching and more constraining coordination of the internal planning of each country.

These two concepts failed to be implemented, because of the internal economic difficulties experienced by the East European countries in the seventies and because of the new patterns in trade brought about by Soviet oil price rises (see chapter 6 on energy). The standstill in economic reforms and the pressure of external constraint made it impossible to liberalise mutual trade. On the other side, the member states did not have the means to undertake major joint projects. The absolute fall in investment in the six East European countries after 1980 (see Appendix, Table 2) made it impossible to free national resources for large-scale common operations. Low-level cooperation therefore was the result. In addition to this, the Polish crisis was seriously disturbing Comecon multilateral mechanisms and demonstrated the lack of institutional solidarity or multilateral assistance in a time of disturbances.

The grand design of technological cooperation: 1984–1988

The following stage of integration is much more difficult to define because of the intertwining of events on the domestic scene and on the international scene, in the Gorbachev era. Just a year before Gorbachev's accession to power, a summit meeting of the communist party leaders was held, in June 1984; it had been advocated by L. Brezhnev already in 1981. The summit launched several new concepts which at first glance seemed to have been created only to justify the specific demands addressed by the USSR to its partners. These concepts were the following: the concertation (*soglasovanie*) of economic policies; the convergence (*sblizhenie*) of the structures of the economic mechanisms; finally, the future development of direct inter-firm or inter-association links, including the creation of joint firms.

In fact, by that time the Soviet Union had built up a huge surplus in transferable roubles (the non-convertible monetary unit of Comecon) since 1975, due to the price increases for oil and raw materials sold to its partners, along with a much slower increase in the prices of manufactured goods supplied by the East European countries. The USSR did not succeed in materialising its gains from improved terms of trade by increasing the value of its imports from East Europe at the same rate as the value of its exports. The specifics of price fixing within Comecon will be discussed later (chapter 6) and also the operation of the socialist monetary system (chapter 8). It will be taken for granted that these mechanisms did not succeed in bringing about a balanced trade between the 'Six' smaller East European countries and the USSR. Thus, a new pattern of socialist integration emerged:

(i)   socialist integration was to be explicitly focussed on the USSR, through a set of bilateral relations between the USSR and each of the Six;

(ii)   it no longer implied the participation of members in joint activities, but structural internal adjustments increasing the complementarity between the Soviet economy and the economies of the smaller countries;

(iii) it relegated market relations to a position of least importance. Trade was seen as large-scale physical compensation between supplies to and from the USSR. Food products and high quality equipment and manufactured consumer goods were meant to balance deliveries of fuels and raw materials. To meet Soviet requirements, the Comecon countries were supposed to adjust through a long-term restructuring of their economies, the final outcome being an all-embracing specialisation within Comecon.

The first move following the 1984 summit was to devise a Comprehensive Programme of Scientific and Technical progress (STP Programme) for technological cooperation up to the year 2000. The STP Programme was adopted in December 1985 so that its provisions might be included in the five-year plans 1986–90. It covered five areas: electronics, automation, nuclear energy, new materials, and biotechnologies. The projects were to be launched both through intergovernmental agreements, and through direct inter-firm contracts. The programme was to initiate an era of technological integration, and to promote the development and manufacturing of articles which up to then had had to be imported from the West.

The launching of this new programme overlapped with the beginning of the Gorbachev era and of the 'restructuring' (*perestroika*) in the Soviet Union. This made it more difficult than ever to reach the goal of *rapprochement* the domestic economic mechanisms, as none of the Six had quite the same conception of reform as the USSR. Hungary and Poland were undoubtedly the closest, but even these countries did not follow exactly the same line, if only because, in the case of Hungary and, partially, Poland, they had initiated it earlier. Bulgaria and Czechoslovakia paid lip-service to the Soviet scheme but with a definite reluctance, especially in the case of Czechoslovakia whose leaders were compelled to praise what they had fought against twenty years earlier after the failure of the 'Prague Spring' and the Soviet-led 'normalisation'. As for the GDR and Romania, both countries were resolutely against any 'bringing nearer' of their economic system to that of the USSR: the GDR because the efficiently centralised German pattern of management through large-scale industrial 'combines' had proved successful, Romania because the Ceaucescu regime was increasingly drifting away from Soviet influence.

All the Eastern European countries, however, as well as the Soviet Union, aimed at making the domestic economies more efficient, and this was supposed to be the basis for the 'concertation of economic policy'. According to the standard wording of the Soviet and East European textbooks, it meant a shift from extensive to intensive growth, that is, rationalisation of factor utilisation, higher technical level and quality of production, as opposed to growth through use of additional labour or capital. Changes in the present industrial structure of the Eastern European countries, however, are not easy to make, because this structure has been shaped according to the growth strategy which was imposed upon them by the Soviet Union in the late forties. High energy-intensive and raw materials-intensive industries have been developed to process energy and raw materials obtained from the USSR. Mass production of machinery capacities have been set so as to satisfy the needs of the

Soviet Union, the poor quality of the production making it impossible to sell these goods on Western markets. Those structures are powerfully protected by domestic heavy industry lobbies. Whereas efficiency considerations would require more flexible mechanisms, the industrial structure inherited from the past both requires and favours a centralised protective pattern of management. This explains why the shift to intensive growth already has a long history, since the end of the sixties, in purpose – but not in implementation.*

The STP Programme aimed at accelerating this shift through joint efforts. 'Direct links' between enterprises were to be set up, and this was the last of Brezhnev's legacies, but they required more flexibility in the integration mechanism. Enterprises belonging to different countries should have been able to exchange goods freely, to fix their contracting prices and currencies. However, the rigid bilateralism in trade, along trade agreements negociated on the inter-governmental level and specifying the quantities and/or the values of the goods exchanged, were strongly impeding the setting of 'direct links', as was the rigidity of the domestic procedures. In fact, a liberalisation of intra-Comecon trade is possible only if and when the *domestic* enterprises have free access to their *domestic* market, which was far from realised in 1985.

All these requirements suggested a redefinition of the principles of Comecon.

Towards a single socialist market? 1988 onwards

A new 'Collective Concept for the International Socialist Division of labour for 1991–2005' was adopted at the 44th Session of the Comecon council in Prague (July 1988). At first glance, the new 'concept' looked very much like the 1971 Comprehensive Programme in the attempt to reconcile plan integration and market integration. But the principle of coordination in planning cannot be understood in 1988 as in 1971, because the nature of the planning process itself has changed. In an increasing number of countries, planning is (or at least is supposed) to be done at the level of the enterprise and no longer at the level of the central authorities. In parallel, at the same session, an agreement was signed between all the Comecon members except Romania 'to ensure the gradual formation of conditions for the free movement of goods, services and other production factors among them, with a view to forming a unified market in the long term once the preconditions for that have been studied'.

In its final phase, the CMEA is thus defining itself as a sort of 'common market' with a set of coordinated economic policies. Is this the logic of an integrated community of the EEC type?*

What Comecon really is

We are again faced with the question already asked in chapter 1. Is it possible to apply the standard set of analytical instruments used in economics when explaining the centrally planned economies? Or, after stating that Marxist analysis does not help much, should one try and devise an alternative *sui generis* type of explanation?

The matter was discussed during several years as a by-product of what has been called 'the subsidy issue': was the Soviet Union subsidising the Eastern European countries through the system of intra-bloc prices, especially in the period 1973–83 when the prices for oil were rising on the world market? The 'subsidy debate' will be discussed later on (chapter 6) along with the problem of oil prices. Here we shall only mention the theoretical background of the debate. The authors who supported the 'subsidy thesis' (Marrese, Vanous, 1983) applied the standard opportunity cost theory to the foreign trade data of the Soviet Union. According to them, the Soviet Union suffered losses because its intra-bloc terms of trade had a different pattern compared to its terms of trade with the West. In intra-bloc trade, the USSR had been selling (mainly oil) at less than world prices and buying (mainly machinery) at higher than world prices. As there was no economic explanation for such behaviour by the USSR, non-economic reasons had to be invoked for the rationale of intra-bloc cohesion and privileged trade. According to the authors, these reasons were, for the Soviet Union, 'unconventional gains from trade' in terms of the political, ideological, and military allegiance of its satellites; for the Eastern European countries, reciprocally, these 'unconventional losses' were compensated for by economic gain. The alternative view is provided by Holzman (1987), followed by Brada (1988). Without discussing the materiality of the subsidies, these authors see them as explicable through the customs union theory. This theory states that the formation of a customs union usually leads to trade creation among partners through the lowering of trade barriers but also to trade diversion at the expense of third nations through tariff discrimination. Holzman argues that the standard theory may be modified so as to accommodate the specific features of centrally planned economies. In these economies, there are no tariffs or explicit quotas; they are not necessary because foreign trade is conducted in the framework of a state monopoly. Historically, the losses from trade diversion, according to Holzman, fell first on Eastern Europe, then (since the late fifties) on the Soviet Union. In addition, the system leads to absolute 'trade destruction' instead of trade creation, with all the countries suffering from the resulting losses.

In both of these approaches, the political factor is present. It is assumed that the Soviet Union had a strong political motivation to form a polarised trade area with Eastern Europe after the Second World War and that its satellites had little or no choice but to agree. But what brings the Comecon countries together *now*?

Among the authors attached to the specifics of socialist integration, Sobell (1984) argues that unlike a market-oriented integration aiming at maximising efficiency, Comecon is an 'international protection system' whose aim is to maximise stability, even at a great economic loss. But then, how can one evaluate the numerous statements in the socialist literature criticising the operation of Comecon precisely for its lack of efficiency? The alternative view is provided by van Brabant (1988). The argument, very much simplified, is as follows: to successfully implement their domestic reforms and sustain their modernisation drive, the centrally planned economies more than ever need to develop their links with the West. But in this case they need to be competitive on Western markets and this competitiveness may be enhanced by a more effective socialist economic integration. How to achieve this, though, remains an open question, which cannot be answered at this point.

Both views assume that socialist integration is a reality, however imperfect. Centrifugal trends are however increasing. In 1988–89, growing dissatisfaction was expressed by several Comecon members, first and foremost Hungary. In this country the question of whether it might be preferable to leave was openly discussed. But to step out is not an easy thing. It was long taken for granted that the cohesion of Comecon was politically imposed by the USSR on its European partners. Should this no longer be the case, Comecon countries have not yet a free choice, because of their lack of competitiveness on Western markets, itself due to a growth strategy shaped after the Second World War. The privileged links within Comecon might then be seen as a trap committing its members to unwillingly play a negative-sum game.

Up to now we have considered the developed part of Comecon, that is, the Six plus the Soviet Union (even though for political reasons Romania has chosen to call herself a developing country). Comecon, besides this group, includes three underdeveloped countries: Cuba, Mongolia, and Vietnam. These countries, according to socialist conceptions, are not among the 'developing countries' group. The socialist system cannot be seen to be reproducing the division between rich and poor nations. The East has no 'North–South' dimension. The only way to get out of the contradiction between doctrine and the reality of underdevelopment within Comecon is to alter reality. Thus, the 1971 Programme assigned to the member states the task of giving preferential aid to Mongolia. Subsequently, Cuba and Vietnam were added for such treatment. The 1988 session of Comecon adopted together with the 'collective concept of international socialist division of labour', a long-term multilateral programme of cooperation with these three less developed states.

Here we see clearly the impasse in which socialist-orientated countries find themselves. Comecon cannot have any 'poor' countries. An extreme gulf between levels of development cannot be tolerated in a socialist community. It must therefore be lessened. This however is expensive. Therefore, beyond a certain limit which it would seem has now been reached, new members cannot be accepted – unless of course they are rich. According to Marx, the revolution was to happen first in highly industralised countries. History showed that Marx was wrong: revolution occurred first in industrially less advanced countries. But nowadays, the association he established between revolution and a high level of industrialisation seems to hold true: once the socialist system became richer, its doors began to close for the poorest.

True, the socialist system is not limited to Comecon. But the group of 'other socialist countries' has no economic unity and its ideological unity is purely formal. Of the five countries concerned, Laos and North Korea are in fact treated like the other developing countries (with proportionally greater aid). China has weak trade relations with Comecon–Europe although these fluctuate according to the political climate and are on the rise since Gorbachev's accession to power. Trade with Albania is negligible. The only really significant partner in this group is Yugoslavia. Relations with Yugoslavia, a country heavily involved in a whole set of sectoral cooperation undertakings with Comecon, are none the less more on the lines of the East–West model (for example, trade is settled in convertible currencies while payments with a 'Western' country such as Finland are done through clearing!).

THE SOUTH

In official texts listing trade partners the developing countries always come immediately after the socialist ones. However, as Table 4 (Appendix) shows, the contribution made by developing countries to socialist trade falls significantly short of that made by the developed countries. The ranking accorded to developing nations is thus an indication of the ideological preference they enjoy.

But why should relations between socialist and developing countries be of a particular and privileged nature? The answer is increasingly complicated. Here once again, we can isolate several stages.

1955–1964. This was the first stage of East–South relations, from decolonisation to the creation of new independent states. Politically, socialist countries assured these countries of their support and solidarity. Economically, considerable aid was granted to a small number of countries with the avowed aim of turning them away from capitalism. This was a period of major projects such as the Aswan dam, which in 1956 the USSR offered to finance after the withdrawal of American aid, and the Bhilai steel complex in India. In 1964, 80 per cent of Soviet cooperation credits went to eight countries: Egypt, Ghana, Iraq, Syria, Algeria, Indonesia, India, and Afghanistan. The ratio between aid given by the socialist countries and aid extended by the capitalist countries was never again to be as high as during this period (Valkenier, 1983).

1964–1976. This period starts with the first UNCTAD (United Nations Conference for Trade and Development) meeting where the Eastern bloc gave unconditional support to the claims of the developing nations, and ended with the fourth UNCTAD meeting where the socialist nations, like the developed capitalist ones, saw themselves confronted by the demands of the South as set out by the 'Group of 77' (which now consists of nearly 130 developing countries, and was founded at the first UNCTAD in Geneva, in 1964). The Eastern bloc countries were then increasingly concerned by their economic interests in the South. At the same time, the initiation of the North–South debate and the seeking of a new international economic order was going ahead without them. Their non-participation in the debate was logical from their point of view as they did not want to be involved as part of the 'North'. Yet, be that as it may, it still appeared as a collective dereliction of world responsibilities in preference for outdated traditional principles.

1976 onwards. Next came the stage of a restrained support for Third World countries. These were no longer considered a homogeneous whole destined sooner or later to opt for the socialist path to development. As Oleg Bogomolov, the director of the Institute of the World Socialist System in Moscow wrote in 1980: 'It would be inaccurate to state that relations between the socialist world and the developing countries are built on the principle of socialist solidarity. No. We deal with states, the majority of which have chosen the capitalist path to development. Only a few of them have opted for socialist orientation' (Bogomolov, 1980, p. 258). Among the countries of the first group, we find the 'intermediate capitalist' countries or 'sub-imperialist centres', as Evgueni Primakov, formerly director of the Institute of World Economy and International Relations (IMEMO), calls them. These countries have in their turn become instruments of capitalist exploitation and their multinational companies are no less imperialist than those situated in the developed nations. These, according to Western terminology, are the 'newly industrialising countries' (Primakov, 1980).

The obligations of the socialist countries have thus become far more qualified. Real solidarity is conceivable only with those countries seen as having a 'socialist orientation' and which, generally speaking, are also the poorest. We have seen earlier that even this might be questioned in the future, should the very notion of 'socialist orientation' be discarded. Which countries does this include for the time being? A systematic count would include, besides the six nations which have become observers since 1976, 13 other countries which come under this heading because they once chose a socialist path to development and maintain political links with socialist countries. These are Algeria, Benin, Burma, the Cape Verde Islands, Congo, Guinea (up to 1984), Guinea-Bissau, Iraq, Madagascar, Mali, Syria, Tanzania, and Zambia (Libya has never been mentioned in this group although it is often considered as a 'client' state from the Soviet point of view). Curiously enough, the only more or less 'official' document to have given this list is the announcement of the delegations which attended the funeral of Iuri Andropov (*Pravda*, 14 February 1984). Since then, Burkina-Faso should probably be added to the list. This group of nations, (including Burkina-Faso and excluding Guinea) accounts for over 250 million inhabitants which is almost 10 per cent of the total population of the developing world (1987 figures).

Socialist orientation, it must be remembered, is a reversible process. Admission to Comecon as an observer is a sign of confidence from its members that the choice is irrevocable. Political circumstances affecting such a choice should not however be overlooked. There is a long list of countries once well disposed to socialism which none the less opted for an alternative choice, from Ghana and Indonesia to Egypt and Somalia. Political take-overs have always ushered in a period of uncertainty, as was the case in Guinea after the death of Sekou Toure in 1984. Close political relations and dynamic trade are not enough to assure a country entry into this group. There are also basic incompatibilities such as Islamic fundamentalism which makes Libya's entry impossible.

The granting of aid to the 'capitalist' Third World is a much less urgent obligation. In 1976 (UNCTAD IV) and 1979 (UNCTAD V) the socialist countries categorically put the responsibility for the crisis and difficulties the developing world was going through on the industrialised capitalist world. The same was stated at UNCTAD VII (1987) regarding the problem of international indebtedness. Such a collective attitude is sometimes criticised in some small Eastern European countries as a political argument which, while certainly convenient, is too easily exploited by the capitalists. The other justification for granting limited aid lies in the economic difficulties experienced by the Eastern European countries in the eighties. Though seldom put forward in explicit terms, this idea very much influences actual policies. Thus, since 1980–81 and up to the fall in oil prices in 1986, the small Eastern European countries have managed to attain great surpluses in their trade with the developing world, by reducing their purchases and stepping up sales especially towards the more solvent Middle East states. The USSR has remained more sensitive to the political aspect of its presence in the Third World, but, for all that, does not automatically pass up economically advantageous opportunities (through arms sales in particular).

Attitudes towards the new international economic order (NIEO) are also influenced by such considerations. Here, once again, the USSR in official stances taken in international organisations, is more positive than other socialist countries towards NIEO theses put forward in the Third World. The NIEO programme is however seen as relatively incoherent and contradictory. It ignores the fundamental difference between capitalism and socialism and distinguishes between 'rich' and 'poor' countries instead, without taking systemic differences into consideration. It does not provide for changes in capitalist production relations (in Marxist terms, in the ownership of capital goods). It is too favourable towards the interests of the multinational firms. Eastern economic literature puts it in even blunter terms. The Polish economist, M. Paszynski, frankly acknowledges that:

> the position of the socialist countries towards the new international economic order has been so far reduced to three basic components: general support for developing countries' demands addressed to developed capitalist countries; refusal to acknowledge the demands that the 'Third World' puts to them; and the absence of a vision of global solutions for the grand problems of the world economy. (Paszynski, 1980)

No unified view on the NIEO exists within the European Comecon countries. Such a position is not to be expected in the near future. First, the interests of the socialist countries in the Third World are divergent depending on the structure of their trade with the South; second, these interests are contrary to the commitments to which the Third World countries would like to make them suscribe. One may also question the relevancy of the whole discussion. The NIEO Programme was launched in the mid-seventies in the framework of the United Nations, and its implementation has never really begun. The socialist countries, therefore, are increasingly resolved to develop their relations with the South on the basis of mutual advantage – without exploitation, but not necessarily with preferential treatment. As an exception, a symbolic gesture may take place. This was the case in 1987, when the Soviet Union finally decided to ratify, after more than ten years of reflection, the agreement on the UN Commodity Fund, conceived at UNCTAD IV (1976), which had been designed to help keep commodity prices stable. Generally speaking, the idea of a special relationship with the developing world gives way to concerns of national interest – just as in relations with the West.

While noteworthy differences remain in the views of the socialist countries on the NIEO, there is indeed much more unity on the question of international interaction. With a growing insistence, these countries ask for a joint discussion of East–West, East–South and North–South issues. This is a position politically unacceptable to most Western countries. What is meant by the interdependence issue is that one should not ask the socialist countries to grant special privileges to their Third

World partners (in terms of access to markets, financial facilities, etc.) while they are themselves discriminated against in world trade and finance by their Western developed partners (see Lavigne, 1988a, chapter 6).*

THE WEST

It has been commonplace to say that East–West trade is by definition very much influenced by the political factor. This seems to be borne out by both sides. *Détente* is supposed to give an impetus to trade and international tension to constrain it. It is thus paradoxical that East–West economic relations turn out to be much less fraught with conflict than East–East or East–South relations. In fact, the East–West scene has been very much influenced by events which occurred in East–South relations (the entry of Soviet troops into Afghanistan, December 1979) or within the Eastern bloc (the imposing of martial law in Poland, December 1981), to mention the two major sources of international tension in the eighties. The history of Comecon has been marked by economic conflict, Romania's resistance to any supra-national concept of integration being the most striking case. East–South relations have always been beset by upheavals, for instance, by the renouncing of socialist orientation.

The paradox is more apparent than real. The rationale behind East–West relations is, first and foremost, an economic one. Economic interests have always dominated in actual business. True, Western governments have often made an issue out of East–West economic relations, and Western media have dramatised such conflicts as, for instance, the one about the gas pipeline (see chapter 6). But economic interests have consistently prevailed over political conflicts, as the actual trends show:

(1) in the initial phase (1955–65), the decision to open up to the West was seen in the East by economists and leaders as an additional factor for economic growth. For the West, particularly Europe, it was seen as creating new outlets;

(2) the period of maximum trade expansion (1966–75) coincided with *détente* coupled with increased economic complementarity: the East sought modernisation by purchasing Western technology so as to increase the effect of internal domestic reforms, while Western com-

panies were finding vast markets for major equipment sales. This was the 'golden age' of East–West trade;

(3)   the slow-down in trade which set in after 1975 went hand-in-hand with growing political tension but was basically due to economic causes. These included the Western recession which meant a reduced market for sales from the East (especially for manufactures), the debt crisis in the East, and the domestic slowdown fuelled by the adjustment policies conducted in Eastern Europe. At the same time, the USSR which was held responsible for the bad political climate was expanding its trade with the West with growing grain purchases and energy sales;

(4)   the beginning of the Gorbachev period saw a gradual improvement in East–West political relations, but a decrease in Soviet–West trade. External constraint was hitting the USSR through the fall in oil prices. Here again, the economic setting has determined the pace of trade.

Are economic interests stronger in the East? This is certainly often said to be the case. For the West, East–West trade has a marginal weight (less than 3 per cent of the total trade of the OECD countries is conducted with the Seven in the eighties); for the East it is quite substantial (25 to 30 per cent on average since 1970).

This is however an overall view. In the *West*, trade with the East is highly concentrated on a small number of companies and products. For the firms in question, orders from the East probably provide for some hundreds of thousands of jobs only in Europe. Loss of Eastern orders can lead to bankruptcy in some cases. As far as products are concerned, grain and gas deals between the USSR and the West have created strong interdependence. Trade with the East is not seen by those engaged in it as second best to trade in industrially developed markets, but as an alternative to trade with developing countries. This alternative offers closer outlets (for Western Europe in particular), often more reliable markets, and, in the case of the USSR, much bigger opportunities and less risk.

The economic interest which *the socialist countries* have in developing East–West trade is certainly more crucial than is the case for Western countries. This is seen not only in the percentage of East–West trade in overall trade. Trade with industrialised countries is more advantageous, for the socialist countries, than intra-Comecon or East–South trade.

Intra-Comecon trade was supposed to develop in line with intra-industrial cooperation according to the ideal scheme of the international socialist division of labour. As this could not be achieved, what holds Comecon together is Eastern Europe's dependence on the USSR for energy and mineral resources. This is neither satisfactory for the USSR nor for Eastern Europe. A tonne of oil sold to the West earns more for the USSR (qualitatively especially) than it would if supplied to its partners. As for Eastern European countries, they feel burdened by the obligation to provide the USSR with products which they could otherwise export (or believe they could) to the West. In relations with the developing world, prospects for expansion are limited as the Third World remains oriented towards the industrialised market economies.

The USSR and the Six therefore do have strong economic motivation to develop trade and cooperation with the West. However, for the West, economic interests are not homogeneous in the East. The USSR is an ideal trading partner for the West. It represents an immense and solvent market. It offers Western Europe the same supplies of energy and minerals as the Third World does with the added benefit of stability. Prospects opened up by Gorbachev's willingness to modernise his country make the USSR market still attractive, even though Soviet opportunities to earn hard currency through oil sales have appeared less promising since the slump in oil prices at the end of 1985. The Six are, on the other hand, far less attractive trading partners. Their supply of 'sensitive' products (semi-finished manufactures such as steel products, textiles, chemicals, consumer goods, and agricultural produce) congests markets where there is already great competition between domestic and Third World producers. As the medium-term prospects for growth in Eastern European exports to the West are not bright, these outlets depend on planned priorities for imports which might be financed through a resumption of borrowing. But though the debt crisis of the early eighties has been overcome, the outlook for East–West trade is gloomy as far as Eastern Europe is concerned.

Figures support these conclusions. Though the Soviet share in total East–West trade, which had reached almost three-fifths in 1983, regained in 1987 its 1980 level (slightly under one-half), the USSR remains by far the leading partner. But, here too, the West is not homogeneous. At one end of the spectrum, one finds the USA, for which trade with the East means just over 0.5 per cent of total trade and 0.02 per cent of GNP. Few companies are involved, and banks have little and decreasing exposure in the East. The business community is hence ready to follow political signals issued by the administration. At the other end, three small European countries have high stakes in trade with the East (Finland, Austria, and Greece). The leading economy of Western Europe, the FRG, conducts over 5 per cent of its trade with the East, the GDR included, and has the lion's share of Central European markets. The FRG gets on average slightly under a quarter of Eastern purchases in the West, the share rising to 30 per cent in Czechoslovakia and Hungary and over 40 per cent in the GDR ('inner-German' trade included, see p. 83–4).

This economic reality is sometimes ackward to acknowedge politically. From the traditional point of view of the socialist system, mutual cooperation with the developing world should take precedence over trade with the developed capitalist world. Moreover, cooperation with the system which is one day to be outstripped and defeated by socialism needs to be politically justified. Lenin introduced the concept of peaceful coexistence in 1919. Almost seventy years later, Gorbachev launched another concept – that of international economic security. In both cases a strong link is established between peace and economic cooperation, and this may be considered as a basis for trade between countries belonging to different systems. The socialist countries never really succeeded in securing a consensus on such principles with their Western partners; the closest they came to it was in 1975, when the Final Act of the Conference for Security and Cooperation in Europe was signed in Helsinki.

For the 'capitalist' states, the need to justify trade with the East is far less pressing. In the past, in a period of détente, it was always easy to advance market logic: business is business and firms are entitled to trade with whomsoever they please. The American government stands alone in having always constantly upheld the link between politics and economics. (The fact that it upheld the link does not mean that it always acted accordingly: US grain policy is a striking illustration of the contradiction between economics and politics.) In the early eighties, the crisis over events in Afghanistan and Poland clearly brought out the clash of views between the USA and its allies. But, are we then to conclude that, as far as Western Europe is concerned, politics do not have any effect on East–West trade? The breaking down of political relations no doubt also created a climate of 'unease' at the time of the 1981–82 recession in this trade, even if the trade recession could, after all, be put down to the economic situation alone. Conversely, the new popularity of the Soviet leader following Gorbachev's accession to power did not entail a boom in trade, but again, there were good economic reasons for that.

In the nineties, East–West economic relations may find a new momentum under the label of the socialist system's (re)integration into the international economic system. This may appear as the combined effect of domestic reforms in the East and of an increasingly stronger feeling in the West that there should be a multilateral approach to the issues of East–West trade and cooperation. What is labelled 'new thinking' in the Soviet Union, along the wording coined by M. S. Gorbachev, is a reassessment of socialism itself. If 'radical' reforms are mean to introduce market methods and ultimately to eradicate central planning, it is irrelevant for a socialist country to conduct economic relations with the capitalist system on the basis of a fundamental difference between capitalism and socialism. Western governments should accordingly assist the East 'so as to sustain the momentum of reform' as was expressed – but only mentioning Poland and Hungary – at the July 1989 Summit of the seven richest industrialised countries in Paris. In 1989, neither side had a clear view of the stakes and outcomes. In the East, the reorientation toward a market economic system had not occurred in all the countries. Only Poland and Hungary were at first openly rejecting the former Soviet-type system. By the end of 1989, the GDR and Czechoslovakia, under the pressure of the people, were taking the same course, while the Soviet leaders were still expressing their commitment to socialism. The assistance expected from the West was also differently understood, meaning food aid (for Poland), financial relief (for Poland and Hungary), management expertise and commercial policy concessions (for both these countries as well as for the USSR). Similarly, under the inaccurate, but largely circulated in the West, idea of 'a Marshall Plan for Eastern Europe' which had already emerged in 1988, various proposals were made, from expanding the participation of the Eastern bloc in international economic organisations to easing access to finance and relaxing rules on technology exports, along with support for the privatisation process in the domestic economies. While the outcome of these trends remains unclear on the eve of the nineties, especially as by the end of 1989 all Eastern European countries except Romania had been taking a new course, economic interests are increasingly interdependent.*

The institutional setting

The institutional framework of the socialist countries' external relations remains very conservative. It mainly consists of a network of bilateral agreements.

The reason for this is to be found basically in the traditional system. It is a requirement born of planning and of state monopoly of foreign trade. From the point of view of the planner, set arrangements with foreign trading partners covering trade for a given period and, when possible, a list of traded goods as well as commercial and financial conditions, defining major cooperation projects, represent security – rigidity being the drawback.

This pattern does not allow for multilateralism. Officially, it should be the very basis of Comecon operations whereas, in fact, multilateral procedures, where they exist within it, are only workable if they are consolidated by bilateral agreements. In relations with the West, multilateralism is still viewed with great suspicion as an attempt by Western states to collectively impose their rules of play. In relations with the developing world, the multilateral approach is well nigh non-existent in spite of the Third World demand for it. In particular, the East has failed to set up a collective system of aid to the Third World, a result both of the inflexibility of their financial mechanisms and the lack of any intra-Comecon consensus on the issue.

THE FRAMEWORK OF INTRA-COMECON TRADE AND COOPERATION

As has been seen already, Comecon bears but an apparent resemblance to the European Economic Community. The EEC is an organisation with supranational powers implementing common policies (agricultural, commercial, monetary, etc.). Trade and cooperation are conducted on the level of firms (both national and multinational) based on the principles of free circulation of goods and services, capital and labour. Comecon has no supra-national powers. It is not a common market, despite the goal of a 'unified market' set in 1988 for the long term. Within each country, enterprises enjoy a still limited autonomy in the field of foreign trade, and multinationals are almost non-existent. The main effective agent in international trade is the state. In the EEC, the state as such only intervenes in

order to regulate trade and to uphold national interests against EC prerogatives or claims by other states. Inter-state confrontation is to be
found in both systems but its significance differs greatly from one system
to the other. The differences are partly due to the weight of the USSR
within Comecon, while within the EEC there is a balance of potential
between the main partners. What does differentiate the two systems
most, however, is that under the socialist system the state and its economic agencies manage and plan production and trade. Inter-state conflicts are thus jeopardising a nation's sovereignty over the production
process itself. In a market economy, integration and common policies
associated with it involve first and foremost the redistribution of means
between states and this is where conflict arises. Two typical examples of
this can be given. In the first instance: the resistance which Romania put
up to a specialisation plan which the USSR sought to impose on it in the
sixties and which would have prevented it from developing its heavy
industry; in the second instance: Great Britain's opposition to EEC decisions fixing its budgetary contribution in the eighties.

Comecon as an institution is not however a body devoid of any real
meaning. It represents an association of states where bilateral procedures
get priority over multilateral ones. The multilateral arrangements are
generally no more than the sum of bilateral agreements negotiated
between pairs of partners. In addition, bilateralism gives priority to the
relations between the USSR and each of its partners, while links between
the Six are looser and less significant.

Table 2 shows the structure of the organisation (see Caillot, 1971;
Lavigne, 1973; Schiavone, 1982; Sobell, 1984; van Brabant, 1988).
Comecon, although set up in 1949, was only granted a charter in 1959.
Its bodies were completed by amendments to the charter, the most
important in 1962 and 1971. In 1987, a major reshuffle took place, along
the line of the changes initiated in the Soviet administration. A number of
committees and commissions were suppressed, some were merged, and
the whole structure was simplified. The number of employees was reduced accordingly.

Unanimity of the interested parties is the basic legal principle of Comecon. Whatever their level, the regulations laid down by Comecon bodies
are only obligatory for member states provided these regulations have
been ratified by the countries concerned according to the domestic legal
provisions of these countries. Ruling adopted unaminously by the interested parties may not be opposed by the countries which have declared

Table 2. *The institutional structure of the Council for Mutual Economic Assistance (Comecon)*

Session of the Council for Mutual Economic Assistance		Banks
		  International Bank for
		    Economic Cooperation
		  International Investment
		    Bank

Executive Committee	Committees:
	  for planning (1971)
	  for scientific and technical
	    cooperation (1971)
	  for machine-building
	    (1984)
	  for foreign economic
	    relations (1987)
	  for electronics (1987)
	  for the agro-industrial
	    complex (1987)
	  for energy and raw
	    materials (1989)
		Institutes
		  of standardisation
		  for the economic problems
		    of the world socialist
		    system
		  for industrial management

Secretariat	Standing commissions	Inter-state economic organisations

The table takes into account the changes introduced by the 43rd Session (1987) reducing the number of the Comecon bodies (the dates between parentheses refer to the dates when a given body was set up).
Source: Pravitel'stvennyi Vestnik (Government Monitor), no. 22, November 1989, p. 10.

themselves not to be concerned in the issue under discussion. Any country, on the other hand, may declare itself concerned in an issue and then has the right to oppose the measure under discussion if it is prejudicial to that country. This is actually a right of veto which can mean that a measure voted for by the majority will be thrown out. This provides a guarantee of national sovereignty but at the same time acts as a formidable stumbling block when it comes to voting on commn policies. This principle also explains just why a great many decisions are implemented outside the formal framework of Comecon by two or more states. The inter-state economic organisations created for cooperation in particular sectors were set up in this manner in the sixties, such as Intermetal, Interchim, etc. In most cases Romania was the country which refused to agree on a particular move, which often did not prevent it from joining the organisation created without its participation. An example of this was the creation of the International Investment Bank, which Romania joined a year after the founding of the bank by the other members.

The unanimity principle thus generates inefficiency in the functioning of Comecon as a multilateral institution. It is a security device for the smaller member states but also a drawback when important collective decisions have to be made. This explains why Comecon institutions have been supplemented by summit conferences of the heads of communist and workers' parties. The conference itself is not a formal institution. It is an expression of the supreme political will of the community of socialist states. Conferences met frequently at the start of the sixties (in 1958, 1962, and 1963) to discuss economic issues, but have only met twice since, in 1969 and 1984, and always at crucial periods for the organisation. In 1958 the Charter was being drafted. In 1962 the basic principles of the international socialist division of labour were adopted. In 1969 the Comprehensive Integration Programme got underway. The year 1984 saw the institutionalisation of Soviet-centric bilateralism in trade and cooperation. The fundamental positions of the Comecon supreme body, the council session, have always been laid down after a conference meeting.

The most important functional bodies of Comecon are the standing commissions preparing specific proposals for specialisation and cooperation. Their recommendations must however be ratified by the member states concerned and by the concluding of bilateral agreements on trade or production cooperation. They are often 'matched' by the inter-state economic organisations created in the sixties, for instance, for the coordination of electric power distribution through a network of high-tension transmission lines linking the power grids of seven European countries (Mir), for trade in specialised steel products (Intermetal) or chemicals (Interchim). The two Comecon banks also belong to this category of bodies.

Comecon bodies issue normative regulations such as multilateral conventions defining the rules of trade, equipment assembly and technical service, transport, etc. They also prepare inter-state agreements on plan coordination.

Trade itself is conducted largely independently of the Comecon agencies. The only interaction lies in the fact that inter-state agreements on trade have to include provisions for specialisation that have been agreed upon in the framework of the sectoral standing commissions. Bilateral flows of trade are determined by five-year trade accords which are broken down into yearly protocols; the protocols establish the quantities and prices of goods traded. This is the case for the largest share of mutual trade flows. For a small part of trade only overall value of trade is agreed upon (e.g. for spare parts, some manufactures). The share of the really 'unaffected' trade is very small, it amounts to a mere 1 per cent of total trade. As for prices, they are always fixed definitively by decisions taken jointly between trading partners. This may be surprising as there do exist objective rules for price fixing in keeping with principles agreed collectively since 1958. The present-day workings of this pricing system will be illustrated in connection with intra-Comecon oil trade. But the 'multilateralism' which such a system might suggest, based as it is on reference to 'world' capitalist prices, exists only in name. Representatives of socialist countries have never sat around the same table to fix prices for mutual trade. Neither has the price of a given product ever been the same throughout the entire Comecon. Bilateral trade agreements involve price bargaining and negotiation on the very nature of reciprocal supplies. Prices tend to be unified when reference to a world price is publicly known and of an incontestable nature (OPEC price for a given grade of oil; commodity prices quoted on the commodity markets). Prices start to differ when the reference becomes uncertain (e.g., for manufactured products for which 'world price' means nothing). There cannot be any automatic equalising of prices as there is no real market and no free circulation of goods within Comecon.

Bilateral bargaining in the content of reciprocal supplies is a complex operation bound up with the domestic planning of each country and the nature of this fake market. Each country has the objective of securing supplies of goods which it does not itself produce (or which it produces at high cost). 'Supply' and 'demand' are therefore determined in the main by the extent to which Comecon is self-sufficient in the products in question. Goods which are in short supply within Comecon as a whole (or seem in short supply, which is different as the 'market' is anything but transparent) are called 'hard' goods. These include energy, raw materials, agricultural produce, and certain technologies. But it may also be any product for which a shortage is feared, or artifically created by the seller. All other goods are 'soft'. Every bilateral trade agreement, therefore, is a combination of hard and soft goods, each country trying to attain a balance for each of these two groups as well as for overall trade (see van Brabant, 1973, who coined the expression of 'structural bilateralism' for this behaviour).

Given this trade pattern, the USSR has always had structurally unbalanced trade with its partners. This lack of balance is reflected in the composition of trade, the USSR being first and foremost a supplier of hard goods (energy and raw materials) and a buyer of manufactures.

Since 1975, the lack of balance also affected the overall value of trade, with the rise in Soviet oil prices causing a surplus. This surplus began to shrink when the trend in oil prices was reversed in intra-CMEA trade, and in 1987 for the first time in twelve years Soviet–East European trade was again balanced overall, but slipped into deficit (for the USSR) in 1988. The structural imbalance between hard and soft goods, however, remains. Herein lies the main explanation for Soviet-centric bilateralism. Bilateral trade agreements which Eastern European countries sign with the Soviet Union are the most important not only because the USSR is the main trading partner of each country (the size factor) but because through its supplies and its purchases it can predetermine the content of the other bilateral trade agreements to a great extent (the structural factor).

The intra-bloc bilateral trade relations determine the actual pattern of trade. The bilateral negotiations and agreements are largely independent of the operation of Comecon as a multilateral organisation.

The difficulties encountered in reforming the Comecon institutions have given rise to various suggestions in the member countries, which range from keeping to the status quo – this was the stance of the GDR under the leadership which was overthrown in November 1989 – to dissolving the organisation altogether. Among the most feasible alternatives, there is the setting up of a smaller 'sub-regional' integrated market, grouping Hungary, Poland, possibly Czechoslovakia, with or without the USSR. Some Soviet authors have suggested that Comecon might be transformed into a kind of OECD, i.e. a rather loose coordinating organisation, while a new international grouping comparable to the EEC might be formed with the participation of the interested European Comecon members, rejoining the previous proposal. Prospects for a market–oriented policy in the GDR and Czechoslovakia, which opened at the end of 1989, might revive ideas about a *Mittel-Europa* free trade area including these two countries along with Hungary and Austria. This does not mean of course that the whole system of commissions, inter-state agencies, etc. is just marking time. Through this network of bodies, international specialisation is promoted on bilateral (over 1,000 agreements in force) and multilateral (150) levels, especially in the machinery trade. The effect of these agreements is limited by their inter-state nature. Though officially encouraged already since 1971, direct links between firms in different countries are still an exception. The 1985 Comprehensive Programme for Scientific and Technical Progress led to the setting up of about 1,600 bilateral links by the end of 1988 between enterprises from different countries, but out of this total only a few became really operational.*

EAST–WEST RELATIONS: AGREEMENTS AND INSTITUTIONS

It is not just French chauvinism to say that the classic institutional model of East–West relations is to be found in the network of agreements and agencies set up between the USSR and France after General de Gaulle's Moscow visit in 1966. This scheme was to serve as a basis for other bilateral relations during the following decade which was marked by a rapid growth of East–West trade.

Such an organisation was an expression of political will as well as of the constraints of state trade. For the East, the framing of trade within agreements, which are themselves overseen by joint commissions, facilitates their inclusion in domestic planning and makes it easier for them to be run by a system of state monopoly of foreign trade. It acts as a bond for the Western partners who have committed themselves to certain principles (the equality of partners, mutual advantage, and the long-term nature of cooperation, with some agreements running to twenty-five years). For Western countries, the signatory governments are establishing their desire to have relations with the East, but the operational aspect of the agreements is far more limited. A socialist state may commit itself to what it undertakes directly. A capitalist state seeks to offer its firms the best chances of conquering a market and helps them especially in the financial field, but it does not act directly. Even in cases of public monopolies (for example, the purchasing of Soviet gas by a nationalised firm which has a monopoly on gas distribution), the position of the Western state is not totally analogous to that of the Soviet state in its relations with the gas exporting agency.

These differences between the two types of signatory states in East–West relations is well known. Each partner plays it up. Official representatives of Western governments are pointing out that they are not empowered to force private firms into concluding trade or cooperation contracts. Representatives from the socialist countries stress that industrial projects which are mentioned in cooperation programmes are indeed part of the plan but that they will be undertaken in cooperation with the capitalist partner offering the best terms according to market laws.

This systemic asymmetry has been compounded by the strengthening of the Common Market. While intra-Comecon developments did not affect the competences of member states in their relations with the outside world, the main partners of the socialist states, for example, the members of the EC, have given up a number of trade prerogatives to the Community.

In the initial phase which preceded the coming into force of the common commercial policy, the inter-governmental framework of East–West relations was constituted by the network of bilateral trade agreements. These began to develop from 1959 onwards and underwent their most intensive development in the period 1966–74. From 1 January 1973, EEC member states could no longer sign or renew trade agreements with third countries. As a result, the network of bilateral trade agreements between states had to disappear. But, according to the letter of the Treaty of Rome, unlike commerce, economic cooperation was not to form part of EC common policies. A convergence of political interests occurred between Western governments and socialist states. Western EC members wanted to retain a margin of manoeuvre in such a politically sensitive area as trade with the East. Socialist countries were eager to remain in a bilateral framework of negotiation. As the bilateral framework could only be retained, according to EC rules, in the field of cooperation, commercial matters were as unconspicuously as possible insinuated into cooperation agreements. Since 1975 the MFN (most favoured nation) clause, obviously a commercial measure, has frequently been included in the cooperation agreements. This inclusion has often taken the form of an exchange of letters included as an appendix to the main agreement. The requirements of business sometimes call for a greater degree of such rule-bending. The USSR has tried to arrange its grain imports on the basis of long-term (five-year) agreements fixing the minimum yearly quantities to be purchased from its main suppliers. These are all non-European with the exception of France. The Soviet desire to place its grain purchases in a conventional framework brings together the planner's usual preference for arrangements that stretch well into the future and the need to protect supplies beforehand from possible sanctions. In October 1982, France, like other grain exporters seeking to secure for themselves a share of the world's largest market, signed an accord (again by exchange of letters) which was nothing less than a commercial agricultural treaty between the two countries and provided for French sales of food and agricultural produce, including 3 million tonnes of grain a year. The arrangement, signed for a three-year period, was again renewed in 1985, to the strong displeasure of the EEC Commission.*

The EEC, in light of this, has indeed to defend its prerogatives on two fronts. Firstly, against its own members who want to maintain room to manoeuvre and also to use the community argument when it suits them. Secondly, against the Eastern bloc countries themselves. On this policy the EEC has had considerable success.

1   The EEC members have less and less power in the commercial field (in particular as concerns the modifying of import contingents from the East); and the creation of the unified European market in 1992 is following the same trend.

2   The EEC managed to involve the entire Eastern bloc, except the USSR and the GDR, in sectoral bilateral agreements on textile and steel (Table 2). With Romania, it signed an agreement on trade in industrial products (1980) and after years of negotiation reached agreements with Hungary, Czechoslovakia (1988), Poland and the USSR (1989). Exploratory talks began with the GDR, also in 1989. Yet the reform trend in the socialist countries is bound to make such accords very difficult to negotiate. For the EEC, these countries remain state trading countries, despite the introduction of reforms allowing for an increasing role of market mechanisms, and hence must meet specific obligations, which the Eastern European countries consider as discriminatory (see chapter 4). Political circumstances also influence the negotiations, either negatively or positively. The negotiations for a renewal of the agreement with Romania were discontinued in March 1989 because of the forced resettlement of the rural population in this country. In July 1989 talks were suspended with Bulgaria on account of the government's policy toward the Turkish minority. The signing of the agreement with Poland was accelerated after a non-Communist government was formed in September 1989. In addition, the sweeping political changes in Eastern Europe and the response they trigger from the West tend to mix commercial arrangements and economic assistance. Thus, the agreements reached with Hungary and Poland were modified so as to provide for an accelerated lifting of trade restrictions already as from January 1990.

3   The EEC has long avoided getting involved in a framework agreement with Comecon, negociation for which was offered by this organisation in 1976. At that time Comecon sought a treaty with the EEC governing the principles of relations between the two groups (this included principles relating to commercial matters), as well as the terms

Table 3. *The EEC and the Comecon countries: autonomous policy and trade arrangements, 1969–1989*

Until 31 December 1969	EEC member states negotiate and sign bilateral trade agreements with third countries

1 January 1970	The EEC common commercial policy comes in force. The Commission is competent:
	    to negotiate and sign trade agreements with third countries
	    to fix the conditions of trade with these countries.
	However, as most bilateral trade agreements with the USSR and Eastern Europe expired at the end of 1969, they had been hastily renewed for 1970–74. The new Community competence therefore applied from 1 January 1973 and took effect *vis-à-vis* Comecon countries from 1 January 1975.

1974	All Eastern European countries ignore the framework agreement proposed to them by the EEC.
1975	The autonomous commercial regime comes into force. Each year a list of quotas open to imports from each Eastern European country and from the USSR is published for each EEC country. Since 1979, the powers of the EEC have been reinforced thus limiting the possibilities of waiving for EEC member states.

1976 onwards	The Eastern European countries sign self-limitation agreements for textiles in the framework of the MFA (multi-fibre arrangements):
	    MFA I (1973–77): agreement with Romania (1976)
	    MFA II (1978–81): agreement with Romania (1977), Hungary (1978), Poland (1979); with Bulgaria (1979) although this country is not a GATT member
	    MFA III (1982–86): agreements with the same countries plus Czechoslovakia (1982)
	    MFA IV (1986–91): same as MFN III.

1978–79	Self-limitation agreements are signed for steel products between the EEC and the Comecon countries with the exception of GDR and the USSR; they are renewed in 1983.
1980	Trade agreement with Romania on industrial products. All negotiations for renewal stopped in 1989.
1988	Agreement with Hungary on trade, cooperation, and the setting up of a joint commission (26 September 1988). Agreement with Czechoslovakia on trade in industrial products (19 December 1988).
1989	Agreement with Poland on trade, cooperation, and the setting up of a joint commission (19 September 1989). Agreement with the USSR on trade and cooperation (initialled 27 November 1989) Additional commercial concessions to Poland and Hungary; removal of trade quotas by 1 January 1990 (November 1989). Negotiations underway of trade agreements with Bulgaria; exploratory talks with the GDR.

Sources: Official documents; press reports.

of economic and monetary cooperation. On certain of these points (economic cooperation) the EEC would not have legal competence either for
issuing regulations or for signing agreements. As regards commerce, on
the other hand, the EEC had legal competence to negotiate with third
states on behalf of its members, but questioned the competence of Comecon for these matters. As for matters of monetary and agricultural
policy, the EEC did not want to negotiate at all. The EEC–Comecon
dialogue came to a deadlock in 1980. It resumed after Gorbachev's
accession to power and was finalised in June 1988 through a 'Joint
Declaration' establishing 'official relations' between the two organisations, and calling for cooperation in areas of 'mutual interest' to be
specified later on. These areas might include standardisation, presentation of statistics, environmental protection, macro-economic forecasts,
to which Comecon countries would like to add transport, energy, and
technology. No substantial economic consequences are to be expected in
the short run. The political significance of such an agreement is great, if
only because it settled the tricky question of the 'territorial clause' which
has long hindered any agreement between the EC and Comecon.

4   The 'territorial clause' is a compulsory component of any treaty
signed by the European Communities. According to the clause, the given
treaty is to be valid on the territory of the EC as defined by its statutory
acts. This means clearly that West Berlin is part of this territory. This is a
point which was long considered as unacceptable by all the Comecon
countries but Romania. These countries treat West Berlin as a special
area under quadripartite administration and not as a part of the Federal
Republic of Germany. This point was solved for the signature of the
1988 Joint Declaration by a concession from Comecon. The technique of
'unilateral reservation' was used, the Comecon countries (except
Romania) reaffirming the existence of the 1971 quadripartite agreement
on Berlin, while having accepted the clause inserted in the Joint
Declaration.

The debate over the 'territorial clause' also points to the anomaly of
GDR–FRG relations. The two Germanies are linked by a 1951 agreement governing their mutual trade as domestic trade which dispenses
with custom duties and under which some of the trade (for a definite
range of goods and specified quotas) is financed through a kind of clearing arrangement (called *swing*) providing for interest-free loans. This
agreement is recognised as an exception by the 1957 Treaty of Rome. It
offers both countries political and economic advantages and grants each

of them privileged access to the economic community to which the other state belongs. It is generally said that the GDR benefits more than the FRG from the agreement, namely because the balance of trade is usually negative for East Germany, which thus gets free loans through the 'swing' system. But one should not overestimate the extent of this advantage. The frontier between the two Germanies is not the 'sieve' by which exported goods from the GDR all end up in Western Europe in violation of community regulations. Re-exportation of both processed and unprocessed goods does exist, in very small quantities, but the bulk of this trade remains 'inter-German'. The FRG keeps a strict control on these movements. Conversely, it is not indeed the leading trading partner of the Eastern bloc solely or mainly because it has greater access to the GDR market, but because it is more competitive in Eastern Europe than its Western competitors. The changes initiated in the GDR in the end of 1989 might however strengthen the position of the FRG. Western assistance to the market-orientated reforms will presumably be provided by the FRG first and foremost. The political moves towards any form of association between the two countries, not to speak of reunification, will also have an economic component.

Are inter-European relations to become a privileged area of East–West trade? The question may be asked as both European integrations have argued upon mutual recognition. In the early seventies when *détente* was expanding, the *rapprochement* between the United States and the Soviet Union suggested in parallel closer relations between Eastern Europe (some advocated the expression of 'Central Europe') and Western Europe on the basis of shared interests. The pattern emerging at the beginning of Gorbachev's era looked different, if only because of the dedication of Gorbachev to the concept of 'the European house'. The unified Western European market of the nineties is seen as providing new opportunities in this respect. The socialist countries certainly dread a new and powerful protectionism which might emerge on the borders of the unified market. But they count on the countries interested in fighting this protectionism, such as Japan, the United States, or the EFTA countries in Europe. And those countries which have not yet finalised trade agreements with the EC are prepared to seek the lifting of the specific barriers hindering Comecon imports into the EC.

The role of the EC was strengthened after the July 1989 Summit of the Seven richest industralised countries, which entrusted the EC Commission with coordinating Western aid to Poland and Hungary. This coordination process may react on the relations between the EC and the mentioned countries. Hungary has officially suggested, in a memorandum to the EC, that it might 'join the European integration process without becoming a member of the EEC' (August 1989). Albeit very vague, such an evolution might be comparable to the strengthening of links between the EFTA (European Free Trade Association) and the EC after 1992. Should other Eastern European countries take the same steps, a new Europe may emerge, different both from the Gorbachev scheme of a 'common European house' and from the post-1992 free-trade Western European space as initially envisaged.*

EAST–SOUTH RELATIONS: THE CONVENTIONAL FRAMEWORK FOR COOPERATION

Economic relations between socialist countries and the developing world are carried on within a network of bilateral agreements on various levels.

First, there are friendship and cooperation treaties usually signed for twenty years between the USSR and socialist-orientated Third World countries. The importance of these treaties is more diplomatic than economic. Some non-socialist-orientated countries have also been involved in such agreements, for example, India (1971), a country 'with a capitalist orientation' but which is yet the main permanent trading partner of the USSR in the Third World, and North Yemen (1984), a neighbour of South Yemen whose position is consolidated by this very fact. The reversibility of socialist orientation has led to certain treaties being annulled. The Soviet–Egyptian agreement of 1971 was annulled in November 1977. Treaties still in force have been concluded with Angola (1971), Iraq (1972), Mozambique (1977), Ethiopia (1978), Afghanistan (1978), South Yemen (1979), Syria (1980), and the Congo (1981).

On the purely economic level, the most general framework is the trade agreement which runs to three or five years with yearly protocols establishing the lists of good exported and imported. Most agreements signed up until 1970 also contained arrangements for settlements in clearing. To-day clearing applies to only a small number of bilateral relations (see chapter 8). Trade agreements link the seven socialist countries of Europe (the USSR included) with slightly over 100 developing countries. There are some 500 agreements, which indicates that not all trade is covered by this framework. Some trade may occur with countries not included in the statistics of the Eastern bloc, which have no diplomatic relations with most of the socialist countries (for instance, Taiwan and Hong Kong).

In addition to trade agreements there are economic cooperation agreements which are much longer term (ten, fifteen, or twenty years). These cooperation agreements generally involve the setting up of joint commissions to coordinate cooperation and possibly even to set up planning concertation if the developing country introduces a planning system. Such accords have been signed with about 80 developing counties.

Multilateralism is very limited. Comecon never foresaw anything similar to the Lomé Conventions between the EEC and African countries. However, several agreements have been concluded on a multilateral basis between Comecon and the Third World. Two were signed in 1975, with Mexico and Iraq; no concrete developments followed. Later on, a new round followed, all with socialist-orientated countries: Nicaragua (1983), Mozambique (1985), Ethiopia, Angola, South Yemen (1986), and Afghanistan (1987) (see p. 55).*

Up to now there has been nothing similar to the International Development Agency within Comecon. Aid is channelled exclusively through bilateral agreements. In 1973, Comecon member states decided to set up a special fund within the framework of the International Investment Bank (one of Comecon's two banks) to finance major projects in the Third World. But the IIB is not the World Bank. The common fund, which was to hold 1,000 million transferable roubles (t.r.) after an initial investment of 100 million roubles, never operated. Another project worked more effectively. This is the grant fund for Third World students, which was also set up in 1973 and which finances Third World students in the educational establishments of socialist countries, so as to supplement the bilateral technical assistance programmes. The reasons why a common fund could never operate, in one case, and why a scholarship fund could actually work, in the other case, are identical and to be found in the nature of the collective money of Comecon (chapter 8).

CHAPTER 3

―――――――― · ――――――――

COOPERATION: SPECIALISATION, COUNTER TRADE, ASSISTANCE

The socialist countries claim to grant cooperation a central position in their international economic relations. Cooperation is based on the principle of mutual advantage with all the countries of the world.

In the field of 'relations among countries having different economic and social systems', to use the terminology accredited to the United Nations by the Eastern bloc, the term cooperation takes on its most symbolic meaning of reciprocal good will. From the famous catch phrase uttered by General de Gaulle, '*détente, entente* and cooperation', to the Final Act of the European Conference on Security and Cooperation, over a period of ten years (1966–75) the word cooperation seemed to win universal acclaim. Since then, for the socialist countries, the dwindling of *détente* has in no way affected the status of cooperation, while for their partners it has become no more than lip-service. The new political climate of East–West relations in the Gorbachev era again promotes the notion of cooperation, associated with aid when it comes to relations with such countries as Poland and Hungary.

Is cooperation really as important as its permanent reassertion suggests? In fact, most of the trade flows are just simple export–import operations. The range of products involved is rather small. The bulk of trade is concentrated on a few large groups of goods which will be examined in Part 2 of this book (chapters 5 to 7).

To put all this under the heading of cooperation is a matter of faith. Strictly speaking, the area of cooperation is very limited. Within Comecon, despite all efforts to intensify it, it is quite marginal, while it should be the driving force of socialist integration. Cooperation with the West aims at setting up trade in a reciprocal framework which would no longer be determined merely by market forces. For the West, such compensation-based cooperation, as it is called in the East, has been identified with counter trade and reluctantly accepted, though compensation deals did not develop at the pace which businessmen feared and which Eastern trade officials expected. Finally, cooperation with the Third World is a vehicle both for economic assistance and for the long-term consolidation of trade relations. The quantification of this assistance is a matter of dispute, and the figures provided by the East are usually considered as too high. Even if these figures were accepted cooperation still would not dominate East–South relations.

Specialisation–cooperation within Comecon

According to the wording of official Comecon documents, a major objective of the organisation is to intensify and extend cooperation between its members. But how is one to understand the concept of cooperation?

In Russian – the official language of Comecon – cooperation is expressed by two terms. These words do not have exactly the same meaning although they are usually translated alike. 'Cooperation A' (let us differentiate between them in this way), or *sotrudnichestvo*, is the most all-encompassing term and is the term used to refer to relations with the West or South as well as within Comecon. 'Cooperation B' or *kooperirovanie* has more technical and micro-economic connotations and is the basic instrument for intra-branch specialisation. Both forms are to be found in the mechanisms of plan coordination.

It becomes increasingly difficult to assess these mechanisms. The failure of Comecon to set up a multilateral system of plan coordination reults in an accumulation of various institutional instruments, which add up rather than replace each other. None of them is officially suppressed, but some in fact become obsolete. In the mid-eighties, the picture was as follows.

1   The five-year 'Concerted Plans for Multilateral Integration Measures' were introduced in the mid-1970s as a new method of coordinating five-year planning, as a compromise between national sovereignty in the field of planning and the goal of promoting integrated planning. The most distinct feature of this method was that for each five-year period each member country had to list the multilaterally concerted relevant provisions in its own national five-year plan. This was meant to avoid what had previously been the stumbling block of plan coordination, namely, the adoption of coordination measures once national plans had already been worked out and were thus unable to integrate the operations envisa-

ged. Ideally the Concerted Plan should have included: the amount of investment funds required for large joint projects; the supplies (in quantity and value) required from each partner to service these projects as well as to comply with the multilateral specialisation agreements; the research and development (R and D) expenses needed for these projects.

It soon appeared that this method did not meet expectations. The first concerted plan for the period 1976–80 was a collection of ten joint investment projects already decided upon, eight of which were located on USSR territory. Two of these (the gas pipeline from Orenburg (South Ural) to the Western border of the USSR, and the high-voltage transmission line between the Ukraine and Hungary) took up 90 per cent of the total financing provided by the USSR and its partners. The second plan, for 1981–85, was adopted with a great delay only in 1981, probably because of the reluctance of the member countries to embark on new joint investments. It mainly comprised specialisation measures and the completion of already undertaken projects, for an amount which was less than one-quarter of the amount financed in the first Concerted Plan (2 billion transferable roubles instead of 9 billion). The third Concerted Plan (1986–90) again combined joint investments and specialisation measures, for an amount which has not been disclosed. The preparation of the fourth plan for 1991–95 was announced at the 44th session of the Comecon council in 1988. This latest document is supposed to integrate the measures included in the Comprehensive Programme for Scientific and Technical Progress as well as in the collective concept of international socialist division of labour. This would not be an easy task. It was decided that taking into account the domestic reforms and the increased rights of the enterprises in several countries, coordination in planning should be achieved on the three levels where planning is conducted. These levels are: the state level (through the offices of planning); the ministerial level; and the level of the enterprises. Given the different degrees of competence attributed to all these bodies in the different countries, coordination in planning is bound to remain a formal exercise in many cases.

2   The 'Long-term Target Programmes' were launched slightly later than the first concerted plan and were supposed to cover the decade of the eighties, with a possible extension up to the end of the century. Five have been signed: for energy and raw materials; for agriculture and the food industry; for machine-building, all these in 1978; and for industrial consumer goods; and transport, signed in 1979. In fact, the programmes

were redundant, along with the 'Concerted Plans' for the major projects concerned. Only the first was ever said to be operational. It included the main projects dealing with energy (gas, nuclear energy) and raw materials (iron ore). This format seems now to have been quietly dropped.

3   Bilateral cooperation programmes are usually signed to supplement and concretise the content of multilateral plans and programmes and besides this, give detailed breakdowns of purely bilateral projects. These bilateral programmes are supposed to cover all bilateral links but information is to be found essentially on those signed between the USSR and its partners, which is consistent with the already mentioned 'radial' pattern of intra-Comecon relations. A first 'round' of programmes had been devised at the end of the Brezhnev era, and signed for the period 1980–90. In the wake of the 1984 summit meeting of Comecon leaders, these bilateral programmes were all revamped in 1984–85 and extended up to 2000. Following the adoption of the Comprehensive Programme of Scientific and Technical Progress, another series of bilateral agreements was negotiated, this time providing for the setting up of 'direct links' between the firms of the countries concerned. Only Romania refused to sign up in this last round – in the previous rounds it was usually the last.

There is thus an interaction between multilateral and bilateral links, the latter being by far more effective than the former, where it is easier for the partners to shun their obligations. In both mechanisms, there is an interaction between 'cooperation A' and 'cooperation B'.

The principal instrument of 'cooperation A' is joint investment. Energy is the leading sector (see chapter 6). These investment projects are, for the most part, situated in the USSR and investments are made as contributions from the Six towards the development of Soviet natural resources against the moral guarantee of future supplies by the USSR. These deals do not involve participation of the Eastern European countries in capital or management. The latest projects (up to 1990 and later) involve Poland (for coal), Czechoslovakia (magnetite). Cuba also receives this kind of contribution for the development of its natural resources (sugar, and nickel deposits). In the case of Cuba, joint investment may be seen as an example of multilateral assistance to development as well as the consolidation of the country's economic integration into Comecon.

After 1980, joint investments seemed to decline. The general shortage of investment resources among the Six and the investment contraction policies introduced after 1981 provided good reasons for a scaling down.

But the 1986–90 Concerted Plan again contains joint investments in gas transport (a pipeline from Yamburg in Siberia to the Western border of the USSR), iron ore extraction (a ferrous oxide mine at Krivoi Rog in the Ukraine), electricity transport (an extension of the linking of the power grids) and other projects of less importance. It seems thus that high-cost priority projects are still pushed forward if and when there are conditions for mutual bargaining. Obviously the partner countries are reluctant to embark on such ventures, and often it is not clear whether all have agreed to participate (for instance, Hungary is said to have pulled out of the Krivoi Rog project in 1987). They take part if it is the only way of getting guaranteed supplies.

However, the general trend of intra-Comecon relations suggests a strong boost given to 'cooperation B' along with an alteration in production and export structures in order to further adapt the Six to their role as suppliers to the USSR. The USSR itself seeks to increase its exports of manufactures in line with its domestic reform. The fall of world oil prices in 1986 made the Soviet Union conscious of the vulnerability of its trade structure, based upon sales of raw materials against imports of manufactures. To be able to export manufactures to the West, the USSR needs first to improve its production capacities, and the Comecon market may serve both as an outlet and as an exercise field to prepare the USSR for the needs of the developed markets.

Comecon is not prepared for such an evolution. Intra-branch and intra-product specialisation is far more recent and less developed than is the case in the EEC. Of overall intra-Comecon trade in machinery, the share of 'specialised trade' (i.e., trade conducted under specialisation agreements) stands at around 40 per cent. But the proportion of trade in spare parts and components is at most 15 per cent, while foreign trade in specialised engineering products among industrialised nations is 45 per cent of total trade in these items.

The development of specialisation has been very slow, and initially concentrated on inter-branch specialisation. In the beginning it followed domestic priorities. Thus, Poland specialised in shipbuilding and railway equipment, Bulgaria in electric trolleys and hoists, Czechoslovakia in heavy machine-building, motorbikes, trams, textile machinery, and shoes, Hungary in medical and pharmaceutical equipment, medicines, and buses, the GDR in tractors, textile machinery, railway rolling-stock, cameras, and precision equipment, Romania in oil-processing equipment. As for the USSR, it could hardly be said to specialise in any specific goods and claimed the ability to supply complete equipment as a field of specialisation. Very soon the Comecon countries became conscious of the high costs of such a pattern. Because of the lack of intra-branch (and intra-product) specialisation, each country still had to manufacture most of the industrial goods it needed, especially in the field of machinery and equipment. At the summit conference of 1984, it was stated that Czechoslovakia manufactured 70 per cent of the world assortment of machinery, Hungary, Poland, and the GDR each manufactured 60 per cent.

Intra-branch and intra-product specialisation has nevertheless developed within Comecon very slowly, along three basic lines.

1   In the initial stage, specialisation was set up for specific items. In the sixties, multilateral specialisation began with non-standard types of intermediate goods or parts which it was irrational to produce in all countries: special types of ball-bearings; non-standard qualities and mouldings of steel; special chemicals. These arrangements were usually reached, in these cases, through the creation of special inter-state organisations rather than through the normal procedure of Comecon recommendations, for which unanimity could not be obtained.

Already in 1971, multilateral cooperation was set up in the motor industry. The Soviet car Zhiguli (known as the Lada for export to the West) has been manufactured since then with the help of seventy different types of parts supplied by the USSR's partners. Bulgaria supplies accumulators, starters, and batteries; Hungary – dashboards and car-radios; Czechoslovakia – headlights; Poland – shock-absorbers. The USSR pays back in vehicles or parts (for example, it supplies parts to Poland for the Fiat models produced there). The other example is cooperation in computers for which an agreement was signed even earlier, in 1969. Seventy-five plants in seven European Comecon countries and Cuba are participating in this programme and specialising according to types of computers and accessory equipment.

In the seventies, this pattern of specialisation was extended through a series of multilateral and bilateral agreements. Machinery was the most favoured area for this. If initially the traditional fields were most involved (machine-tools, textile machinery, tractors), later specialisation covered high-technology sectors (micro-electronics, robot technology). In 1979 a multilateral agreement was concluded for nuclear power machinery between the Comecon Seven and Yugoslavia. At the moment the USSR manufactures 50 per cent of the related equipment, and shares the production of reactors only with Czechoslovakia; Bulgaria specialises in equipment for environmental protection, Hungary in repair and maintenance equipment, GDR in transport, Poland in heat-generating equipment, Romania in water cooling installations, and, finally, Yugoslavia in cranes and hoists. After the Chernobyl accident in 1986, the agreement was updated and revised; it was finally extended to 2000 in 1987. Other branches are covered including special steels, non-ferrous metals, chemicals which are necessary for various stages in the production of olefins; the final aim being to create an 'olefin belt' incorporating nineteen chemical firms by the year 1990.

This type of specialisation comes up against difficulties which have so far limited its efficiency.

(a) The Comecon institutional mechanisms do not provide sufficient penalties for failure to meet specialisation commitments. Once a specialisation agreement is concluded, the suppliers of the product covered by the agreement have to increase their production potential to meet the needs of the buyers, and conversely, the countries which have agreed to stop domestic production have to purchase the specialised item from the producer. But if any party fails to meet its commitments there is no real sanction. The fact that responsibility lies with the country, and not the firms, is a considerable obstacle, which could be removed were direct inter-firm cooperation to develop.

(b) There is inadequate integration of research and production. A typical case is the automobile industry. Its modernisation comes from outside in the form of contracts with Western firms (e.g., in 1984 the USSR concluded a contract with Fiat for the modernisation of its Togliatti plant, and in 1987 with Volkswagen to modernise the Moskvitch so as to make it saleable in the West). Specialisation is then adapted to meet the needs of production modernisation and export. A better coupling of research and production within the Comecon countries might emerge as a consequence of Western technology export restrictions, if they are not relaxed.

(c) Intra-Comecon pricing has a deterrent effect. As there are no indisputable 'world prices' to which one may refer for intra-Comecon price fixing for spare parts or machinery, one has to use contractual bargaining prices, which tend to be pushed up. This leads national producers to themselves manufacture parts even when specialisation has been accepted. In the case of the Zhiguli agreements, mutual supplies are based upon barter: a given quantity of parts amounts to a complete car.

2   The second direction is bound up with the problems of energy and

raw materials. Since the start of the eighties, the USSR has been urging its partners to restructure their production so as to abandon high energy and raw materials intensive production and to specialise in less energy intensive products. This division of labour would mean that the most energy intensive production was concentrated on Soviet territory. Already in 1979 an agreement was reached for the chemical industry. The first phase of this agreement, concluded in 1979, for the period 1981–85, was to cover 15 per cent of intra-Comecon chemical trade, with balanced flows of imports from and exports to the USSR. The USSR committed itself to supply Eastern Europe with ammonia, methanol, synthetic rubber, and polyethylene in exchange for low energy intensive chemicals. Symbolic of this strategy was the decision to construct a plant processing yeasts out of paraffin oil with the cooperation of three European countries (the GDR, Czechoslovakia, and Poland) as well as Cuba.

The general applicability of such a scheme could be questioned. All the Eastern European countries have developed heavy industry beyond their needs and are high consumers of raw materials and energy. Any restructuring therefore would have to be a long and difficult business. The energy-saving schemes initiated in Eastern Europe have remained largely ineffective, except in the GDR whose consumption of energy and metal per capita however remains well above that of the FGR. In 1985 the Comecon session decided to launch a general programme of cooperation for a 'rational utilisation of material resources' up to 2000. It contains over 100 energy and raw materials saving schemes, including recycling of materials as well as substitution measures, with gas and solid fuels being substituted for oil.

3   The third direction is 'strategic' specialisation in the machine-building industry. A multilateral agreement concluded in 1980 defines seven fields of specialisation: new systems for controlling production processes; machines and mechanisms aiming to replace manual labour; modern mining and excavating techniques; energy-saving machinery and technology; precision metal-working and steel processing equipment; production of universal machine-tools; systems for integrated mechanisation in agriculture. As may be seen from this list, specialisation is not directed towards a specific branch or product but aims to solve a complex group of problems. Later on, in 1985, a general multilateral agreement in machine-building especially concerned with robotics expanded the previously agreed upon commitments to the field of flexible automated systems. A new Comecon committee for machine-building was created

the same year, suggesting that coordination in this field is to be ensured primarily through national ministries rather than on the micro-level.

Specialisation is a risky undertaking as it may lead countries to fore-sake vital elements of their industrial base leaving these to partners who may then not be able to meet their obligations. This explains why the most industrialised Comecon countries have to cover an excessively wide range of products in machine-building – all the while complaining about it. Specialisation requires direct links between production units. It can only develop if it is brought about by the constraint of the market, otherwise countries find it safer and more convenient to maintain the whole range of production, even if this costs more. The only hard con-straint within Comecon is, not the constraint of the market, but the need for Soviet supplies of energy and raw materials, itself resulting from the pattern of growth imposed upon Eastern Europe by the USSR after the Second World War. Comecon countries first try to get additional supplies from the USSR, whatever the price. Setting up specialisation is not the main concern. Therefore, the USSR influences the whole specialisation process, including specialisation among the Six. This is why pressure is exerted through the bilateral programmes which the USSR concludes with each one of its partners. Smaller Comecon states try to obtain advantages in counterpart of their agreement to intra-Comecon speciali-sation–cooperation schemes. Here, the counterpart is to buy more from the USSR. As we will see now, in East–West industrial cooperation, the Eastern countries also look for *quid pro quos*: but here, the *quid pro quo* is to sell more to the West, in return for imports from the West.*

East–West: cooperation and compensation

Throughout the decade 1971 to 1980, industrial cooperation seemed to be both the political symbol of *détente* and the economic instrument which allowed structural problems in East–West economic relations to be overcome. The most comprehensive and meaningful definition of industrial cooperation is still that given by the United Nations Economic Commission for Europe, in its *Analytical Report on Industrial Coopera-tion among ECE Countries* (ECE–UN), Geneva, 1973):

> Industrial cooperation in an East–West context denotes the economic rela-tionship and activities arising from (a) contracts extending over a number of years between partners belonging to different economic systems which go beyond the straightforward sale or purchase of goods and services to

include a set of complementary or reciprocally matching operations (in production, in the development and transfer of technology, in marketing, etc.; and from (b) contracts between such partners which have been identified as industrial cooperation by governments in bilateral or multilateral agreements.

though this definition does not draw a clear-cut line between industrial cooperation and conventional trade.

Throughout the decade 1971 to 1980, industrial cooperation seemed to be both the political symbol of *détente* and the economic instrument which allowed structural problems in East–West economic relations to be overcome.

The motivation lying behind industrial cooperation has been analysed repeatedly. The main motivation for the Western partner appeared to be the quest for markets as it enabled the West to sell its technologies where it could not actually sell its products directly. Unlike the case of North–South cooperation, the attempt to benefit from the differential costs of factors appeared as a very secondary factor, if indeed it existed at all. Cost considerations can be seen in certain operations of the workshop-subsidiary type, as when Renault had its transmissions for the Estafette van made in Romania, as well as in sub-contracting or joint manufacturing operations concluded with the Eastern European countries in the field of the small mechanical, or clothing industries. Such operations, though numerous, are usually of low unitary value. Overall, cost determinants are weak, contrary to a rather common view according to which the low level of wages, coupled with greater security in so far as the local labour force does not go on strike, is an advantage for the capitalist partner. In fact, the Western partner has no way of knowing or controlling their socialist partner's costs. Production costs are impossible to compare owing to differences in cost-evaluation accounting methods, to the non-convertibility of socialist currencies, as well as to the secrecy and the more or less arbitrary nature of conversion coefficients used to calculate foreign currency costs from domestic costs. Even for Hungary and Poland, who have introduced a commercial exchange rate, which in principle corresponds to purchasing power parities (at least for products exported), differences in the structure of production costs distort the comparisons. Finally, for the operation of joint firms especially, the socialist partner often insists upon retaining the average wage level in the Western partner's country as a basis for evaluating labour costs. In this case the local workers are paid according to the wage level in the socialist country, and the difference between the accounting wage and the salary really paid goes into the state budget, which annihilates any advantage to be derived from wage differentials.

The outcome of industrial cooperation is the net value of the goods which the Western firm gets in return. The cost can be seen as a trade-off between obtaining increased outlets and having to absorb a reverse flow of products or components. In other words: does the amount of the reverse flow exceed that of the outward flow? Does the operation go beyond the reimbursement period? Is the net cost of the product supplied in return lower than domestic costs in the Western country?

For socialist countries, the overriding advantage of industrial cooperation is the access it gives to technology, its follow-up, and possibly managerial know-how. The foreign currency savings have increasingly become a strong motivation.

Is it possible to distinguish this cross trade of products and services, implying an access to a market in return for the purchase of goods, from ordinary compensation?

The analyses of industrial cooperation have gradually become less sophisticated. In the early seventies the ECE set out different cases of industrial cooperation: the granting of licences with payment in products, the delivery of turn-key factories in return for products, joint manufacturing, sub-contracting, and operations in association. A new classification was provided in a 1980 document which considerably simplified the breakdown of categories. Essentially, it distinguished between the delivery of turn-key plants in return for products and all other forms of cooperation. Another dividing line was between cooperation in which the product supplied belonged to the group of raw materials or semi-finished products, and cooperation involving payment in manufactures. Finally, with the expansion of the joint venture format once the USSR adopted legislation on the subject, one could draw a line between industrial cooperation through joint ventures with equity participation, and all other forms.

The wording of industrial cooperation now really only appears in the language of inter-governmental agreements and international organisations for East–West dialogue such as the ECE. It is valued by Eastern Europe and the USSR as both a means of safeguarding *détente* and an instrument for increasing trade. As for their Western partners, every time they hear industrial cooperation, they translate this by compensation.

But is compensation really the evil it is supposed to be? Does it deserve the mythical status it had gained at the start of the eighties? Compensation is assumed to account for an important and increasing proportion of East–West trade. It is associated with the financial and commercial 'underdevelopment' of the East, i.e., inferior quality products, the inability to promote modern marketing techniques with advertising, distribution networks and after-sales service, and the non-convertibility of currencies along with high hard-currency debt. Should one be so much afraid of it, and is it an everlasting curse on East–West trade? Let us look at what compensation really is: how to measure it, the forms it takes, what the future holds for it.

AN EVALUATION

Quantitative evaluations of compensation are most inaccurate. In the mid-seventies, estimates diverged between 3 and 70 per cent of East–West trade (Wild, 1981, 83). Later on, the range of estimates narrowed, but did not gain in creditworthiness. Several international organisations suggested figures. The OECD claimed that compensation accounted for 4.8 per cent of world exports in 1983 (2 per cent of trade between industrial countries, 15 per cent of East–West trade, 30 per cent of East–South trade and 10 per cent of South–South trade) (OECD, 1985). According to the GATT, compensation amounted to at most 8 per cent of world trade, not taking into account intra-Comecon trade or South–South relations (restricted study, quoted in the *Financial Times*, 16 May 1984). According to the IMF, in 1983–84 compensation deals accounted for 5 to 10 per cent of world trade. Apart from these estimates, there is a vast literature offering data on compensation. Many of these studies are 'restricted' or said to be so. National agencies in developed countries prepare confidential reports; banks, and consulting organisations, offer studies to their clients. Journals, magazines, and newspapers regularly publish stories, which are usually very attractive because the matter is picturesque, even offering a perfume of scandal from time to time; among the most serious sources in this category one must quote the annual survey of the *Financial Times*. Why are the estimates so divergent?

(1) Methodological approximations affect the evaluation of the share of compensation in trade. Do we mean the total amount of compensation sought in general when dealing with a given country (for example: 'Romania asks for 100 per cent compensation', etc.), or the amount of

Table 4. *Buy-back agreements and compensation evaluations: different methods*

	A. Volume of Western exports under buy-back agreements (1968–80)		B. Volume of Western imports under buy-back agreements (1969–80)		C. Volume of Soviet exports under buy-back agreements (1980–5)	
	million dollars	%	million dollars	%	million dollars	%
Gas	3,500	17.8	13,050	39.5	20,749	82.2
Oil	325	1.7	2,536	7.7	764	3.0
Coal	1,250	6.3	2,603	7.9	317	1.5
Wood, paper pulp, paper	750	3.8	1,900	5.8	567	2.2
Chemicals	10,105	51.3	9,726	29.4	2,790	11.1
Ferrous metals	2,910	14.8			n.d.	n.d.
Non-ferrous metals	850	4.3	3,220	9.7	n.d.	n.d.
Total	19,690	100	33,035	100	25,248	100

Note: These data are not directly comparable as set C relates to the Soviet trade only while sets A and B relate to overall East European and Soviet compensation trade.
Sources: A. UN–ECE: 'Large-scale and long-term compensation agreements in East–West trade', *Economic Bulletin for Europe*, vol. 34, no. 2, June 1982, special issue 'Reciprocal trading arrangements in East–West trade', p. 174.
  B. OECD: *East–West trade, Recent developments in countertrade*, Paris, 1981, p. 32.
  C. Borin (Vadim), 'Cooperation on a compensation basis', *Foreign Trade* (USSR), no. 2, 1988, p. 31 (conversion in dollars).

compensation agreed to by contract after generally tough negotiations? Businessmen are usually warned of high rates of compensation to be asked for by their socialist partner (Western banks often issue tables showing the amounts requested by a particular country, which may vary from 20 to 120 per cent or even more according to the country and the type of deal). When the rate of compensation exceeds 100 per cent it means that the country (or enterprise, or foreign trade organisation) wishes to cover not only the value of the import financed by compensation, but also other local expenses. These requests are rarely satisfied. Most often, the compensation arrangement provides for a rate of less than 100 per cent. Moreover, the compensation eventually implemented is frequently lower, because the socialist partner has not been able to provide the goods concerned. An example of this was one of the very first deals of this sort concluded with the Soviet Union. In 1972, France supplied the USSR with a turn-key plant which was to process cellulose. The plant was to be paid for by deliveries of cellulose – a product very much needed by French paper manufacturers. However, the USSR was never able to deliver the product as the domestic market was itself short of cellulose. Nevertheless, the contract was for years mentioned as an example of successful compensation!

Another methodological bias is introduced by the way the ratios of compensation are computed: in percentages of 'total trade', 'exports' (of the Western partner? of the East European partner?), or imports.

One should add that most of these evaluations are made by Western agencies, firms, or experts. The estimates by Comecon countries are much more recent. The Soviet trend towards *glasnost* has prompted the publication of data. According to the Soviet monthly *Foreign Trade* the share of the Soviet exports according to compensation contracts in total Soviet exports increased from 11 per cent in 1980 to 22 per cent in 1985 (*Foreign Trade*, no. 2, 1988: 31).

(2) There are no specific statistics for compensation trade as distinct from 'normal' cash-for-goods trade. The goods traded in the framework of compensation deals are registered in customs data exactly as other products. One has then to apply special methods of investigation and to question the actors in international trade: enterprises, banks, trade companies, counter-trade firms. Business confidentiality comes into play. Firms which practise counter trade for others are naturally shy about it. The exporters of equipment who obtain deals through compensation are also secretive because counter trade is a component of their competitiveness. On the other hand, studies on compensation sometimes aim at showing that it is an anomaly jeopardising the conduct of 'normal trade' and therefore tend to exaggerate it.

In view of these numerous estimates, my opinion is that the figure of 20 per cent for the ratio between the amount of compensation deals resulting in actual imports from the USSR and Eastern Europe, and the amount of total exports to this area, is really a maximum. Normal trade is therefore the rule, not the exception. And whereas at the beginning of the eighties it was suggested that this ratio would increase, it seems now that a peak was indeed reached in this period.

THE FORMS OF COMPENSATION

Within compensation, we find basically two forms: buy-back and counter-purchase.

1 *Buy-back* was the first to appear at the close of the sixties. It involved major equipment sales against resultant products, raw materials

or intermediary goods or, more rarely, manufactures. This form is called in Eastern Europe 'cooperation on the basis of compensation'.

Contracts of this kind have a number of features in common. The basic contract is for a large amount and mainly concerns the commodities sector. Western sales are mainly, but not exclusively, turn-key plants. Sales of small equipment or, exceptionally, of intermediate goods, are also to be found (in the latter these are generally semi-products to be used in plants sold by the West). Cooperation of this type developed mainly in the first half of the seventies in the chemical industry which, between 1970 and 1980, accounted for over half the compensation deals relating to Western equipment sales. These deals were primarily linked to the modernisation programmes being introduced in the USSR and Eastern Europe. Given the scaling down of investment in these countries in the eighties, the sales of turn-key plants gave way increasingly to separate machinery sales while the engineering expertise was supplied by the Eastern partner.

In the buy-back deals, the contract for the sale of equipment is coupled with long-term credit which enables the supplier to be paid, whatever the buy-back conditions. Usually this is an officially backed export credit, although ordinary bank credits or mixed credits are also to be found. Finally, the buy-back contract provides the supplier with products manufactured by the equipment sold. The concept of 'resultant product' is to be broadly understood, hence its application in contracts for pipelines paid for by gas or oil. The link is usually more specific in intermediate product sectors (i.e., chemical products, ferrous and non-ferrous metals, paper pulp). The ECE–UN has long been reluctant to consider the pipelines-against-gas contracts with the Soviet Union as industrial cooperation. It has done so since 1980. As for the Soviet Union, such contracts have been considered as 'cooperation on a compensatory basis' from their very beginning (the first contract was signed with Austria in 1968). The USSR considers that 100 per cent of the gas it exports comes under the heading of buy-back and accounts for 80 per cent of total deliveries made in the framework of compensation arrangements for the period 1975 to 1985.

Buy-back deals always involve at least two separate contracts (if there is no credit equipment is sometimes paid for in cash) and most often three. Usually the buy-back comes after the sale of equipment. It does occur that the purchase obligation coincides with the sale itself. This is the case in chemical compensation deals, when equipment sales are conditional upon the buying back of products similar to those being manufactured, which are supplied by other already operational factories. The buy-back period may very much exceed the period laid down for reimbursement of the operation. The major gas contracts with the USSR provide an illustration of this. Purchasing deals cover periods of twenty to twenty-five years. The total cumulated value of the product sales is naturally a multiple of the value of the original equipment sale. Here we can see clearly just how certain methods of presenting statistics can distort evaluations of compensation. When one evaluates compensation from the total of planned Soviet and Eastern European exports signed for under buy-back agreements for a given period, this distorts reality, not only because a proportion of these sales may never take place (buy-back agreements may be revised if domestic demand is too high) but also because a considerable proportion of sales fall outside the framework of compensation strictly speaking (see table 4).

In the eighties a new situation emerged – 'the compensation of compensation'. Since 1980–81, owing to their imports of oil and gas, the USSR's major clients (France, the FRG, and Italy in particular) developed large deficits with the USSR. They began to ask for compensation, i.e., for additional purchase of goods by the USSR in return for the gas sold, which was itself supplied in return for the equipment originally purchased. The question may then be asked: where to stop when measuring the scope of compensation?

In the industrial manufacturing sector, the value of compensation is generally inferior to the value of the equipment supplied. The evaluation of compensation is particularly difficult here. Studies published agree in putting compensation in the manufacturing industry at around 20 per cent of total compensation. This is very probably an under-estimation in the absence of information on small and medium deals (those under $1 million). Accurate classification of the operation is also problematic in this field. For example, does sub-contracting figure in this category? It obviously does when the sub-contractor is working on machinery supplied by the Western partner. Is the same then to be said of deals involving the reimportation of goods after processing, where the Western exporter supplies not only machines but also such items as cloth and accessories, and the Eastern European enterprise produces jeans, men's suits or ladies' underwear? How is one to class coproduction and specialisation in machine-building, electric engineering, or electronics?

Virtually all these deals involve the counter-delivery of a finished product or its joint marketing. Let us take the case of the contract between a French firm (Citroen SA) and the GDR for the delivery of a factory for the manufacture of constant velocity drive-shafts with an 80 per cent compensation in parts supplied by the German firm (ECE–UN, 1982: 10–11). This is obviously a case for industrial cooperation rather than sheer compensation. The partners were both quite satisfied with the deal and even when the plant was completed, cross-deliveries of a wide range of automobile parts went on.

2 *Counter-purchase* which started later, at the beginning of the seventies, and is especially practised by the Eastern European countries, is the form of compensation most dreaded by Western operators. The main contract provides for sales of equipment as well as of semi-finished products and consumer goods. This contract does not usually contain provisions for credit. It is however settled in hard currency and thus it is distinct from pure barter which does not involve payment in currency. Barter deals were exceptional up to the start of the eighties. They have been revived since, especially in deals involving developing and Eastern European countries which have rescheduled their foreign debt. In the case of rescheduling, all hard currency revenues are in principle allocated to the servicing of the debt. Barter allows the indebted country to export goods so as to get first-priority imports in kind, and to avoid the servicing of debt. In Eastern Europe, Poland and Romania in the eighties resorted to this kind of deal. Even in barter operations, there may be financial arrangements. The most usual practice is for the exporter to open a trustee account in a bank. Revenues from the sale of bartered goods are put into the account, from which the exporter is paid once he has made his deliveries.

The counter-purchase contract is negotiated simultaneously with the main contract. It concerns goods which have no direct connection with the basic deal. Businessmen faced with this constraint complain particularly of the following:

(i) Compensation demands are not always expressed immediately. The Western businessman may be presented with such demands at the very end of the negotiations, with little if any means to avoid it except by jeopardising the whole deal. It is therefore preferable that negotiations on the total value of the counter-purchase take place at the outset. This has already been agreed upon in institutional arrangements, such as the Hungary–EEC agreement signed in September 1988. A similar provision is included in the document concluded in January 1989 at the Vienna review meeting of the Conference on Security and Cooperation in Europe (CSCE) (see below p. 112).

(ii) The choice of products eligible for counter-purchase is limited and does not include those goods which the country could export most easily through the normal channels. Commodities are seldom involved in counter-purchasing. Usually semi-finished products or manufactured goods are traded that way. This is why there has been very little counter-purchasing in trade with the USSR up to now as the favourite Soviet method was buy-back based upon a small range of commodities such as natural gas, coal, and wood. However, lately, commodities have been included in counter-purchase deals, especially oil, following the trend observed for the counter-trade deals of developing countries.

The availability of products for counter-purchase is very much linked to the organisation of foreign trade. Very often the Western partner cannot choose from the whole range of goods in principle offered for compensation, but only from a narrower range proposed by the specific FTO (Foreign Trade Organisation) with which he is dealing. Some countries (such as Hungary) are more flexible in this respect and have set up general purpose FTOs offering a very large choice of goods.

(iii) The Western partner always faces marketing problems. When the partner is the exporter himself (of machinery or intermediate goods) the product offered is more often than not unrelated to his own industry and cannot be easily incorporated in his activities. He may use the services of a specialised trading company but the Eastern European FTOs usually are very reluctant to accept the intervention of such companies. When they do accept it, marketing is still a problem because the Eastern partners do not wish to meet competition with their own goods on their traditional markets when counter-purchased goods are resold on third markets by trade houses. The Eastern partners therefore often request territorial clauses to be included in the counter-purchase contract, limiting the area of possible resale.

(iv) The price of the products is usually overestimated. As they can only be sold off with reductions, the Western operator suffers a loss which he cannot always allow for in his costs.

(v) Penalties, which are usually in the range of 10–15 per cent but may be higher, are enforced for failure to carry out the counter-purchase, even when the main reason for it is the bad quality or limited choice of goods on offer. Nevertheless, the Western partner may deliberately choose to pay the penalty rather than buy the goods. In this case, the counter-purchase obligation just means an additional cost added to the main contract.

(vi) The counter-purchase has to take place by a certain deadline which may be very short; some countries such as the GDR extend the period to as much as two years.

(vii) All the problems previously stated affect the small and medium enterprises more than the large ones.

The general impression one gets from talking to Western exporters is that compensation by counter-purchasing is increasing and its conditions are becoming increasingly constraining. This is offset by the stance taken by certain Eastern European countries which declare their hostility to compensation (this is particularly true for Hungary). Romania, on the other hand, has actually included compensation in its foreign trade code.

(3) How then is one to look on *compensation in general*? I feel that the phenomenon must be stripped of certain myths by taking a view which runs deliberately counter to the most widely held opinions.

(i) It is not simply the demands, the commercial under-development and the financial difficulties of the Eastern European partner which have given rise to compensation. After all, it is the Western partner who starts out because he wants to sell.

(ii) Unlike buy-back which, even if it presents major difficulties, can be estimated since it involves large sums and receives quite a lot of publicity, counter-purchase cannot be clearly set out in tables. Such estimates as are made for counter-purchasing are the result of extrapolations from extremely limited figures obtained from commercial firms, research institutes, and businessmen. They are of no scientific value, a point which is admitted (see OECD, 1981: 28), but this has in no way stopped the generalisations being made. This is all the more true of the form of compensation which is said to be spreading again recently, having disappeared from international practice – barter. As has been mentioned, barter is said to have developed in trade with countries such as Poland since it started rescheduling its debt. In this case, it is often the Western exporter who insists on barter so as to be sure of being paid! However barter is an illegal practice in many countries, including France, as it violates exchange control regulations. In such a situation, it is hard to see how barter may be spotted from the figures!

(iii) It is an exaggeration to say that the goods offered as compensation pose a threat to national production. The buy-back deals obviously do not as they are mostly devised to get needed primary or intermediate goods. The majority of the counter-purchase deals end up in the developing world even though Eastern Europe introduces non-reexportation clauses into contracts.

(iv) A large proportion of counter-purchase deals are never actually implemented, either because none of the products are acceptable to the Western partner or because it has deliberately opted to pay the penalty.

Why then has the myth that compensation is widespread and damaging so taken hold of public opinion? The reason is that, in the West, it is in everyone's interests to be up in arms against compensation. The governments have their political reasons. Eastern Europe accuses them of protectionism and discrimination; the West strikes back complaining about compensation. Western exporters make compensation part of their competitiveness. The ability to integrate it into one's strategy brings dividends and it is therefore in their interest to stress the difficulties. The same is true of commercial firms which live off compensation and derive profits from it. All these reasons have the same effect of making the phenomenon seem more widespread than it is while presenting it in its worst light. All this obliterates straightforward commonsense: nobody has to accept compensation. Any businessman presented with a compensation request may just walk away. If he does not, then it means that his increased (by compensation) transaction costs are still enabling him to derive a profit or some other advantage from the deal. Of course the deal may seem less advantageous than it might have been *without* compensation; but so it would have been with a better price, or more quantities purchased. Why blame compensation alone?

Both businessmen and governments have now in fact grown used to the practice of compensation, which is a common occurrence. Any attempt to speculate on its future requires an examination of the adaptations already made in this field.

THE FUTURE OF COMPENSATION

The first question to ask is the following: is compensation really increasing? For many years that seemed just obvious. At the end of the eighties, it seems much less so. The number of countries, as well as the number of goods, involved in counter trade are increasing. But, as a consequence, the counter trade activity itself is losing its specificity and its frontiers are becoming more and more fuzzy.

(1) Compensation is deeply linked with bilateralism. Any trend of world trade away from bilateralism should therefore reduce the scope of compensation. But world trade is becoming more and more bilateral, in the sense that all export-oriented countries in the world are less and less ready to accept a deficit with a given partner (the USA being a special case). They do not adjust as in the textbooks, seeking a surplus with one group of partners so as to cover their deficit with the other. They try to achieve a balance, when possible, with each of their partners (the fact that they do not always succeed does not mean that they are not trying). For instance, before agreeing, in 1986 to import large quantities of Norwegian gas for twenty years, the French government asked for a firm commitment from the Norwegian government to increase purchases of French investment goods. Between developed industrial countries, compensation deals are the rule for large transactions involving military or aerospace equipment; in this case, they are designated as 'offset' deals – which only looks more respectable but amounts to the same thing. Most of the bulk sales of airplanes thus involve orders in which the buyer supplies the seller with components or alternative goods partly 'offsetting' the cost of the main goods sold. Should we reach a situation when each country would exert pressure on each partner with which it is in imbalance, we might say that compensation has invaded world trade in general, and the prospects for this are not so remote.

(2) Specifically in East–West trade, however, the pressure for compensation seemed to decrease parallel to its increase in other relations. Two factors provoked a surge in counter trade arrangements in general. The first was the debt crisis of the developing countries, which became obvious in 1982 after Mexico's default. A growing number of countries were from then on subject to rescheduling under the control of the IMF, which meant that export revenues had to be channelled primarily to the servicing of the debt, namely, to the interest payments. So as to escape this commitment, the indebted countries frequently resorted to compensation in its crudest form, i.e. barter, which does not result in currency inflows but covers some imports. This prompted counter trade deals in North–South and particularly in South–South relations. The second factor, adding to the first, was the fall in world oil prices. Prior to 1985–86, oil was seldom included in the lists of goods suitable for counter trade, as it sold well for hard currency. It was even specifically excluded from these lists as in the case of the first coherent state regulation of compensation, which was adopted by Indonesia in 1982 (and followed by other South

Asian countries) so as to promote non-oil exports. But after the decrease in oil prices, the oil exporters began to press for counter trade in oil, thus frequently lowering prices still more.

Both crises – debt and oil – had as a common outcome the effect of involving an increasing range of goods in counter trade. Anything that can be sold is offered: oil, grain (in the case of Latin America), but also intermediate goods such as textiles, steel products, chemicals, and manufactured goods including equipment and vehicle components. The purchases covered by barter or counter trade are also diversifying. While, initially, in the seventies, equipment goods were the main item, raw materials are now bought this way (in particular, oil by non-oil exporters), and large construction projects have become major objects of counter trade arrangements.

One is thus left with the impression that counter trade is expanding forever, the only limit being the overall volume of world trade. In East– West trade, the picture is mixed, Romania strongly increased compensation because it wanted to devote most of its hard currency earnings to the pre-payment of its debt to the West by 1990. About 75 per cent of Romanian imports, it is said, will be covered by barter by the end of the eighties. The Soviet Union has developed counter trade since the fall in oil prices. The other Comecon countries seem to try and keep compensation demands within 'reasonable' limits, i.e., in the range of 20 per cent of the value of the Western export. Compensation is better monitored, and looks less pervasive perhaps because it is no longer a special feature of East–West relations only.

First, we are witnessing the development of 'preventive' arrangements which incorporate compensation deals in the general strategy of Western firms.

In 'preliminary compensation' or precompensation, also called *junctim* in the FRG and Austria where it is especially practised, purchases made from Eastern European FTOs (foreign trade organisations) are entered on 'evidence' accounts, which means that it is possible at a later date to export goods to the value of the precompensated amount. When such operations are carried out by specialised trading companies, these 'compensation rights' are sold to exporters against a commission. In this case, from the point of view of the businessman, compensation is only felt as an additional transaction cost, and the exporter need not bother about the compensation itself at all. Major Western firms are increasingly conducting this kind of operation on their own account.

In the intermediate goods sector (chemicals and steel, in particular), major firms have set general agreements covering all their transactions with an Eastern European country or with the USSR on a long-term basis. In France, the firm Rhone-Poulenc signed two such agreements with the USSR in 1976 and 1980. The second of these covers the period 1980 to 1990 and provides for a total of 30 billion francs in overall trade. No pre-established link has been introduced between the supplies and the counter-traded purchases. In principle, trade should be balanced; in fact, there is a surplus for Rhone-Poulenc. Is it still compensation? The executives of the firm contend that it is not; they say it is just good business. But their less clever competitors argue that it is just word-play. In any case, this is not an isolated example. Firms such as Montedison and Dow Chemical Europe (chemicals), Finsider and Krupp (steel) have operated in this way. Outside Europe, one may refer to the deal between Romania and the Hancock company in Australia, providing for supplies of iron ore to Romania against railway carriages, mining equipment, and various other goods that will be handled by a Hong Kong trading company. The deal is supposed to cover a fifteen-year period and imply a total of about $1 billion in each direction (*Financial Times*, 9 December 1988).

Secondly, banks and specialised traders are increasingly involved in such deals, with growing sophistication. Nearly all major banks have now a counter trade department acting as consultant and offering support services, and often engaging itself in mainstream deals. Specialised trading houses, often linked with banks, range from small companies to large groups expanding in different countries, such as the German-based Metallgesellschaft. In Western Germany, more than 200 compensation houses may be found. In 1988, a trading house (Warning and Partner), the BHF Bank, and a company (Stinnes) set up a large compensation subsidiary in Frankfurt, Integrated Services GmbH.

Complex financial packages are becoming regular features. They generally derive from the practice of *switch*, or 'financial barter' as it has often been referred to, which appeared in the seventies. Switch trading involves the existence of a bilateral clearing agreement between an Eastern European country and a developing country. The Eastern European country has a surplus in clearing with its developing partner. It pays the Western exporter with its clearing surplus. The Western partner sells its assets in clearing currency to a switch dealer, with a discount, against payment in hard currency. The switch dealer (usually based in Austria, Switzerland, or Great Britain) thus holds a right of purchase in kind, which he may use for buying goods specified in the bilateral clearing agreement (such as coffee, bananas, oranges, etc.). The goods are then resold in any country. Such operations involve a discount which may range up to 40 per cent of the value of the initial clearing asset depending on the solvency of the debtor and the type of goods offered. The case described here is a straightforward one and can hardly be found in practice any more. Specialised traders buy and sell compensation rights and clearing balances. The resulting packages may involve a great number of partners throughout the world.

The debt crisis in the developing world might bring about new types of financial compensation; one may consider as such the 'debt-for-exports swap' or the 'debt-for-equity swap'. In such cases, some specified exports of the indebted country, or some capital assets (in the form of equity participation in domestic enterprises), may be offered in payment of part of the debt. Poland and Hungary have been mentioned as potentially eligible for such deals. In July 1988, the rescheduling agreement signed between Poland and the creditor banks provided for such debt-for-equity swaps. The equity participation, according to the agreement, may be taken in existing enterprises or in joint ventures to be founded.

Thirdly, governments may intervene to organise or facilitate compensation. This involves relatively interventionist administrative structures. Thus, in France the *Association pour le développement des échanges compensés* (ACECO) was set up in 1977 with the backing of nationalised banks and the administration. Much earlier, in 1968, the Evidenzbüro was set up in Austria on a government initiative and with backing from the banks, in order to facilitate 'precompensation' deals, and the role of the Evidenzbüro has subsequently been greatly extended. Institutions of this kind, which are not trading companies, above all provide information and contacts. In Great Britain, the Ministry of Trade and Industry has published a guide for exporters since 1984, and advises operators on compensation.

The US Department of Commerce barely tolerates counter trade. However, its analysts have tried to identify the products available for import from the East which are also in demand in the West. A study published in 1977 drew up a list of the fifty products most often sold for hard currency for each of the Eastern European countries. The list set out those products likely to find lucrative 'openings' in the West: Polish sports equipment, German machine-tools, etc. (Lenz–Kravalis, 1977). Similar studies have been produced since then by private consultants, including in the Soviet case because the Soviet Union is since 1986 willing to expand its offer of manufactures (PlanEcon 1988).

Fourthly, could international concertation play a role here? To date, such concertation as exists has not gone beyond the stage of information gathering (ECE, OECD). The EEC does not explicitly integrate this point in objectives set out in its common trade policy. However, while the Commission has limited itself to recommending that member states do not institutionalise compensation (which certain member states neverthe- less did, for example, France in its cooperation agreement with the USSR in 1979), the European Parliament has proposed that the Commission establish a 'code of conduct' for compensation operations, backed by sanctions should there be market disruption, and a bureau to monitor compensation agreements, which in general 'should be declared' (European Parliament, Session Documents, 28 July 1982, quoted by L. Van Hoof, 1983: 119–20). The EEC seems however to have moved towards a recognition of compensation. The trade agreement with Hung- ary signed in 1988 specifies that counter trade practices may create distortions in foreign trade and must be regarded as temporary and exceptional. The contracting parties agree to avoid such practices, but should they be used, all necessary information should be provided.

The IMF estimates that counter trade is currently used by half its members. It is looked on as a form of trade and exchange restriction and is particularly condemned in cases of debt rescheduling by a member state (e.g., Romania in 1982–83). As has been seen, export revenue must go to all creditors without discrimination as debt service. Compensation could be seen as a kind of misappropriation of these earnings. But the new financial procedures such as debt-for-equity swaps or debt-for- exports swaps are just an officialisation of compensation. GATT has been very cautious over the question of compensation which, as a pro- cedure of private business, is beyond its scope. GATT is concerned, however, when compensated trade is enjoying exemptions from the application of tariff legislation. Such exemptions are illegal. Before the EEC common trade policy came into power effectively, certain East– West bilateral agreements, particularly those signed by the FRG, were excluding from the quota, products imported under industrial coopera- tion agreements. The exclusion of these products, a measure sub- sequently forbidden in principle, was none the less tolerated for several years. Particular GATT codes in certain areas of international trade (aircraft, public contracts) where compensatory practices abound, remain silent on this issue. A confidential GATT study merely suggests that signatory states should refrain from bringing pressure to bear on buyers, pointing out that imports should be guided exclusively by trade considerations.

Eastern policy in this field is no better coordinated. This is more to be expected, as Comecon has no common trade policy as such. However, in 1978, a book published in Moscow mentioned the possibility of having a unified compensation strategy, justifying this in the following terms: 'this would allow us to determine not only methods for the common planning of exportable production to Western markets, but also the mechanism for dividing corresponding foreign currency revenues between the member states' (Shmelev, 1978: 206–7). It is doubtful if such common planning would be acceptable to the smaller Comecon countries.

In 1983, for the first time, a debate arose between the East and the West on this issue. The framework for these talks was a review meeting of the CSCE (Conference on Security and Cooperation in Europe) held in Madrid, and the final document mentioned compensation as a reality to be accounted for. The original text of the Final Act (Helsinki, 1975) does not mention compensation but in fact deals with it when listing the forms of industrial cooperation, in the optimistic tone of that period. Since 1975, Basket 2 (for economic cooperation) of the Final Act has largely been forgotten with attention focussing on the military-security and the human rights baskets. Basket 2 has again come under discussion in 1986, at the review meeting of the CSCE in Vienna, and with it the concept of compensation emerged. It remained limited to the information issue, more data on compensation being requested by the Western delegations. Some Comecon countries, for example Poland and Hungary, seemed willing to open a dialogue on this basis. However, from the point of view of Comecon members, the compensation issue should not be tackled in isolation but linked with the whole topic of cooperation – including joint ventures. As a result, the final document signed on Basket 2 in January 1989 mentions compensation, expressing the wish that compensation requests 'be addressed at the beginning of the negotiations and' . . . 'dealt with in a flexible way, especially regarding the choice of products', with special consideration for the 'concerns of small and medium-sized enterprises'.

East–South: cooperation and assistance

Relations between the socialist countries and the Third World are dominated by an increasingly ambiguous concept of cooperation. Until 1975, cooperation was based on a few principles:

(1) Trade is the primary form of cooperation. It is based on the natural complementarity between developing nations which provide raw materials and socialist countries which offer industrial products.

(2) Trade goes hand in hand with economic cooperation which provides the Third World with the means of industrialisation without involving any claim on the natural resources of the developing nations.

(3) Cooperation has the aim of facilitating the spread of world socialism. It is therefore carried out primarily with countries having a large public sector and it aims at developing this public sector. When possible, it is integrated into the national planning of the Third World country. It seeks to promote economic growth based upon the development of infrastructures and industry, similar to the growth strategy followed in the past by the socialist countries themselves.

These principles have been called into question in two ways: by the increase in demands coming from the Third World, voiced in bilateral relations as well as within the framework of UNCTAD from 1976 onwards, and by the socialist countries' awareness of their own interests in East–South relations.

In demands from developing nations for more active cooperation with the socialist countries, financial problems have been given priority. The East has been called on to improve the conditions and terms of loans to the developing world, and to increase the proportion of convertible currencies in the total sum of resources earmarked for financial assistance to developing nations (the platform of the 'Group of 77' presented at UNCTAD VII, Belgrade, 1983). These claims have supplemented those put forward in 1976, which sought trade restructuring and qualitatively improved economic cooperation.

The response by the 'rich' (as they are sometimes called in Third World literature) socialist countries came in two stages and introduced a significant change of outlook.

Until 1982, the East's collective declarations (in UN or UNCTAD fora) simply affirmed the specific nature of their aid which could not be estimated in quantitative terms according to 'capitalist' measurements. In the second stage, heralded by a Soviet declaration at the UN, they exposed themselves to evaluation by the West by stating that if one summed up all the forms of aid granted by them to the Third World using capitalist standards, then the socialist countries would come out proportionally in the forefront of 'donors', from the point of view of the ratio of aid to GNP.

These two arguments follow different rationales. The same reality lies behind both. It may be summed up as follows. East–South trade is small; its share in the foreign trade of the South is marginal (about 5 per cent), and it is negligible in world trade (about 1 per cent), the main partners of the South are the developed countries of the North. Cooperation based upon trade finds its limits here. In addition, the level of development in the socialist countries is too low to have a sizeable impact on the development of the Third World, especially as the most advanced countries in the socialist system – Czechoslovakia and the GDR – are the least involved in trade with the South. Finally, the magnitude of the problems faced by the developing world and especially the indebtedness crisis prevents the socialist countries from offering workable solutions, and their own difficulties in this field preclude a workable participation in international attempts to solve these problems.

Let us now examine whether the East's assistance is unique in its nature, and significant in its amount.

A 'UNIQUE' ASSISTANCE?

Is there really anything specific in the nature of East–South relations based on aid through trade and the advantages gained through economic cooperation? The two criticisms most often aimed at the socialist countries may be summed up in the following arguments:

(a)   East–South trade has the same structure as North–South trade (this structure may be even more exaggerated).
(b)   The aims of East–South cooperation are no more altruistic than those of the North's investment in the South. Cooperation basically tends to guarantee the socialist countries privileged access to the South's raw materials.

Do East–South and North–South trade display the same commodity composition?

Broadly speaking, the answer is yes. The socialist countries sell manufactured goods (this covers about two-thirds of their exports) to the Third World and purchase primary goods (this accounts for 90 per cent of their imports).

This similarity in overall structure conceals deep qualitative differences. On the export side, the manufactured goods sold to the South by the East are quite distinct from the Western supplies, and in chapter 6 on technologies we shall elaborate on that. On the import side, within the primary commodities, food imports have a larger share than is the case for the West, and oil imports have a different pattern. But the main question – the one which emerges most in East–South debates – relates to the low share of manufactures in imports from the South.

The proportion of manufactured goods purchased from the Third World has dropped since 1974–75 and only slightly increased since 1985. In both cases, this expresses primarily the movements in oil and commodity prices rather than changes in the composition of trade in real terms as far as the Six are concerned. For the USSR, there has been a marked shift towards an increase of manufactured goods purchased in the South, but only from some countries.

Two questions may be asked here: why don't the countries of the East purchase more industrial products, and are they really to be 'blamed' for acting as they do?

The main reason for the low proportion of industrial products lies in planning priorities. Foreign trade loans aim first and foremost at providing those raw materials vital to the economy. Manufactures actually produced in the developing world do not have the same priority; they can be produced by the East. No doubt, Comecon countries, through bilateral agreements with certain Third World countries, have undertaken to increase their purchases of such goods. The USSR is the only country to have actually increased its purchases of manufactures, in particular from India and Pakistan. Overall, the imports of such goods by the Soviet Union account for a third of its purchases from Asia (excluding Middle East Asia).

Studies published in the East increasingly insist on the need to develop this kind of trade with the South. The main argument put forward to this effect is not that the South must be helped to sell off its manufactures, but that it is in the interest of the socialist countries to integrate in the international division of labour in the manner of the highly industrialised nations, by importing unsophisticated products and specialising in the manufacture of sophisticated goods. It is even in theory more rational for socialist countries to act in this way if one assumes that the labour shortages which they claim do indeed exist and that labour-saving restructuring is necessary. Soviet economists propose to supplement this policy by investments in the Third World aimed at creating export industries oriented towards the Comecon countries which would then no longer develop such industries in their own countries. This design comes up against obstacles, especially for Eastern European countries. Their adjustment policies have led them since 1981–82 to reduce greatly their imports from the Third World, starting with those products which are dispensable. On the other hand, any attempt at specialisation in high quality goods comes up against the actual structure of their industry. Restructuring would require investment in modern industries. Such investment is impossible in a period of slowdown and overall reduction of fixed capital formation; once investment resumes, existing branches have to be taken care of in order of priority.

Moreover, should the Eastern European countries really be placed in the dock on this issue? The commodity composition of their imports depends greatly on the nature of their partners. These partners are predominantly exporters of primary goods. Eastern Europe and the USSR have only limited trade with the newly industrialising countries. Their trade with the Asian NIEs (newly industrialising economies, a term which was substituted in 1988 for NICs, newly industrialising countries) is small as these countries are politically hostile to the East. True, this may change, as Singapore, South Korea, Hong Kong, even Taiwan, are making overtures to Comecon. But one may say that the 'Four Dragons' have already reached a level of development, in any case, of diversification and quality, higher than any of their East European partners, and should East–South cooperation take place between these countries, it would be between a developed South and a less developed East. As for the Latin American NIEs, they have a large surplus with the East due to their sales of food products (and certain minerals) and Eastern Europe is reluctant to increase its deficit by additional purchases of second priority manufactures.

Is the main aim of economic cooperation to guarantee access to the South's raw materials?

The usual format of economic cooperation is that of a long-term credit in kind, in the form of equipment supplies, which are reimbursable over eight to twelve years with the scheduling for repayment starting to run two or three years after completion of the project. Interest is usually set at 2–3.5 per cent. Reimbursement is also generally made in kind, either through delivery of traditional export goods or in products stemming from the cooperation. The larger part of the credits extended by the East go towards heavy industry (see chapter 5 on technology). Such cooperation has allowed the countries receiving aid to develop their industrial production base (power, steel smelting, the mining industry). Have the socialist countries benefited in relation to supplies received in return?

The USSR is far and away the greatest provider of cooperation credits (as high as 80 per cent total credits extended by Comecon). It has used this mechanism selectively to secure guaranteed supplies of some raw materials.

One has to recall here that the Soviet Union is a major producer and exporter of most of the minerals extracted in the world. For a range of commodities (especially non-ferrous metals) the Soviet Union acts erratically, making strategic purchases the amount of which fluctuates widely from one year to the next and cannot be traced through Soviet statistics as such data have disappeared from the foreign trade yearbooks since the mid-seventies. The difficulty is increased by the fact that many of these purchases are made on the open market. For a smaller number of minerals, the Soviet Union has developed a long-time supply policy. This applies mainly to bauxite and phosphate rock, but also, increasingly, to some strategic metals.

The USSR depends on imports for about 45–50 per cent of its needs for bauxite. Its first move in this field was an agreement concluded with Guinea in 1969. According to this agreement the Soviet Union was to develop bauxite extraction in Kindia, 90 per cent of the production was to be supplied to the USSR from 1974 up to the year 2005, of which 55 per cent would be compensation for the supply of equipment and the construction of a railway from the mine to the coast, and the rest to be on commercial terms. The capacity of the mine has been extended and since 1986 the annual output amounts to 3 million tonnes (a third of the total production in the country, which accounts for one quarter of world reserves). Along the same lines, the USSR has concluded cooperation agreements with other bauxite producers in the developing world, such as India, Indonesia and Jamaica.

Unlike bauxite, phosphate rock is abundant in the Soviet Union. The costs of extraction are growing due to the unfavourable location of the fields. The USSR is becoming a net importer of this mineral. It is not quite clear whether the agreement with Morocco signed in 1978 for developing the phosphate field of Meskala is being implemented. It provided for supplies of equipment and a credit of $2 billion, partly in hard currencies, to be repaid through supplies of phosphate for thirty years. Agreements have been concluded by the USSR and some Eastern European countries with other phosphate producers such as Syria, Egypt, Tunisia, and Angola.

The Six are, however, less prone to expand this type of cooperation. True, they are highly import-dependent for raw materials, but their major supplier remains the Soviet Union. The Third World is a residual supplier in so far as the Soviet Union has been reducing its sales since the mid-seventies, or is not able itself to export such goods (tin, bauxite and phosphate rock). When they do engage in cooperation in this field, they are involved in direct investment more often than the USSR.

Joint companies have developed between FTOs of socialist countries and (public or private) enterprises of the Third World (see chapter 4). According to a study by Carl McMillan (1987), among the 231 joint companies existing in the Third World in 1983 with equity capital from the CMEA European countries, 20 were concerned with extraction and processing of raw materials. Romania had, in this category, the greatest number of joint ventures (12 companies out of a total of 20), followed by Bulgaria (4), Hungary (3) and the USSR (1). Czechoslovakia, Poland, and the GDR had none. The differences between the countries originate from divergent conceptions of the risks occurring in such ventures, and also from differences in capacities and expertise in the field of mining.

Cooperation, including direct investment which remains marginal compared to the magnitude of standard credit-based cooperation, is certainly spurred on by the desire to find outlets for equipment goods not marketable in the West. But this aim is not the major one, if only because cooperation, unlike direct trade, does not result in immediate inflows of hard currency. Neither are the USSR and the Eastern European countries mainly motivated, at least until now, by the desire of obtaining low-cost manufactures. Both the limited share of the manufactured goods sector in the areas of cooperation and the poor experience of the Comecon countries in basing their decisions on cost considerations might explain this, although in the future things may change in relation with the economic reforms. The reforms should prompt more attention to production costs and a restructuring of production which might create new forms of cooperation with the Third World, parallel to new patterns of trade suggested in the previous section.

As it is, the main economic interest in cooperation from the point of view of the socialist countries and particularly the Soviet Union, remains foreign sources of raw materials. From the point of view of the Third World, it is a form of aid as it should help the benefiting countries to develop their basic industries. How can one estimate this help?

THE CONTROVERSY OVER AID

Socialist aid to the developing world has given rise to a generally unfavourable appreciation in Western studies on the subject. The following points have been stressed.

1   Aid is small as a percentage of the GNP of the donor nations. For the 1970–80 decade, it has been estimated at 0.09–0.16 per cent for the USSR and 0.06–0.12 for the Six. Even taking into account a reevaluation of the estimates following the Soviet statements of 1982, the Western figures remain much lower than the percentages claimed by the socialist countries, as well as below those of the Western countries (average aid figures for the Western world are 0.35 per cent of the GNP of the relevant countries).

2   Aid is small when compared to the total official development aid received by the Third World (7 per cent of this total in 1980, 10 per cent in 1985, according to the OECD).

3   Aid is extended on harder terms than Western official development aid. The OECD computes the 'grant element' included in credits according to a complex formula taking into account the period of the loan, the interest rate, the grace period, the rescheduling or annulling of the debt. On this basis the 'grant element' in Western assistance is supposed to amount to about 90 per cent, whereas it is slightly over 50 per cent for Comecon aid in the mid-eighties. There are very few grants in Comecon practice, and this has shocked Western public opinion when considering the food assistance extended to Ethiopia. Notwithstanding the fact that Ethiopia is an observer in the CMEA and a socialist-orientated country,

it got very little emergency help from the socialist countries during the worst period of the famine in 1984. However, the computation of the grant element does not take into account preferential prices, nor the fact that the loans are generally reimbursed in kind. One has to note that of late, repayment in dollars is sometimes included in the agreements: such is the case for a $350 million loan extended by the USSR to Algeria beginning in 1986 for financing twenty-two projects, including follow-on and repair of former Soviet-built items such as oil and gas pipelines; Algeria is to pay back over a thirteen-year period with 50 per cent of it in dollars.

Aid conditions are naturally much better for the developing socialist countries and especially Comecon members (Mongolia, Cuba, Vietnam) which according to the 'socialist' classification do not belong to the developing world, but are included in the group of developing countries in the Western studies.

4   Aid may, in exceptional cases, be granted in hard currency. Generally, it is linked to the import of equipment from the donor country. The local expenses for installation are seldom financed, which often prevents the beneficiary from actually using a committed credit.

5   Aid is very much concentrated on the donor side. The USSR extends over 80 per cent of it (85 per cent in 1985 (according to OECD)). The GDR accounts for 30 per cent of the rest, followed by Czechoslovakia and Bulgaria (for the latter, mainly in the form of technical assistance). Hungary, Poland, and Romania contribute very little.

6   Aid is also strongly concentrated on the side of the beneficiaries. Most of these are the aforementioned countries not belonging to the 'developing' world according to the standard Comecon concept: Cuba, Vietnam, Mongolia and Cambodia absorb 70 per cent of total aid in the eighties. If one adds the socialist-orientated countries (often called 'client states' in Western publications), and, in particular, Afghanistan, Ethiopia, South Yemen, and since 1982 Nicaragua, one gets a share of 85 per cent. Not much is left for other grantees. These other recipients satisfy the following criteria:

neighbouring countries of the USSR (India, Iraq, Iran up to 1979, Turkey, Pakistan, Syria);
suppliers of crucial raw materials (Iraq, also belonging to the previous group, Nigeria, Algeria, Guinea up to 1984, the year when Sekou Touré died).

7 Multilateral development aid is almost non-existent as has been mentioned in chapter 2.

For quite a long period the socialist countries refrained from giving figures for their aid, arguing that it could not be compared to the so-called 'aid' of the capitalist countries. As long as the call for data originated in the West, this position could be maintained. Even when the 'Group of 77' asked the socialist countries to allocate 1 per cent (later on, 0.7 per cent in public aid) of their GNP to development aid, exactly as the 'rich' industrially developed countries of the capitalist system, the Soviet and Eastern European stand remained unchanged. 'There is no reason, and cannot be any, for presenting the Soviet Union and the other socialist states with the same demands as those which the developing countries submit to the developed capitalist states, including the request of allocating a given share of the GNP to economic assistance', declared the Soviet representative to the 36th Session of the General Assembly of the United Nations in October 1976.

However, in 1982, the Soviet delegation to UN ECOSOC (Economic and Social Council), soon followed by other communist countries, disclosed two figures, for the first time: one was the absolute amount of aid (30 billion roubles for the period 1976 to 1980); the second was its share in GNP (1 per cent in the same period). Bulgaria, the GDR, and Czechoslovakia provided similar data for the UNCTAD VI the following year, but with a smaller percentage of aid in GNP (between 0.73 and 0.79 per cent). These statements were subsequently repeated in various United Nations bodies, without altering the initial position of the socialist countries. Thus, the Bulgarian statement mentioned that 'such figures do not mean in any way that Bulgaria is prepared to alter its principle position according to which the targets for financial aid are not applicable to the cooperation and assistance which it extends to developing countries, due to the nature and to the modalities of this cooperation and assistance' (UNCTAD, doc. TD/291, 7 June 1983).

These statements were a challenge to the agencies which up to then gave estimates of Comecon aid. Just to discard them was difficult; to recompute the aid in line with these new data seemed very hazardous.

The Western sources available for estimates of Soviet and East European development aid include national agencies such as the CIA and the Department of State in the USA, the UK Foreign Office, and multilateral bodies. The most systematic and open investigation is available from the OECD: a summary of information is given annually in the report by the chairman of the Development Assistance Committee, *Development Co-operation*. The new Soviet data are discussed from 1983 onwards. In addition the OECD has prepared several reports on the topic, with a restricted distribution.

Some of the conclusions of the published Western discussions of Soviet data are reviewed below.

Computations are based on the commitments of the socialist countries. It is not so easy to trace them: one has to read many journals, and identify all the announcements of loans or contracts published in the press. The USSR publishes a compendium (*Sbornik*) of all international agreements concluded by the Soviet Union with foreign countries, unfortunately it is published a long time afterwards. Information published in the press is rarely exhaustive (in particular, on the conditions of and delays in repayment). Then one has to follow the implementation of the accord to compute the annual gross disbursements. As information is rarely available, one has to combine some published data (such as the Soviet figures on deliveries of complete equipment in the framework of cooperation) and assumptions on the actual disbursements. Finally repayments have to be subtracted from gross disbursements, so as to get the net drawings of the developing countries. This is a very tricky part of the computation, and the OECD has ceased to publish its estimates on this point. The OECD has stated that in 1981 the USSR extended a *negative net* aid to the developing countries (reimbursements exceeding disbursements). It also seems that in 1982–83 the net aid of the Eastern European countries was negative. Since then the trend seems to have been reversed. To give an example: in 1983 Soviet deliveries of equipment in the framework of cooperation agreements amounted to two-thirds of the value of Soviet imports of goods produced with equipment earlier delivered by the USSR. But the Soviet deliveries of equipment are just part of what is supplied on the basis of cooperation accords; as far as imports are concerned, part of the flow of goods in compensation for Soviet equipment are sold as commercial deals. Thus statistics have to be used with great care. The most detailed investigation of Soviet statistics is due to a British researcher (Bach, 1987).

The socialist countries have indeed supplied some information, not in the form of figures, but in clarification of their assumptions:

> the concept of 'developing country' is the one retained in the West, in other words it includes developing socialist countries, just for the sake of demonstration;

loans with a concessional element of not less than 25 per cent were retained;
assistance includes the training of cadres and the supply of experts;
it also includes advantages granted 'in the sphere of foreign trade', such as: favorable terms for technology transfers; preferential prices for exports (lower than 'normal' prices) and imports (higher than 'normal'), as well as preferential marine freight tariffs. These items are not considered as aid in OECD concepts.

When the OECD experts tried to recompute Soviet and Eastern European aid using the available statistics and following the methodological assumptions stated by the socialist countries, they obtained figures significantly higher than the earlier ones, but still much lower than the lump sum amounts offered by the individual socialist countries after 1982. Is it possible to reconcile the two sets of figures?

Let us, for instance, discuss the Soviet figure for the year 1981. The amount of aid extended is said to have been 8.1 billion roubles. According to the Soviet explanations, these are 'devisa-roubles' (d.r.), i.e. the accounting roubles used in foreign trade statistics (and *not* the domestic Soviet monetary unit), the value of which in dollars is obtained by multiplying them by the official rate of exchange of the dollar, i.e., in 1981, $1.38 for 1 d.r. Thus r.8.1 billion means $11.2 billion, whereas the highest OECD estimate for this year is $2.4 billion.

If we assume that this sum is equivalent to 1.3 per cent of the Soviet GNP as the Soviets claim, then the implied value of GNP in 1981 would be r.630 billion, and $860 billion at the official rate of exchange. In roubles, the figure would be consistent with the Soviet data on the net material product (NMP), which amounts to r.482 billion (one usually considers that GNP=1.3 NMP because the Soviet concept of NMP does not include the services, whose value is conventionally estimated in Western sources as of about one-quarter of GNP calculated according to Western standards). But this consistency is itself misleading as it would imply that the devisa-rouble (used for the estimate of aid) and the domestic rouble (used in NMP data) are equal, whcih cannot be the case. What demonstrates this is the fact that the GNP figure in dollars which we thus get is very low. It yields a GNP per capita of $2,330 whereas the figure given by the World Bank for the year 1980 was already $4,550! Finally, we know that the GNP referred to is not the actual one but the (unpublished) figure by which the UN Secretariat calculates the Soviet contribution to the costs of the organisation.

I have tried elsewhere (Lavigne, ed., 1988) to assess the amount of Soviet aid in 1981 from Soviet sources, itemising the components of aid. Recomputation yields the following results:

if all Soviet loans are supposed to be granted at a minimum concessionary element of 25 per cent, and if one retains as 'credits extended' the value of Soviet equipment delivered in the framework of cooperation, one gets 1,606 million roubles. Note that I do not follow the method of some other experts, who first estimate the commitments and then the extensions (or effective drawings), which is not easy because the published sources usually do not provide the actual time periods of the utilisation of the loans (see Bach, 1985: 270);

the grants and contributions to international organisations are supposed to amount at most to 10 per cent of the value of the equipment supplied on credit, i.e., to 161 million roubles;

the amount of technical assistance is itself divided between:

(a)   the cost of *experts*. Should one take the Western figure for the number of experts in 1981 (about 80,000), and the Soviet estimate of the actual cost of these experts to the developing countries, which is said to amount to 25–40 per cent of the cost of Western experts (by reference to the United Nations norms), the difference between the Western norm and the cost of the Soviet expert would be tantamount to an aid. This would account for r.1.0 to 1.6 billion;

(b)   aid in the form of *training* students from the Third World in the USSR. Should this number be 60,000 (Soviet data), and the annual cost of a student in the USSR estimates, on the basis of Western norms, r.9–10,000 per year, this would yield r.500 to r.600 million;

(c)   aid in the form of training on the spot. Taking the figure of 100,000 technicians trained in a year (which is consistent with the overall figures given by the USSR), aid according to this might be estimated at r.100 to r.150 million;

aid 'in the sphere of foreign trade'. The only computable item here is aid to Cuba. The USSR sells oil to Cuba at subsidised prices, and buys sugar (and also nickel) at much over world prices. Subsidised oil is also sold to Mongolia and Vietnam. For the year 1981 the price subsidies to Cuba amount to about r.2 million.

Taking the lowest figures we get an amount of r.5.4 billion, that is, $7.3 billion. This is still well under the Soviet figure (by 35 per cent), but largely over the OECD estimate, which amounts to 33 per cent of our estimate. The ratio of our figure to the Soviet GNP for 1981 would be 0.85 per cent – which would put the Soviet Union at the level of the most generous donors in the world, which are the Scandinavian countries.

Our computation may be compared with that of Q. Bach for the years 1976–80. He gets a rather close figure of 0.67 per cent of the Soviet GNP for total Soviet aid, but the ratio drops to 0.23 if one takes into account only the items which would qualify as aid by Western standards (i.e., excluding the cost of Soviet experts, and of all price and foreign trade subsidies). He ends with the conclusion that 'the Soviet claim remains an enigma' (Bach, 1985, 272). Indeed, so it is – as a claim. And notwithstanding *glasnost*, it has been renewed, and substantially increased, for the recent years, at UNCTAD VII in Geneva in July 1987.

Leaving the figures aside, new qualitative trends in cooperation are obvious. Aid is to be concentrated in favour of developing socialist countries (i.e. Vietnam, Mongolia, Cuba, as the other Comecon members have pledged to do in July 1988), and of socialist-orientated countries. As for the other Third World partners, normal commercial credits tend to supersede cooperation credits. These commercial loans are granted for a shorter period (for five years from the delivery of equipment) at a higher rate of 4–5 per cent or even more. They too may be repayable in kind, and since the fall in the world oil prices in 1986 it is assumed that a growing flow of oil from OPEC countries to the USSR and Eastern Europe is indeed traded that way. In parallel, reflection on past cooperation credits leads to a reappraisal which is more and more often negative. A more limited aid, better monitored in the benefiting countries, more selective in its objectives, is advocated in the Soviet post-Gorbachev literature. The discussion in the Supreme Soviet over the 1990 budget for the first time questioned the very principle of foreign aid. Some deputies pointed out that aid to the developing countries was almost equal to the amount of the social bill subsidising health, education and all kinds of social transfers to the Soviet population, and they called for drastic cuts in the economic assistance budget (*Moscow News*, 3 December 1989: 6).*

In this chapter, we have seen that cooperation has quite different meanings according to its direction. Is a magic 'synthesis' possible? – the very principle of aid is questioned.

A FALSE SYNTHESIS: TRIPARTITE EAST–WEST–SOUTH COOPERATION

Tripartite East–West–South cooperation has been much more publicised then implemented in practice. The socialist countries strongly insist on these experiences. Politically, they mean cooperation between different socio-economic systems; economically, they suggest that the East is advanced enough, from the point of view of technology, to assist the South at par with the West (North). Finally, it allows increased East–West cooperation. However there are many limits to tripartite cooperation. The Western companies make use of it as a last resort, when there is no other way to penetrate a given market in a developing country. The role of the Eastern partner is often secondary. This is why the cases are to be found mainly in the 'rewarding' Third World, that is, in the countries rich in raw materials and energy (for instance, Middle East countries), as P. Gutman (1981) remarks. A study of UNCTAD, based upon the research of P. Gutman, notes that of about 300 projects recorded at the end of 1982, the Middle East accounted for more than 50 per cent (mainly concentrated in Algeria, Iran, Iraq), and among industrial activities, the energy sector (generation of electricity, refinery of oil, extraction of gas) accounted for 40 per cent (UNCTAD, 1984).

Tripartite cooperation is for these reasons a minor factor in East–West relations. If we consider that it accounts for 4–10 per cent of East–West industrial cooperation and that East–West cooperation itself amounts to 3–4 per cent of East–West trade, then tripartite industrial cooperation should amount to an average of 0.25 per cent of East–West trade!

Tripartite industrial cooperation (TIC) is cooperation between the East and the West in the South, rather than with the South. In 90 per cent of cases it takes the form of the sale of turn-key plants or equipment. Contribution by the developing country is nil or low (assembly or civil engineering). In the West, the countries most involved are the FRG, which has the commanding lead, France, Italy, Finland, and Austria. In other words, they are those Western European nations which are also the leading partners in East–West trade or who reserve a large proportion of their foreign trade for Eastern trade. In the East, the main protagonists are the USSR, as far as the amount of the contract is concerned; Hungary, Poland and, quite some way behind them Romania as far as concerns the number of operations. The latter three countries are also those most involved in direct investment in the developing countries. The GDR and Czechoslovakia are not very involved in TIC deals since their level of technical know-how enables them to undertake bilateral operations more easily and also because their relations with the developing world are limited.

Generally, the instigator of most of these operations is the Eastern country which seeks a Western partner for the most advanced high technology and for design engineering. It is much more rare to find the Western firm approaching the East to take advantage of political or marketing opportunities, this being the case particularly in state-trading Third World countries.

The difficulties which the Eastern countries find in achieving successful integration in North–South relations through tripartite cooperation point to their inadequate control over the multinationalisation process. The foreign trade reforms underway in all these countries, along with the domestic reform movement, are meant to improve this control through an opening up of their economies.

CHAPTER 4

TRADE MECHANISMS AND POLICIES: FROM STATE TRADING TO MARKET

It is usually said that all socialist countries apply the principle of state monopoly of foreign trade. According to this principle, in the traditional foreign trade mechanism which was valid everywhere up to the beginning of the eighties, specialised organisations attached to the Ministry of Foreign Trade and/or to industrial ministries handle trade relations with foreign partners. This principle applies to all trade, whatever the direction, to socialist or non-socialist countries. These foreign trade organisations (FTOs) act like a screen between the foreign partner and the domestic enterprise. With the former, they deal on the basis of world prices and in foreign currencies (either convertible or non-convertible depending on the trade zone). With the latter, they deal in domestic prices and in domestic currency. The FTOs usually specialise in products or groups of products: food, raw materials and semi-finished goods, consumer goods, machinery, and others (licences, tourism, transport, representations, etc.). Each country has approximately forty to sixty such FTOs. These are monopolies not only because of their exclusive right to trade for a given range of goods, but also because of the amounts of trade which they handle. This is true in particular for the Soviet FTOs. Export-khleb, which imports and exports grain, is the single largest grain importer in the world, and Soyuzneftexport, which trades in oil, is the largest oil exporter. They each have turnovers of several billion dollars.

However, since the reforms initiated in the Eastern European countries in the seventies, followed by the maelstrom of Soviet reforms since 1986, this picture is no longer true. We shall look first at these reforms, which have altered the monopoly of foreign trade without quite suppressing it, although some of these countries now claim to be treated as market economies in the field of trade. A particular aspect of these reforms has consisted in the introduction of laws allowing for joint ventures.

Although the joint ventures may be seen as a form of cooperation, we have included them in this chapter as their operation is narrowly linked with the foreign trade mechanism. Finally, we shall see how these reforms have changed the involvement of the socialist countries in world trade. This raises the very political issue of protectionism. The West usually considers that state trading is protectionist by nature, while the East complains about discrimination which is imposed on socialist countries on the basis of an obsolete understanding of their foreign trade and economic system. So who is protectionist, indeed, and are the barriers resulting from this double protectionism to be eliminated in the near future?

Reforms in the foreign trade mechanisms

The changes in the traditional state trading system stem from two major ideas, to be found also in domestic economic reforms. First, foreign trade is now considered as an economic activity of the enterprise, and not as a set of administrative procedures. Therefore, production enterprises have to be involved directly in the foreign trade process, either through a closer cooperation with the FTOs or by trading on their own account. Second, the production units have to be interested in the outcome of their foreign trade activity just as they are in the outcome of their domestic activity, through material incentives. Foreign trade will not be successful if conducted through plan directives. We find here the twin ideas of autonomy and incentives which lie at the bottom of the domestic reforms (Table 5).

In spite of these reforms, the FTOs still remain in most countries. Western businessmen have some trouble understanding with whom to deal in an intricate network of agencies and firms with changed or uncertain competences. This section will thus end with some 'intructions' for their use.

THE GRADUAL INTEGRATION OF FOREIGN TRADE
AND PRODUCTION

Reforms have started everywhere with the creation of a closer relationship between FTOs and manufacturing firms, while the principle of state monopoly is retained, at least to begin with. The degree of flexibility in state monopoly depends on the extent to which the domestic reform itself

Table 5. *The foreign trade reforms in the Eastern countries (main provisions)*

	Bulgaria	Czecho-slovakia	GDR	Hungary	Poland	Romania	USSR
Organisation of foreign trade							
FTOs subordinated to the Ministry of Foreign Trade or Foreign Economic Relations	X	X	X	X	X	X	X
FTOs subordinated to industrial ministries and other state agencies	X	X		X			X
FTOs attached to a combine or enterprise	X	X	X[a]	X			X
Enterprises granted rights to trade on their own	X	X[a]	X[a]	X	X		X
Incentives to export							
Subsidies on export prices	X	X	X	X	X	X	X
Use of conversion coefficients	X	X	X		X		X
Rights to retain a part of hard currency gains	X			X	X	X	X
Export credits in domestic currency		X[a]		X	X		
Bonus funds	X				X	X	X
Credits in hard currency	X	X[a]		X	X	X	X[b]

a Only on an experimental basis.
b Only for joint ventures.
Source: Author's elaboration from various sources on the foreign trade reforms; a comparable, slightly different table is to be found in Haendcke-Hoppe (1988). The table relates to the status of the reforms in 1989.

has liberalised economic activity. Has state monopoly utterly vanished in some cases? The Hungarians, for instance, claim they have succeeded in shifting to a market-type operation in trade. Does this hold true, and is state monopoly bound to wither altogether?

In *Hungary*, in the wake of the overall liberalization of the economic system since 1980, about 340 industrial, marketing and service firms have been authorised to carry out foreign trade deals on the export and/or the import side, on the basis of a general licence, supplementing the 38 existing FTOs. In addition, industrial firms have obtained specific authorisations to import or export. The number of such authorisations totalled almost 400 in 1981, 700 in 1983, and over 1,300 in 1987. New regulations have been introduced in 1988. From 1988 on, all enterprises, whatever their activity, may export and import on condition that they register at the Ministry of Foreign Trade for the goods or services which they want to export or import. In 1989, the number of enterprises engaged in foreign trade had already soared to 600, including private firms, and this number should reach 1,000 in 1990. However, not all goods or services may be traded this way. In trade with socialist countries, the enterprises still have tasks assigned from above, due to the necessity of implementing agreements concluded with the other Comecon countries. In trade with capitalist countries, about 58 per cent of Hungarian exports and 48 per cent of imports are covered by restrictions, meaning that the non-specialised (in foreign trade) agencies cannot obtain rights to export or import the relevant goods. Not only bureaucratic structures impede the liberalisation of foreign trade. Firm managers especially appreciate the newly acquired rights in certain fields, for example, in the import of spare parts of specific semi-finished products. However, it has been noticed that firms prefer to trade through the FTOs for traditional foreign trade deals, e.g., for the import of raw materials and essential semi-finished goods and for the export of traditional goods. On the other hand, since 1982 over half the equipment exports have been carried out by the manufacturing firms themselves (Salgo, 1986).

These developments were stimulated in Hungary by the awareness that, due to rigid structures, the potential of the country was not being fully used.

A striking example is the Rubik's cube case. This began as a success story. This cube has on each of its six sides nine squares articulated on three different axes which must be manipulated so as to end up with a different colour on each side of the cube. This invention by a Hungarian mathematician was initially marketed by an industrial cooperative in association with an American firm, Ideal Toy, for sales on the capitalist market. Although exports by the toy industry quadrupled over a few years largely due to the success of this magic cube, this very success highlighted its weak points. The small production unit found it impossible to keep up with the huge increase in demand (with 5,000 cubes sold in 1977 and a demand of 10 million on foreign markets in 1981). Export was carried out through a foreign firm with considerable losses in profits for the Hungarian partner. In the initial transaction the Hungarian cooperative was paid $2 for each cube to be resold at $10 in the United States. In 1979, the toy industry did not have access to foreign markets.

Since 1980, the Hungarian system has shown increased creativeness in the field of foreign trade. It was in that year that the first agency of a new kind was created. Generalimpex was authorised to import and export all kinds of products in order to break down the rigidity of the traditional FTOs specialising in given products. This was meant to stimulate exports to non-socialist countries, to develop relations with small capitalist enterprises and to establish, when needed, compensation arrangements. This move paved the way for the 'despecialisation' of the FTOs but not without reluctance on their part. In fact these FTOs tried – and partly succeeded – to organise a sort of boycott of Generalimpex by potential suppliers or buyers. Competition indeed played its role here, but in an oligopolistic, cartel-type way, which was neither expected nor looked for by the authorities.

Also in 1980, thirty-eight FTOs and enterprises (from light and heavy industry and agriculture) got together to set up Interinvest with a capital of 100 million forint to make investments linked to foreign trade operations (warehouse construction, packaging, pooling freight truck transportation, etc.). Medicor, the large Hungarian agency for the export of pharmaceutical products and medical equipment, has also created a firm, Medinvest, in partnership with three other firms and the State Bank for Development, to provide engineering services for the export of complete medical installations.

The field of representation has not been neglected either. Since 1980, Hungarian firms have been authorised to have representation abroad. Likewise, specialised firms represent foreign interests in Hungary with greater dynamism than in other socialist countries. Ten firms are operating, in addition to the permanent representatives of large Western firms.

The best known is Interag, set up already in 1958. Interag does not limit itself to representation alone, although this activity brings it large profits – for instance, Interag represents Shell and its network of service stations in Hungary, as well as fifty or so other Western firms. It also exports small turn-key plants, in the chemical, timber, and metal industries. In 1978, it created a holding company in Luxembourg called Globinvest which buys shares in small Western firms, the first such operation realised being the purchase of 72 per cent of the shares of a Danish television company.

Finally, the regional dimension of export is taken into account. In 1982, a network of officials was set up in the regions with the task of promoting the exports of small local firms and coordinating their operations while 'discovering' those articles most suitable for export, such as local handicrafts, tools, etc. An example of this was the association of a hotel complex and an agricultural cooperative on the border with Austria for the manufacture of ready cooked foods and preserves for the Austrian and West German markets.

In 1982, once again, Hungarian legislation made it possible for Hungarian firms and foreign companies to set up joint ventures in zones with off-shore status. This innovation did not immediately bring an expansion in joint venture creation. Favourable tax provisions implemented in 1986, followed in 1988 by a new law on companies allowing private persons to take part in joint ventures, should give a new impetus to this format, especially for small units. By the end of 1988, the number of joint ventures exceeded 200 (see p. 159). It had increased up to over 700 by the end of 1989.

Despite these developments, in the Hungarian case, it does not seem that state trading and state monopoly of foreign trade is about to be eliminated. The state has retained extensive regulating powers, in the specific 'bargaining-type' planning which operates in Hungary. The enterprises themselves are reluctant to take risks as a protective environment protects them from external or internal competition. The other East European countries have not even gone this far.

In *Poland*, reforms tending towards an increase in the rights of firms to undertake foreign trade have not yet proved fruitful. Reform had begun earlier than in other countries, but experiments with 'pilot firms' which got underway in 1973 were shelved almost immediately due to the world crisis and the growing indebtedness of the country. In the framework of the Polish economic reform of 1982, enterprises in the manufacturing industry were granted the right to export directly if they held a trade permit delivered by the Ministry of Foreign Trade. The granting of the permit was subject to certain criteria: the enterprise had to export at least 5 per cent of its production (since 1988; originally, 25 per cent), or a minimum amount, which was initially fixed at 1 billion zlotys (since 1988: 4 billion). Other firms are supposed to be able to choose between FTOs in order to make the FTOs compete with each other. In 1988 the right to export or import on their own account without any prior permit was granted to firms supplying or buying specific goods according to a list drawn by the Ministry of Foreign Trade (78 export goods, 20 import goods). Finally, beginning in 1989, no permit is necessary except for importing or exporting specific goods. On the import side the list mainly includes food items, medicines, and some strategic raw materials. On the export side it includes all raw materials and all goods which are subject to quotas and restrictions on Western markets. The FTOs themselves have been reorganised. The traditional FTOs have been retained only for coal and strategic raw materials. For other goods, they have been transformed into FTCs (foreign trade companies) in which the Polish state has the majority of shares.

As a result of these measures, already by 1987, 250 state enterprises, 45 cooperatives, and 200 small firms had the right to trade with foreign partners. By the end of 1988, the overall number of such units exceeded 1,700. One can hardly say, however, that these measures helped to reduce the scope of the state monopoly. In the light of Poland's financial constraints, the enterprises have better access to foreign trade and are more likely to secure the import goods they need if they use the FTOs or FTCs. They do not really compete with the FTOs in the field of foreign trade. In fact, even with the liberalisation process, export or import transactions remain subject to licensing. Up to 1988, a licence had to be issued by the Ministry of Foreign Trade for each transaction, since then general licences may be issued for transactions similar in kind.

In 1988, the Ministry of Foreign Trade became a Ministry of Economic Cooperation with Foreign Countries, probably to follow the Soviet model. As in Hungary, a new law passed at the end of 1988 on economic activity allows private persons to set up companies and to participate in joint ventures.

Bulgaria has several times reformed its foreign trade organisation – in 1978, 1979, 1982, and 1986 – along with the rather disorderly pace of its economic reform. Since 1982, different types of foreign trade organisations have come into existence: the FTO attached to a branch ministry (this disappeared in 1987 with the suppression of the branch ministries themselves); the FTO which caters for different firms or is directly geared to the requirements of one; the 'service' FTO attached to the Ministry of Trade (which since 1986 has merged both ministries of foreign and domestic trade) undertaking transit or middlemen operations. Several FTOs specialising in engineering have been set up, particularly for the export of complete sets of equipment to developing or socialist countries. For example, Bulmedprom (1982) unites the Academy of Medicine, the specialised FTO Maimex and two firms for the export of medical and hospital equipment. Within the framework of the new economic units set up since 1980, which are associations of firms with specific interests, foreign trade fares well. Thus the Economic Association of Bulgarian Industry established in 1980 (which one may compare in its intentions to the Confederation of British Industry) and which brings twenty-six firms and banks together, seeks to assist members in adapting to foreign demand and gaining a foothold in foreign markets. With its help, four Bulgarian firms founded a foreign investment company in 1982, whose first operation was the purchase of the German company, Roperwerk. There thus seems to be a decentralisation of foreign trade management in Bulgaria. One must remember that the industrial structure is very concentrated in Bulgaria, with about 140 'economic associations' only. The devolution of foreign trade rights is by no means the end of the foreign trade monopoly. True, the decision adopted in December 1988 by the Bulgarian Communist Party plenum suggests a deep restructuring of industry with the so-called 'firm' to become the new unit of management. The outcome of the following legislation adopted in January 1989 is yet far from clear.

As in Bulgaria, in *Czechoslovakia* the law on economic relations with foreign countries (April 1980) closely followed the adoption of the 'set of measures for the improvement of planning and management' (January 1980). It provided for a closer linking of FTOs and 'large economic units' (associations of firms). Three limited experiments followed this law. The first involved the incorporation of FTOs previously attached to the Ministry of Foreign Trade, in five of these 'large units'. The second linked four 'units' to the relevant FTOs through association contracts. The third experiment involved firms producing traditional exports (jewellery, crystal, and china) and went only as far as introducing greater incentives. When Czechoslovakia decided to follow the Soviet path of *prestavba* (the

Czech word for *perestroika*), the foreign trade sector also benefited from some decentralisation. According to measures taken at the end of 1986, about a quarter of the Czechoslovak export of machinery was transferred to the competence of the production enterprises and is no longer controlled by the Ministry of Foreign Trade. The Czechoslovak law on the socialist enterprise adopted in 1988, following the Soviet model of 1987, embodies increased rights for the enterprises in the field of foreign trade. However, knowing the reluctance of the Czechoslovak leadership to abandon the traditional principles of central planning, one may doubt that radical changes will soon affect the foreign trade sector.

In *Romania*, the December 1980 law 'on the strengthening of self-management and financial autonomy in foreign trade' amended the 1971 law on foreign trade activities and economic, scientific, and technical cooperation. According to the 1980 law, most of the 55 FTOs were directly subordinated to branch industrial ministries, or incorporated in the large enterprises, and only 9 remained directly subordinated to the Ministry of Foreign Trade and Economic Cooperation. A further 'reform' re-centralised the system and reattached the FTOs to the Ministry of Foreign Trade (Lhomel, 1987).

In the *GDR*, the restructuring of industry into 'combines' (148 since 1979) has brought about the reorganisation of foreign trade. In 1984, of the 53 FTOs, these combines have absorbed 22 (these are major industrial units such as Carl Zeiss Iena, Robotron, the Magdeburg engineering works, etc.), 20 come under an industrial ministry and cater for the enterprises subordinated to that ministry, while another 5 are still attached to the Ministry of Foreign Trade, mainly in the field of service trade. In 1981 the FTOs subordinated to ministries were sub-divided into narrowly specialised so-called 'firms' (in the chemical, electrotechnical, and electronic industries), each one working for a combine. Sixty-four combines benefited from this last measure, mainly in the chemical and machine-tools industry. In 1990 all combines are to be allowed to export and import, and should be granted the right of borrowing in hard currency.

In all the various reforms carried out by the Eastern European countries, there is above all a desire to integrate production and marketing activities. The Ministries of Foreign Trade have had their functions considerably reduced on the micro-economic level, while basically retaining their controlling and coordinating role at the macro-economic level.

The real autonomy of the enterprise in the foreign trade field is still to come.

Up to 1986, the *USSR* appeared to be far behind these changes. In May 1978 a decree on the management of FTOs did not go any further than delegating to FTO deputy directors in charge of so-called 'firms' the right to sign contracts. Each FTO was thus divided up into specialised departments which have been called 'firms' to create the illusion of some kind of business-like management. But this was no more than a way of detailing the product mix for which the FTO was competent. For example, the FTO Raznoexport which markets various consumer goods was subdivided into 9 firms: clothing, millinery, footwear, haberdashery, electrical appliances, glass and china, toys and musical instruments, sports equipment, and tobacco. These entities were completely subordinated to the FTO and the Ministry of Foreign Trade. Enterprises were formally involved in the management of the FTOs, as they became members of a 'management board' created in each FTO but endowed with consultative powers only, without any power in the field of trade. In 1978, 20 industrial ministries obtained the right to set up directorates for foreign economic relations, and foreign trade departments but only to manage transport and delivery business (*zagranpostavki*) or turn-key plant sales involving supplies from different ministries (*zarubezhstroy*).

All this changed dramatically in 1986. The restructuring of foreign trade was launched by a joint decree, issued by the Central Committee of the Communist Party and the Council of Ministers on 19 August 1986, followed by various regulations and decisions in 1987 and 1988. The reform also included the rules on the operation of joint enterprises, which will be examined later (pp. 165–70), and the law on the socialist enterprise of 30 June 1987, of which article 19 deals with the powers of the enterprise in foreign trade. The last stage of the Soviet foreign trade reform is the Decree of the Council of Ministers published on 2 December 1988, 'On the further development of the foreign economic activities conducted by state, cooperative and other social enterprises, associations and organisations.' This decree was followed by technical implementation measures in March 1989, which, however, mark a step backwards from the intended liberalisation.

The Soviet approach is characteristic in the way it has integrated foreign trade and domestic economic reforms. Unlike the situation in other countries, foreign trade reform was not a by-product of domestic reform but came first, under the pressure of the external constraint. In 1986, following the fall in world oil prices, it became obvious that the standard Soviet export model, oriented towards the export of oil and gas as hard-currency earners, was no longer valid. Thus it was decided to prepare a restructuring of Soviet exports, and to create conditions allowing Soviet industry to develop the export of manufactured goods. However, it made little sense to give the Soviet enterprises increased rights in the field of foreign trade while in the management of their domestic activity they had hardly any autonomy. Thus, the measures adopted in the field of foreign trade remained essentially declarative; their actual implementation is subject to the developments occurring in the *perestroika* process. The following measures have been decided upon in 1986.

1   Foreign trade activities are controlled and coordinated through a new body, the State Commission on Foreign Economic Relations (the acronym in Russian is GVK). The new body is a sort of super ministry whose chairman has the rank of deputy prime minister. It may be compared to other 'super-bodies' created in the course of the *perestroika*, such as the Gosagroprom for agriculture (replaced in 1989 by a State Commisssion for Food and Procurement), or the coordinating agencies for the machinery industry, and the construction sector.

2   The current management of foreign trade is conducted by a new Ministry of Foreign Economic Relations. This ministry results from the merger, in January 1988, of the former Ministry of Foreign Trade and the State Committee for Foreign Economic Relations (*GKES*), which used to deal with cooperation agreements with developing and socialist countries (see chapter 2, p. 86). The aim of such a merger is to integrate trade *stricto sensu*, and cooperation activities. Again, to symbolise this widening of perspective, the Foreign Trade Bank has changed its name and become the Bank for Foreign Economic Activities (Russian acronym Vneshnekonombank or VEB).

3   In the framework at the state monopoly on foreign trade, foreign trade rights were given to 21 ministries and central agencies and to individual enterprises of which there were 68 in 1987 and more than 90 at the end of 1988. In addition, the federated Soviet Republics also got foreign trade rights of their own, allowing them to set up their FTOs. The distribution of competences between the revamped traditional actors (the Ministry of Foreign Economic Relations and its FTOs) and the new

actors (industrial ministries and enterprises) had a rationale. The traditional procedures still applied to trade in raw materials, fuels, and food products, to imports of turn-key plants and large sets of machinery, and cooperation based upon inter-governmental agreements. The new format mainly concerned trade in manufactured goods (and primarily machinery and chemicals). In 1987, approximately 25 per cent of Soviet foreign trade was affected by these changes.

This restructuring has opened an era of intense confusion in the Soviet foreign trade sector. Many FTOs have been reorganised, and their staff transferred to the ministries and agencies newly endowed with foreign trade rights. The internal departments of the FTOs (the so-called 'firms') have been transferred to the enterprises which gained the right to trade with foreign partners. For foreign businessmen trading with the USSR, this was not an easy thing. Their network of familiar partners was dissolved; the former staff did not always join the new agencies, for different reasons. Many foreign trade civil servants were affected by the anti-corruption campaign and found themselves in jail. Others were reluctant to leave Moscow and to train inexperienced managers in remote provinces in foreign trade techniques. Thus, the industrial enterprises often had to organise a foreign trade department out of nothing. For instance, the prestigious ZIL enterprise manufacturing trucks in Moscow had to set up its foreign economic relations service by incorporating people from the protocol service, and from the transport division which up to then was merely concerned with sending trucks abroad once the contracts were concluded by the relevant FTO, Avtoexport.

For the East European partners of the USSR, Soviet reforms also create difficulties. These partners were used to the rigidities of the Soviet system, which hindered the degree of autonomy of enterprises in the most 'liberalised' countries such as Hungary, but was at least familiar. Following the Soviet reforms, East European agencies were supposed to trade with ministries or enterprises instead of FTOs without knowing exactly what they were, though they might have been expected to understand the changes better than the 'capitalist' partners of the USSR. Moreover, they had to adjust to the new willingness of the USSR to upgrade its machinery and industrial goods exports. As the Soviet enterprises newly engaged in direct foreign trade activity were obviously not competitive on the Western markets, their most natural outlet was in the East

European countries, but in most cases their overtures were received without any enthusiasm. The discussions at the CMEA meetings in 1987 and 1988 reflect this state of mind.

The late 1988 decree and its implementation measures hardly clarify the matter.

As from 1 April 1989, this decree gives *all* enterprises and organisations (state, cooperative, or belonging to 'social organisations' such as trade unions, associations, etc.) 'which are competitive on foreign markets' the right of access to foreign markets. This right is subject only to registration. Imports have to be financed by exports. The GVK is entitled to deprive any enterprise of this right in cases of 'unfair competition' (indeed a surprising wording) or of 'activities damaging to the interests of the state'. To conduct foreign trade operations, the enterprises may set up any type of organisations: 'unions, consortia, various associations, joint stock companies, merchant houses and others, with the participation of the producers (of goods and services), the foreign trade organisations, and if needed with the participation of banks, supply organisations and other'.

These rights are, however, very unlikely to be finalised. Less than three months later, by a decree of 7 March 1989 'on measures ensuring state regulation of foreign economic activities', a general ban was placed on any barter or trading activity; the enterprises or cooperatives can only buy what they will use, or sell what they have produced. This ban also applies to joint ventures unless they are specifically authorised by the Ministry of Foreign Economic Relations. Cooperatives are totally excluded from such activities. State enterprises may engage in trading only on the basis of relevant regulations in the framework of the activities they are registered for. Already, complaints are numerous. Angry enterprises stress that to limit trade to buying or selling one's own product is quite unproductive. The alternative is to use the state FTOs which are considered quite ineffective. Unofficially, it is said that already in January and February 1989, a lot of cooperatives engaged in such activities, especially buying abroad and reselling in the Soviet Union video equipment, and computers, with huge returns, as the domestic prices for such goods are very high.

The right to export to import is however not extended to producers or users of goods the trade of which is to be regulated centrally. As before, the FTOs of the Ministry of Foreign Economic Relations are to manage the export of fuels and raw materials, the import of agricultural goods, raw materials, a large share of the intermediate goods (for instance, tubes for pipelines), and equipment for new projects. This already excludes from free trading 80 per cent of Soviet exports to OECD countries, and probably more than 50 per cent of Soviet imports to begin with. In addition, export and import rights are to be limited by non-tariff restrictions. In such cases, a licence is needed in addition to the registration. The list of relevant goods was given in a regulation issued by the State Commission for Foreign Economic Activities (GVK), on 20 March 1989. This includes 8 commodity and services groups for import and 30 groups for export. On the restricted import list, we find medicines and pesticides; virtually all cultural, artistic and intellectual goods (printed material, video material, movies, cassettes; services linked with the organisation of all types of shows, concerts, etc.); the hiring of foreign labour; and all financial services. The export list includes, as expected, all raw materials, most of the chemicals, virtually all food products, medicines and medical equipment, intellectual property (patents and licences), art and cultural services, and financial services. Some imports and exports are totally forbidden to enterprises, such as military equipment, drugs, and precious metals.

Finally, for all the goods produced under the procedure of a 'state order' (*goszakaz*), that is, earmarked for the domestic market, the enterprises will not be free to divert a part of their production to the foreign markets. Taking all this into account, there might be cases when a Soviet enterprise will contract with a foreign partner, then be unable to fulfil its obligations.

In principle, the right to export or import is given irrespective of the country of destination or origin. But here again, there might be difficulties, in particular, for those enterprises which would like to trade with Finland (for many Soviet enterprises, a more familiar partner than other Western countries). As Finland and the USSR have a bilateral payment by clearing agreement, with the USSR having a deficit since 1986, and being urged to cut it, Soviet enterprises exporting to Finland with the aim of importing later on might well have their assets in Finnish marks blocked, and their import rights suppressed. More generally, it is to be expected that in all cases where the Soviet Union has a deficit with a given country, the enterprise which manages to export to this country might be strongly persuaded to use its hard currency rights for imports from any country where the USSR has a surplus.

These measures, along with regulations expanding the foreign trade rights of the Soviet republics and local bodies, apparently brought about dramatic results. By October 1989 more than 9,000 Soviet participants (i.e., enterprises, cooperatives, republican, and local foreign trade organisations) had already registered to perform foreign trade business. But as well in the Soviet case as for the other Eastern countries, the efficiency of such a liberalisation depends on the incentives provided.*

INCENTIVES TO EXPORT

In traditional foreign trade management payment was made to enterprises by the FTOs at domestic prices and in domestic currency for their exports. This payment might include the particular expenses incurred for a specific order (better quality packaging, different paintwork, additional parts for a machine, etc.). Apart from this, there was no distinction between working for export and for the domestic market.

This traditional pattern was altered much earlier in Eastern Europe than in the USSR, along different lines. Incentive procedures were introduced to encourage firms to export, especially to countries with convertible currencies. These procedures go hand in hand with an overall reduction in compulsory planning indices for foreign trade. The incentive system is designed to support the centralised policy decisions as to the direction of exports and their composition. It does not mean a departure *per se* from the principle of state monopoly of foreign trade and has to be seen as basically a change in the instruments of central regulation.

Two questions may be raised here. The first: to *whom should incentives be directed?* When both the FTO and the enterprise participate in foreign trade, bonuses are usually shared between them accordingly. They accrue to the enterprise when the latter exports at its own risk and on its own account.

The second question: *how are incentives to be organised?* If socialist exports are to be competitive on foreign markets, exporters should be more involved in gaining revenue from their foreign currency earnings. These proceeds may be converted into domestic currency at a realistic rate of exchange. In addition, the enterprise may have the right to retain a share in the total amount of hard currency earned, or may be given other means to earn foreign currency.

There are various ways of *dividing incentives* between the FTO and the enterprise. The most frequently employed is the commission contract. The FTO is paid for its part, once its management costs have been covered, by a net payment proportional to the value of the transaction, and by a share in the net profit gained from export. In the case of imports, the profit sharing applies to the reduction in price, i.e., the enterprises and the FTO agree on a ceiling price for imports, and if this price can be reduced they share the difference. Other more complex methods may be used. In Hungary, what is referred to as a *pool* contract is used especially for exports. Here, the enterprise and the FTO undertake a foreign trade deal at joint expense with their respective production and marketing costs taken into account; they not only cooperate in the field of foreign trade but also share production risks.

The *nature* of the incentive is linked with the degree of autonomy allowed to the enterprise in the field of foreign trade. When autonomy is limited, granting an export incentive is a way of rewarding the enterprise for an adequate implementation of the foreign trade plan. The enterprise is then paid according to its earnings in foreign currency, converted into domestic currency at a realistic rate of exchange. When the enterprise is allowed to operate on foreign markets directly, it has to be able to import as well as to export, so as to buy abroad the investment goods required for a successful export strategy. This may be achieved through a retention right to part of the foreign currency earnings. The ultimate stage of the process is logically internal convertibility, allowing resident enterprises to buy and sell foreign currency. Such convertibility is officially to be introduced in Hungary and Poland at the beginning of 1990.*

SPECIAL EXPORT PRICES

When the enterprise is to be stimulated through export incentives, it is no longer paid for its exports at domestic prices, but on the basis of its foreign currency earnings. All countries may use this method, even in cases where domestic prices are still fixed independently of foreign prices. The exporting firm receives the equivalent in domestic currency of its foreign currency earnings converted by means of a coefficient. The coefficient is usually determined as the average cost (in domestic currency) required to obtain one unit of foreign currency from export for a weighted basked of exports (see chapter 1). It may be therefore that earnings in domestic currency, once calculated in this way, turn out to be below the price which would be obtained on the domestic market. In this case a subsidy may be used as a bonus over and above the average conversion coefficient. A set of differentiated coefficients thus emerge, by currency areas and often by products or groups of products, so as to stimulate exports.

Western experts and also economists from socialist countries have often argued that such coefficients ought to be calculated as the marginal cost of earning a unit of foreign currency. This would avoid the need for subsidies; some enterprises would earn very high profits, but these might then be taxed if necessary.

The GDR is the only country which by 1989 had not significantly integrated the foreign trade results of the enterprises (combines) into the overall results of the enterprise activity. However, conversion coefficients are applied to calculate the amount of export earnings. These coefficients are only differentiated by currency areas (convertible currencies, clearing, transferable roubles), but subsidies over the coefficient do apply if the calculated price is inferior to the usual domestic one.

For the countries which have introduced a 'realistic' exchange rate deriving from the conversion coefficients (Hungary since 1976; Romania, with some reservations as to the 'realism' of the rate, since 1981; Poland since 1982; and Czechoslovakia since 1989) this new commercial rate replaced both the former 'official' overvalued rate and the multiple conversion coefficients. However, subsidies did not altogether disappear. The case of Hungary is significant. When it was decided, in 1980, that Hungary's domestic wholesale prices (for around 60 per cent of output from the processing industry) would be fixed as so-called 'competitive prices' based on world prices, firms which could only make a loss if they respected these prices obtained subsidies which were 10–16 per cent of the total price plus an 'exchange rate subsidy' equal to up to 20 per cent of the current rate. In principle, export subsidies are gradually to be phased out in Hungary. However the fulfilment of this policy aim could be difficult as at the same time exports are being encouraged as much as possible. Poland has also committed itself to phase out subsidies except for agricultural goods and shipbuilding. But it is very difficult to assess the actual operation of the complicated Polish system of 'Price Equalization Account' which has the aim of insulating domestic producers from the adverse effect of world prices.

The USSR is moving towards the introduction of a 'realistic exchange rate' as from 1 January 1991. Already, since 1987, the export proceeds have been recalculated in domestic currency by using special differentiated currency coefficients (DCC) applied to the official foreign exchange rate for converting values expressed in foreign prices. Here the Soviet Union follows what was already for a time the practise of other Eastern European countries. But it does so in much greater confusion. There are a great number of coefficients, up to 3,000, and perhaps even more. The rates vary from 0.2 to 6.6 (a coefficient of 1 means that the rate applied is the official rate of exchange, for instance, at the end of 1988, $1=r.0.6. A coefficient of 2 means that the amount of roubles allotted for 1 dollar is doubled, i.e., equal to r.1.2 for $1). The reason for this is that domestic prices in the USSR are still more irrational than in other countries, with relative prices diverging widely from the relative 'world' prices. The coefficients are supposed to be reduced in number when the price reform is implemented, but this will not be the case before 1991 at best. The price reform itself is supposed to 'bring nearer' the Soviet and the world relative prices, but the very concept of 'world prices' is highly controversial, especially for manufactured goods. The wording suggests mainly that the domestic prices for raw materials (food included) should be raised, and the prices for manufactured goods decreased. But apart from this principle, there is no precise concept for this reform, which in turn should command the revision of the currency coefficients and ultimately the introduction of a rational exchange rate for the rouble. For the time being, the wide divergence of the coefficients distorts the measure of the efficiency of exports and may create perverse effects (encouraging costly exports or discouraging efficient imports).

In fact, the coefficients never really worked in the USSR, for various reasons underlined in the Soviet press:

The coefficients were simply not applied in most cases, and the enterprises were paid as usual on the basis of domestic prices. Only 3 per cent of the earnings in hard currency were treated that way. If we assume that, anyhow, at most only 20 per cent of the hard currency earnings could be concerned, according to the range of goods and the number of enterprises involved, then we should conclude that 15 per cent of the relevant transactions were treated accordingly to the new rules. As for imports, they were simply ignored.

Enterprises did not like the coefficients because when they were applied to exports they frequently led to a price lower than the domestic price. The enterprises then asked for a revision, and usually got it, but just to the level of their costs, yielding no profits.

The ministries did not like them either because when 'revising' the coefficients for their enterprises they had in fact to support the burden of the corresponding subsidy.

The Ministry of Finance hated the coefficients because it understood that a wide use of the DCCs would entail large losses. Here one has to recall the rationale of the old system (see chapter 1). On an accounting basis, the export earnings (let them be called X_f) and the import disbursements (M_f) were converted into roubles using the official rate of exchange. The enterprises were paid or had to pay at domestic prices (X_d for exports and M_d for imports). The FTOs 'bought' the export production from the enterprises, realising a net result of (X_f-X_d) on the export side, and 'sold' the import goods, realizing a net result of (M_d-M_f). The net outcome (or *Preisausgleich*) of foreign trade was thus $S=(X_f-X_d)+(M_d-M_f)$.

While the revenues from exports were limited just because of the over-valuation of the rouble (however, domestic prices for the exported goods were so low, especially for fuels, that even thus a gain was to be achieved), the imports yielded an enormous gain because domestic prices of goods imported (especially machinery) were many times higher than the foreign trade prices converted in roubles at the official rate. The budget thus gained a very large income. This has been shown convincingly by Igor Birman (1981) among others. Having lost a large amount of taxes on liquor sales, the Ministry of Finance is still less inclined to accept the loss of such a reliable income!

Finally, for a large range of goods it was simply impossible to calculate coefficients, namely for consumption goods, spare parts, components of machinery, etc.

What was the final result of all this? There was no incentive to export; at best the enterprises succeeded in having their expenses covered. The December 1988 decree is in fact substituting for this system another one, based upon an exchange rate reform. In the meantime (i.e., during 1989), the coefficients are 'to disappear gradually'. Does it really matter? It would if the present system had any coherence and logic. As everything is solved on a case-by-case basis, the suppression of the coefficients will probably not decrease the present confusion, as they will remain in the hidden form of *ad hoc* subsidies.

'Before the shift to accounting with a new rate of exchange, and beginning from 1 January 1990, there will be a 100 per cent bonus to the rate of exchange of the free convertible currencies against the rouble' (text of the December 1988 decree). In 1990, there will thus only be a unification of the coefficients (*vis-à-vis* the 'dollar' area) through the introduction of a 100 per cent bonus over the present official exchange rate of the rouble. This new rate will be used for converting the export gains of the Soviet state enterprises into roubles for their accounts. As for many enterprises the new rate will not ensure export profitability, probably, there will again be a set of additional subsidies to the new rate. The final phase, i.e., the introduction of a new rate of exchange in January 1991, will bring the Soviet Union to the point where Hungary, Poland and Czechoslovakia are already, with the same reservations and probably the same type of more or less hidden subsidies to non-competitive enterprises. By the end of 1989, the Soviet authorities seemed however to be contemplating a two-tier commercial exchange rate already for 1990, close to the present official rate for raw materials and fuels, and 5 times that official rate, in roubles per dollar, for manufactured goods. This would clearly act as an export subsidy to the producers of manufactured goods, and also delay the implementation of a single rate perhaps well after 1991.*

In all the countries under review, there is no symmetry between the modes of calculating export earnings and import costs. In most countries, these are still being calculated at domestic prices, which are themselves fixed on the basis of a domestic cost plus a profit margin. This principle applies generally to raw materials and energy and may sometimes also apply to manufactured goods (the GDR, Czechoslovakia). Hungary is the country where the repercussions of world prices on domestic prices is the greatest. This means that, when importing, firms pay the world price on the capitalist market after conversion in forints at the current rate of exchange. When they import energy and raw materials from the Comecon (principally from the USSR) they also pay the world price, and the difference between this and the actual price of the imports is put into an adjustment fund. This rule was however suspended when the intra-Comecon price for oil and some raw materials began to exceed the world price (as from 1986), and the enterprises had then to pay the highest price, i.e., the Comecon price, not without protest.

As in the case of sales on the domestic market, firms and export-import agencies are able to draw on their net gains to constitute a bonus and incentives fund. The proportion of earnings transferred to this fund varies according to the degree of implementation of the export plan if such a plan still formally exists (Romania, GDR, and Czechoslovakia).

RETENTION OF HARD CURRENCY EARNINGS

In most countries, enterprises may now retain a part of their hard currency earnings, with which they may purchase from abroad the intermediate goods they require to expand their exports, and finance such expenses as participation in trade fairs, etc. In most cases this is a *right* to a certain amount of hard currency, not the immediate availability of the currency itself. The distinction is far from trivial. Generally speaking, the rate of retention is usually small, and the right to use the retained currency is subject to dire restrictions.

In *Bulgaria* the retention rate amounts to 1 per cent of the currency earned for planned exports and 70 per cent of the earnings above the plan when the export plan is overfulfilled. In *Poland*, the rate fixed in 1982 amounted to 20 per cent of the hard currency earnings and was lowered to 16 per cent in 1987. In fact, in most cases, the enterprises could not obtain the currency they were entitled to, and the debt of the state towards the enterprises has been 'rescheduled' over the period 1988–95. In the *GDR*, some combines may retain up to 25 per cent of their net gains; the rate is 12.5 per cent if the export plan is not totally fulfilled. Sixteen combines had this right in 1988 (in the machine-building sector mainly). This should be applied to ninety combines in the future. In *Czechoslovakia*, the retention principle was introduced in 1981, and applied to both the FTOs and the enterprises, only for the overfulfilment of the foreign trade plan (with distinct rates for the overfulfilment of the export plan in hard currency and in domestic prices!). In any case, the rates are very low, and cannot exceed 6 per cent of the earnings for the export plan in hard currency and 2 per cent for the export plan in domestic prices.

Here again, the Soviet case exemplifies the difficulties of such measures in a system of tight exchange control.

This was the great novelty of the 1986 resolution. Enterprises were to retain a share of their earnings, again, differentiated according to goods, in principle from 2 per cent to 80 per cent (the latter for sophisticated machinery), in fact never higher than 50 per cent. But, by no means did it amount to an immediate availability of hard currency. The 1987 earnings (amounting to the equivalent of r.900 million according to the official rate, i.e., $1.4 billion, or 7 per cent of the total hard currency earnings through exports to developed countries and 36 per cent of the non-fuel earnings) were available only beginning from 1 April 1988. Even so, they were not really 'available'. The enterprises had to deposit the corresponding amounts in a special account, which granted them a *right* on their hard currency earnings. It was very difficult to make that right. Why was this? Because the enterprises had to 'buy back' their own hard currency account, using for this earmarked funds which were to be taken from their profits. Although no overall statistical figure is available, the estimate which emerges from numerous Soviet articles is that the enterprises succeeded in recovering at most 10–15 per cent of their legitimate earnings.

The December 1988 decree did not improve this procedure. It just provided for a quicker availability of the foreign exchange earnings (they are available as soon as they are earned) and fixed a series of special rates (for the enterprises of the Agroprom system, sub-contractors of exporting enterprises, city councils, and republican and regional authorities, etc.). However, beginning from 1991, the logic of the whole system will be reversed: instead of fixing the share of foreign currency earnings retainable by the state enterprises, the government will fix the share of these earnings to be handed to the state, the rest being kept by the enterprises.

The foreign currency resources are to be spent on imports, and also used to send enterprise workers (specialists, experts, commercial agents) abroad.

The decree provided in addition that 10 per cent of the foreign currency retained might be spent according to the decision of the workers' collective of the given enterprise, to buy abroad consumer goods, medicines, and goods to be used 'to strengthen the material base of social and cultural activities'. A similar measure was taken in Romania in 1978 – and has since been dropped. Will this act as an incentive if the effective rights of the enterprises are not guaranteed? In addition to the already mentioned difficulties, a range of problems arise here as an enterprise is obviously not a department store: how will the imported goods be resold (with or without a tax? tax is very high on such goods as clothing, shoes, etc.), to whom (only to the workers of the enterprise? to other consumers?). Knowing the huge demand for such goods in the USSR, one may imagine the worst – speculation, corruption, intrusion of the authorities, etc.*

CURRENCY AUCTIONS

All the previous incentives are just substitutes for *internal convertibility* allowing any domestic enterprise to buy foreign currency so as to engage in foreign trade activities, or to sell it at a good rate. Hungary is the only country which has come near to this. Already, in 1976, it had opened a kind of credit line to firms with a sum of 45 billion forints (at that time, approximately $1 billion) for the period 1976–80. The scheme was renewed for the period 1981–85, but was soon curtailed due to balance of payments difficulties. The enterprises allowed to engage in foreign trade activities may buy the currency they need for their imports from the National Bank, but only to buy authorised goods. This excludes the bulk of equipment. The foreign exchange monopoly is strictly maintained although the banking system itself has been decentralised. It was decided to introduce in 1989 a small foreign currency market between commercial banks and the National Bank; this market should be fully operational by 1990. By 1990, also, most of the restrictions on hard-currency imports are to be lifted. This will bring about an increase in imports and a worsening of the trade balance, which might then require some kind of restrictive regulation.

A proxy to internal convertibility is a currency auction market. This has been introduced first in *Poland*, in 1983. Such auctions have taken place twice a month since 1987 (before then, they were irregular). The bidders put forward those projects for which they required imports. A selection committee grants hard currency, at the current official rate, to the highest bidder. The criteria followed by the committee include the value of the exports resulting from the imports to be made, the value and the type of the goods to be exported. All the enterprises of the socialised sector (state and cooperative) may take part in the auctions. Hard currency is provided by the enterprises wishing to sell their hard currency rights. The total price paid by a given buyer is the contract price in zlotys paid to the seller of hard currency rights, the price paid to the Export Development Bank for the purchase of the corresponding amount of currency, at the official rate, and the fee paid to the Bank. The dollar/zloty rates derived from these auction prices are very near the black market rates, i.e., four to five times the official commercial rate. In fact the mechanism is described here in a very simplified way, and one can identify several channels through which enterprises can actually have access to hard currency, thus creating a segmented 'market' for hard currency.

Bulgaria introduced a somewhat different procedure in 1988. A special agency, the Currency Auction Association, has been set up jointly by the Ministry of Economy and Planning and the Bulgarian National Bank. The bids are secret starting from a minimum set by the authorities and by the enterprises selling their hard currency. The hard currency goes to those offering the highest interest rates. At the first auction, the highest offers amounted to about fourteen times the official rate.

Following the Polish and Bulgarian practice, the Soviet reform of December 1988 provides for auctions of hard currency to be organised under the auspices of the Bank for Foreign Trade Activities. These auctions would offer hard currency sold by enterprises or cooperatives, as well as 'from centralised funds'. As foreign experiences show, such auctions, especially if they are conducted on a rather narrow basis and if demand largely exceeds supply, lead to an exchange rate sometimes higher than that on the black market. Even so, it may be advantageous in cases when the enterprise may hope to legally 'recover' only 10 per cent of the hard currency it is entitled to as in the procedure described above. The first currency auctions took place on 3 November 1989. As expected the number of enterprises willing to sell hard currency was much smaller (31) than that of the prospective buyers (210), and the average rate was close to the black market one, i.e., slightly under 10 roubles for 1 dollar.*

ARE THE REFORMS TO BOOST TRADE?

The foreign trade reforms are obviously meant to give a new impetus, first and foremost, to East–West trade. However, all these countries are realising a large share of their foreign trade within Comecon. What are the consequences in this field?

It has been stated often that in Comecon trade there had to be an alignment of trade procedures along the practice followed by the most traditional partner. If one country has given its enterprises the right of access to foreign markets and another country still retains the traditional FTO system, it is likely that the more liberal country will have to conduct its trade with its partner also through an FTO. This is precisely why the 1988 session of Comecon has so strongly insisted upon the crucial importance of 'direct links' between enterprises of different Comecon countries.

This is not only a question of enterprise rights. The whole incentive system set up for trade with the West is in contradiction with the intra-Comecon system. In trade with the West the authorities want to stimulate exports. In trade with Comecon they have to limit exports (otherwise a country may have a surplus in transferable roubles (t.r.) which it would not be able to use). Conversely, they have to constrain imports in hard currency and to encourage transferable rouble imports – should the enterprises be lucky enough to secure imports from their partners in addition to what has been agreed already in bilateral foreign trade protocols. A typical example of the consequences of liberalisation is the 'customs war' which raged during the autumn of 1988 between Czechoslovakia and its Comecon partners. The liberalisation of tourism and exchange controls in the USSR brought an enormous number of Soviet tourists in addition to the usual Hungarian, Polish, and East German tourists, and sales of consumer goods flourished. What would have been a bonanza in capitalist conditions turned into a nightmare for the Czech authorities. The inflow of non-convertible foreign currency translated into earnings in transferable roubles – through a conversion according to the non-commercial rate, which is unfavourable to Czechoslovakia. And the surpluses in transferable roubles could not be used for additional purchases in other Comecon countries. The country took then a rational measure under these circumstances; in September, an embargo was put on the export of a range of consumer goods. What seems absurd from the point of view of a market mechanism is perfectly understandable here.

However, this means that, until a reform of the Comecon mechanisms takes place, the authorities of the most market-oriented Comecon countries will exhibit schizophrenic behaviour, encouraging or discouraging their enterprises to export according to the currency area. This in turn may have disastrous consequences. The reforms are aiming to transform the enterprises into competitive units. Whatever they might achieve on the capitalist markets will have no spillover effect on the Comecon market.

Will the reforms be successful in relations with the West? The perceptions of the West are mixed. As the reforms are meant first and foremost to expand Eastern exports, exporting Western businessmen experience them mainly through barter or joint venture demands, both being substitutes for standard direct exports. In the field of Western exports, the scene has changed less, except for the fact that the restructuring of foreign trade has strongly affected traditional links. Typically, a Western businessman used to spend much time in finding the right FTO, and building his personal network of partners – sometimes with the help of bribery, but not so often as in state trading with developing countries. The officials in charge used to keep their jobs for many years, which eased relations once business links became established.

In countries where the reforms went further, these links were broken. New partners appeared, not quite as reliable as they were, often, in the case of the enterprises, not well aware of their rights and duties. In the traditional FTOs, job cuts and reshuffling of competences also disrupted the former relationships. It has become much more difficult to trade with the East: it is no longer a traditional system, but not yet a market in the capitalist sense. Apart from the structural, financial, and political obstacles which constrain trade with the East, the reforms, paradoxically, create an additional one. The art of selling to Comecon is thus to be learned anew as is the art of selling to the West. Both sides need expertise. This is even more obvious in the field of joint ventures.

Joint ventures

A 'joint venture' is a partnership with a clearly defined purpose established between two or more business enterprises in which management and (in general) equity are shared between foreign and national partners. This form of cooperation, with the joint venture located on the territory of a socialist country, emerged in East–West practice at the beginning of the seventies. It developed rather marginally at first, but suddenly got much more attention when in 1987 the USSR decided to join the group of countries which had legislation on such entities.

This format is not the only type of multinational developed by the socialist countries. Much earlier, they established a network of companies on the territory of developed capitalist countries, totally owned by them on the basis of Western regulations, or with shared capital. They have also spread such companies in the Third World. With much less success, they have attempted to create 'socialist multinationals' within Comecon itself.

Let us first introduce some remarks on the multinational concept itself. The multinational, we should not forget, was analysed as early as 1917 by Lenin in *Imperialism, the Highest Stage of Capitalism*. In Lenin's understanding, imperialism was characterised, among other criteria, by the fact that 'the division of the world through international trusts had begun'. Present-day works by economists in socialist countries approach the multinational phenomenon from three different angles:

(a) in keeping with the Leninist line, works on the activities of multinational enterprises with the developing world stress the 'exploitative' nature of these activities;

(b) as part of analyses referring to the capitalist firm, 'managerial' studies on multinationals, which are very in-depth and fully documented, analyse their operation and internal planning mechanisms as well as their organisational structures without denying their efficiency from a capitalist point of view;

(c) in the framework of East–West relations, the studies (first, especially those of economists from the smaller Eastern European countries and, later on, the analyses of the Soviet economists) stress the role of the multinationals, which is seen as not necessarily a negative one.

One of the first comprehensive articles on the subject was published in a Hungarian journal, and a heated debate arose between the leftist French adversary of the multinationals, Arghiri Emmanuel, and the author of the article, the Hungarian economist A. Blaho (Blaho, 1978). Blaho advances the following arguments against Emmanuel's accusations (which hint at the socialist countries' collusion with the multinationals): the socialist countries may effectively control the multinationals by state monopoly of foreign trade; industrial cooperation, including that conducted with multinationals, creates employment in the West; subsidiaries of the multinationals in countries where the setting up of joint ventures is allowed, are subject to planning controls; and, finally, such cooperation does not make the East into strike-breakers in the West, since it accounts for only a small proportion of East–West trade. For all that, Blaho does regret the absence of coordination among Comecon countries in facing this problem. A clear, common strategy is called for. As far as tripartite cooperation or the setting up of joint ventures within the developing world are concerned according to Blaho:

> We must clarify the motives for creating firms belonging to the socialist countries within the developing states, we must show that our interests are different from those of the capitalist world and point out the more progressive significance of their activity compared with capitalist firms when it comes to aiding the autonomous development of the developing nations. (Blaho, 1978: 430).

The ambiguity of these tenets is revealing. Is the multinational phenomenon a good or bad one? Is it both? International division of labour goes hand in hand with the transnationalisation of production which has proved efficient in the increasing of specialisation, facilitating the development of advanced industrial branches and even, to some extent, resolving the problems arising from world crises and recessions. These are recurrent themes in Soviet economic literature which refers to Lenin's words on 'the progressive character of big capital against small production'. On the other hand, however, transnationalisation is said to distort international economic relations, aggravating the contradictions within capitalism. It all then boils down to the question of how to make use of the advantages the transnationals offer, without having to cope with the disadvantages.

Whether the socialist countries want it or not, the multinationals are present in their countries, in any case, in the wake of East–West trade. Obviously, it is not difficult to show their role in this trade where usually only large units from both sides are in contact, excluding or limiting the part played by small or medium-sized firms. The major Western multinationals are almost all involved in trade with the East, in particular in relations with the USSR (Krasznai, 1982).

When it comes to direct investment, the reality of the 'multinational phenomenon' imposes itself more crudely, encroaching on certain fundamental principles of the socialist system, such as the primacy of collective ownership of the means of production. Shortly after the Bolshevik Revolution in the USSR, Soviet capital was allowed to be invested abroad in the form of joint ventures on the territory of capitalist countries. There was also a recognition during the New Economic Policy (NEP) period, that Soviet territory could host joint ventures with capitalist capital. However, in the thirties this last form of participation was seen as contrary to the principles of socialism and abolished. It reappeared from 1971 on, first in several small socialist countries, along with a long-term compromise with the laws of collective ownership. It did not, however, bring with it all the advantages foreseen. It has spread also to relations with developing countries, although, once again, direct investment in the Third World has long been seen as an imperialist practice.

Finally, the socialist countries have raised the question of the possibility of introducing, within Comecon itself, a multinationalisation of production as efficient as the capitalist one. This last attempt has until now been more of a series of disappointing experiments than a move towards socialist integration.

EAST–WEST MULTINATIONAL ENTITIES

These are of two types. The first and most developed consists of the participation of socialist enterprises (foreign trade organisations, banks) in capitalist enterprises (banks). The USSR has been involved in such arrangements since before the Second World War. The other European socialist nations developed this form of intervention at the end of the sixties. Such joint ventures generally have a majority participation by the East. In the case of the USSR, this participation may often be as much as 99 per cent. Most of these companies deal with marketing and after-sales services and have become extensions of export-import organisations abroad, to look after the follow-up of machinery and transport equipment sales, to ensure any necessary adaptation to the requirements and preferences of the users as well as to guarantee the supply of spare parts. There are also international transport firms (sea, land and air), insurance companies, and banks. A large network of banks with Eastern European capital has been set up in the West, Soviet banks being the most numerous as well as the most powerful, the two oldest and largest being the Moscow Narodny Bank based in London and the Banque Commerciale pour l'Europe du Nord (Eurobank) in Paris, the latter having created the 'eurodollar' in the late fifties.

Development of production enterprises with the participation of socialist capital is still poor. One of the few studies to be available on this subject points out that at the end of 1983, only 34 out of 484 companies with socialist capital based in the West had production activities (McMillan, 1987: 35). Hungary has been the most active Comecon country in promoting such investments abroad, especially in the field of medical equipment and electric lighting. The lighting firm Tungsram even managed to set up a joint venture in the United States in 1978 (with 49 per cent Hungarian participation) which in 1982 had 5 per cent of the electric bulb market in that country (see p. 165).

In the eighties, the investment drive of the socialist countries in the West declined due to the overall decrease in investment. One may expect a revival with the extension of the direct right of access to foreign markets for Soviet and Eastern European enterprises.

The second type of East–West multinational entities are constituted by the joint ventures on the territory of the socialist countries (see ECE/UN, 1988).

Table 6 shows the main features of the regulations on joint ventures in the six socialist countries allowing this type of coenterprise. Up to the mid-eighties, the development of these companies fell short of the forecasts and hopes of the host countries. Foreign capital was not very attracted by this scheme and industrial cooperation without equity participation proved more fruitful. However, the launching of legislation on joint ventures in the USSR in the beginning of 1987 stirred enormous expectations.

To start with, the initial aims and motivations of both parties are quite different.

For the socialist countries, hosting foreign capital meant opening up to the West. This political goodwill was expressed in Basket II of the Conference for Security and Cooperation in Europe, and the Final Act of the CSCE (Helsinki, 1975) mentioned joint ventures as one of the forms of industrial cooperation to be developed. At the beginning of the seventies, the main motive of the countries which introduced such regulations was to get Western technology at the lowest cost. Later on, a change occurred in the motives. It became essential to promote exports in hard currency when the indebtedness of these countries began to soar. When the USSR decided to accept joint ventures on its territory, along with the export concern and the desire to obtain advanced technology, there was quite clearly an educational motive: the joint venture was supposed to teach capitalist efficiency to Soviet managers, quite in line with the objectives defined by Lenin as early as 1922.

On the Western side, joint ventures have been seen as a means of reaching aims otherwise unattainable, or very difficult to attain. The first of these aims is market extension. A joint venture is often to be preferred to crude compensation, and, moreover, the Western partner hopes to obtain easier access to other CMEA countries. At any rate he expects to be treated as a privileged supplier. This seems to be the case for traditional partners of the USSR (in chemical, petrochemical, and metal processing industries) which have entered joint venture schemes without enthusiasm, rather as a proof of their good will and on a limited scope, so as to remain among the partners first considered for big traditional trade deals, if and when resumed. Second, the Western firm expects an improvement in the use of production capacities and a reduction of production costs as in any type of industrial cooperation. It may also expect increased profits and an extension of the product cycle should the joint venture manufacture an item no longer processed by the Western partner.

Table 6. *East–West joint ventures located in the East (1971–1988)*

	Romania	Hungary	Bulgaria	Poland	Czechoslovakia	USSR
Date of legislation	1971, 1972	1972, 1977, 1979, 1982 (law on customs free zones), 1986, 1988	1980, 1987 (law on customs free zones), 1988	1976, 1979, 1982, 1986, 1988	1986 (information on relevant legislation); 1981 (special Act)	1986, 1987 (Jan., Sept.), 1988, 1989
Maximum of foreign equity share	49%	49% in principle exceptions allowed	no limit	49%, no maximum limit in 1988 law	49% in 1986–88; since, higher share allowed but not encouraged	49%; exceptions allowed in 1988 law
Supplies on domestic markets	in hard currency	as local enterprises	as local enterprises	as local enterprises	as local enterprises	according to the contract, in hard currency or roubles
on foreign markets	without any restrictions	with a licence	with a licence	with a licence	with a licence	without any restriction
Sales on domestic markets	in hard currency	through wholesale firms	direct sales	direct sales	direct sales	according to the contract, in hard currency or roubles
on foreign markets	without restrictions, in hard currency	with a foreign trade licence	with a foreign trade licence	with a foreign trade licence	with a foreign trade licence	without any restriction
Planning	done by the firm on approval by authorities	done by the firm	done by the firm	done by the firm	done by the firm	done by the firm

Labour and wages						
locals	wages in lei according to local rates; the joint enterprise has to pay the corresponding amount in hard currency	as fixed in the labour contract both for locals and for foreign employees	according to the local rules	as fixed in the contract and in zlotys for all; foreigners may transfer their wages abroad up to 50% of the total and provided there is hard currency	Czechoslovak law and rules for all	according to the decisions of the joint venture, both for locals and foreigners; foreign wages may be transferred abroad only if there is hard currency
foreigners	as defined by contract		as defined by contract			
Taxes on profits	30% (plus 10% in case of transfer abroad)	40%	20% (plus 10% in case of transfer abroad)	40% to 10% (1988 law)	40% (plus 25% on dividends transferred or not)	30% (plus 20% if transferred abroad)
Grace measures	negotiated case by case; no payment on 1st year of profits, 15–30% on the 2 following years	negotiated case by case; for major interest objects, no taxes for first 5 years, then 20%	negotiated case by case	no taxes for 1st 3 years; then 0.4% rate reduction for each 1% exported	exemptions possible	no taxes for 1st two years of profits; other exemptions
Number of cases	9 (founded 1972–1987; 4 have ceased their activity since then)	over 200 (most of them under the 1982 law)	25	over 700 under the 1976–79 laws; over 50 in 1986–88	11	191 on 1 January 1989

Sources: Relevant legislations; ECE/UN, 'East–West Joint Ventures', 1988, and *East–West Joint Ventures News*, quarterly information letter, from February 1989; various press reports.
Unless otherwise specified, all statements refer to the last legislation put into application.

Looking at Table 6, and summing up the developments up to 1988, we may state that both sides have been largely frustrated in their hopes. Joint ventures have not taken a large share of foreign trade or investment. A Soviet author (Rodina, 1988: 15) contends that the overall amount of direct foreign investment attracted does not exceed, for Eastern Europe, half a billion dollars, i.e., 0.1 to 0.2 per cent of total capital invested in these countries (for the period 1972–87). For the Soviet Union, the 191 joint ventures set up in 1987–88 account for an overall amount of statutory capital of over r.800 million (about $1.3 billion) 37.5 per cent being invested by the Western partners. The ventures registered in 1989 seem larger in size but involving less Western participation. While the capital of the 727 ventures recorded by 1 August 1989 amounts to r.4,267 billion, the share of foreign partners amounts to only 950 (22.3 per cent). The ventures located in the USSR and Eastern Europe still account for a negligible share of East–West trade overall. In most cases, their contribution to technology transfers has been limited. One has to remember that Cocom restrictions on high technology transfers remain of course valid for joint ventures as well. The Western partners have not, on the whole, witnessed a substantial extension of their markets. This may be due to the fact that the bulk of the joint venture laws appeared or were fully implemented during the period (1981–85) when the Eastern European countries adjusted to their indebtedness crises through severe cuts in imports. The profits have usually been lower than the expectations. Overall, standard industrial cooperation without equity participation has proved to be more fruitful. There are several reasons for such a failure:

(i) The field of activity was initially too limited, for instance in Hungary where the first law (1972) excluded industry from the joint venture format. In all countries, the trend is towards a very large definition of the fields open to joint ventures. Preferential fields are sometimes named, usually in high technology sectors (Czechoslovakia, USSR).

(ii) Potential capitalist partners have often been badly informed, with different reasons for inadequate information: frequent changes, heavy legislation (before Czechoslovakia implemented a new law in 1989, Western partners had to get acquainted with twenty-four acts, some of them dating back to the forties), and most often the fact that almost all the regulations are negotiable case by case. Hungary created an information service only in 1984 so as to answer foreign capitalists' questions and guide them through the intricacies of regulations, which are obscure to Hungarian citizens as well. Polish legislation has a special feature in this respect. The first regulations were issued to lure capitalist of Polish origin (belonging to the 'Polonia' scattered all over the world). It was probably easier for members of the Polonia to develop entrepreneurship in a country where they understood the language and the mood. But the outcome was a great number of small family firms (many of them totally 'foreign'-owned), mostly in services, the hotel industry and small industries. The limited scope of the law induced the Polish authorities to enact new rules (in 1986) so as to attract larger investments not linked to considerations of family or origin.

(iii) The guarantees offered are not satisfactory. There may be a guarantee in the case of liquidation of the joint venture. Hungary has concluded several bilateral agreements from 1986 on with its Western partner countries so as to protect the investments of these countries against the political risk of nationalisation of foreign capital or of non-repatriation of capital. Czechoslovakia and the USSR are following the same procedures. But many prospective foreign investors are requesting a guarantee of safe operation of the joint venture protecting them against the risks of an environment which is felt as potentially insecure (disruption of supplies due to the inconsistencies of planning, etc.).

(iv) Such advantages as were offered (tax deductions, reduced costs) were deemed insufficient when the risks involved were played off against any profit which stood to be made. Here, it is worth pointing out that the advantages which accompany low wages are not great. Of course, Eastern European salaries are below Western ones. However, the host country, and this was particularly true of Romania, often calculates the cost of manpower to be borne by the capitalist partner on the basis of the salaries of the Western country in question. Local workers are not paid at this level. The difference between the reference salary (in foreign currency and indexed on the average level of wages in the given industry in the Western partner's country) and the salary actually paid to the locals (in domestic currency and in accordance with national norms of pay) goes to the host country and thus constitutes a kind of supplementary non-tax levy. Other countries gradually abandon the rule according to which the local workers must not be paid more than if they worked in a domestic enterprise. The new Soviet regulations (in force since January 1989) leave to the joint venture the right to decide upon the level of wages paid to local workers, so as to provide for additional incentives. In this case, the cost of the increased wages will be borne by the joint venture, and the increase will go to the workers and not to the state. However, in both solutions – let us call them the Romanian one and the Soviet one – labour can definitely not be considered as a cheap input.

(v) Taxes have initially been devised on a level lower than in the capitalist countries, with incentives for reinvestment in the firm, for export, or for the choice of selected priority sectors. However, they have been perceived as exceedingly high when compared with Third World regulations. In most cases the regulations now allow for a negotiation of the tax rate, and the grace period is extended to two or more years following the first profitable year. This would suggest that hardly any taxes on profits are paid at all.

(vi) The division of the market between partners raises some difficulties. For the socialist countries, the initial motive for setting up such enterprises is to obtain hard currency revenue from exports. This runs counter to the desires of the Western partners seeking ways of dividing up the market in which goods manufactured in the East do not compete with their own production in their usual markets.

In fact, most of these obstacles are of a systemic nature. The operation of a joint venture in a socialist environment poses the problem of how to make compatible the free enterprise and a planned regime. Hence, two solutions are to be envisaged. Either the joint venture is seen as a foreign enclave in the socialist production system. Romania never departed from this scheme, which usually requires a double accounting system (in domestic currency and in foreign currency). This is also the case of Hungarian (since 1982) and Bulgarian (since 1987) offshore joint ventures. Or, conversely, the joint venture is considered as a domestic enterprise, subject to the national law, operating with the same constraints but not necessarily the same rights. In the Soviet Union, the co-enterprise is regarded at the same time as a domestic enterprise (a legal entity subject to the Soviet law) and as an alien body which cannot benefit from the advantages of guaranteed planned supplies. This ambiguity generates many problems, some of which are shown below (p. 167). Let us now review the national solutions.

Romania was the first country to provide for legislation which appears now as the less flexible one. Four of the nine firms initially set up have had to close down. The largest in terms of capital invested is Oltcit, a firm set up by Citroen, France (36 per cent participation), and two Romanian firms for the manufacture of a motor car designed by Citroen, the Axel. The contract was signed in 1976 providing for the construction of a plant capable of turning out 130,000 vehicles per year, 65,000 of which would be sent back for marketing by Citroen. There were considerable setbacks during realisation of the project owing to technical difficulties in constructing the plant, the inadequate skills of the Romanian workers, and, since 1981, Romania's financial problems, which meant that Citroen was asked for further credits for the completion of the last section. The model was eventually launched in 1981 and has been marketed since 1984. Factory capacity as well as marketing conditions have been altered since the original contract was signed, with the French firm buying back more than half of the production, which itself amounted to little more than one-third of the initial capacity.

In *Bulgaria*, legislation is relatively recent and in spite of its flexibility has not attracted many takers. Bulgarian rules lay down that it is up to the partners to decide whether or not a joint venture has legal personality. Among the few firms established, the most important is the one created by the Japanese firm Fujitsu Fanuc and the Bulgarian FTO Mashinoexport for the maintenance of numerical control equipment manufactured by the Japanese firm with its Bulgarian concessionary company, and the equipping of machine tools based in Eastern Europe. The new company laws adopted in Bulgaria in January and February 1989 may help to develop joint stock companies with foreign participation in the country. Private foreign persons are also allowed to set up a joint venture in Bulgaria.

Initial *Hungarian* legislation in 1972 only gave rise to three firms in five years, with the participation of Volvo (mini-jeep manufacture), Siemens (after-sales service and joint research development for computers sold in Hungary), and Corning USA (for the manufacture of medical equipment). Two of these, Volcom and Radelcor, have in fact ceased to function; Siecontact is the only one to have survived. The setting up of joint ventures really started after the passing of the 1979 and 1982 laws. The main partners in these operations are West German, Swiss, and Austrian, which may be seen as evidence of cultural and traditional links apart from strictly economic considerations. The Central European International Bank (1979) is a particular case. Hungarian participation in it is low (34 per cent), the rest of the capital being divided into six shares of 11 per cent each between two Japanese banks, and German, Austrian, Italian, and French banks. It is located in Budapest with an off-shore status. It specialises in international financing deals and provides services to Western investors operating in Hungary. It is no doubt the success of this bank that made Hungary decide in 1982 to adopt a regulation on customs free zones so as to stimulate the growth of joint ventures with foreign status and management. The number of joint ventures strongly increased in 1985–88. At the end of 1988, the Hungarian Parliament passed two laws, a Company Act and a Foreign Investment Act, which came into force at the beginning of 1989. These acts combined should facilitate the setting up of joint ventures by Hungarian individuals. The Foreign Investment Act allows joint ventures in the field of trading. It provides tax incentives for joint ventures operating in fields of high priority, or in the case where the annual profit is small. In this second case the tax relief should encourage the setting up of such ventures by small enterprises.

Poland has altered its legislation several times since 1976, making it more restrictive in 1979, and then providing more favorable terms for foreign capital since 1982. The need to revive the small private firm and to provide the population with products not available on the national market (such as toothpaste, zip fasteners, and shaving cream) has joined the initial aim of developing production for export. These 'Polonina' firms have not lived up to the hopes put in them, producing low-quality goods and low-performance processes. Besides this, the authorities feared the emergence of *nouveaux-riches* cashing in on opportunities offered by an economy in which serious shortages and a black-market network had become endemic. The 1986 law was meant to attract other partners to different sectors, namely high-technology engineering industries. The lack of enthusiasm among investors prompted the authorities to relax the rules, especially the tax rules, and to ease conditions on the resale of hard currency earnings, as of 1 January 1989. The new law ('On Economic Activity with the participation of foreign parties') of 23 December 1988 is in fact a mix of the previous legislation, both favouring small joint ventures wholly foreign-owned (however, with a minimum amount of investment), and larger companies (joint stock or limited liability) in priority sectors.

For both *Hungary* and *Poland* a new pattern emerged in 1989. Both countries want to attract new Western capital so as to assist the restructuring of the domestic economy and to provide some debt relief. Joint ventures have thus to be supplemented with fully capitalist-owned firms. While Poland did not manage to attract a significant amount of fresh capital in that way, Hungary offered a list of fifty-three Hungarian enterprises for sale to the West in February 1989 and already in this first year sold several companies. The light bulb manufacturing firm Tungsram was sold to the US conglomerate General Electric in November, and several other deals were concluded before with US firms and banks, in particular the purchase of the trade company Intercooperation and the contribution to the first leverage buy-out (of a state stationery firm) realised in the East. This gives a new dimension to foreign investment in the East, which might in the future both accelerate the privatisation of the former centrally planned economies and entail a partial solution to the problem of foreign debt.

The main feature of the *Czechoslovak* approach is its cautiousness. The joint ventures were admitted in 1986 only and for three years the rules applied to joint ventures were in fact a compendium of various texts providing a legal framework. As from 1 January 1989, there is a single legal framework, the Act 'On Enterprises with foreign property participation'. The new Act does not limit foreign equity to a share of 49 per cent as previously, but it is to be expected that the authorities will dissuade the partners from giving too high a share to the capitalist party. The Western partners are not particularly attracted even by favorable fiscal rules: the Czechoslovak regulations are the most dissuasive. A few sectors are to be developed through joint ventures, including electronics, machine-tools, special chemicals, and tourism.

The case of the *Soviet Union* is certainly the most fascinating. The recognition of the joint venture format was part of a foreign trade reform launched in 1986, as a harbinger of *perestroika* which occurred from 1987 on. It also meant a revival of Leninist ideas on the necessity to learn from Western managers through mixed companies. The spirit of the NEP, the New Economic Policy, was thus felt both in the domestic economy – turning to the market – and in the foreign trade sector.

The legislation on the joint ventures developed in several stages. The decree setting the framework of the foreign reform, of 19 August 1986, barely mentioned the possibility of creating co-enterprises with Western (as well as with socialist) participation. Later on, a decree of 13 January 1987 provided the first comprehensive set of rules, along with a great number of contradictions and obscurities which were only partly lifted in September 1987 by a new set of regulations. Finally the 2 December 1988 decree relaxed several constraints without totally satisfying the Western partners. It also created new uncertainties in launching a reform of the foreign exchange regulations, the impact of which on the operation of joint ventures remains unclear. It had however an immediate impact on the setting up of joint ventures. In January–July 1989, 546 new ventures were finalised, as compared with 191 formed in 1987 and 1988. This surge was attributed by the Soviet officials to the relaxation of previous constraints. But Western businessmen argue that such developments are due to the fact that the new regulations were expected. Many operators just waited for them to be enacted. Most of these new ventures are very small in the size of their assets. This is not the case of the framework agreement signed on 31 March 1989 between a consortium of six US firms and the USSR, which might involve $5 to $10 billion of US investments over the next fifteen years. In this case, the momentum came from a specific, *ad hoc* settlement of the problems linked with the setting of joint ventures.

Very few Soviet joint ventures are actually operating, at most 5 per cent of those set up according to conservative estimates. What is certainly astonishing is that so many Western firms – by comparison with the East European experience – have agreed to play the game with so little clarification. The ranking of the Western partners is more or less in line with their share in Soviet trade, with some differences. According to a census at 1 August 1989, on a total of 747 ventures FGR, West Berlin included, had 135, Finland 94, the USA 73, Great Britain 56, Austria 53, Italy 51, Switzerland 36, Sweden and France 31 each, Japan 24. Although acquiring technology was claimed as one of the first motives, most of the ventures do not belong to high technology industries. On the mentioned total of 747, the 'social' complex comes first with 228 enterprises (hotels, restaurants, medical and household services). Then comes the food processing industry and the chemical and wood industry (53 each), the light industry, i.e., clothing and footwear (35), machine-building (24). True, a large number of ventures (78) are mentioned under the heading of 'Personal computers and software', but these are mostly small-size service ventures. Another single heading (161 enterprises) lumps together consulting activities, engineering, teaching and training, trading services (data compiled by the Soviet Chamber of Commerce and Industry).

Is this good news for the Western investors? Not quite so as one of the basic principles of the joint venture is that any transfer of hard currency abroad must be generated by an export gain. True, it is also said that the joint ventures must create import substitutes and help to eliminate 'irrational imports'.

The Soviet joint venture, unlike its East European counterparts, has no legal definition other than being a co-enterprise (*sovmestnoe pred-*

priiatie). It is not a joint stock company or a limited liability company, or anything else that is legally identifiable. This is probably not too worrying compared to the other drawbacks but it is still disturbing. A law on joint stock companies is expected in 1990 which may settle the question.

The USSR–Western joint venture is supposed to act as a domestic enterprise while not being integrated into the domestic framework. Let us mention the most tricky consequences of this situation, in the fields of supplies and sales, payment, decision-making and tax treatment.

The joint venture is free to buy and sell on foreign markets (with the provision that, if buying, it has to 'earn' the hard currency to do so), while not all Soviet enterprises have yet the same right. But it was not initially free to buy and sell on the domestic market, precisely because the latter is not a market and because the co-enterprise cannot be included in the planned system of sales and supplies (which is itself in the process of being altered). The January 1987 decree has thus to state that access to the domestic market had to be managed, for a joint venture, by the foreign trade organisations, *but* with settlements in domestic roubles . . . *but* with a reference to world prices! The decree of September 1987 changed the rules: the joint ventures may buy and sell freely on the Soviet market (it may be advisable, however, to have an agreement with domestic trade organisations), including in hard currency, which a domestic enterprise is not entitled to do. If the joint enterprise uses roubles on the domestic market, it may trade either in Soviet domestic prices, or in 'contractual' prices referring to 'world prices', which necessarily means the use of an implicit foreign exchange coefficient. If and when the joint venture uses hard currency, this has to be converted in roubles for accounting purposes: the question of the rate of exchange thus emerges.

When the Soviet trade representatives abroad first explained the contents of the new regulations they stressed that there should be no currency problems as all the accounting of the enterprise was to be in roubles, and that every time one would need a conversion of roubles in hard currency the official rate of exchange would be used. Nevertheless, the joint venture was entitled to have bank accounts both in roubles and in hard currency. In fact, exactly as in the case of the Soviet enterprises whose foreign trade activity was to be regulated through the ill-fated DCCs (differentiated currency coefficients), the joint venture was to use implicit foreign exchange multipliers. The equity capital was to be accounted in roubles at the official rate of exchange 'taking into consideration world prices'. This indeed meant pricing the Soviet assets at artificial prices in roubles so as to obtain, after conversion at the official rate of exchange, an estimate comparable to the value of the Western partner's assets. It also created difficulty in the case where the Western partner contributed its share in the form of cash. In this case, the conversion into roubles at the official rate clearly appeared as very disadvantageous due to the over-valuation of the rouble.

In the field no clarification emerged; on the contrary, the announcement of foreign exchange measures (see p. 147) is related to export-import commercial transactions. Does it apply also to the operation of joint ventures? Obviously not in the first stage, when the differentiated conversion coefficients are to be unified and replaced with a uniform bonus of 100 per cent over the present exchange rate; perhaps in the second stage, beginning from 1991, when a new exchange rate is to be applied. In this case, the assets contributed in foreign exchange should be reevaluated, and conversely the sales of joint ventures on the domestic market in roubles would yield much less hard currency – unless those domestic sales were made in hard currency, in which case they would generate at least twice the previous amount on the rouble account!

This is not only a question of accounting. All transfers in hard currency (repatriation of profits, of salaries for foreign employees, payments for imports) must be 'earned' beforehand through gains in hard currency. Sales in hard currency on the domestic market provide for such revenues, presumably in the cases when the production of the joint venture is an import substitute. (But who decides that it is?) Another solution is to save hard currency, and here the December 1988 decree offers an opportunity by providing that the payment for rents and other services supplied to the foreign workers of a joint enterprise is made in Soviet roubles 'except in the cases provided for in decisions of the Council of Ministers of the USSR'. (This is indeed good news, especially if 'in Soviet roubles' also means – which should be the case – 'at Soviet prices'. But what are the exceptions? There are some hints that these might be for joint ventures established in special economic zones.) As it is, the rule of a 'hard currency pay-off' is certainly felt as most constraining by the foreign partners.

The Western businessmen complained very much about the provision that the equity share of the foreign partner could not exceed 49 per cent. This has been relaxed since December 1988, and presumably did not bother them so much before, as the average share in the joint ventures formed up to the beginning of 1989 was 37.5 per cent. More significant is the fact that from now on a foreign citizen may be chosen as chairman or general director, something which was forbidden in the initial regulation. All important decisions have to be taken by the board with an unanimous vote: no side may impose its will. Among the questions to be solved by the joint enterprise, there is labour and wages management, which was previously regulated by Soviet law for Soviet employees. The joint enterprise may decide upon all matters involving labour (hiring and firing of workers, forms and amounts of salaries, bonuses in roubles included); this is very important because it allows the joint enterprise to give its *Soviet* wage-earners a treatment different from the rules applied in purely *Soviet* enterprises. It also may comfort the Western businessmen, who were afraid of being obliged to hire too many workers and of finding labour productivity lower than they expected.

The Soviet Union has followed the practice of the other socialist countries, reducing taxation on profits from a rather high level (initially, a tax of 30 per cent was to be levied after the first two years of operation, coupled with a 20 per cent tax on that part of the profits transferred abroad). From 1 January 1989, the additional tax on profits transferred abroad by the foreign partner may be reduced or waived by the Ministry of Finance, in particular for enterprises producing consumer goods, medicines, and high-technology goods. Already in September 1987, it was decided that the tax should be imposed only following the first two profitable years, which may allow most of the ventures to escape taxation for quite a long time.

In the same spirit, the goods imported by the joint enterprise for expanding production may benefit from preferential tariff treatment or even be totally tariff-free (what exactly does 'may' mean?).

All this might attract more Western partners, especially as the Soviet partners are now better motivated as well. The quantity of red tape with which a joint venture has to deal is reduced as the authorisations are now to be obtained at the lowest level (i.e., the relevant ministry, or, for the cooperatives, the regional authorities). But this will be the case only if the system on the whole appears more reliable.

The question of joint ventures is related to the setting of customs free areas, as in the case of Hungary. The Far East economic region has been selected to get the status of 'a zone of joint entrepreneurship' during the first quarter of 1989. Indeed, there have been indications that another special zone was to be set up in the area of the Saimaa canal between

Lappeenranta (Finland) and Leningrad. Later on the tentative territory of the zone was shifted to the more developed border region of Vyborg. The whole matter still remains very obscure. The Soviet authorities have not yet made up their minds on what the suitable format of such zones should be: territorial, sectoral, or functional. In the first case the model would be the Chinese special zones. But there are some limitations to this, because, unlike in the Chinese case, the border regions of the USSR are not the most economically active (the Leningrad region is an exception). The Far East zone clearly provides an opening on the Pacific area, not on the West. The Black Sea area would give opportunities mainly in the field of tourism. The sectoral conception supported by Academician Bogomolov from the Institute of the World Socialist System advocates the setting up of free zones for high technology activities, and this is what the Saimaa zone is meant for. But to attract high-tech industries to a rather unsuitable place, with severe climatic conditions and no housing or infra-structure capacities, does not seem promising. The 'functional conception' would draw on the Hungarian model and prompt the setting up of off-shore banks, perhaps trading firms, which might be located in Moscow.

Finally the GDR is to join the other countries in organising joint ventures on its territory. The authorities consistently opposed such a move until 1989, arguing that industrial cooperation was better suited to the country's industrial organisation. The new GDR joint venture model should be a conservative one, at least in the beginning, allowing for only 49 per cent foreign equity participation.*

SOCIALIST MULTINATIONALS

The Complex Integration Programme raised the question of setting up joint bodies between the socialist countries, called 'international business associations', which were to match, in the international area, the national associations of enterprises set up following the post-1965 reforms. These bodies, created by inter-state agreement, do not involve joint ownership. Ownership remains national; only management is common. Four bodies of this kind were set up between 1972 and 1978, two of them, Interatominstrument and Interatomenergo, in the field of nuclear energy use. Intertekhimvolokno had the task of coordinating the production of chemical fibres, and Intertextilmash, the production of machinery for the textile industry. With the exception of Interatominstrument (for after-sales servicing of laboratory installations using nuclear energy), such entities have never become genuine enterprises, remaining basically in the field of research-development and coordination.

The second format, that of joint enterprises, predates the 1971 Programme (Matejka, 1988). It is most often bilateral, following the example of the Polish–Hungarian firm Haldex, set up in 1959 for the exploitation of Polish slag-heaps through a Hungarian coal-recovery process (see Lavigne, 1977). About fifty bilateral enterprises of this type are in principle operative as at the end of 1988. The first to be set up following the 1971 Programme was the German–Polish firm 'Przijazn-Freundschaft' (i.e., Friendship) in the Polish town of Zawiercie, which manufactures cotton yarn using technology from the GDR (Gilbert, 1984). A certain impulse was given to this format when the USSR adopted, in 1987, on the same day as the regulations on joint enterprises with capitalist countries, a separate text on joint enterprises and international associations on Soviet territory, with the participation of other Comecon countries. However, these enterprises meet with great difficulties in operation. The most publicised instance has been the case of a venture (which seems to be a case for a 'direct link' rather than a joint enterprise proper) associating a Soviet and a Bulgarian enterprise for the manufacture of textile machinery with numerical control, as the chairman, a very active and loud-voiced Georgian called Kabaidze, amply provided the newspapers with information on all the bureaucratic obstacles he met.

There are very few 'multinational enterprises' involving several nations. The first to be set up in 1978 was Interlichter which uses barge-carriers and barges for joint transport by sea and river (shipping on the Danube and to South East Asia). In 1985, along with the adoption of the Programme for Scientific and Technical Progress, an international enterprise called Inter-Robot was set up to coordinate the production of industrial robots within Comecon. A Soviet–Czech bilateral enterprise, Robot, had been set up just one year before. However, Inter-Robot was not to have a successful start, as the GDR, the country most advanced in the field, declined to join, basically to avoid sharing its advances with other countries, and probably too because of disagreements with the USSR on the very conception of the robot industry.

Thirdly, there are more fuzzy groupings of a non-equity partnership type, bringing two or more firms together for the coordination of research-development, export-import, investment, services, and environmental protection.

To this already complex construction, the 1987 Soviet regulations added still more confusion. Although these regulations are Soviet and not international, they are meant to shape the format of joint entities within Comecon as the Soviet Union is certainly more eager than any Comecon member to push them through. The 1987 decree speaks of 'joint business organisations' which seems to be an amalgamation of the first two formats described above, the third one seemingly dropped altogether.

A detailed description of the existing joint entities would clearly indicate the aims which the socialist countries are seeking: a more efficient management of common interest services (for example, Interport, a Polish–German port authority set up in 1973; Medunion, a multilateral organisation for the marketing of medical equipment, which includes the Seven except for Bulgaria and Romania); and the promotion of inter-branch specialisation in such branches as camera films, domestic detergents, refined oil products, etc.

The inefficiency of these 'multinationals' may be put down to several causes:

(1) The issue of ownership still remains an obstacle. It turns out to be more difficult to give up a portion of national collective ownership to a 'brother' state than to a capitalist country. The legal procedures for participation in equity capital between socialist countries have not yet been laid down completely. The Soviet regulations of 1987 rely on the concept of 'co-ownership', a notion legally inconsistent. The emerging company laws which have been adopted since 1988 in various countries compound the difficulty.

(2) National planning of the state where the joint enterprise has its headquarters may infringe on the rights of the latter. To avoid this, there are usually provisions according to which the joint enterprise has a privileged access to the allocation of investment goods, raw materials, etc. The joint enterprise thus remains an enclave in the host country. If this format develops, conflicts between national planning and the management of the joint enterprise will inevitably arise. But one may as well say that the very risk of such conflicts hampers the creation of such enterprises. Would the withering away of domestic planning itself make things easier? Not necessarily. True, the scope of central planning is shrinking in most Eastern countries, but in various ways.

(3) The non-convertibility of socialist currencies and the arbitrary nature of rates of exchange between them makes accounting and management of joint ventures extremely difficult. In most cases *ad hoc* rates are

applied, and differentiated according to the accounting operations, though the principle of a gradual unification of these rates was stated as early as 1973. In 1987 and 1988, the Soviet Union agreed with four of its partners (Czechoslovakia, Hungary, Bulgaria, and Mongolia) to apply a single exchange rate for all operations resulting from 'direct links' between enterprises, including coenterprises.

The 'direct links' just mentioned are a substitute for real joint ventures. Although there were supposedly hundreds of those 'bilateral direct links' between enterprises at the end of 1988, very few were really operational. Here again the lack of a 'common market' and of a truly common currency impedes the setting up of workable inter-enterprise relations.*

EAST–SOUTH MULTINATIONAL GROUPINGS

Joint companies have developed between the FTOs of the socialist countries and the public or private enterprises of the Third World. According to a study by Carl McMillan (1987), there were 231 joint companies in the Third World in 1983 that had equity capital from the CMEA European countries. Apart from resource exploitation, the main fields of direct investment by socialist countries in the Third World are assembly and manufacturing, construction and engineering services, and import-export operations.

The overall value of capital invested is low, between $1 and $2 billion in 1983 according to educated guesses by Carl McMillan (1987). The equity share of the East is generally a minority share. Associations are often, though not always, sought with state-owned firms. The Eastern countries are motivated by access to markets (especially for their technology), access to resources (raw materials and, especially for the USSR, fishing resources), and in some cases by the existence of low-cost labour. Usually these firms are bilateral companies. Some organisations in socialist countries, however, do appear to be genuinely multinational, such as Dal, the Polish organisation for foreign trade, which has branches in twenty-three countries.

This form of cooperation was looked on with suspicion in the beginning, because of the political positions developed in the Third World against foreign investment, positions which were shared and supported by the socialist countries. Nowadays these ventures are approved of in the Soviet or CMEA publications. What about the traditional analysis of these ventures as neo-colonialist, in Marxist literature? The answer is that such an analysis is not relevant here. The joint venture is temporary, it generally ends with the Third World country buying the shares of its socialist partners.

The weakness of multinational inter-enterprise links in the Third World has systemic as well as developmental causes. The socialist states conduct business in the Third World mainly through their FTOs, as their enterprises have not as yet either the capacity or the will to take action on their own. Due to their level of development, these countries are not as attractive to the Third World as the developed market economies. A very recent trend, beginning in 1987–88, and due to these structural reasons, is emerging. Among the most developed countries of the Third World, some are beginning to set up joint ventures in the socialist countries. India has been one of the first countries to take advantage of Soviet regulations on joint ventures in the USSR, and set up a restaurant in Moscow in 1987. India might help the USSR to develop light industry and services in Central Asia and Siberia. In 1988, South Korea proposed joint ventures to the USSR and Hungary in the automobile industry. The pattern of East–South relations is thus definitely drifting away from a North–South model – or else toward a reverse one.

Trade policies: who is protectionist?

Systemic and development issues are again at the centre of the debate on trade policies. How should the socialist countries be treated in international trade? As state trading countries to which special rules of a discriminatory nature should be applied? As 'intermediate' or 'relatively poor' countries which one should involve in the international trade system through specific preferences?

Up to now, the East has been considered as a group of state trading countries. Whatever adaptations have been introduced in state trade, the USSR and Eastern European countries are not seen in the same light as other nations in international trade relations, the rules of which have been established by the market economies. When the Eastern countries declare that they seek to grant foreign trade rights to their enterprises, to open their economies to the influences of the world market, they are clearly not believed. The conditions laid down for their accession to Gatt are a clear illustration of this. State monopoly and planning are seen as basically protectionist mechanisms and as such, fundamentally incompatible with the rules of free trade. The East–West dispute which raged for years centres on this one point: the East feels itself the victim of discriminatory practices, whereas it does not discriminate against its partners.

ARE SOCIALIST COUNTRIES PROTECTIONIST BY NATURE OF THEIR SYSTEM?

In a very simplified approach, the traditional planning of foreign trade aims to determine the economy's import needs for a given period, and the required export cover.

In such an approach protectionist in itself? Not necessarily, according to the standard Western definition of protectionism. One might conceive of an optimal foreign trade plan in which import quotas would be fixed at the level they would reach in an open economy, through the application of the neo-classical theory on international specialisation. Efficiency criteria devised by socialist economists implicitly refer to comparative advantages.

In actual fact, the determining of import volumes does not follow such rules, for several reasons.

(1) Even if he wanted to, the planner could not operate this way. The inadequacy of domestic price-fixing and of the exchange rates would not allow him to achieve an optimum calculated in this manner. This is actually one of the reasons which encouraged some Eastern European nations to seek a rationalisation of this system, by linking domestic and foreign prices, calculating a 'realistic' rate of exchange.

(2) The very fact that import requirements are the starting point from which the overall volume of foreign trade is calculated shows an autarkical attitude as it implies that self-sufficiency is sought first and foremost. This is what F. Holzman call a 'trade aversion' (Holzman, 1976: 24–26), and suggests a protectionist attitude.

(3) Finally, imports from Comecon are privileged and imports from the outside world are therefore discriminated against. This is a consequence of domestic planning and of the way Comecon mechanisms operate. In domestic planning of foreign trade, preference is given to imports which do not require hard currency, if the relevant goods may be obtained from Comecon suppliers as well as from external suppliers. If these goods cannot be obtained from Comecon suppliers, in particular when there are quality requirements, or if they can be obtained but not in the needed quantities, then and only then will external suppliers be preferred. For

goods obtainable from Comecon suppliers, the bilateral procedure of negotiating foreign trade agreements within Comecon may lead the importers to scale down their demands, as the potential exporters will not be willing to supply goods for a greater value than their own import needs, or to supply 'hard goods' against 'soft goods' (see chapter 2). One has to remember that, as the settlements are being made in a clearing currency, nobody wishes to maintain a surplus.

We may certainly speak of a regional preference, but this preference is very different from that which results from regional integrated groupings that are accepted and recognised by GATT as allowing exceptions from the non-discrimination rule (art. XXIV on customs unions and free trade areas). GATT only recognises 'market' integration groupings. Comecon is not a market. The Comecon preference is not based upon economic optimum considerations, it is rather imposed upon its members by virtue (sin?) of its specific mechanisms. Every Comecon country would prefer to import from the West, but is prevented from doing so mainly by its inability to offer tradeable goods. The typical strategy will then be to try and import from Eastern partners everything possible among the goods needed, while diverting to the West all saleable exports. The limit of such a strategy is the willingness of the exporting partners to expand their sales beyond their own imports.

Thus, the operation of Comecon differs greatly from that of a regional union of market economies. The discriminatory nature of such a union is based on protection at the point of entry (common external tariff, a common policy of quantitative restrictions or preferences). Within the union, there is a free circulation of goods and means of production. Comecon is in this sense less protected than the EEC. It has neither a common external tariff nor a common trade policy. Within the Comecon area, there is no free circulation of goods, but a network of bilateral trade and specialisation agreements supplemented by a set of multilateral specialisation agreements. Little is known of this dual network owing to the incomplete information at our disposal both on domestic foreign trade plans and on the actual impact of trade and specialisation agreements.

The Eastern countries deny that this secrecy is overwhelming. They claim that Western partners may get sufficient information from the foreign trade organisations. In addition, the FTOs are supposed to play the market without discrimination as planned imports from non-Comecon countries are not designated beforehand to any particular country.

The way the FTOs actually operate, it would seem, is as follows. Western suppliers compete for large orders and the contract goes to those firms offering the best quality, price, and finance conditions. It should however be added that pressure to keep the balance of trade in equilibrium is very real for the FTOs at the micro-level, as it is at the macro-level for the planner. This pressure is even greater in the case when individual enterprises are granted the right to import. They generally have to balance their imports and their exports – this is what the Soviet legislation of 1987–88 calls a 'hard currency self-supporting system'). Demands for compensation are bound to increase, and appear as a powerful form of bilateral protectionism.

Finally, even when competition might exist between foreign suppliers, there is no competition between the foreign suppliers and the domestic producers. There are two reasons for that.

First, the importer cannot really chose between the foreign supplier and the domestic producer. In the traditional centrally planned economy, the domestic enterprise is allocated goods, with strict specification of domestic and foreign suppliers. When the domestic allocation mechanism and the foreign trade monopoly are relaxed, which is indeed the case in most of the Eastern countries now, the relaxation affects first the export activities and only marginally affects the importer, whose autonomous decision-making powers are nil or severely limited.

Second, the link between domestic and foreign prices is not sufficient, even when it does exist, to allow any competition to be effectively practised. Let us take the case of Hungary. The so-called 'competitive' prices introduced in 1980 had the aim of stimulating exporters to reduce their costs because the export price was to determine the domestic price. The aim was not to encourage importers to prefer cheaper foreign goods to domestic goods. In all the socialist countries, the national producers are constantly criticised for supplying high-cost, low-quality, non-competitive (with the West) production. At the same time, they are effectively protected from any competition. They generally are of such a size that they have an actual monopoly on the goods they offer. (This is why the reforms insist upon the need to develop a network of small enterprises.) The domestic producers are also protected from competition with the outside world: not only because of balance of payments considerations, but because the whole domestic production system is inefficient. It is impossible, however, to wind up the inefficient producer: should one take this step, the whole production system would go bankrupt.

To sum up, Eastern countries *are* protectionist. One may even find here the usual grounds for protectionism: the existence of a regional union, balance of payments (trade) considerations, protection of infant industry (with many infants!). This protectionism is *systemic* and uses instruments different from the standard ones used by a market economy. In the traditional centrally planned economy, these instruments are planning and monopoly of foreign trade, on which is superimposed the intra-Comecon preference.

Do reforms improve things and lessen this specific type of protectionism, when planning is relaxed, when domestic prices are linked with world prices, when gradually more and more economic agents are allowed to trade, and finally, when the binding intra-Comecon links are relaxed and when Comecon's share of foreign trade is kept at a level low enough to prevent it determining the bulk of trade? The question emerged in actual trade policy when the Eastern countries began to apply for GATT membership.

TRADE POLICIES: MEMBERSHIP IN GATT AND AGREEMENTS WITH THE EEC

Gatt membership and negotiation of trade and cooperation agreements with the EEC are closely linked since the EEC is the main partner of the East within GATT.

For all the Eastern European countries up to now, membership in GATT was achieved before reaching agreement with the EEC. This might change in the future, in the case that Bulgaria and the GDR happen to conclude an agreement with the EEC before being admitted into GATT, as will be the case for the USSR. The last country to join GATT (to-date) was Hungary in 1973. Hungary was then applying its 1968 reform called the 'new economic mechanism' and succeeded in convincing GATT accession protocol negotiators (first and foremost the EEC) to admit this country on terms of a quasi-market economy in spite of its planned economy characteristcs. Hungary was considered as meeting normal conditions of entry to the group of so-called free trade nations, these conditions basically being the lowering of customs duties. Subsequently Hungary was very careful to comply with GATT rules, even when enforcing restrictions. The drastic cuts on imports introduced in 1982 were duly notified to GATT, on account of balance of payments difficulties which are a case for temporary restrictions (art. XVIII of the Agreement).

This was not the case for Poland and Romania which had entered GATT in 1967 and 1972 respectively. These countries had no customs duties when they became members, and, in any case, there was no question of their being treated as market economies. In exchange for the advantages which GATT membership offered them, they were called upon to guarantee greater access to their (non-) 'market' for GATT countries. For Poland, this meant a commitment to increase its imports from the GATT contracting parties by at least 7 per cent per year. For Romania, the growth rate of Romanian imports from the contracting parties was not to be below the rate laid down by the five-year plan for the country's overall foreign trade growth. In other words, this saw the introduction of a *reciprocity* clause to make sure that state trading countries did actually provide advantages on the level of those they were offered.

GATT negotiators assumed from the outset that the socialist countries could not offer *identical* advantages to what they were getting in acceding to GATT (the benefit of the MFN clause, putting aside the special case of the USA). In consequence, they had to offer *equivalent*, or *reciprocal* advantages. This notion of reciprocity had been included after tremendous struggles in the Final Act of the Conference on Security and Cooperation in Europe (Helsinki, 1975). It means essentially that a CPE cannot grant tariff concessions, even when it has a tariff. This is because the tariff is always bound to be meaningless in the framework of a state trading system, for two reasons: there is no automatic connection between domestic and external prices; there are no independent import decisions made by economic agents distinct from the state. For this reason, the Gatt negotiators argued, one had to devise concessions bringing about an increase in trade, equivalent to what a tariff reduction might entail. Hungary managed to avoid such concessions, under the assumption that its tariff was meaningful. But this was mainly an act of political good will from the Western side. When Hungary began negotiating a trade agreement with the EEC in 1984 and claiming that its membership in GATT should entail the suppression of all quantitiative restrictions still existing in its trade with EEC member countries, the EEC Commission was not prepared to accept this argument. Finally, concessions from both sides allowed the agreement to be finalised in 1988, with the elimination of quantitative restrictions on imports from Hungary scheduled up to the end of 1995. In November 1989, in the framework of the aid package extended by the EEC to Hungary, it was agreed to lift all quantitative restrictions by January 1990.*

Czechoslovakia, a founding member of GATT, remained a sleeping partner. This did not prevent it from reaching an agreement with the EEC, a few weeks after Hungary, at the end of 1988, without having significantly reactivated its role in GATT. The agreement with Czechoslovakia covers only trade in industrial goods; it excludes cooperation, and trade in agricultural goods. It provides for an expanding of the list of quota-free exports to the EEC. In return, Czechoslovakia has committed itself to improve business conditions for Western businessmen.

The trade and cooperation agreement with Poland was signed in September 1989, and benefited from the overall mobilisation of the EC countries in favour of this country. By 1994–5, all quantitative restrictions except for a few more sensitive products were to be eliminated according to the original arrangements, but two months later, in November 1989, the EC agreed to lift the restrictions as soon as the beginning of 1990. The negotiations with Bulgaria stopped at a preliminary stage in July 1989 and were to resume when Bulgaria would adopt a more liberal stance towards its Turkish minority. Exploratory talks have been held with the GDR and may take a new course in 1990 if still closer links than already exist develop between the two German states.

The case of the USSR is to be seen in the light of these experiences. The USSR approached GATT in 1982 and 1984 to request observer status, already granted to Bulgaria. The reluctant response which these requests were met with were not of an economic nature. The USSR hardly exports any sensitive products for which it is in need of concessions, at least in the traditional structure of Soviet foreign trade. At the time of the first Soviet applications, Soviet imports from the West were still increasing, unlike the case of Eastern Europe. As the Soviet approaches were informal, there was no need for explicit rejection. Unofficially, it was felt that even the passive presence of the USSR in GATT deliberations could give rise to political malaise within the organisation.

In 1986, when the multilateral negotiations for the Uruguay Round were to begin, the USSR applied once again, but to participate in the negotiations, without having observer status. Its request was rejected on strong opposition from the United States Trade Representative, claiming that 'the Soviet international trading system [was] at fundamental, practical and philosophical variance with the principles and practices of GATT'. Should this be taken at face value, then one should clearly exclude almost all the CPEs (centrally planned economies) from GATT, and perhaps even Hungary. However the very dimensions and political importance of the Soviet Union gave a different meaning to its potential membership.

The Soviet Union, and the smaller CPEs, see an essential symbolic gain in getting the right to the most favoured nation clause. This right, which results from membership in GATT, is seen as a sign of international respectability. The right to avail oneself of the clause is not tantamount to the actual benefit from the clause. Without being a GATT member, the USSR is already benefiting *de facto* from the clause in trade relations with most of its partners. Conversely, it would not automatically get the most favoured nation treatment from the USA even if (or just because) becoming a member of GATT. In addition, contrary to the other CPEs of Eastern Europe (and China) the USSR does not urgently need the clause, at least until its export structure will remain dominated by fuels, which is bound to be the case for some time notwithstanding the present reform of the foreign trade mechanism.

Nevertheless the Soviet Union was eager to reach an agreement with the EEC in all fields where the EEC has competence, and in 1989 had submitted proposals not only for trade matters but also in the field of cooperation in energy, transport, environmental protection, and facilitation of business contacts. As in the case of Hungary, the USSR was specifically claiming that its foreign trade reforms met the requirements a country had to satisfy to be treated along the same lines as a market economy. The draft trade and cooperation agreement signed in November 1989 even included cooperation in the field of nuclear energy. It provided for the elimination of quantitative restrictions over the 1990–95 period. It brought the USSR closer to GATT membership, and the observer status was to be granted in May 1990.

The Soviet Union thus reaped the results of a market-oriented trade reform. The 2 December 1988 decree was indeed one step away from a *planned* regulation of foreign trade, and towards a *market* regulation using instruments resorted to in market economies as well. A new tariff code is to be introduced and a new tariff is to be applied from 1 January

1990. The decree very candidly stated that among other reasons the recourse to tariff instruments strengthens 'the basis of the international commercial negotiations, namely with the GATT and the EEC'.

The basis for the new tariff nomenclature is the Harmonised Commodity Description and Coding System which allows for coordination between the SITC and the Brussels classification used by the EEC countries. Poland too has implemented this system, in the new tariff which has been in effect since 1 January 1989. One should note that many Western countries have not yet put this system in operation, while preparing it since 1985. The Soviet enterprises have never had to be concerned with *any* nomenclature, as the 1961 tariff was in fact not operational!

In addition, the Soviet Union has introduced a system of non-tariff restrictions, again 'to achieve favorable results in international commercial negotiations' (decree of 1988). These are both export and import restrictions. Up to now, such limitations were only set for private movements of goods.

A new situation has emerged. The traditional centrally planned economies were displaying a specific 'trade aversion' which was implemented through non-market protectionist instruments. They were asked to remove these instruments through non-market type concessions. Moving towards reforms, they have first to introduce market-type protectionist measures so as to abolish them *vis-à-vis* their Western partners.

The old concept of 'reciprocity' so strongly criticised by the socialist countries remains, but in a modified form. What is increasingly asked from these countries is the creation of favourable business conditions for the development of trade, through quite practical measures concerning accommodation, communication, visa procedures, and customs clearance for businessmen. This is included in multilateral documents such as the January 1989 final text adopted by the participants in the CSCE in Vienna, as well as in bilateral agreements such as the EEC–Hungary agreement of September 1988.

The issue of protectionism is not relevant only in the East–West context. It is also present in East–South trade and cooperation relations.

This is an issue hardly debated. Some Eastern European countries are rather claiming the status of developing countries for themselves, from the developed market economies. Partial preferences were granted to Romania (1974) and claimed by Hungary and Bulgaria without success.

Poland might get some preferences as from 1990, within the aid package from the EC. The general trend is indeed to consider Eastern European countries as relatively developed countries, which might be expected to grant rather than claim preferences. The Third World countries themselves have repeatedly asked the socialist countries, since UNCTAD IV in 1976, to increase their imports of manufactures from their developing partners. Is the low level of imports of manufactured goods to be attributed to protectionist practices from the East? Since 1 January 1965, the USSR has done away with all customs duties for imports from the Third World, and the other Comecon countries have considerably lowered their duties between 1972 and 1976. This political gesture, the significance of which was greatly reduced by the introduction of a generalised system of preferences by EEC member states, failed to open East European markets to the Third World. Manufactured goods of the Third World are similar to those produced by the East European countries, and are not priority products in import plans. The 'systemic protection' also applies to non-priority raw materials, such as coffee, cocoa, and tea. This is why the developing countries are demanding more efficient measures, with the inclusion of quantities of goods and products to be bought from the Third World to feature clearly in import planning by socialist countries. For their part, Eastern countries, and the USSR in particular, prefer to cover this through bilateral agreements with specific countries (India, Pakistan, Turkey). There is nothing in view of the type of a 'Lome' agreement between Comecon and the Third World. For such an agreement to be possible, Comecon should first turn into a common market, a state not to be achieved in a near future.

IS THE EAST DISCRIMINATED AGAINST BY THE WEST?

The socialist countries are increasingly eager to show their dedication to market mechanisms because they want the discriminatory protectionism against them to end. As we have seen, this is not an easy task. Basically none of them has completely succeeded in getting rid of its state trading image. What is at stake?

In all international fora devoted to international trade, the East complains of discriminatory restrictions, i.e., applied exclusively to the socialist countries. Here one has to distinguish carefully between two types of discrimination: discrimination which affects Eastern countries as communist regimes and is particularly practised by the United States; and, discrimination meant to protect Western countries from the disruptive action of state trading countries.

The first type boils down to the use of the most favoured nation clause as a political weapon. Without going into the details of American legislation, it should be remembered that since 1951, MFN status has been exceptional in relations between the USA and the communist regimes. The USSR, which enjoyed this status between 1935 and 1951, saw it reintroduced only during the golden age of Soviet–American relations (1972–74). Since then the USSR no longer enjoys this status, having so to speak, a record of offences. It is denied the MFN status because of its communist nature, according to a law passed in 1951; because it has restricted the rights of its citizens to emigrate, according to the Jackson–Vanik amendment to the Trade Bill of 1974; because of events such as the invasion of Afghanistan (1979) and the imposition of the martial law in Poland (1981) for which the USSR was held responsible by the USA. In 1989, a debate emerged in the United States as to the suitability of restoring the USSR to the most favoured treatment, as almost all the reasons but the first one for denying it this treatment had disappeared due to the political changes which had occurred since 1985. According to the US legislation, the extension of the most favoured treatment requires a waiver of the Jackson–Vanik amendment and the ratification of a new bilateral trade agreement. A waiver to the Jackson–Vanik amendment was considered by the US in 1989 for the first time. The rest of Eastern Europe has enjoyed various status levels. Poland obtained the reintroduction of the MFN status in 1960, the year J. F. Kennedy, a Catholic president, was elected. It lost it in 1981 and regained it in 1987. Romania has enjoyed it since 1975, but later on periodically threatened to lose it by its emigration policy. The tax put on Jewish emigration in 1981 almost lost Romania the benefit of the clause. In an exceptional move, Romania itself decided to end its status in 1988, obviously to avoid a scrutiny of its human rights policy from the Congress of the United States. Hungary, in 1978, obtained both the application of the clause and the return of the Crown of St Stephen which had been kept in the USA since the end of the Second World War. However, the MFN treatment had to be confirmed every year. In 1989 the USA agreed to extend it on a permanent basis. For these countries the advantage of the clause is not purely symbolic. Due to the high tariffs applied in the USA to goods from countries which do not enjoy MFN status, export opportunities may strongly increase if the clause is applied.*

In relations with Western Europe, and the EEC in particular, the significance of the MFN clause is quite different. The Eastern countries are strongly attached to the principle. In fact, practically all these countries benefit from it. Prior to 1973, bilateral trade agreements between the Comecon countries and the Western European countries provided for the MFN treatment quasi automatically. Since the effective coming into force of the EEC's common trade policy, bilateral trade agreements have disappeared but the clause has been unofficially maintained by exchange of letters or the inclusion of appendices in bilateral cooperation agreements, overriding the spirit, if not the letter, of EEC regulations (see chapter 2). The question is bound to become purely academic sooner or later, when the EEC has trade agreements with all its Eastern partners.

The MFN treatment does not offer that many advantages, and certainly less in relations with the EEC than with the USA. The MFN clause, extending to the beneficiary country all advantages, privileges, or immunities granted to any other country applies strictly only to tariff treatment. EEC tariffs are low. The main obstacles to trade are of a non-tariff nature, and, as such, are not affected by the clause. Even with the benefit of the MFN clause, the Eastern countries are certainly affected by an implicit discrimination. They are indeed, along with major developed countries such as Japan or the USA, the main trading partners still subject to the EEC common external tariff. Western Europe is a free-trade zone. The developing world enjoys preferential treatment under various schemes.

Unlike the USA, Western Europe has never made use of the MFN clause as a sanction or a leverage. The protectionist instruments of the EEC are basically of two kinds: quantitative restrictions and anti-dumping measures.

Quantitative restrictions (QRs)

Quantitative restrictions are either imposed unilaterally by the 'autonomous regime' (since 1975), or negotiated with Eastern European countries (with Romania an agreement was reached on industrial goods in 1980, and is now obsolete; in the new round of agreements between the EEC and the Eastern European countries, the QRs are to be gradually lifted between 1990 and 1995). One may add to these QRs the agreements signed for textile (within the Multi-Fibre Arrangements) and the voluntary export restraint arrangements for steel and some agricultural goods.

Within the autonomous policy of the EEC, there was a trend towards liberalisation up until 1977. Since then, the number of quota-free tariff items has levelled out. When the quotas are expressed in money values the increases have been shown to be inferior to the rise in prices; the quotas in physical units remain stable.

Two questions arise here. Were such quotas discriminatory? Were they harmful?

The Eastern experts insist on the discriminatory nature of the quotas. According to the Hungarian economist, A. Inotai, between 1973 and 1980 the share of sensitive products (chemicals and compounds, fertilisers, plastics, textiles, steel products, clothing) has dropped in exports to the West from Czechoslovakia and Romania, has remained stable for Poland and has only increased for Hungary (Inotai, 1982: 26–27 and 98). In a later study the same author claims that out of 774 QRs applying to Hungary in the mid-eighties 88 per cent discriminated against Hungary (Hamori and Inotai, eds, 1987: 56). Do the QRs explain the decrease in market shares? A study undertaken by the Economic Commission for Europe of the United Nations suggests that the drop was significant but might be explained as well by a fall in demand (*Economic Bulletin for Europe*, 1981, vol. 33, no. 4: 34). Later studies by the ECE confirm this drop but attribute this to a loss of competitiveness compared to the newly industrialised economies (ECE UN, 1982 and 1983); a US expert reaches similar conclusions (Poznanski, 1986). According to another frequently used argument in the West, QRs cannot be as damaging as claimed because in fact, most of the quotas are underutilised. The study (Hamori, Inotai, eds, 1987) quoted above shows that for 1985, 42 per cent of the total number of import quotas extended to Hungary were utilised over 90 per cent; fully utilised quotas were 'rare birds' but really restricted trade (p. 64). The loss in markets seems obvious both for goods covered by quotas and for goods covered by voluntary export restraints or general arrangements of the same kind (textiles and steel) (see Matejka, 1988).

To the already mentioned restrictions one has to add all those resulting from administrative barriers, norms, sanitary rules, etc., all restrictions with which Eastern countries tend to be less familiar than other partners of the Western countries; to this the West replies by listing obstacles stemming from the state trading bureaucracy, the lack of the usual business facilities available, and so on. In any case, the debate cannot be decided either way objectively. Where the East claims that there is discrimination, the West answers with references to lack of productivity and competitiveness in the East.

The question is particularly topical in view of the single European market of 1993. The Eastern countries dread this deadline as they fear being the first victims of the enlargement of the Western markets. The single market is intensively studied in its potential consequences (Gorski, Chebotareva, 1988). The ECE/UN, in a 1989 study, acknowledged that the competition of the internal market could indeed have adverse effects (ECE/UN, 1989). In any case, three years before the deadline, some crucial questions are not yet settled on the EEC side. One of them concerns the QRs remaining in force after 1992.

The bilateral agreements already signed provide for a gradual elimination of the QRs. For the remaining restrictions (Article 115 of the Treaty of Rome) the national import quotas should be replaced by Community-wide quotas, but agreement is far from being reached among the EEC countries themselves.

Anti-dumping

Anti-dumping policies are strongly resented by the Eastern European countries and the USSR. These countries consider that every time they manage to increase their share of the Western markets through price competition, the anti-dumping rules are applied to them with prejudice. In fact, out of 278 investigations conducted by the European Community on dumping cases between 1981 and the first half of 1987, 132 concerned the centrally planned economies; out of 175 anti-dumping actions (including the imposition of definitive duties and minimum price undertakings), 87 concerned these economies (Kelly *et al.*, 1988: 120).

Dumping is defined by GATT as selling at a price below the 'normal value' of the product. Eastern Europe has often been accused of dumping practices, with proceedings usually brought by associations of national or European producers or by the EEC Commission itself. In a large number of cases, the proceedings have resulted in price undertakings (not to export below a given price level), or in voluntary export restraints. Towards the Eastern countries as in general practice, anti-dumping action is increasingly used as an instrument of trade policy (Kelly *et al.*: 11). The socialist countries claim that here again, they have been discriminated against. They are even beginning to strike back. A Soviet foreign trade organisation, Tekhnointorg, introduced a complaint in the European Court of Justice in June 1988 against the EEC, because of the countervailing duty imposed on refrigerators imported from the USSR.

Most frequently, the products susceptible to dumping have one or more of the following characteristics: (a) they are simple products using standard technology; (b) they are produced in developed countries by backward industries with obsolete or uncompetitive manufacturing conditions; (c) Eastern Europe has managed to rapidly increase its share of the market with these products. Examples of this are:

(1) electric motors (getting a third of the EEC market between 1967 and 1974, with prices undercutting those of the national producers in the importing countries by 25 to 55 per cent). This was the first really spectacular case of Eastern European dumping. It is not history; again in 1987, following an anti-dumping action, a countervailing duty was imposed on imports of motors from the six Eastern European countries;

(2) watches (especially Soviet);

(3) polyvinyl chloride, penetration of which increased by five times between 1975 and 1980; other chemicals (an investigation was thus launched in March 1989 into sales of fertilisers from Romania, Hungary, and Poland, whose imports doubled between 1984 and 1988 with a market share rising from 1.4 to 4.4 per cent (*Financial Times*, 7 March 1989);

(4) electrical appliances (vacuum cleaners, fridges, light bulbs);

(5) various steel products;

(6) wood-fibre panels.

What prompts the East to denounce discrimination is that the prices of the socialist countries are suspect from the outset. Their domestic price-fixing methods are called arbitrary, and as soon as their export prices fall below those of the competitors they are immediately accused of dumping. The procedure used to prove dumping totally ignores Eastern price-fixing rules (in other words, the premise is that in a planned economy, no 'normal value' can exist) and 'reconstitutes' a theoretical selling price by referring to production conditions in a non-EEC market economy (Spain before joining EEC, Austria, the Scandinavian countries). Outside the EEC, the golf cart case brilliantly described by F. Holzman, which saw anti-dumping procedures brought against Poland, obviously meant to protect domestic producers, illustrates the arbitrary nature of such reconstructions (one had then to figure a purely theoretical case of golf cart production made in Spain – which does not manufacture electrical golf carts – so as to 'prove' that Polish domestic production prices could not possibly be as low as claimed (Holzman, 1987).

Eastern Europe would certainly stand a better chance of winning its case if it provided better information on the price-fixing rules. In any case, it is in the interests of these countries to promote sales not through mark-down prices but through a positive marketing policy.

The liberalisation of state trading regulations is, however, bound to increase, rather than decrease, the number of anti-dumping cases. The opening of the Single European Market may have the same effect as from 1993. In the East, enterprises granted foreign trade rights and urgently needing to import might develop a policy of selling at any cost. This is explicitly provided for in the Soviet decree on foreign trade of December 1988. The decree mentions that foreign trade rights may be cancelled in case of 'unfair competition'. How can this be clarified? The enterprises will not be allowed to sell at any cost and price. First because it would be contrary to the interests of the economy – it would amount to earning hard currency at black market rates. Second, because the authorities nevertheless fear that many an enterprise might be strongly tempted to do so, which would trigger, should it succeed in selling, a host of anti-dumping suits from the Western partners, just at a time when the Soviet Union wants to look respectable.

On the EEC side, there might be a surge of anti-dumping deals so as to compensate for the effects of lifting QRs. Some Eastern European countries already fear that. It might also be expected that in the same vein the area of 'grey' restrictions, such as a vast array of technical norms, may considerably expand.

PART II

———— · ————

COMMODITIES AND STRATEGIES

Three groups of products and commodities have a major share in the international trade of the socialist countries. These are: technologies, energy, and food products. This of course does not exhaust the list of goods traded by the socialist countries, especially the smaller East European countries. The latter are actively trading in intermediate goods (steel products, chemicals, textiles) as well as in consumer goods.

In a political economy approach however, the trinity of goods primarily exported and imported by the Soviet Union is shaping the pattern of trade for the whole bloc. The purchases and sales of these goods determine a set of interactions worldwide, allow for political pressure and leverage, and sometimes provoke open conflict. Machinery, oil, and grain thus form the core of the international political economy of the socialist system.

CHAPTER 5

·

TECHNOLOGIES

In keeping with convention, by 'technology' is meant anything which falls under Class 7 of the SITC (Standard International Trade Classification) i.e., 'machinery and transport equipment'. Obviously several other definitions are possible and will be referred to further on. The basic definition used here allows us to get an idea of the share and the direction of technology trade in the East's foreign trade. Referring to Table 5 (Appendix) it is possible to outline the following major areas.

1 The East purchases technology from the West, those goods accounting for about a third of their total purchases between 1970 and 1980. Since then this proportion has been tending to drop.

2 Eastern Europe and the USSR export technology to the Third World, this accounting for two-fifths of their sales in 1970, and one-third since the early eighties. Figures are not quite reliable due to the 'unallocated residue' of Soviet exports to the developing world. The difference between total Soviet exports to the developing countries and exports to identified Third World countries amounts to more than a half the sales to the Third World. If we suppose that this residue is made up mainly by arms sales and if we include this under 'technology', then the percentages given above should be increased.

3 Machinery and equipment account for over 50 per cent of the mutual trade of the CMEA European countries. Here. however, an important distinction must be drawn between the USSR and the Six. The Six sell such products among themselves, for a share amounting to 50–55 per cent of their mutual trade. They also sell machinery to the Soviet Union, as half of their supplies to that country. On the other hand, of total exports to its partners, the USSR supplies a relatively small share of technology, the bulk of its sales being made up of energy and raw materials.

Equipment is traded within the CMEA increasingly on the basis of bilateral and multilateral specialisation agreements. Most often it is produced in the socialist countries themselves. However, it may happen that equipment produced in the West is reexported within the CMEA, particularly by the Six to the USSR. For example, the construction of the Orenburg gas pipeline, the most important intra-CMEA cooperation venture undertaken during the seventies, was achieved with Western equipment imported by the Six in hard currency and resold to the USSR in transferable roubles, against the Soviet commitment to provide long-term supplies of gas to the CMEA countries. In addition, national equipment is often produced on the basis of Western technology transferred to the East under different forms (the sale of licenses, of turn-key plants, or of individual items). Thus, one gets the following technology trade interactions:

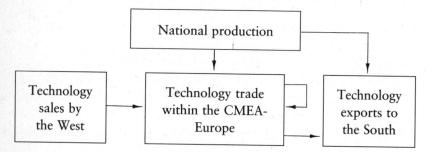

Such interaction is often seen in terms of levels of dependence. It is very widely assumed that the technological backwardness of the USSR and Eastern European countries makes it impossible for them to rely on national production or joint cooperation-specialisation efforts, to reach the level of the major industrial nations. According to this view, they are therefore forced to employ in their economy, as well as to export, older, less sophisticated technology. Only a great flood of advanced Western techniques could held them to catch up. This leads to policy recommendations: in the case of East–West tension, restrictions on sales of Western technology are seen as a particularly effective weapon.

Let us therefore ask the following questions:

(a) How is the East's technological backwardness to be assessed?
(b) Is the contribution made by Western technological imports crucial to the growth of these countries?

(c) How efficient are policies placing embargoes and restrictions on technological transfers to the East?

(d) How much might intra-CMEA specialisation and cooperation programmes contribute?

(e) What features characterise East–South technology transfers?

The East–West technological gap

The claim that such a gap exists is often heard, but to measure the gap is very difficult. Two approaches exist in Western works on the subject. The first approach tends to analyse the implementation of technical progress in the USSR and evaluate the results shown by the economy. The measure of the contribution of technical progress to growth is based on a reconstructed production function from Soviet statistics and is supplemented with a description of the institutional mechanisms for innovation in the USSR. The other approach is to make a direct comparison of technological levels reached in the East and the West according to types of technology or industrial branches. Most often such studies are made for the Soviet case. The technological potential and efficiency of the Eastern European countries is assumed to be comparable to the Soviet Union's performance in this field. This approach underestimates the contributions of the USSR's more industrialised partners, particularly those of the GDR and Czechoslovakia (see Wienert and Slater, 1986: 123–24).

The measurement of the effects of technical progress in the USSR by use of a *production function* has been attempted by several American economists (in particular, Bergson, Desai, and Weitzman). Whatever the methodology and types of functions used, all conclusions agree entirely on the fact that there has been a decline in the overall productivity of factors. This is, moreover, in line with analyses carried out by Soviet authors, which express this in terms of a deceleration of production and investment efficiency. The contribution of technical progress was low in the past, no more than 15–25 per cent of total growth between 1950 and 1969 (Weitzman, 1970: 685), which fits in with the fact that until that point growth was mainly of an extensive type. When the 'extensive' sources of growth run out (i.e., one can no longer increase investment or manpower), one would need a much higher rate of technical progress to keep the growth of the Soviet economy at a level, say, of 2–3 per cent per annum. Until now, as far as technical progress in the strictest sense is concerned, Soviet performance appears 'to have been within the range of Western experience but inferior to that expected of a Western country at a comparable stage of development' (Bergson, 1983: 65). In other words, in the past, technical progress should have been more rapid in view of the USSR's initially low level, according to Bergson. According to Desai, it was indeed more rapid (Desai, 1976: 378) which also goes to underline the difficulties of accurate assessment.

Evaluation based on the always questionable results of a production function must be complemented by a qualitative assessment of the innovation process in the Soviet Union (see Berliner, 1976; Gicquiau, 1988). The advantages of a planned system are not negligible here. It provides the opportunity to selectively orientate investment towards the branches which most embody technological progress, as well as to ensure priority financing of research. In 1975, for instance, as a percentage of GNP, research financing accounted for 3.7 per cent compared to 2.2 per cent for the USA and FRG, and 1.5 per cent for France (see Bergson, 1983: 54). Finally, there is very little 'business secrecy' which might hinder the development of research. Along with these advantages, there is the prestigious position which science enjoys in the USSR, especially in the field of fundamental research, where the advances made by Soviet researchers are incontestable in certain fields (especially mathematics, plasma physics, nuclear physics, etc.) However, there are powerful forces curbing technological progress and its implementation, quite different from the problems holding up research and development in the West.

Among these forces is the priority given to defence. The main point here is not the production of total research spent on defence and space research, which American experts put at 50 per cent and British experts even higher (Kaser, 1988: 161), but the fact that the split between the civil and the military sector forbids cooperation between them, and spill-over from the defence sector. This is perhaps not enough to explain why the Soviet housewife has never heard of Teflon pots and pans, but the point is that her American counterpart has been able to take advantage of such techniques for a long time thanks to spin-offs from research on materials for military aircraft! Some experts (Cooper, in Amann and Cooper, 1986) consider that the separation between civilian and military industry has been exaggerated in Western writings. This is true in the sense that the military industry contributes to the production of civilian goods. But this contribution is not of the same kind as in the West. Enterprises in the military sectors are allowed to manufacture goods for the civilian sector, mainly consumer goods. They do so using their extra work force and materials, not their advanced technology. Even in such conditions, the goods manufactured by enterprises from the defence sector are better than the similar goods produced in the civilian sector. The consumers are well aware of this superiority in quality and try to select the items produced by the military industry when they can find them in the shops. In addition to allowing military enterprises to produce consumer goods, the gradual dismantling of the military industry and the conversion of the defence industries into civilian producers have been initiated in the USSR in 1988, and followed by Hungary. But again, the first steps are in line with tradition. A part of the factory manufacturing the MiG-29 fighter aircraft was converted to civilian activities and now manufacturers food processors, chandeliers, and toys. This does not entail spin-off effects, although it may be quite useful from the consumer's point of view. According to the director of the factory, the only really high technology item manufactured by the enterprise is a machine for packaging sugar (*Pravitel'stvennyi Vestnik* [Government Monitor] 1989, no. 4, 'The fighter and the toys').

Secondly, there is a traditional separation in the USSR (and in most Eastern European countries as well) between research and development carried on in research institutes and the application of this to mass production. Enterprises are not called upon to be innovative. The system of indicators used in production, as well as the price-fixing rules, encourage them to stick to routine. Around 1973–74, there were attempts to further integrate mass production and research by setting up units called 'research-production units', however the result was of no real significance. Another factor which serves to perpetuate this tendency to carry on with things as they are in the absence of internal or external competition. All this leads to excessively long delays between the appearance of an invention and its introduction in the economy. In the USSR, one out of four inventions is industrially developed in under two years, as against two out of three in the USA and FRG (Bergson, 1983: 62). The number of prototypes is steadily decreasing since 1971 (Gicquiau 1988: 10). Close reading of Soviet economic publications provides a wealth of illustrations of these characteristics within the system, and an OECD study also provides quite a number (Gomulka *et al.*, 1984: 39–42).

Is this to change under Gorbachev's rule? The priority to be given to efficient R and D and to its implementation in mass production has been stressed by the new leadership. Along with a reorganisation of the

academic research system (including a rise in salary for young researchers, mandatory retirement after seventy, and more flexibility in scientific
contacts with foreign countries), the ministerial research networks were
transferred in 1988 to 'self-supporting' schemes on the basis of contracts
with industry. But the traditional factors of Soviet technological retarda-
tion have not all been removed (Sinclair, ed., 1988).

How is one to make a more exact assessment of the technological lag
stemming from these factors? Here we must look at *direct comparisons*
for each technique or sector of technology in the West and East (most
usually in the USSR). The Centre for Russian and East European Studies
(CREES) of the University of Birmingham has carried out important
studies on this subject involving the collaboration of economists and
specialists of different technologies (see Amann, Cooper and Davies,
1977, and also Amann and Cooper, 1982). Table 7 allows a comparison
between the USSR and the USA from the point of view both of the date of
a given innovation and its actual implementation in industry (according
to Amann, Cooper and Davies, 1977: 55).

Table 7 clearly shows that even when the USSR leads the USA in a
basic invention, delays in implementing use of the invention in industry
are always more lengthy. Delays are only the same length in one case,
that of numerically controlled machine tools.

Can we conclude that the USSR is 'lagging behind' the industrialised
countries in the majority of industrial techniques? Is this gap to be
bridged, or is it growing wider?

Here we come into a highly subjective area which is very difficult to
quantify. Besides the dates of the innovations and the time taken for their
implementation, other characteristics of the equipment such as reliability, productivity, etc. must be considered. For example, one constant
feature of Soviet equipment is its great weight in comparison with
Western equipment for the same task, due to the abiding propensity of
planning in 'tonnes', which though officially abolished in 1965, has
survived all the reforms including Gorbachev's *perestroika*, and is still
referred to in Soviet articles. The use of a tonnage indicator discourages
the utilisation of lighter materials (e.g. plastics) in the construction of
such machines, which would only make it more difficult for enterprises to
fulfil their plans. The quality of intermediary products (metal, chemicals,
textiles) should also be taken into account as the often inferior quality of
such products lowers equipment performances.

Below we give a resumé of the conclusions drawn by several sectoral

Table 7. *Comparison of speed with which innovation is implemented in the USSR and the USA*

Technological field	USSR	USA
Oxygen steel-making:		
First industrial installation year	1956	1954
Number of years between first industrial installation and year output of oxygen steel reaching 20% of total steel output	16 years	12 years
Continuous casting of steel		
First industrial installation year	1955	1962
Number of years before procedure used for 5% of total steel output	17 years	7 years
Synthetic fibres		
Year first produced commercially (nylon)	1948	1938
Year output of synthetic fibres as a proportion of total chemical fibres output reaching 20%	25 years later	21 years later
Numerically controlled machine tools (ncmt)		
Year of first prototype	1958	1952
Number of years passed between ncmt used for 1% of mt output	13 years	13 years
Nuclear power stations		
First year commercial power	1954	1957
Number of years passed before procedure used for 2% of electricity output	21 years	14 years

Source: Amann, Cooper, Davies (1977), pp. 55–57.

studies (see Zaleski and Wienert, 1980; Zaleski, 1981; Amann and Cooper, 1986; Gicquiau, 1988).

Machine-tools

The USSR is the world's leading producer of machine-tools (over 250,000 in 1982 compared to under 70,000 in the USA) although its production has been on the wane since the end of the seventies. Of this total, there were 10,600 numerically controlled machines, that is, under 5 per cent compared to 10 per cent in the USA. In 1987, 156,200 machine-tools were produced, of which 13.5 per cent were numerically controlled, while the corresponding figures for the USA were 95,000 and 30 per cent. In the light of these figures, it is impossible to speak about backwardness in general terms. However, the machine pool is mainly composed of metal-cutting equipment, barely a quarter of the annual output of machine-tools is composed of metal-forming machines, compared to almost a third in the US case. About half the existing pool is over ten years of age. Chronic shortages in the production of spare parts means that around one-third of that stock of machines is under repair at any one time. Production is highly standardised with the same model being continued for fifteen to twenty years. It is up to the consumers to manufacture the particular devices they require. According to the Soviet experts themselves, in 1985, 14 per cent of the machine-tools reached the world technological level.

Computers

Computer production got underway in the USSR in 1953. This makes the Soviet Union one of the first countries to have developed such production, yet this field is known as one in which Soviet backwardness is greatest, which explains the political significance of controls on Western exports to the USSR. The extent to which the USSR lags behind can be seen in the paucity of the computer pool (accounting for probably less than 5 per cent of the world computer pool, if the potential of both the USSR and Eastern Europe are taken together). The development of micro-computing in the West means that quantitative comparisons are increasingly meaningless; the very underdevelopment of the USSR in this field is the most worrying aspect of its backwardness (see Snell in Amann and Cooper, eds., 1986). There were, at the end of 1988, at best 300,000, more likely about 200,000 personal computers; to match the developed nations' capacities the USSR ought to have more than 24 million. The USSR does not build 32-bit micro-processors; the Soviets claimed in 1988 to have designed one and were looking for Western cooperation to develop it. The USSR accounts for less than 3 per cent of the world production of micro-processors, and is lagging behind its Comecon partner, the GDR, which in 1988 announced the starting of large-scale production of 256-kilobit memories, while heading for the industrial production of 1-megabit memory chips.

The Soviet lag in comparison with the West is usually put in the Western press as anywhere between two and ten years, even fifteen for mainframe computers and super-computers. It can be seen in the following figures. Since the start of the seventies, the USSR has begun, in cooperation with its CMEA partners, to produce 'third generation' computers (with integrated circuits) called ES computers, which in Russian refers to 'Unified System'. The first models (series 1), launched in 1971–73, in terms of memory and calculation speed corresponded to the IBM-360 launched in the USA in 1964–65. The models of series 2 developed in 1978 met the standards of the IBM-370 produced in the USA in 1970–72. It is possible that, since 1980, the accent put on intra-Comecon cooperation in this field will help to bridge this gap. Reports from professionals regularly speak of great progress in reducing the lag, but one may wonder if such reports, widely quoted in the US press, are not more part of the political context, and as such, an attempt to justify export restrictions. Moreover, as in other fields, the failings of the Soviet system are not due solely to technology, in its stricter sense. The upkeep of the computer pool suffers from the same shortcomings as the pool of productive equipment in general. Training of computer experts falls very short of requirements. Public awareness drives, particularly among the younger generation, in the field of computers, so greatly stimulated in the West by the micro-processing boom, have hardly got off the ground. The owning of personal computers, even if their mass production was possible, is hardly likely for political reasons. There is a plan for introducing micro-computers in schools on a large scale, which was launched under Andropov, but this does not yet mean that everybody is soon to be allowed to buy a PC if he so wishes. Gicquiau (1988) states that for the period 1986–88 the total supply of PCs for sale to the public had not exceeded 3,000. In any case the PCs are sold without monitors, without software, and the floppy disks are almost impossible to find! The restrictions put on printing activities of individuals and cooperatives in 1988 are already a sign of political caution in this field. Software production is undertaken entirely on an individual, non-industrialised basis by the administrations and firms which require it, often with recourse to the 'second economy' or, since 1988, to the new cooperatives which have flourished in this area. The small capitalist software producers, or groups and associations of software users, which have sprung up in the industrialised world, have been for a long time incompatible with the USSR's industrial structure, concentrated as it is on major firms. Here also, the development of the cooperatives after 1988 might bring some flexibility, although software production is to be kept under state control. The joint ventures developed since 1987 occasionally deal with such activities. An instance is the first Soviet-French-Italian venture 'Interquadro' for computer services using French hardware, Italian marketing, and Soviet mathematical skills. But such small-scale experiments are clearly not enough to overcome powerful obstacles to an expansion of this sector.

Energy equipment

Shortcomings in Soviet production were highlighted in 1981–82, during
the 'gas pipeline case' (see chapter 6) and, for nuclear power equipment,
by the Chernobyl case. The greatest weaknesses of the Soviet techniques
do not belong to the nuclear field, spectacular though the Chernobyl
accident was, but to the oil and gas sector. Drilling is one such sector.
With the exhaustion of Soviet oil reserves, drilling must be undertaken to
ever-greater depths and through increasingly difficult geographical
strata, while the performance of Soviet equipment in these conditions is
inferior to that of German, Japanese, or French equipment. It is acknowledged that only one-third of the drilling equipment may be considered as
meeting world standards (Gicquiau, 1988: 12). For the transport of
hydrocarbons, the USSR has manufactured the majority of pipes required
for the network (in 1987: 86,400 km of oil pipelines and 197,000 km of
gas pipelines) as well as the compressors for them. But it was only in
1983 that the USSR began the production of large diameter 56-inch
pipes. Only in 1981 did it start production of 16 and 25mw turbines
(OTA, 1981: 63). Finally, in this sector as in others, the USSR is failing to
produce, or is producing insufficient computerised surveillance and
assistance equipment for the main technological process.

Nuclear energy equipment production was considered as an altogether
self-sufficient branch until the Chernobyl accident, which prompted the
Soviets to turn to the West for help in designing atomic power stations
using high temperature reactors, and for checking security devices on its
pressurised water reactors (October 1988).

What are the conclusions to be drawn from this analysis? Most experts
feel that there is a gap between the USSR and the West, less at the
prototype stage than at the application stage, and that this gap is not
growing any smaller – at best it is remaining stable. This conclusion
should, however, be qualified by several comments.

The main cause of this technological gap lies in the organisation of
research and of industrial production in the USSR, as well as in the
specific nature of centralised planning. The Gorbachev leadership is
deeply committed to change both. The very fact that many indicators of
modernisation deteriorated in 1987 (for instance, the number of new
types of machinery created per year, the share of them surpassing the best
world standards) only shows that the statistics are more credible than
before; and some of these indicators did improve in 1988, for example,

the share of new machinery in total machine-building production. This might also be said of the very harsh criticisms expressed in press articles about the state of Soviet R and D, which shows greater *glasnost* or openness. But, in any case, the outcome of such measures as are undertaken since 1986 cannot quickly be felt.

In any case, the Soviet 'lag' is neither absolute nor generalised. In certain sectors of R and D, Soviet industry is known for its good performance, for example, continuous steel casting, high-voltage power transmission (Hewett, 1988: 216–18), special coatings, welding, electromagnetic casting of aluminium, and specialised ships. It may also be suggested, however with many reservations, that the characteristics of basic Soviet equipment (extreme standardisation, robustness, lack of sophistication) correspond more to the needs of consumers (in the USSR and those countries to which it exports, i.e., Eastern Europe and the developing world) than do the characteristics of more sophisticated equipment made in the West. This is also the basis for the statement according to which the USSR should not complain so much about restrictions on high technology exports, as what it needs is more standard technology and the skills for using it rationally, rather than very advanced equipment which is often doomed to remain idle.

In this context, it is therefore possible to speak of Soviet and Eastern European technological dependance on imports from the West?

Technology transfers and economic growth in the Soviet Union and Eastern Europe

It is first necessary to define the meaning of the term 'technology transfer'. It may be defined as 'a process whereby the productivity of resources of one country can be increased by the transmission from other countries of information or of products and processes embodying that information' (Hanson, 1981: 14); or as 'a process whereby innovations (new products or know-how) achieved in one country are transferred to another to be used there' (Zaleski and Wienert, 1980: 12).

The transfer may be made in the form of incorporated technology (in equipment or products), or non-incorporated technology (the providing of information, the sale of patents and licences, technical assistance). It may increase the potential of the recipient country, or it may not; the outcome of the process is irrelevant to the definition. According to the nature of the transfer, it may be considered as negotiable, i.e., commercial (the purchase and sale of products, industrial cooperation) or non-negotiable (the reading of scientific texts, the once-and-for-all acquisition of a given piece of equipment for copying and reproduction, industrial espionage).

The second form is impossible to assess and very difficult to control. The myth of the non-negotiable transfer from West to East is deeply rooted in public opinion and maintained in periods of political tension, to the point of giving credence to the idea that the USSR and Eastern Europe have been modernised thanks to the secret copying of Western machinery. As 'theories', these ideas belong to the realm of folklore and the spy thriller, even if isolated cases of this do indeed exist. The 'Farewell Case' which emerged in 1983, motivated the expulsion of forty-seven diplomats from the Soviet Embassy in Paris, and was, later on, cleverly arranged by talented journalists, is a good example of tremendous fiction associated with rather disappointing relevations on the way the KGB collected information from the West in 1979–80 (see Labbé in Bertsch, 1988: 201). Something quite different is the systematic gleaning of accessible scientific documentation from journals, from trade fairs and exhibition brochures, including reports read at conferences, and interviews with specialists, etc. Experts from the East do indeed familiarise themselves with new techniques, with irreproachable effi-ciency. If we in the West were more efficient in reading all the material available from the East (and if more of us were trained to do so) we too might learn much more than we used to do.

The impact of non-negotiable transfers cannot be seriously assessed. True, one often finds statements of the type 'spying has allowed the Soviet Union to reduce its lag in (whatsoever) field by x years, or to save y million (billion) roubles (dollars) in domestic expenses (imports)', but this cannot be taken as a scientific assessment. Should we indulge in impressionistic statements, our guess would be that the Soviet 'spies' are likely to be on average as (little) efficient as any Soviet worker performing a task for an administration, and that, once obtained, if any, valuable information is very likely to be used in the same (inefficient) way as even quite valuable domestic innovations are, just kept aside because there is not enough incentives to make a productive use of it.

This section is thus to be limited to negotiable transfers and in particu-lar to the transfers of incorporated technology.

Trade of patents and pure (non-incorporated) licences is indeed also very difficult to measure. Statistics for these items are almost non-existent in the East and highly inaccurate in the West. According to a Soviet author (Simanovsky, 1980), the USSR and Eastern Europe's share in the world licence trade was 10 per cent at the end of the seventies, but this total also includes intra-CMEA movements. A compilation by a British author (Hill, 1983: 33–36) which deals with data up to 1976, shows that in 1975 the East had purchased a little under 2,000 licences for around $240 million and had sold 700 licences for $30 million. The USSR and Poland figure as the main buyers, followed by Czechoslovakia and Hungary; Czechoslovakia is the main seller, followed by the USSR, Hungary and the GDR. These figures, which are both old and questionable, suggest that the flow of licences is probably ten times higher from West to East than *vice versa*, but do not allow for any analysis of the impact of such transfers. The final OECD study on East–West technology transfer closing a series of country studies (Wienert and Slater, 1986) is quite cautious in commenting on comparable data borrowed from UN/ECE surveys and various other sources. The OECD study also identifies the USSR, Poland and Czechoslovakia as the main buyers of licences, but unlike Hill's study it puts the GDR in the list; Hungary is the most active Eastern country in incorporating licencing agreements in industrial cooperation (Wienert and Slater, 1986: chapter 7). It suggest that the main shift in licencing arrangements between the seventies and the eighties is the tying of licencing contracts to the export of goods manufactured under the licence, instead of using the licence primarily for domestic production.

As in the OECD study, we are obliged to keep to a circumscribed view, which is the only really practicable one, i.e., the effects of equipment sales (class 7 of the SITC).

A question immediately arises here, however. Should all products of class 7 be taken into consideration or should one concentrate on high technology sales only? The first method has the advantage of (apparent) simplicity in its favour. The second is of greater practical use if we are seeking to obtain a list of high-technology products whose export to the USSR should be limited in terms of trade policy, or of politics generally.

THE IMPACT OF EQUIPMENT TRANSFERS

A certain number of works have evaluated the impact of the import of machines from the West and have reached differing conclusions. These studies use very different methodologies, and are not always comparable.

For the USSR, the American economists, D. Green and H. Levine, have calculated the effects of the import of Western machinery on Soviet economic growth within the framework of their econometric model Sovmod, for the period 1960–74 and (projected) 1975–80. They used a production function of the Cobb–Douglas type. They estimated the ratio between accumulated capital of Western origin and total capital stock in industry to be 1.5–2 per cent. For the oil, chemical and engineering industries, the figure reaches 3–6 per cent. The productivity of imported equipment is fourteen times greater than the marginal productivity of Soviet equipment, so that for an annual growth rate of 6.6 per cent of industrial production, 1.2 per cent (i.e. almost 20 per cent) can be attributed to imported equipment. (A later calculation for the period 1973–78, using Sovmod III version, yields a ratio of 8 to 1 for the productivity of imported equipment compared to that of domestic equipment). On the other hand, S. Rosefielde, covering the same period (1960–73) considers that the contribution of Western imports has been negligible. According to this study, technical progress born of Soviet research and development has been the principal motor of growth. One American author, M. Weitzman, acknowledges that 'so far, we cannot determine any influence of technology transfer on Soviet economic growth using existent data. It's too bad, but nothing consistent seems to emerge from the numbers' (Weitzman, 1979: 168). The British economist, S. Gomulka, using a different method which does not refer to a production function, comes to the conclusion that the import of Western machines has contributed 0.3–0.6 percentage points to Soviet economic growth and 1–3 points annually in the other Eastern European countries. A survey of these studies may be found in Hanson (1981: 144–45) and Gomulka, Nove and Holliday (1984: 20–28). Later, Brada and Hoffman (1985) show that the productivity of imported machinery cannot be proven to be significantly higher than that of domestic versions. However, this may be due to the fact that the Western equipment is not fully used. Also, the use of Western equipment may help to increase the efficiency of the domestic technology. The final OECD study (Wienert and Slater, 1986; chapter 8) adds a few references which do not change the general picture ('Western capital goods make an appreciable contribution to Eastern economic performance, though it is not always possible to pinpoint it', p. 395).

The difficulties of these studies and the misleading nature of their results lie, first and foremost, in a methodological problem which is difficult to solve and which has already been raised in chapter 1. In order to estimate the contribution to Soviet growth, for instance, made by imported equipment, this equipment must be valued in domestic currency and we must calculate the price in domestic roubles from dollars (or 'devisa-roubles', which comes to the same thing). We must then assume that available Soviet information on capital stock is reliable, something which is certainly open to question (see Lavigne, 1968). Finally, we have all the technical problems of econometric studies, particularly problems associated with the use of production functions. In conclusion, it will be noted that, in spite of the generally negative view authors take of the efficiency of the Soviet system, it is still felt that imported equipment has an effect after one or two years. Yet, even the most cursory reading of Soviet publications shows that imported equipment is often under-employed and installed only after long delays.

Researchers have then two alternative options. Either they concentrate on the qualitative side; or they limit themselves to cases which allow them to work on 'physical' figures.

Some authors consider that the import of equipment is privileged because it saves time and thus acts as an 'economic accelerator' to fight against domestic delays (Sokoloff, 1983: 158). Businessmen confirm this view, especially in the case of the import of turn-key plants (this form of import was however dramatically curtailed in the eighties). As all the tasks of coordinating deliveries of subcontractors, installing the whole complex of machinery, controlling the initial operation of the plant, instead of being undertaken by various agencies under the conditions of administrative planning, are entirely performed by the Western supplier, the gain in time may be of five to ten years. The Western supplier must deliver everything to strict deadlines which are to be met at the risk of penalties, and he must also guarantee the perfect functioning of the equipment supplied. If this much is asked from the Soviet supplier, deliveries will not arrive in time, some supplies will be faulty, there will be no spare parts, etc. Zaleski confirms: 'Soviet machinery imports serve above all ... to provide a kind of spare tyre for faults in centralised administrative planning. Catching up in the technological race is most probably of only secondary importance' (Zaleski, 1980: 354).

Sectoral studies only corroborate these findings. The seminal one is the study by Hanson on fertilisers, to which he returns in a 1981 work. The chemical industry in general absorbed a quarter of machinery purchases from the West between 1960 and 1977. The introduction of chemicals in agriculture was raised as a priority as early as 1958. The USSR had at its disposal the entire range of raw materials necessary but lacked production capacities and only had traditional technologies. The import option was taken up. For the most part this meant the import of turn-key plants. L. Kostandov, the man who for twenty years was minister of the chemical industry and whom his Western partners are unanimous in considering one of the century's great businessman, played a determining role here. The impact of such an individual signals that crucial decisions may be determined by a subjective factor and not only by policy choices. According to Hanson, at the close of the seventies, half of the ammonia production came from plants imported from the West. The proportion is about the same for urea production and even greater for artificial fertilisers. On the other hand, the USSR is not very dependent on the outside world for potash processing equipment. As for the production of phosphate fertilisers, imported technology is mainly Polish and this is a case for successful intra-Comecon cooperation. Hanson concludes that 'given the situation of a backward agriculture and a backward chemical industry . . . the mixture of domestic inputs, imported from both Eastern and Western Europe in the various sub-branches of this industry . . . suggests that the application of this (technology imports) policy has been particularly well-handled' (Hanson, 1981: 181).

A complete presentation of case studies carried out in particular branches is provided in Gomulka *et al.* (1984) by Holliday (pp. 74–77). It shows the USSR's great dependence on technological imports for a certain number of branches besides the chemical industry (the automobile industry, oil and gas, textiles, clothing, wood processing and paper pulp industry). Conclusions differ as to future import developments. Most authors are of the opinion that this dependence will continue into the future, no doubt for a rather long time. Others opt for a growing measure of autonomy.

This leads us to the prospects for a growth in machinery imports by the socialist countries. Developments in the share of SITC class 7 in total imports from the West since 1975 (see Table 5, Appendix), as well as trends in its volume, do not provide for a clear picture.

Why has there been a drop in imports of equipment, especially in the eighties? Many reasons may be suggested. Financial difficulties encouraged import substitution when possible. The deflationary policies adopted by certain small Eastern European countries led to a dramatic fall in domestic investment along with cuts in imports. The costs of introducing foreign techniques became more widely acknowledged and led to the abandoning of certain types of imports. Finally, for investments made in the form of industrial cooperation with the West, there is a growing desire to include some domestic technology, which can be explained both by the wish to avoid hold-ups due to Western restrictions on high technology exports and by the attempt to gain a fuller mastery of the production process.

This fall in imports went hand in hand with a change in the nature of the purchases. There has been a shift from the purchase of turn-key plants to the purchase of individual items of equipment, or the concluding of contracts for revamping operations. According to Hanson, this sees the end of the era of growth stemming from imports (Hanson, 1982; see chapter 1). In the French case, there has been indeed a dramatic fall in the share of major contracts with the East, which in 1973–77 amounted on average to over 18 per cent of the French total sales of large equipment abroad, and in 1983 to only 3 per cent (*Moci*, 16 April 1983: 20–21).

At the close of the eighties, as a decade before, there is a need to deal separately with the Soviet and the East European cases. Eastern European countries have experienced more or less harshly the difficulties of adjustment in the first part of the eighties. They resumed investment and machinery imports in the mid-eighties. Already in 1987 the share of machinery and equipment accounted for 36 per cent of total imports from the West, unparalleled since the mid-sixties (*Economic Bulletin for Europe*, 1988, vol. 40: 33). Within this commodity group, the growth of trade relating to transport equipment (cars and aircraft) is particularly striking. The first deals in airliner sales occurred in 1988 (Boeing to Poland and Romania, Airbus to GDR), and also the resumption of talks between Western (including Japanese, and Korean) carmakers and Eastern countries (Poland, Czechoslovakia, Hungary) for complex deals involving a radical modernising of the car industry through industrial cooperation and export-oriented, currency-saving contractual provisions. As for the Soviet Union, while the *perestroika* spirit might clearly allow for large imports of machinery, class 7 imports declined steadily from 1985, and seem to have borne the brunt of the adjustment required by the falling price of oil. Some improvement in Soviet imports of equipment was noticeable in 1988. The course taken by the leadership in favour of consumption, and the cuts decided on in domestic investment, should, however, lead to a concentration of imports machinery on equipment for light and food industry.

This is not to say that technology trade is now in an impasse. But, in the future, any new large deals will have to be self-financed and/or contribute significantly to domestic modernisation. Western exporters will thus have to be imaginative in terms of financial arrangements, technology transfer provisions and market-sharing schemes, all this in dealing with a much larger group of decentralised partners than before. The East is no longer self-centred as in the seventies, but self-confident enough to claim to play the role of a newly industrialising economic region. Such an expression to be found in the East European press as 'we are a new Singapore', inaccurate as it may seem, shows a definite change in attitude. The East no longer pretends to be a partner of equal strength, but wants to make the best out of its real assets. Compared to the former 'NICs', it has some indisputable advantages, such as the geographical proximity and undeniable cultural links with Western Europe, its major target. There is a long way to go, however. Studies have shown that the Eastern European countries have lost significant market shares on the Western market to the NICs in the seventies and early eighties (Poznanski, 1986; and ECE/UN, 1982, 1983 and 1989: see chapter 4). The OECD project (Wienert and Slater, 1986, chapter 8) on East–West technology transfer concluded that the 'boomerang effect', i.e., the impact of machinery imports from the West on Eastern exports has been very weak for Eastern Europe, and only partly significant for the USSR.

Future developments are, however, largely dependent on the relaxation of Western export controls. This issue is linked with the impact of high technology, to which we now turn.

THE IMPACT OF ADVANCED TECHNOLOGY IMPORTS

What is 'high' or 'advanced' technology exactly? There exists no universally accepted definition. Studies by the OECD (1970) and the Economic Commission for Europe (ECE/UN 1976 and 1977) have identified 'high research-intensive' goods as opposed to high labour-, capital-, or natural resource-intensive. This classification is further qualified in a volume published in 1980 by the OECD (Zaleski-Wienert, 1980: 80ff) which compares it to the list compiled in 1977 in the United States by the Bureau of East–West Trade (which became, in 1981, the Office of Trade and Investment Analysis) of the Department of Commerce. This list is regularly updated for 'Quantification of Western Exports of High-Technology Products to Communist Countries' (see Martens, 1986). The US list is somewhat narrower and more specific than the lists constructed in the same country for an overall analysis of high technology trade and retains only the 'strategic' items. The retained items belong to the following categories (all from SITC classes 7 and 8): aircraft and parts, nuclear reactors, computers and office equipment, metal-working machine-tools, glass-working machinery, roller-bearings, telecommunications equipment, optical and medical instruments, measuring and control instruments, tubes, transistors, photocells, photographic films, etc.

Whatever the definition, high technology is not a major item in total exports to the East, and its share strongly declined in the eighties as the share of capital goods exports overall. According to a French study (Haegel, 1983), the share of high technology exports in total exports of the OECD countries rose to 14 per cent in 1977 then steadily decreased to less than 9 per cent in 1981 – the study stops there; due to the tightening of export controls from 1982 on we may assume that it has remained at this level, if not lower, since then. The shares of the Western suppliers and of the Eastern buyers on this market are roughly in line with their shares in East–West trade in general. One may note, however, that the FRG's share is higher, both in the direction of the USSR and of Eastern Europe (30 per cent and over 40 per cent respectively as a total of Western exports of these items, for the period 1975–81, against 20 and 25 per cent of total exports to the East).

Studies carried out by the Office of Technology Assessment attached to the US Congress (OTA, 1979 revised 1983, and 1981) as well as studies published under the aegis of the Congress (1979 and 1986) have compiled a register of the qualitative characteristics of high technology imports by the USSR. Thus, in the field of energy, the USSR imports electronic surveillance and monitoring equipment for oil and gas prospecting and transportation, sophisticated drilling equipment such as submersible pumps or recovery technology (*gazlift* supplied by French firms), deep-drilling pipes and the equipment used in laying them, large-diameter pipes for hydrocarbon transportation and the compression stations this requires. In the field of machine-tools, the USSR imports special, highly sophisticated machines, especially numerically controlled machines. As for computers, around 4 per cent of the pool at the end of the seventies was of Western origin. Large purchases of computers were made especially during the years 1972–78. Half of these were bought directly from the USA but if we consider the origin of computer equipment purchased elsewhere, 85 per cent of it comprised American material (Tasky, 1979: 518). These imports have covered the types of equipment not manufactured in the USSR, which have better performance and are sold with software not yet developed in the USSR. This flow of exports was strongly affected by the policy of restrictions on such exports in the eighties.

Restrictions on Western technological exports to the East

In the area of East–West relations, this is definitely the subject which, since 1980, has given rise to most writing, much of it polemicised. Among these writings, the articles in the press have often tipped over into sensationalism.

Let us first outline the multilateral 'institutional' framework of the restrictions policy. At its centre is Cocom, set up in 1949 under pressure from the USA, which, since 1947, has declared an embargo on the export of strategic goods to communist countries. The Exports Control Act of 1949 laid down a code for the implementation of this policy on the national US level. As dispensers of Marshall Aid, the USA persuaded their allies to set up a consultative group (Coordinating Committee for Multilateral Export Controls, hence Cocom) which started to operate in 1950. Cocom membership is made up of all NATO countries except Iceland, and plus Japan. The neutral countries, Switzerland, Austria, Sweden, and Finland, are therefore not members; Spain was admitted in 1986, two years after joining Nato. This body has its headquarters in Paris, in an annex of the US embassy. It has a modest budget ($600,000 to $700,000 in 1983, according to D. Marsh in the *Financial Times* of 30 December 1983) and a small secretariat with a staff of fifteen. The secrecy which members seek to preserve in their always informal functions, has been reduced somewhat in the last few years. A permanent committee meets regularly (once or twice in a fortnight) to revise the lists of products subject to restrictions and consider appeals for special dispensation. This committee includes the representatives of the member states, who are officials of their respective embassies in Paris (in the case of France, it is an official of the Ministry of Foreign Affairs). Often, experts are required to participate in technical meetings and are sent by the national ministries (of Defence or Industry) or approached as consultants for their expertise in a given technical field. Regular, high-level ministerial meetings, held every two years since 1982, evaluate the activities of the organisation. The USA would like to transform Cocom into a genuine international organisation with greater visibility and codified rules of conduct. Their allies oppose this, particularly the host country which has never officially recognised the existence of Cocom on its territory. However, some moves have been made in this direction, such as setting up an executive committee meeting twice a year, at the beginning of 1988.

Cocom's basic function lies in the compiling of lists of products under restriction. In actual fact, there are three lists: the munitions list (military and associated materials), the atomic energy list (fissile material, reactors, etc.), and the industrial list. The latter breaks down into a further three sections: products subject to embargo, exportable products subject to quotas, products subject to surveillance and information exchange.

The industrial list of commodities subject to embargo, for which a licence must be agreed upon when any Cocom member proposes any of its items for export to communist countries, divides up into ten groups: metal-working machinery, oil and petro-chemical equipment, electrical and power-generating equipment, general industrial equipment, transportation equipment, precision and electronic instruments, metals and minerals, chemicals and metalloids, petroleum products, rubber and associated products. The list has been revised every two or three years since 1949. Until 1976 there was a reduction in the number of the individual items within these groups (from 270 items overall to 149). Obviously, it is impossible to determine accurately the proportion of goods subject to embargo in overall Western exports to the East. In principle, it should be nil! But exceptions have been granted. In 1977, the last year for which data is available, the value of such exceptions reached 0.8 per cent of total exports from OECD countries to the East, and 5 per cent of advanced technology exports. To this must be added the 'leaks'. These include the exports of products under Cocom embargo by members themselves, either directly or by reexportation circuits and sales originating in non-member states, in particular Sweden and Switzerland. The press often carries reports of complex circuitious routes of this kind. For example, at the start of 1984, checks intercepted American computer equipment sold to a German firm, which had been sent to South Africa then reexported to Sweden, from where it was probably to be sent to the USSR (*International Herald Tribune*, 25 May 1984). Such cases are probably not exceptional, but to then extrapolate that they represent an important share of technological sales to the USSR would be stretching the imagination. The figure of 3–5 per cent as a percentage of exports subjected to embargo in total Western sales to the USSR, quoted by the *Financial Times* (David Buchan, 24 January 1984) is probably exaggerated. For all that, it is impossible to confirm or disprove it completely.

The recent development of embargoes has brought about two new features which did not exist at the end of the seventies: the use of embargos as a sanction and the appearance of deep splits between the USA and their allies on the concept of embargoes.

FROM THE SECURITY EMBARGO TO THE SANCTION EMBARGO

The idea of sanctions was totally absent from initial objectives for imposing embargoes. The USA was not seeking to 'punish' the USSR in any way just after the war. They sought to weaken it so as to bring about the downfall of the new communist system. The main purpose of the controls was to deprive the USSR and its allies of goods which could be used for military purposes as well as goods which were likely to boost their economic growth.

The difficulty lies in the definition of the strategic criteria. What is a strategic product? On what basis is its export to be limited? These questions were greatly debated in the USA at a time (1975–76) when Cocom seemed destined to dissolve sooner or later and when exceptions granted to products which actually figured on the industrial list were becoming more and more numerous. The general idea was that one should primarily control 'dual-use' technologies with military as well as civilian applications. An official report called 'the Bucy Report' (*An Analysis of Export Control*, 1976) defined 'critical technologies' as 'technologies that would make a significant contribution to the military potential of any country and that may prove detrimental to US national security'. On this basis, the 1979 Export Administration Act adopted by the Congress of the United States recommended that the Secretary of Defense should develop a list of 'militarily critical technologies' which might be integrated in the US Commodity Control list, which is itself significantly larger than the Cocom list (McIntyre, 1987: 116). This integration was never achieved. Later on, a National Academy of Sciences Report (*Balancing the National Interest*, 1987) recommended that the US and the other Cocom members develop a 'community of common controls in dual use technology' (Nau, 1987: 390). The report used the wording 'strategic' rather than 'critical' and included among the strategic goods and technologies, apart from military items, 'items in which proscribed nations have a deficiency that hinders [the] development and production [of military items] that they are not likely to overcome within a reasonable period' (quoted from Bertsch, ed. 1987: 447). Finally, if one assumes that these 'critical', 'strategic', 'dual-use' technologies are bound to be 'high' technologies one also has to solve the definition problem of what is to be considered as 'high'.

The definition problems having been solved, the rationale of *national security* restrictions is, however, still not clarified.

1   If the primary objective is to curb military advancement, restrictions must be concentrated on all technologies with military applications (including dual-use technologies) and on these alone, with a no-exceptions policy. This idea proves very difficult in practice. It requires perfect concertation, and no leaks. It also requires an agreement as to what constitutes technologies with military applications, which are not necessarily advanced technologies. For example, all sales of truck factories to the East would be proscribed, as all trucks may have military uses. Great controversy arose over the giant Kama truck factory constructed in the USSR with Western credits at the start of the seventies. On the other hand, a whole multitude of advanced non-military technologies may have military applications, electronic games included.

2   If the idea of national security is understood in a broader sense, the East should be deprived of access to all advanced technologies which they do not have or which they have not sufficiently developed. In this case, all goods embodying standard technology may be exported, even if they may be used by the military (i.e. transport equipment), but transfers of advanced technology should be stopped. However, it often proves difficult to separate advanced technology from the industrial equipment incorporating it (e.g., electronic surveillance equipment which is part of a traditional installation; or a procedure for processing a raw material or intermediary product, delivered along with certain equipment). Industrialists have managed to adapt these requirements. An example of the first case is an episode in the gas pipeline affair. In 1980, France concluded a contract for delivery to the USSR (by the Thomson company) of surveillance equipment for the Euro-Siberian gas pipeline after several weeks of hold-ups in negotiations while more 'simplified' techniques than initially agreed upon were sought. The second case is

illustrated by another French deal. After the withdrawal of the American steel company Armco, which was to construct a silicon-plating factory in association with Nippon Steel, in the wake of the restrictions introduced by the Carter administration in 1980, the Creusot-Loire company signed the contract with the USSR though the French government had undertaken not to substitute for withdrawn American supplies. The French argument which though logical was not accepted by the Americans, justified the contract on the grounds that purely Soviet technology and know-how would be used in the manufacture of the silicon-plated sheet metal, with France supplying only the equipment.

3   Another version of the 'national security' argument runs as follows: all technological exports (even traditional ones) should be curbed in areas of decisive importance for the potential of the country. This was one of the arguments put forward in the case of the Siberian gas pipeline. Since the development of energy production is crucial for the USSR, as it determines its future hard currency gains, the USSR should be deprived of all Western energy equipment.

4   'National security' might be extended to economic security considerations in the form of the 'rope' argument (after the famous words attributed to Lenin although nobody could ever convincingly demonstrate the source, 'the capitalists will sell us the rope with which to hang them'). According to this rationale, one should avoid selling the East technologies which it could use to compete with Western countries on Western markets. There are few areas where this could pose a real threat. However this would suggest the following policies: (a) a stricter embargo on all equipment allowing mass production, whatever the technology, for instance, the sales of chemical turn-key plants in the seventies undoubtedly created an export potential which proved competitive on Western markets. Looking toward the nineties, such a rationale would lead to strict control on equipment sales and joint ventures in the field of car manufacturing, and such plans developed by Western (German and Italian), Japanese and Korean car-makers have already been attacked in the USA; (b) it would logically lead to stricter control on sales to the smaller East European countries because they are more competitive than the USSR.

5   The 'national security' argument could run into new contradictions. Nuclear equipment is on the Cocom list and the only exception has been the sale of nuclear reactors by Canada to Romania in the seventies. In October 1988 two West German factories agreed to supply a nuclear

reactor to the USSR, pending Cocom exception. This unique deal, as the USSR has up to 1988 exclusively relied on its own technology, raises complex issues. Clearly, nuclear power equipment might be used for the defence industry. But, the aim pursued by the Soviet government is to increase safety in nuclear reactors by using Western technology. Should one forbid the deal at the risk of contributing indirectly to a new Chernobyl?

The *sanction argument* (which in US official wording is euphemistically called the 'foreign policy' argument) as a rationale for embargo emerged at the end of the seventies. The national security and the sanction arguments overlap. An embargo on high-technology sales may be justified on both grounds. On the other hand, sanctions may include measures other than embargoes on high technology, and actually have done so (see Table 8). But the 'sanction' argument has its own logic.

The demise of *détente* in the mid-seventies brought about the use of sanctions, following a period when rather than punishing the USSR for its acts, one sought to influence its behaviour through *linkage* (linking commercial or financial advantages to political concessions) or *leverage* (pressure through economic arguments).

The sanctions, as Table 8 shows, have had little impact on the East (and more impact on the Eastern European countries than on the USSR, contrary to the aims they pursued). They have had a damaging impact on the Western economies (through contract losses) and on the Western alliance. There are several reasons for this:

1 They have been followed reluctantly by the allies of the United States. The pipeline case (see chapter 6 on energy) makes the point. More generally, the EEC, which agreed to follow the grain embargo (which only really affected France among the EEC members) did not join the embargo on all sales of energy equipment decided by the US in December 1981 (including items not on the Cocom list). The only sanction the EEC agreed upon was a ban on manufactured imports from the USSR, which in principle could not affect more than 2 per cent of imports and in fact was implemented only marginally because it did not apply to contracts already signed. The only compliance with the US demands was the 'no-exception' policy decided in March 1980, according to which Cocom committed itself not to grant any exceptions for items on the industrial list.

2 Sanctions have created lasting acrimony between the US and Western Europe (and also within Western Europe). The Pegard case in

Table 8. *The rationale of US economic sanctions against the USSR and Poland*

Date of events triggering sanctions	Circumstances giving rise to sanction	Sanction	Country sanctioned	Effects
End 1974	Denial of the right or opportunity to emigrate ('Jackson–Vanik Amendment') relates in fact to Jewish emigration	Deprivation of MFN treatment Non-eligibility for US government supported export credits	All countries; in fact, specifically the USSR	MFN status lost for the USSR until (?) US officially supported credits not available to the USSR
July 1978	Trials against dissidents in the USSR	Ban placed on sale of a computer for the Olympic Games of 1980 Surveillance of all sales of oil equipment	USSR	USSR turns to French, German and British suppliers From Sept. 1978, sales resume (with a Dresser licence for the manufacture of drilling equipment)
Dec. 1979	Entry of Soviet troops in Afghanistan	Partial embargo on grain exports (joined by the EEC)	USSR	The USSR turns to other suppliers (Canada, Argentina). Embargo lifted in Apr. 1981
		Boycott of 1980 Moscow Olympic Games	USSR	Games held with 79 nations. In 1984, USSR and Eastern Europe boycott Los Angeles Games
		Embargo on sales of superphosphates by the US (sales linked to compensation agreement with Occidental Petroleum)	USSR	USSR has difficulties in producing fertilisers. Turns to other suppliers (possibly also US suppliers through intermediaries). Does not suspend its own ammonia deliveries. Embargo lifted Apr. 1981
		Stricter rules on licencing of high-technology exports	USSR	No major project affected. Some shifting away to Western European suppliers

Date	Event		Measures	Effects
13 Dec. 1981	Martial Law declared in Poland	USSR	Restraints on fishing and landing rights, scaling down of bilateral exchanges	Symbolic effect as far as bilateral exchanges are concerned. Fishing rights partly reestablished July 1984
		Poland	Annulment of MFN status Non-renewal of Poland's line of credit insurance from the Exim Bank Halt of official US food aid Suspension of Polish landing rights in the US Tighter Cocom restrictions (concertation sought with Allies)	Substantially damaging effects, in particular for food aid. Sanctions lifted in July 1984, except for the MFN status (reestablished in 1987) and the access to US credit (reestablished in 1989)
		USSR	Increased controls on exports of oil and gas equipment; suspension of issuance of export licences Postponement of negotiations on a new long-term grain agreement Suspension of negotiations on a new maritime agreement, Aeroflot service suspension, non-renewal of US–Soviet exchange agreements Tighter Cocom restrictions; 'no-exceptions principle' agreed upon in concertation with Cocom members (Jan. 1982)	US fails to achieve suspension of gas pipeline contracts concluded between their Allies and the USSR (in 1982) Ban on oil and gas equipment lifted in Jan. 1987 New grain agreement signed 25 Aug. 1983 Resumption of exchange cultural programs in 1986 No-exceptions principle lifted in 1989

Source: John P. Hardt, Kate S. Tomlinson, 'The potential role of Western policy towards Eastern Europe in East–West trade', in A. Becker (ed.), *Economic Relations with the USSR, Issues for the Western Alliance*, Lexington, D. C. Heath, 1983: 76–133; information on post-1982 events collected from the press and various sources.

Belgium (in 1984) when Belgium was forced to withdraw an export authorisation delivered to a machine-building company to sell a sophisticated machine-tool in the USSR, created a political anti-American sensation in that country. Western European countries have much more at stake in terms of deals with the USSR and Eastern Europe than has the USA. Industrial employment, and sometimes the survival of some Western firms, depends on contracts with the East. In Europe it was suggested that the US government might use Cocom rules to reduce the threats posed to US firms by competition with European firms on the Soviet market. Even if this is probably not the case the thought exists, and it is fuelled by some disturbing facts. For instance, on the eve of a presidential election, the firm Caterpillar was allowed to deliver pipe-laying bulldozers despite restrictions on sales of energy equipment (1980) and, in similar circumstances, in 1984, an export licence was grated to sell submersible drilling pipes to the USSR. The Toshiba case in 1987, when Toshiba was accused of having sold the USSR advanced milling machines that allowed it to develop submarines with quieter propellers, was a clear failure for the US government. The sanctions against the Japanese firm, which were meant to ban Toshiba products from sales in the USA, had to be reduced to symbolic measures – a three-year ban on government contracts – as American firms dependent on Toshiba supplies successfully lobbied against the general ban.

3   Although Cocom rules have been followed more effectively in the eighties than in the seventies, there have been many leaks through non-members (often concerning exports from Cocom members diverted to the East). In consequence, the US government has exerted definite pressure on non-Cocom members to make them comply with Cocom rules. Austria, Sweden and Switzerland bowed to the pressure and, following them, Singapore, India, Korea, Australia – the latter country applied for membership in April 1989. The growing number of significant technology exporters should become a matter of increasing concern. If one assumes that the East is gradually being overtaken in high technology by the newly industrialising economies, then, according to this logic, more countries should be added to the list. The Latin American NIEs (Brazil, Argentina, Mexico) might be eligible. Notwithstanding the fact that the developing countries concerned are (with the exception of India) either strongly opposed to the communist regimes or at least not well disposed towards them, they do not disregard the Soviet and East European market and their potential role as suppliers of high technology might

become actual. But, in this case, the controls will be increasingly difficult to manage.

4 The final problem, when embargoes are used as sanctions and not exclusively on national security grounds, is when to end them. The Gorbachev policies exemplify the problem. Assuming that the 'no-exceptions' rule was a sanction against the invasion of Afghanistan (let us add, Polish martial law), why should it be continued when the Soviet troops have pulled out of Afghanistan and when national reconciliation is virtually achieved in Poland? The same applies to Poland itself. All this leads to questions about the future of Cocom itself.

WHAT FUTURE FOR COCOM?

Since 1980 Cocom has undoubtedly strengthened. The no-exception policy was a major development in this sense. The revised lists of 1984 only continued this development. Restrictions were applied more broadly to industrial robots, computers, software, telecommunications equipment (with the export of modern exchanges frozen up to 1988). Sales of pure silicon and equipment for its production have been totally banned so as to hold up the development of miniaturised electronic chip production. Though the USA has not managed to give Cocom formal status, an executive committee was set up in 1988 (see above p. 213). In 1984, it was agreed that the industrial list should be reviewed on an ongoing basis, a quarter of the entries being reviewed annually, and particular entries being reviewed any time any member requests it. Domestic controls have been strengthened in some countries, as in France since 1981.

The development of *perestroika* in the USSR, the growing political liberalisation in Hungary and Poland, as well as the increased openness about Cocom in the East, particularly in the USSR where it was hardly mentioned at all during the Brezhnev period, now challenge the West. Already in 1984, Czechoslovakia had submitted a complaint to Gatt, calling the strategic embargo a violation of Gatt regulations as it was an illegal customs barrier. While in the past the East simply officially ignored Cocom, almost all the Cocom countries have been complaining about it since the mid-eighties.

After having long resisted pressure from some of the Western countries to ease Cocom restrictions, the US administration has gradually agreed to relax some of them. Already, since 1987, personal computers (of 8-bit capacity and some 16-bit) may be sold, but the 32-bit machines are still under control. This decision was extended to most of the commonly used 16-bit micro-computers in August 1989, allowing the West German firm Siemans to finalise a historic deal with the USSR, whereby 300,000 personal computers are to be supplied. Sales or leasing of aircraft to the GDR, Poland and Romania by Airbus and Boeing were accepted by Cocom in 1988, and were under discussion concerning the USSR. In September 1988, during review of the computers and telecommunications equipment list, it was agreed to allow the sales of exchanges and digital switches (only for equipment in use in the West already in 1984, excluding the most recent technologies), but in this very sensitive field, the negotiations for contracts with the USSR for assembling or building digital telephone lines have been suspended due to Cocom disapproval in 1989 (Siemens in FRG and Alcatel in France were concerned). Restrictions on sales to China have been relaxed. China has even been granted, in 1989, the status of 'cooperating country', meaning that it has agreed not to supply high technology to the USSR, as for instance Singapore and Hong Kong and South Korea had agreed before. But the general view of the US administration remains reluctant, though the 'no exception rule' was lifted in July 1989.

The fate of Cocom might be affected by the implementation of the single European Market. It will be impossible, as from 1993, to monitor sales of strategic goods within the EEC. There might thus be a *de facto* alignment of the stringency of controls on the countries which have the most lenient legislation (Portugal and Greece). There will be increased pressure from business groups in Western Germany to request a general easing of controls. However, the EC is not competent to regulate this matter, unlike in the case of import restrictions, and one could not replace national controls by an agreed-upon Community control.

Finally, the development of joint ventures as a growing form of industrial East–West cooperation might also make export controls more difficult.*

The pressure towards the withering away of controls is matched by the growing desire of the East to intensify East–West technological cooperation, as intra-Comecon cooperation meets growing difficulties.

Intra-Comecon technology transfers

Would it be realistic for the socialist countries to turn to Comecon to develop the technologies which the West refuses to supply? This question can actually be broken down into two: do these countries have sufficient potential to collectively replace what the West might give them? Do intra-Comecon technical and scientific cooperation mechanisms provide the level of efficiency required by this?

The first question has been largely answered. The East–West technology gap is relative, and varies according to country and product. The bridging or widening of this gap does not depend primarily on the policy of importing Western technologies. Poor innovation incentives and inadequate liaison between research and production go a long way towards explaining why this gap is a lasting one. According to their official statistics, the Eastern countries account for 20 per cent of patents for inventions and author's certificates registered worldwide, and for a third of the world's researchers. But a large share of these inventions (at least 50 per cent; two-thirds in the case of the USSR) never result in actual production or even in the building of prototypes.

In chapter 2 we saw how the socialist countries intended to increase their technological cooperation through the implementation of a programme for scientific and technical progress adopted in 1985. The first three years of operation were not successful and the programme has had to be scaled down, along with projects aiming to save it through cooperation with the West.

The inefficiency of intra-Comecon technology transfers, highlighted by the shortcomings of the 1985 STP Programme, can be put down to several causes:

Unequal technological levels between partners

Three countries have an overall lead: the GDR and Czechoslovakia (for the level of their industrial development) and the USSR (for the scale of research-development potential). If we take machinery and equipment sales as indicators of technological transfers, then the GDR, at the end of the seventies, was the main supplier with 23 per cent of all sales, the USSR following (20 per cent) and then Czechoslovakia (18 per cent) (Simai, 1984: 77). A study by the ECE–UN ranks the three countries differently. In 1983, the GDR accounted for 25 per cent of intra-Comecon sales of investment goods, Czechoslovakia for 19 per cent and the USSR for 14 per cent, a point behind Poland (15 per cent) (ECE–UN, 1986). The fall in the USSR share may be attributed to the fact that all countries increased their supplies to the USSR so as to pay for their oil imports, the price of oil having strongly increased in the eighties.

In the field of scientific and technical cooperation, a 'Moscow–Berlin' line can be seen (Samson, 1984: 96). The USSR carries out 40 per cent of its scientific and technical cooperation within Comecon with the GDR, while 80 per cent of the GDR's total research is undertaken with the USSR. The GDR uses the USSR's research potential as a large-scale scientific laboratory which it could hardly develop singlehanded. The USSR has priority access to advanced technologies developed in the GDR (especially in the field of micro-electronics and robots). The GDR and Czechoslovakia are the only Comecon countries to carry on intra-product specialisation in chemicals and in the machine-building industry. The most technologically advanced member states naturally baulk at diffusing their know-how without due compensation. The GDR was reproached for not making available to other members the 500,000 or so new technological processes which it introduces into its industry annually (Shastitko–Simanovski, 1983: 209). The technological level of products traded within Comecon hence match the lowest standards achieved within the bloc. According to the same source, 90 per cent of specialisation agreements concluded within Comecon involve outmoded manufactures which have long been routinely used.

The outward-looking orientation of trade in technology

When Eastern Europe and the USSR purchase technology from the West they then seek to reexport the resultant products primarily to the West in order to make their initial purchases pay off. The proportion of such goods in Comecon sales is far smaller. V. Sobell has shown that all the equipment primarily imported from Comecon consists of traditional goods with low R and D content (buses, lorries, tractors, passenger cars, railway wagons: for all these goods the share of Comecon in total imports by Comecon members was over 90 per cent in 1980). Conversely, where the share of non-Comecon imports was high (over 30 per cent) in total imports of the area, the relevant groups of equipment consisted of relatively complex machinery (energy equipment, chemical equipment, machine tools, ships, instruments) (Sobell, 1986: 145). The USSR, which imports half of the equipment sold in intra-Comecon deals, is the first to suffer the effects of this distribution, which explains its increasingly insistent demand for products which meet world quality standards.

Poor remuneration from intra-Comecon transfers

After Comecon was set up, one of the very first principles jointly adopted, the 'Sofia' principle (August 1949) laid down that the trade of non-incorporated technology (patents, licences, know-how, technical documentation) would be done at no cost in the spirit of socialist internationalism. During the period when this principle was being applied, a great circulation of technical documentation was taking place within Comecon, which was very difficult to put a value on (estimates range from 15 to 20 billion of dollar equivalents between 1950 and 1970; Lavigne, 1976). The principle was gradually done away with between 1968 and 1971. Only the under-developed Comecon countries are still entitled to free material. Licence deals started in earnest mainly among the three leading nations (the GDR, Czechoslovakia, and the USSR). At the same time, in keeping with the guidelines of the Complex Programme of 1971, scientific and technical cooperation developed rapidly. In the decade following the adoption of the programme, over 20,000 joint fundamental and applied research projects were completed with the participation of over 3,000 research centres. However, like licence sales, this joint research ran into the difficulty of establishing a price for the results of scientific activity. It is impossible to apply the usual intra-Comecon price-fixing principle by reference to world prices. Thus, research costs are used as the starting point. The problem of the non-convertibility of socialist currencies is here critical. According to which rates is national spending in domestic currency to be converted to a common unit? What profit margin is to be applied? In actual practice, these problems are solved by bargaining on an *ad hoc* basis. Remuneration from research is not usually profitable enough to give any dynamism to cooperation. As in other areas of intra-Comecon trade, transactions involve remuneration in kind, technology being a 'hard' good like grain or oil. A Soviet author has even proposed the setting up of a 'technological clearing': the valuation of the technology transfers would be made by an international group of experts, and the transfers would be estimated on the basis of 'marks'; the clearing balance would be computed annually for each participant, and could be settled through transfers of goods and services (Bykov, in Bogomolov and Bykov, 1986).

As a result the member countries refrain from engaging in cooperation. When they do, they tend to include outdated themes in joint projects. At the same time they pursue their own research, which results in a large-scale duplication of research, which is supposed to entail annual losses of 5 to 7 billion roubles (Shastitko, 1988: 53). The share of industrially applied research in the total number of joint research projects is only 30 per cent which is even less than within each country.

The absence of efficient socialist multinationals curbs the transmission of innovations

In the capitalist world, multinationals are a powerful vehicle of innovation. The socialist countries have sought to develop such entities (chapter 4). A whole set of joint bodies has been gradually set up. In the sixties these were mainly inter-governmental economic organisations. The 1971 Integration Programme prompted the creation of 'international business associations' then R and D coordinating centres appeared, based on the principle that a leading research institute in a country coordinates Comecon research on priority problems (Sobell, 1986: 150). The 1985 Programme for Scientific and Technical Progress entailed the setting up of a host of new entities: multinational scientific and technical associations of which Interrobot, already mentioned, was the first example, and various types of bilateral joint enterprises, joint engineering bureaus, etc., to which one may add the network of 'direct links' between Comecon enterprises which in theory couples hundreds of firms, but mostly consists of 'paper links'. Management difficulties limit the actual contribution these bodies can make to scientific integration (Blaha, 1988).

Intra-Comecon transfers are of a lower efficiency than the overall potential of those countries should give rise to. Limitations within intra-Comecon trade, such as irrational prices, bureaucratic rigidities, monetary inconvertibility, add to the effects of the inequality of technological potential. Finally, divergent domestic interests militate against a common approach of scientific cooperation.

East–South technological transfer

The socialist countries do not draw a definite line between technology transfers and East–South economic cooperation. They do distinguish between the transfer of technology embodied in machinery and equipment and technical assistance.

TRANSFERRED TECHNOLOGIES

We are dealing here with the transfer of civilian technologies. Of course one can argue that in this type of transfer too, there are 'dual-use' technologies. The arms sales of the USSR (and of some Eastern European countries) are certainly not negligible, and have an economic aspect as they provide hard currency (see chapter 8; and Després, 1988).

There are various forms of civilian technology transfer to the South. Generally, transfers are embodied in machinery supplies. These supplies are either commercial sales usually supported by export credits, or cooperation deliveries. The oldest form of cooperation is the large project of the Aswam dam (Egypt) type. Dams, irrigation facilities, steel mills, oil refineries, cement plants, and also silos, hospitals, airports, are standard examples. This form still accounts for about 40 per cent of the total amount of Soviet assistance in the eighties. A new trend in this cooperation is the growing involvement of the most developed of the developing countries, in the actual realisation of the projects. One may compare this with the increasing insistence of the socialist countries themselves on using their own technology in turn-key projects with Western countries. This has been observed in the case of Argentina (for the building of hydro-electric and thermal power stations), and of Algeria. Some more sophisticated forms of technological transfer are beginning to appear, such as sub-contracting, and co-production, mainly for assembling machinery and transport equipment. As has been seen in chapter 4, East–South joint companies have also developed. These companies may be considered as vehicles of technological transfer when they operate in the industrial field.

According to sources from the socialist countries, they have assisted the South in delivering equipment which produces a large share of domestic production in some fields. The equipment supplied and installations built by socialist countries accounted for 100 per cent of oil production and refining in Syria, 90 per cent of steel production in Algeria, 55 to 90 per cent of electricity generation in Syria, Afghanistan, Egypt, etc.

The cooperation agreements signed up to 1980 with Eastern European countries allow the Third World countries to manufacture 30 million tons of steel per year, to produce 22 million tonnes of coal, 67 million tonnes of oil, and to run 3 million km of railroads. (For the USSR at the end of 1987, see Table 9.)

Table 9. *Capacities built in the Third World with the assistance of the USSR*

	Provided for in the agreements	Put into operation
Power stations (thousand mw)	27	9
Coal (million tons)[a]	94	5
Pig iron (million tons)[a]	25	16
Steel (million tons)[a]	23	16
Oil products (million tons)[a]	30	23
Tractors (thousand units)	11	11
Railroads (thousand km)	2.7	2.2
Roads (thousand km)	2.6	2.1

[a] of annual production
Source: *The USSR and Foreign Countries, 1987, A Statistical Compendium*, Moscow, 1988. The figures are surprisingly lower, for some items, than the former published data.

For all the socialist countries, from the total number of the projects provided for in the agreements since the beginning (that is, from the mid-fifties), energy and industry account for 79.4 per cent of the total, agriculture 4 per cent, transport 5.4 per cent, geological exploration 4.9 per cent, social projects (hospitals, schools, etc.), 5.3 per cent.

How useful to the Third World is the assistance of the socialist countries?

Quite simply, first of all, it *does exist*. Particularly in the beginning of their involvement in the Third World, the socialist countries substituted for the former colonial powers in offering a cooperation which the latter did not want to supply (the case of the Aswan dam is typical), especially in some sensitive sectors such as the steel or oil industry. Due to opposition from Western lobbies or cartels, the steel industries of India, Iran, Algeria, Egypt, Sri Lanka, and the oil refineries of Iraq, Syria, India, would never have been in position to develop, were it not for the help of the socialist world.

The socialist countries often contend that their cooperation is more efficient for the industrial take-off of the benefiting countries. The cooperation, it is stated, does not aim at high profits as is the case with private investments; it is not designed for the selling off of surpluses; it is not devised to flatter the taste for luxury of some Third World leaders. However, one may recall that the Third World indeed provides outlets for goods unsaleable on Western markets.

Is it possible to say that socialist technologies, outdated as they often are, are adapted to the needs of the South? Two sets of conflicting views are to be found here. According to the first, the machinery supplied is obsolete, of low quality, and inappropriate. Some anecdotes are currently cited, such as the case of the Soviet snow-ploughs delivered to Guinea (in fact, the snow-ploughs were part of a shipment of locomotives; in the USSR locomotives are always built with snow-ploughs). Outside the industrial sector it is worse: the Soviet hotels built in Africa operate in an even more inefficient way than in the Soviet Union. Conversely, it is indisputable that heavy industry capacities do supply needed goods (minerals extracted, steel, oil products, etc.). In addition, the assistance of the East differs from Western aid in some important aspects:

it is indeed more appropriate, because of its organisation, for technology transfers to the public sector;

it is more complete: a turn-key plant is supplied with technical assistance and a more lasting follow-up;

there are fewer restrictions to technology transfers, less classified non-transferred items; the benefiting country may use the transferred technology in cooperation with other countries. Thus, India has used Soviet techniques in the field of steel manufacturing in its cooperation with Nigeria;

Western assistance often involves multinationals, with a specific behaviour ('imports' by the subsidiaries from the 'home' firm are overvalued, their 'exports' are undervalued); this is not to be found in the case of socialist assistance. Conversely, traditional management in the East means increased costs: the deliveries are delayed, overspending occurs in the course of the implementation of a project, etc.;

the smaller CMEA countries have contributed to break the Western monopoly in some protected areas such as the pharmaceutical industry, which has considerably lowered the price of drugs in some developing countries (India, and Latin American countries).

A different question is the way in which the recipient country uses the assistance. This issue was raised in 1986 when the General Secretary of the Vietnamese Communist Party acknowledged that hundreds of millions of roubles of Soviet aid had been spent in an unproductive way: 'the potential of our country as well as the great assistance of the Soviet Union and other fraternal socialist states have been seriously wasted and are running the risk of being lost little by little' (*International Herald Tribune* quoting the Vietnamese press agency, 26 October 1986).

The overall balance is not easy to establish. The drawbacks of socialist assistance are in many ways identical to the domestic inadequacies of their own developmental model, and reflect the rigidities of state trading proceedings. The advantages may be attributed to systemic features (in particular, to the weak role of the market), and also to a deliberate aid policy.

TECHNICAL ASSISTANCE

In situ training is included in large cooperation projects. However, it is not always financed as part of the contract and the socialist countries often require a separate financing partly in hard currency, which does not please the developing countries. The USSR has often concluded special cooperation contracts for technical assistance in addition to its large project financing. Such special contracts provide for the establishment of a technical school and the training of specialists for a certain time, but not always for the building of the school itself, nor for training once the project has been completed.

Overall, up to the early eighties the socialist countries have built in the Third World 56 specialised technical schools and colleges (the USSR only: 50) and about 300 training centres (the USSR: 260). Schools of the first type have trained 76,000 engineers and cadres, and the training centres, 386,000 technicians and qualified workers. To these figures one has to add the workers trained on the building sites. According to a Soviet source, the total number of persons trained in the developing countries with the help of the USSR had reached, as of the end of 1982, 1.4 million. To this one has to add 300,000 persons trained with the help of the other socialist countries. Another source cites 2 million persons overall, and 1.5 for the USSR only. Data published in the West yield much smaller figures.

It is equally difficult to estimate the number of students trained in the socialist countries.

This type of training has a multilateral aspect. A Joint Scholarship Fund (the amount of which has never been made public) was set up in 1973 within the CMEA. Already, by 1974, 400 students had been trained, and in 1982, more than 4,000 students of 57 countries were studying at universities in the socialist countries; more than 500 were said to have completed their studies at this date.

In addition, each socialist country sets up programmes for Third World students in its national academic system or in special *ad hoc* faculties such as the University Patrice Lumumba for Friendship among Peoples in Moscow, which was established in 1960. In the USSR education is free (it applies to tuition, accommodation, and medical expenses). The GDR has several specialised institutions (for tropical agriculture) which admit students from developing countries. Similar institutions exist in Czechoslovakia and Hungary. The USSR and the GDR account for more than 80 per cent of the total flow of students. Annually, the USSR gives scholarships (data for the early eighties) to about 60,000 students to be trained in universities and professional high schools; the GDR accepts about 6,000 grantees; Czechoslovakia and Hungary, slightly over 4,000 each; overall, 80,000 students benefit from grants yearly, which leaves almost nothing for the other three East European countries. Africa accounts for more than 50 per cent of the total number of students (the countries with a socialist orientation provide the bulk of the trainees). These students are not always happy with the conditions of their stay, even apart from the climate (the difference between Moscow and Brazzaville or Addis-Ababa is enormous in winter); when they are taught in special schools they complain about lower standards of education; when they are mixed with local students they are facing hostile reactions from people who are not accustomed to multiracial foreign communities as in the Western world.

The number of experts is also controversial. The data from different sources are not consistent; usually numbers of persons are given, without indication of the length of the stay. Overall (and with a certain approximation) the number of civilian experts from socialist countries in the Third World has been multiplied by 20 between 1960 and 1982 (from slightly over 5,000 to 100,000, two-thirds of them being at work in North Africa and the Middle East). These experts are not free of charge for the Third World countries, which have to pay for them, partly in convertible currency; the question of their cost to the Third World, compared to that of Western experts, is a debated issue in the controversy about the amount of assistance extended by the socialist countries.

CHAPTER 6

—————— · ——————

ENERGY

Energy stands at the very centre of the international economic relations of the socialist system. It involves the countries under this system in a complex web of vital interactions. Its principal elements are as follows.
1 The USSR is the world's leading oil producer (since 1974) and natural gas producer (since 1983) and holds third place after the USA and China for coal production. It holds between 20 and 40 per cent of world reserves of these fuels. In 1987, it provided about 15 per cent of world coal production, 22 per cent of oil production, and 40 per cent of natural gas production.

The USSR is also the world's second largest oil exporter (after Saudi Arabia), and the leading exporter of gas. In fact historical continuity can be seen here. In 1900, Russia was the world's leading oil exporter, accounting for 30 per cent of world sales (Goldman, 1980).
2 The Six have production capacities which are greatly inferior and unevenly distributed (Poland has coal, Romania has oil and the GDR has brown coal). They depend almost totally on the USSR for supplies of gas, and to a very large extent, oil and coal.
3 The 1973 and 1979 oil price explosions, and the subsequent rise of these prices between 1973 and 1983, followed by the price fall of 1986, have all caused upheavals in the USSR's relations with the West. Energy has become the main source of hard currency for the USSR. The drop in oil prices has forced the USSR, from 1986 on, to increase its supplies so as to limit its hard currency losses. The Soviet export-dependence on oil sales appears thus to be quite strong. At the same time, however, the long-term development of energy production is impossible without the help of major investment requiring reliance on Western technologies.
4 The Third World plays an important role in the international energy relations of Eastern Europe, in two different ways. Firstly, the USSR supplies oil to certain developing countries. This is an example of

inverted North–South relations where, in exchange, the USSR buys manufactures from them (e.g., USSR–India trade). Secondly, since 1973–74 OPEC members have become important partners of the East. Contrary to a widespread view, however, increasing oil purchases are not first and foremost intended to make up for deficient Soviet supplies. Oil is basically a trading currency in a complex interplay of transactions in which the USSR itself and Eastern Europe above all seek to earn hard currencies in reexport trade.

We shall first look at the energy situation in the USSR and Eastern Europe, then analyse the central position which energy enjoys in the different directions of trade.

The energy situation in the USSR and Eastern Europe

Tables 10 and 11 show the structure and development of primary energy production and consumption in the USSR and Eastern Europe. They pinpoint the contrast between the situation in the USSR and the situation in the Six.

1 *Eastern Europe* (the Six) would seem to be poor in energy. This is not exactly the case if we examine table 10. Overall, for the zone and for the total energy sources, this area covers some 80 per cent of its needs through its own production. The level of self-sufficiency is comparable with that of the USA, almost double that of the EEC, and ten times greater than that of Japan.

Having made this general remark, it should be qualified in several ways.

The degree of self-sufficiency varies greatly from country to country. While it is over 100 per cent for Poland, it is only about 33 per cent for Bulgaria. It also varies greatly according to the fuel. Overall, the entire area is self-sufficient in *coal*. This situation is obviously due to the presence of Poland, which alone accounts for over four-fifths of the coal mined by the Six. The 'Five', however, cover two-thirds of their consumption through domestic coal production, and even more if one includes lignite production which is mined in all these countries, although the GDR is the principal producer (56 per cent of total production). Poland alone still has sizeable deposits with which to increase its coal output. Potential for an increase in lignite output is common to all, but only the GDR, the world's leading producer, has concentrated its economic strategy since 1981 on a rapid increase in mining output.

The world energy crisis prompted the countries of Eastern Europe to

Table 10. *The energy situation in the USSR and Eastern Europe: production, domestic consumption and net trade*

	Bulgaria		
	1970	1982	1987
Coal (millions of t)			
production (1)	0.4	0.3	0.2
net imports (2)=imports less exports	5.5	7.7	7.3
apparent consumption (3)=(1)+(2)	5.9	8.0	7.5
dependence rate (4)=(2)/(3)	93.2	96.3	97.3
Lignite (millions of t)			
production (1)	28.9	31.9	36.6
net imports (2)=imports less exports			
apparent consumption (3)=(1)+(2)	28.9	31.9	36.6
dependence rate (4)=(2)/(3)	0.0	0.0	0.0
Oil and oil products(millions t)			
production (1) (only crude oil)	0.3	0.1	0.0
net imports (2)=imports less exports	8.2	12.0	
apparent consumption (3)=(1)+(2)	8.5	12.1	
dependence rate (4)=(2)/(3)	96.5	99.2	
Natural gas (billions of cubic metres)			
production (1)	0.5	0.2	0.0
net imports (2)=imports less exports		4.2	6.1
apparent consumption (3)=(1)+(2)	0.5	6.5	6.1
dependence rate (4)=(2)/(3)	0.0	95.7	100.0

	Poland		
	1970	1982	1987
Coal (millions of t)			
production (1)	140.1	189.3	193.0
net imports (2)=imports less exports	−27.7	−30.2	−32.2
apparent consumption (3)=(1)+(2)	112.4	139.1	160.8
dependence rate (4)=(2)/(3)	124.6	119.0	120.0
Lignite (millions of t)			
production (1)	32.8	37.7	73.0
net imports (2)=imports less exports			
apparent consumption (3)=(1)+(2)	32.8	37.7	73.0
dependence rate (4)=(2)/(3)	0.0	0.0	0.0
Oil and oil products(millions t)			
production (1) (only crude oil)	0.4	0.3	0.2
net imports (2)=imports less exports	8.1	15.7	17.1
apparent consumption (3)=(1)+(2)	8.5	16.0	17.3
dependence rate (4)=(2)/(3)	95.3	98.1	98.8
Natural gas (billions of cubic metres)			
production (1)	5.0	5.5	5.3
net imports (2)=imports less exports	1.0	5.6	7.5
apparent consumption (3)=(1)+(2)	6.0	11.1	12.8
dependence rate (4)=(2)/(3)	16.7	50.5	58.6

Notes: Negative net imports denote net exports. In this case apparent consumption is lower than production, and the ratio (4) is calculated as the ratio between production (1) and apparent consumption (3), indicating a rate of self-sufficiency.

Czechoslovakia			GDR			Hungary		
1970	1982	1987	1970	1982	1987	1970	1982	1987
28.2	27.5	25.7	1.0			4.2	3.0	2.4
1.5	0.4	0.9	8.2	8.5	9.0	2.4	2.5	3.0
29.7	27.9	26.6	9.2	8.5	9.0	6.6	5.5	5.4
5.1	1.4	3.4	89.1	100.0	100.0	36.4	45.5	55.3
81.3	97.1	100.3	261.5	276.6	309.0	23.7	23.0	20.4
81.3	97.1	100.3	261.5	276.6	309.0	23.7	23.0	20.4
0.0	0.0	0.0	0.0	0.0	0.0	0.0	0.0	0.0
0.2	0.1	0.1	0.1	0.1	0.0	1.9	2.0	1.9
10.1	16.7	18.5	9.1	17.5	17.2	4.5	7.9	10.0
10.3	16.8	18.6	9.2	17.6	17.2	6.4	9.9	11.9
98.1	99.4	99.5	98.8	99.4	100.0	70.3	79.8	84.1
1.2	0.6	0.8	4.3	8.5	5.0	3.5	6.6	7.1
1.3	8.5	10.6	0.2	6.5	7.0	0.2	3.9	4.8
2.5	9.1	11.4	4.5	15.0	12.0	3.7	10.6	11.9
52.0	97.4	93.0	4.4	43.3	58.3	5.4	36.8	40.3

Romania			The Six			The USSR		
1970	1982	1987	1970	1982	1987	1970	1982	1987
8.1	8.4	8.7	182.0	228.5	230.0	432.7	488.0	519.0
3.1	3.3		−7.0	−7.8		−17.4	−28.0	−25.9
11.2	11.7		175.0	220.7		415.3	460.0	493.1
27.7	28.2		104.0	103.5		104.2	106.1	105.3
14.7	29.5	42.8	442.9	495.2	582.1	147.7	162.7	161.0
14.7	29.5	42.8	442.9	495.2	582.1	147.7	162.7	161.0
0.0	0.0	0.0	0.0	0.0	0.0	0.0	0.0	0.0
13.4	11.7	10.5	16.3	14.3	12.7	353.0	612.6	624.0
−3.0	4.4	5.2	37.0	74.2	68.0	−63.3	−114.2	−122.9
10.4	16.1	15.7	53.3	88.5	80.7	289.7	498.4	501.1
128.9	27.3	33.1	69.4	83.8	84.3	121.9	122.9	124.5
25.0	37.3	36.3	39.5	58.7	54.5	184.4	466.7	678.0
−0.2	1.3	3.3	2.5	30.3	39.3	0.3	−58.7	−82.8
24.8	38.6	39.6	42.0	89.0	93.8	198.2	408.0	595.2
100.8	3.4	8.3	6.0	34.0	41.9	0.2	114.4	113.9

Sources: John B. Hannigan, Carl H. McMillan, *East European Responses to the Energy Crisis*, Institute of Soviet and East European Studies, Carleton University, Ottawa, Research Report no. 21, 1983: 102–9. ECE/UN, Geneva, Data file on energy. For 1987, Soviet and East European national statistics have been used; see also Nissanke, in Chadwick, Long, Nissanke (1987: 117ff)

Table 11. *The structure of energy consumption: an East–West comparison*

	Bulgaria	Czecho-slovakia	GDR	Hungary	Poland	Romania	The Six	The USSR	OECD countries
1970									
Coal	50.9	74.6	86.0	53.1	82.7	19.9	68.8	43.4	18.5
Oil	44.4	18.1	12.3	28.0	10.4	25.8	18.0	33.5	53.5
Gas	2.0	3.4	0.7	13.8	6.3	54.0	11.4	21.7	20.5
Electricity	2.8	3.9	1.0	5.1	0.7	0.2	1.8	1.4	7.6
1985									
Coal		59.2	75.1				56.5	22.9	22.4
Oil		21.4	n.a.				21.0	33.4	42.6
Gas		12.0	n.a.				18.1	35.6	19.8
Electricity		7.0	n.a.				4.8	6.1	15.8

Sources: For 1970, 'Situation et perspectives du bilan énergétique de l'URSS et de l'Est européen', *Le Courrier des Pays de l'Est*, no. 216, March 1978: 10–13; for 1985, *Energie Internationale 1987–1988* (1987); Bethkenhagen (1987); Soviet national statistics.

maintain and even develop their coal production in very unfavourable conditions. This policy has had repercussions on the environment, especially in the zone of traditionally mined deposits in Central Europe (southern GDR and Poland, northern Czechoslovakia). Coal pollution has led to the spread of 'acid rain', devastating forests in these areas and threatening those of the FRG.

The level of dependency on the outside world is highest when it comes to *oil*. One country stands out as an important producer, namely Romania. Romanian production reached around 15 million tonnes in 1977 and has been in steady decline ever since. Romania is also alone in importing large quantities of oil to reexport in the form of refined products. The difference between total oil and petroleum products imports and net imports, which corresponds to (re)exports, lies somewhere between 1 to 4 million tonnes for each of the 'Five' in the eighties (with this figure varying from country to country). In the case of Romania, this margin of difference of 6 million tonnes in 1975 reached 9 million in 1980, dropping subsequently to a little under 7 million tonnes. Total imports began to surpass production from 1979 on. Romania has considerable refining capacity (for around 30 million tonnes of crude oil). This obtains foreign currency for the country through the sale of refined products, while also forcing it to import oil, for which, unlike the other Eastern European countries, it must pay totally in hard currency or in 'hard goods'.

Gas production has risen sharply in three countries, namely Hungary, the GDR and Romania. In all countries, with the exception of Romania, the level of dependence has considerably risen due to the increasing share of gas in the energy balance.

The structure of energy consumption in Eastern Europe (Table 11) is characterised by the proportionally large amount of coal, which was twice that of the USSR and almost three times that of Western Europe at the beginning of the eighties. The share of coal was lost however to oil between 1970 and 1980. Oil still none the less accounts for only a quarter of energy consumption (while in the USSR it accounts for a third and in developed market economies it comprises between 40 and 50 per cent). Electricity (of either hydraulic or nuclear origin) accounts for a very small fraction of energy consumption, and only Hungary's consumption is equivalent, proportionally speaking, to that of the USSR. As in production, structures vary enormously from country to country. Poland, Czechoslovakia and the GDR depend greatly on coal. Hungary gives priority to oil, just as Romania does to gas (which is mainly gas from oil).

This consumption is very high in comparison to that of Western Europe (Table 12) whether per capita consumption, or consumption per unit of gross national product, is taken as the indicator. How can this situation be accounted for? Two principal reasons are involved here. The first is the high degree of self-sufficiency along with access to cheap supplies which, while they became more expensive after the energy crisis, did not do so to the same extent or as early as in Western Europe. The second reason is bound up with the rigidity of domestic planning. In no country in Eastern Europe has the increase of domestic energy prices immediately followed foreign price movements. It was not until the eighties that any substantial price rise occurred in most of these countries. Domestic consumers were therefore under no great pressure to make savings in this field. Such savings as there were, were achieved through administrative measures which affected first the population (heating restrictions, power black-outs, petrol rationing) with only a very slight impact, given the low consumption of this sector. Industry too was affected mainly through the establishing of energy-consumption norms per item manufactured. The overall affect of such measures was still poor. The GDR obtained the best results in this field. The studies published in socialist countries generally stress the large 'reserves' which would allow even greater energy savings to be achieved. It is however unrealistic to think that consumption can be brought back into line with the average level in Western Europe. Industry as a whole is structurally dominated by high energy-intensive branches as a result of a postwar growth strategy giving priority to heavy industry. Moreover, production processes in Eastern Europe are more energy-intensive on average than they are in Western Europe, due to obsolescent equipment. In order to reduce consumption, therefore, what is needed is major investment, something very difficult to achieve; in actual fact, there has been a tendency for investment to fall since 1981 in almost all these countries, with a recovery beginning in 1985–86 at a modest pace.

2 In spite of the USSR's great energy-output potential, there has been much speculation as to the future, especially since the onset of the crisis. The whole balance of relations between the USSR and Eastern Europe depends on future energy production, as does the USSR's hard currency revenue, and, therefore, its ability to import from industrialised market economies.

Table 12. *A comparison of energy consumption between East and West (1979–1986)*

	Change in energy consumption in kg of oil equivalent per $1 of NMP (GNP) in 1979–86 1979=100	Energy consumption in 1979 (kg of oil eq. per £1 of GNP)
GDR	80.5	0.76
Czechoslovakia	91.3	0.86
Poland	110.5	1.04
Bulgaria	82.8	0.97
Romania	78.0	1.50
Hungary	89.8	0.69
USSR	92.9	0.80
FRG	88.2	0.34
USA	86.4	0.66
France	80.0	0.35
Italy	89.1	0.37
Japan	85.3	0.34
Great Britain	85.0	0.40

Sources: Column 1: ECE/UN *Economic Survey of Europe*, 1986–87 and 1988–89, for changes in energy intensity of NMP (Net Material Product) of the East; for the changes in energy intensity of the GNP in the West, OECD sources (for energy consumption) and World Bank (GNP).

Column 2: United Nations, *Yearbook of World Energy*, 1979; *World Bank Atlas*, 1981, for GNP data on Western countries; estimates on GNP for Eastern countries from Marer, 1985.

There is, in particular, much speculation over oil. Vast resources of coal (about 20 per cent of world deposits) and gas (about 40 per cent) guarantee future production. Their development requires considerable investment due to the fact that, as with all Soviet natural resources, the greatest deposits are in remote Siberia, and unfavourable geological and climatic factors render them less accessible. The gas field discovered in 1989 in the Barents Sea, which is supposedly equal to the proven reserves of the UK and Norway, might also be very difficult to develop. In the medium term, Soviet financial capacity relies on petroleum-based resources, rather than on substituting oil by gas, coal or nuclear power (see Hewett, 1987; Bethkenhagen, 1987).

The first forecasts of a medium-term drop in Soviet oil output came from the CIA in 1977. They estimated that, by 1985, the USSR would be a net importer and that its production would be 500 million tonnes at the most. These highly controversial forecasts were subsequently modified, and the predicted peak in Soviet oil production postponed. True, in 1984–5, Soviet production declined. It resumed growth in 1986 and 1987, and again stopped in 1988. These fluctuations are a sign of serious difficulties, mainly due to the energy policy itself. The ratio between the reserves and annual production dropped from 25 in 1970 to 14 in 1984. Although energy savings would be much cheaper than a forced growth in supplies, this latter strategy is however still applied. Investments are made in exploitation drilling rather than in exploration. New fields are east of the Urals, while energy is consumed mainly in the West, hence transport costs are rising. Investment and production costs are also increasing, because of geological conditions (drilling has to go deeper and deeper), of climatic constraints (when drilling is conducted in permafrost areas), of technological shortcomings due to production methods based upon water-flooding (Dienes, 1987). Finally, the sector was certainly among the most badly managed in Soviet industry, and this allowed the minister for the oil industry to be made a scapegoat in 1985.

In any case, there is no doubt that it is indeed possible to increase production through better management of existing deposits. At the same time it is possible to find ways of achieving supplementary exportable surplus through consumption savings. Overall energy consumption in the USSR rose by 5.7 per cent annually between 1971–5, by 4.2 per cent in 1976–80, by 2.7 per cent in 1981–85. The target for 1986–90 is to meet 51 per cent of fuel and energy requirements by savings and substitution (mainly of nuclear power) (Tretyakova, Kostinsky, 1987: 549). In 1986–87 energy consumption rose at a slightly greater pace than in 1981–85, but it slowed down in 1988. Awareness about this issue is growing in the USSR, where experts have established that the overspending of energy amounts to 40 per cent of all primary energy produced in the USSR (*Ekonomicheskaia Gazeta*, April 1989: 5).

The energy situation seemed serious enough to the authorities to justify their working out an energy programme which was adopted as early as 1983, and referred to by the chairman of the USSR's Gosplan as the 'second Goelro plan', alluding to the plan for the general electrification of Russia which in 1920 saw the start of all planning in the USSR. This programme provided for the development of Soviet energy up to the year 2000 and contained several basic orientations: strict energy savings; the modernisation of equipment; the acceleration of power production (especially nuclear); the stabilisation of oil production; the development of gas to meet domestic and import requirements; cooperation with the countries of Comecon, Western Europe and Japan (but not the United States!). The Gorbachev policy has consisted in upgrading investments in the oil sector while maintaining high targets for other primary sources of energy, thus complying with traditional Soviet policies, although with better management methods. Western experts are generally cautious to pessimistic on the future of the oil industry and, in consequence, on the hard currency earnings which it might be able to generate in the future, taking into account Soviet commitments to Eastern Europe (Stern, 1987; Bethkenhagen, 1987). One should add to the traditional determinants of the energy policy, a new factor. *Perestroika* has led, in the USSR, as well as in some other Eastern countries and especially Hungary, to the emergence of 'green' opinion groups which actively protest against the development of nuclear energy and, in the Soviet Union, against the oil policy as well, and attempt to stop the development of the huge oil fields in Tenghiz (West Kazakhstan). There is thus now in the USSR an anti-oil lobby, bound to remain powerless against the domestic oil lobby which may count on the support of Western suppliers of oil equipment.*

Energy – the nucleus of intra-CMEA relations

Energy dominates East–East relations. It stands at the heart of the disturbances in commercial trade between the Six and the USSR since 1975. Energy is also the main area of economic cooperation between CMEA member states and, as such, is the very nucleus of socialist integration.

TRADE

The share of Soviet supplies in the total energy imports of its partners was very high in 1970 (70 per cent approximately) and rose higher still in 1980 to 77 per cent, maintaining a slight increase since then. For oil, the proportion of Soviet supplies decreased until 1980, then has increased (from 87 per cent in 1970 to 75 per cent in 1980 and 81 per cent in 1986). If we exclude Romania which imported very little Soviet oil up to 1980, but afterwards bought increasing quantities from the USSR, the corresponding figures are 92, 88 and 90 per cent. The share of Soviet gas in the gas imports of Eastern Europe has risen from 86 per cent in 1970 to 99.3 per cent in 1980, as also have electricity exports. The amount of electricity exported by the USSR has tripled from 1970 to 1980, and has increased by 80 per cent from 1980 to 1988. Oil has the most vital place in the overall list of Soviet energy exports (in value) to European Comecon countries (Table 13).

The determining event in energy relations was the first oil shock which

Table 13. *Energy trade of the USSR and the Six*

	1973	1975	1980	1985	1986	1987	1988
Share of fuels in the exports of the USSR, in % of total value, to:							
the Comecon–Six	22.0	26.3	40.8	55.5	52.2	50.7	43.6
the OECD countries	34.3	54.0	71.3	74.3	62.3	64.5	57.0
the developing countries	2.3	10.5	15.5	14.9	8.9	11.2	9.6
Exports of Soviet oil and oil products (million t), to:							
the Comecon–Six	55.3	63.3	80.3	70.1	81.1	79.8	77.4
the OECD countries	46.4	47.9	55.7	67.5	75.5	83.9	97.5
the developing countries	3.6	4.5	6.2	9.1	9.5	12.6	12.0
Exports of oil and oil products by the Six to the OECD countries	8.3	10.0	19.7	16.0	19.4	20.0	19.2
Soviet gas exports (billion cm) to:							
the Comecon–Six	4.9	11.3	29.5	37.5	37.2	39.3	40.9
Western Europe	2.0	8.0	26.0	34.2	37.9	40.2	40.9
Import of oil from developing countries (million t)							
by the USSR	11.9	6.5	3.5	12.4	14.1	13.7	19.8
by the Six	9.3	9.4	12.4	n.a.	n.a.	n.a.	n.a.

Note: This table does not cover trade with all countries of the world. In particular, it does not include oil trade with Cuba and Yugoslavia.

Exports of oil and oil products are taken together. Separate data are not easily to be found and often vary according to sources. The institutes which publish such data usually refer to their energy data bank (for instance DIW (Deutsche Institut für Wirtschaftsforschung, the West Berlin based institute, or PlanEcon in Washington). In the future, it may be easier to disaggregate this trade as the USSR has resumed in 1988 the publication of separate figures (for 1986 and 1987). The trade in oil products averages 25–30 per cent of total trade in this group. The share of products is higher in exports to OECD countries (it usually remains in the range of 40–45 per cent) than in exports to the Comecon countries (it averages 10 per cent of total oil and oil products exports).

Data on oil trade of the Six with the developing countries since 1985 has not been included. The data available display wide variations, due to the increasing lack of openness of most of the countries on this account. In particular, the re-export trade (purchase of oil in the South and resale to the West) is very difficult to assess.

Source: This table has used a number of sources, cross-checking them. The figures provided in numerous articles and reports by Jochen Bethkenhagen, the DIW energy specialist, have been used; also *PlanEcon Report* (in particular Jan Vanous, 'Long-Term Trends in Energy Consumption and Trade in the Soviet Union and Eastern Europe', vol. 2, nos. 12–13, 31 March 1986; 'Soviet Energy Trade during 1986–88', vol. 5, nos. 32–33, 18 August 1989); see also Hewett (1984), Chadwick *et al.* (1987). Recent Soviet sources include the yearbook *Vneshniaia Torgovlia SSSR v 1987 g.*, Moscow 1988, as well as the statistical compendium *SSSR i zarubezhnye strany, 1987*, Moscow, 1988.

made the USSR seek a revision of Comecon price-fixing rules. Up to this point, international socialist prices were worked out on the basis of world prices, and frozen for five years at the average world price of the previous five years. Thus, in 1973 and 1974, the Comecon countries were using prices fixed for the 1971–75 period on the basis of the average world prices of 1965–69. From 1975, i.e., one year before the next price revision was due, and one year after the oil-price explosion on world markets, a new principle was adopted on the recommendation of the USSR (called the Moscow principle because the decision was taken at a meeting of the Comecon Executive Committee held in Moscow). Prices were to be renegotiated every year, still based on average world prices of the five preceding years. For 1975 however, an exception was made. The price for 1975 was computed as the average world price of the three preceding years (1972–74). This was meant to achieve an immediate impact of the 1973–4 increases in world prices already on the 1975 Comecon price, which would not have been the case if one had taken the 1970–74 five-year average.

The most remarkable result was the immediate doubling of Soviet oil prices (other energy forms also increased in price but to a lesser extent). However, the staggered introduction of oil price rises in this system of prices based on a 'sliding' average of world prices, had the result of keeping Soviet export prices at a level which was always below world prices, as table 14 shows, until 1985.

Even if we consider that 1975–84 was an exceptional decade from the point of view of the conditions under which intra-Comecon energy trade was being conducted, the changes which started in 1975 were to have far-reaching consequences on trade as a whole between the USSR and the Six.

The decade of high oil prices: 1975–1984

1 *The subsidy issue* came to the fore dramatically. Through energy prices which for ten years had remained constantly below world prices, the USSR seemed to have granted its partners a kind of indirect and very large 'subsidy'. The size of this subsidy can be calculated from the 'opportunity cost' incurred by the USSR as, by exporting to the West the oil it sold to the Six, the USSR could have made extra hard currency gains. A comparison of world oil prices in dollars and intra-Comecon prices in transferable roubles has of course to use an exchange rate to

Table 14. *Price of Soviet oil sold to the European members of Comecon (1972–1988)*

Years	(1) Actual price (TR/t)	(2) Calculated price (TR/t)	(3) Current world price (TR/t)	(4) Current world price ($/t)	(5) Ratio (1)/(3)
1972	14–17	12	15	18	103
1973	15–17	12	18	24	89
1974	15–18	12	64	85	28
1975	31–38	32	61	85	57
1976	34–41	35	68	91	55
1977	44–50	45	67	91	70
1978	54–60	56	65	93	88
1979	63–72	64	83	127	83
1980	72–76	70	144	222	51
1981	92–103	87	172	239	57
1982	106–22	107	181	250	63
1983	127–45	129	162	219	84
1984	148–68	148	168	213	94
1985	170–80	166	152	184	108
1986	151–72 (average 153)	167	82	117	220
1987	144–53 (average 148)	149	83	130	193
1988	122–33	129	65	107	189

Sources and methodology: Column 1 is the actual price paid by the Comecon Six for the Soviet oil. The USSR stopped in 1976 to publish data on both quantities and values of oil sold to its partners, which allowed to calculate the price, or more precisely the unit value, of the oil sold. In 1988, the Soviet Union resumed the publication of such data, beginning with 1986 and 1987 figures. We have used those figures to calculate the yearly unit values and the average price. For the years 1976–85, we have used various information such as figures occasionally given in the East European press or even leaked by experts. For each year the lowest and highest figures are given. We have also checked our findings against those of our colleagues; see in particular Anita Tiraspolsky, 'Le Prix du pétrole livré par l'URSS aux pay du Caem', *Le Courrier des pays de l'Est*, no. 229, May 1979: 50, and 'Quel pétrole pour quelle croissance en Europe de l'Est', *ibid.*, no. 280, January 1984: 18; Jochen Bethkenhagen, 'Oil and Natural Gas in CMEA Intra-Bloc Trade', *Economic Bulletin*, DIW, no. 12, February 1984; Dietz (1986: 283); van Brabant (*Osteuropa Wirtschaft*, 1985: 173).

Columns 2, 3 and 4: first we derived the average world market price in dollars/t from the price of a barrel of the Arabian Light crude, using as a conversion key 1t=7.34 barrels. The price was then converted into transferable roubles by applying the official exchange rate in dollars for 1 rouble: 1.21 (1972), 1.36 (1973), 1.32 (1974), 1.38 (1975), 1.33 (1976), 1.36 (1977), 1.44 (1978), 1.53 (1979), 1.54 (1980), 1.39 (1981), 1.38 (1982), 1.35 (1983), 1.26 (1984), 1.21 (1985), 1.42 (1986), 1.58 (1987), 1.65 (1988). The 'calculated price' (col. 2) is the average TR price of the five preceding years (the three preceding, for 1975).

Column 5 is the ratio between (1) – taking the average price – and (3).

convert dollar prices into rouble prices. Should one use the official exchange rate, which obviously overvalues the rouble? It must be borne in mind that the transferable rouble prices are obtained by taking the average world price in dollars. For each year, the world price is converted into roubles according to the official rouble/dollar exchange rate, and the average over five years is then computed. In principle, the same calculation method should be applied in order to determine intra-Comecon prices for manufactures acquired by the USSR in exchange for its energy supplies. As has been mentioned already (chapter 2), in fact, prices of manufactured goods are fixed on the basis of bilateral bargaining between the buyer and the seller, each trying to document its claims as to the lowest/highest possible price through various evidence referring to prices currently applied in Western trade. As indicated by a study carried out by American econometricians (Marrese and Vanous, 1983) which really launched the subsidy debate, and supported on this point by earlier works by Hungarian (Ausch, 1972) and American (Hewett, 1974) economists, intra-Comecon machinery and equipment prices seem overestimated compared to world prices for comparable goods, especially if we consider the generally inferior quality of the goods in question. In this case, whatever the rate of exchange applied, the relative price of oil in terms of the machinery it can buy has indeed been much lower in Soviet–East European trade than in Soviet–Western trade for the years 1973–84.

This issue has certainly been the main one in the discussions conducted among Western experts, and has resulted in a vast amount of literature during the period 1983–87 (see the bibliography, and Brada, 1985, for a survey of the first phase of the debate). Soviet authors never really took part in the debate. Eastern European authors voiced their disagreement in discussions with their colleagues and in conferences; one of the few written expressions is to be found in Köves (1983). Köves strongly dismisses the theory of subsidisation, on the basis that the Eastern European countries have had imposed on them the Soviet inefficient and high energy-intensive strategy of development and therefore have not been able to catch up with modernisation, thus suffering dynamic losses for which a low oil price was quite an insufficient and inadequate compensation.

What then is the subsidy granted by the USSR? Basing our evaluation on the years 1974–80, a period for which data are available from different sources, both Soviet and Western, the lowest estimate (by a Soviet source) is $24 billion. The highest estimate (by Marrese and Vanous) is over $56 billion. If we continue this calculation for the years 1981–84, basing our evaluation solely on the opportunity cost linked to oil sales, this would yield an additional $16 billion.

2 Along with this 'advantage' which the Six obtained, they have also

experienced a considerable deterioration of their terms of trade with the USSR, as by application of the 1975 rule, the prices of their exports to the USSR have risen less rapidly than the prices of their imports. This phenomenon may be compared to the deterioration in terms of trade between industrialised market economies and oil exporting developing nations after 1973. According to Soviet statistics, between 1974 and 1985 the USSR's terms of trade improved by 62 per cent. Western Western estimations on terms of trade with the Six are comparable (Dietz, 1986, has a figure of 46 per cent for the period 1973–82). It should be pointed out that over the twenty-year period preceding the oil crisis, 1955–74, the USSR's terms of trade with its Comecon partners fell by 20 per cent (Hewett, 1974). The oil shocks therefore allowed the USSR to reverse a development which had for a long time been to its detriment.

This improvement in the USSR's terms of trade was also accompanied by a more rapid increase in Soviet purchases (+6.2 per cent annually between 1974 and 1983) than in its sales (+2.4 per cent) in volume. Eastern European countries had to compensate for the energy price rise by stepping up the volume of their exports. For all that, compensation was far from being total.

3 Since 1975, the value of Soviet sales has surpassed the value of Soviet purchases. This *surplus* went against the rules which hold that trade should be balanced (and generally is among Eastern European countries) within Comecon. It might be assumed that the 1975 surplus was due to price modifications at the start of 1975, when foreign trade annual protocols between countries had already defined trade balances in old prices. However, over the following years, this imbalance only increased. The USSR surplus reached r.18.3 billion for the period 1975–86, amounting to about 8 per cent of the cumulated value of Soviet exports to the Six for the whole period. As the transferable rouble is not a convertible currency, this sum could not be used for purchases outside the Comecon zone. For the USSR it therefore represented a foregone gain which must be added on to the opportunity cost born of the relationship between world and Comecon prices.

During the period following 1975 and up to 1986, the Soviet Union often pointed out the need to balance bilateral trade. The trade debt of the Eastern European countries is covered by a long-term credit granted by the USSR at a special rate (2 per cent per annum) for a period of ten years, for which reimbursement in goods began in 1985. Poland obtained a later deadline. The Eastern European countries were therefore expected to cope with pressure to export to the USSR more products adapted to its needs, and it was never so strongly expressed as in the Comecon Summit Declaration of 1984.

4 Price movements have led to a modification of the *commodity composition* of Soviet sales to the Six. Energy exports accounted for only 14 per cent of the USSR's exports to the European Comecon countries in 1970; rose to 26 per cent in 1975; to 50 per cent in 1982; and then remained at the same level until 1986.

5 In *physical quantities*, Soviet supplies have developed differently according to the type of fuel and to the importing country. For 1970–80, oil sales more than doubled (from 34 to 72 million tonnes), with the greatest rise in the case of Bulgaria (a rise of 150 per cent). Romania is a particular case. It only started purchasing oil from the Soviets in 1979 (400,000 tonnes). Gas sales have been multiplied by a factor of twelve in this period, though it is true that they began at a very low level. Here again, Bulgaria had the greatest increase, followed by Czechoslovakia.

After 1980 developments changed. During preparations for commercial trade agreements for 1981–85, the USSR announced that annual sales of oil and oil products should keep the level they obtained in 1980 as their ceiling. At the end of 1981 a 10 per cent drop in oil exports was announced for 1982. This drop was partly compensated for by a rise in gas supplies. The USSR, it would seem, has indeed adopted a policy of long-term stabilisation of fuel sales to European socialist countries, and the supplies declined until 1985 (Table 13). Despite a rebound in 1986–88, the quantities of oil and oil products sold to the Six had not quite reached the 1980 level by 1988. The only country in which imports of oil increased sharply in 1986 (these imports more than trebled) is Romania; they were again reduced in 1987.

6 Although all the countries suffer the effects described, there is a great inequality in the treatment various countries receive. Two countries have had advantages up to 1984–85, namely, Czechoslovakia and the GDR. In 1966, Czechoslovakia concluded a cooperation agreement with the USSR for equipment deliveries to the USSR, which would in return provide Czechoslovakia with 60 million tonnes of oil at the fixed price of 15 transferable roubles per tonne over a fifteen-year period from 1971 to 1984. This had, from 1975, the effect of bringing the average price paid per tonne below the central intra-Comecon price (reduced-price supplies accounting for about a quarter of total supplies to Czechoslovakia). The GDR was granted a similar agreement concluded in 1967.

The differences between the price charged to each country may have other causes. The intra-Comecon price for each product contains transport costs which differ for each country. It is impossible to give an accurate breakdown of this transport margin. Secondly, although very small, a proportion of Soviet supplies is paid for at world prices and in dollars. This covers tonnage supplied over and above the quotas laid down in the bilateral trade agreements. Obviously, for each country concerned, such supplies increased the average price calculated in transferable roubles up to 1985. It is impossible to ascertain the proportion of supplies or the sums involved in these dollar sales. Hungary has long been alone in publishing its dollar trade with Comecon countries; as from 1981 there are also Polish figures. But as there is no breakdown into countries or goods in either of these cases, we cannot calculate figures for oil. Partial figures are occasionally given in the Hungarian press. Thus, in 1979, Hungary bought 1 million tonnes of oil from the USSR in hard currency. The only country about which there can be no doubt on this score is Romania. It paid for all its oil in this way up to 1985. Since then, it has shifted to rouble trade but with barter arrangements.

We should look at the case of Cuba, though it is situated outside the European Comecon. Cuba sells its sugar to the USSR at above the world rate, which is a considerable advantage when the rate is steadily falling. It receives oil from USSR and also from Venezuela in keeping with the terms of an agreement signed with the USSR, which in return supplies equivalent quantities of oil to Spain which is a client of Venezuela. (A similar agreement with Mexico could never be finalised.) Cuba pays the USSR for this oil at a price which has long remained below that charged to European Comecon members (up to 1986). Since the signing of an agreement in 1976, oil and sugar prices have been indexed so that Cuba's terms of trade with the USSR remain stable, and the Cuban price for oil paid to the USSR does not follow the same trends as the Comecon price (Mesa-Lago, Gil, 1988).

The reversal in the trend of world prices after 1985 raises two questions concerning the future of the USSR–Comecon energy trade.

The reverse price shock after 1985

Although oil prices began to decline already in 1983 (March) on the world market, they collapsed at the end of 1985 and in 1986 the gap between Comecon and world market prices was reversed. Comecon prices went on increasing, according to the intra-Comecon price formula which was not altered. In actual fact, a reverse picture emerged as compared with the decade 1975–84:

(i) the intra-Comecon price for oil exceeded the world price and would not reach its level before 1991 should the trend in world oil prices go on;

(ii) it began, however, to decrease as from 1988, for the first time since 1975;

(iii) the terms of trade of the USSR with its Comecon partners declined, beginning in 1987, by approximately 5 per cent in 1987 and 1988;

(iv) the Soviet Union was in deficit with its Eastern European partners, for the first time since 1973, in 1988, for r.2.4 billion, i.e., 7 per cent of its imports from the Comecon–Six in that year.

Should we then say that the USSR is now being subsidised by its Comecon partners? The parallel between the two periods stops here. It is very difficult to find any evidence of Eastern Europe subsidising the USSR. The Eastern European authors who were critical of the subsidy theory do not consider that there has been any change in their relation to the USSR. Eastern Europe did not feel the lower (as compared to world) price of Soviet oil as a favour in the past and, since 1986, it has not felt the higher (again, as compared to world) price of oil as a loss. Why so? Some authors (Vanous, 1988: 5) state that the price of Soviet oil *still* remained lower than world prices should we apply a realistic rate of exchange to the transferable rouble. True, the official rate of exchange may be overvaluing the rouble, but the problem does not lie there. The point is that the two areas of trade, inside and outside Comecon, are strictly non-comparable. In trade with the non-socialist world, prices matter. In trade within Comecon, quantities and the nature (hard or soft) of the goods traded matter first and foremost (see Merkin, 1988).

What is then the future of USSR–Comecon energy trade and, hence, the future of intra-Comecon trade in general?

Two very different issues are raised here. The first has to do with the volume of Soviet supplies. As we have seen, there is little doubt that the USSR intends to bring pressure to bear for these supplies to be lowered, and this is especially true in the case of oil. There are several reasons for this: to economise on Soviet oil resources, an area in which growth is a problem, to push Eastern European countries to make energy savings, and to link energy (and raw material) supplies to return supplies of quality manufactures. Independently of this pressure, the needs of the Eastern European countries have been diminishing in the early eighties, not only due to the effects of economy drives, but in general terms owing to the slowdown in growth which was felt already in 1976–80 and which has accelerated in 1981–85. But investments resumed in the second part of the eighties, and already in 1986–88 energy consumption grew faster, while energy intensity of production decreased less, than in the previous five-year period (see table 12). The oil problem may be alleviated by other energy sources increasingly replacing oil in the future. Intra-Comecon cooperation programmes add weight to this hypothesis. But in this case the cost of such a substitution for Eastern Europe has to be taken into account, both in terms of adapting their domestic equipment to different energy carriers, and in terms of participating in Soviet investments in this field.

What became obvious already in 1988 was that while the USSR agreed for more than ten years to remain a creditor in transferable roubles, Eastern European countries were not ready to turn into structural creditors of the USSR. A downward adjustment of intra-CMEA trade is thus to be expected if Soviet exports to Comecon do not increase, and this is already noticeable since 1987 (appendix, table 3).

The second issue concerns price levels and calculations. We have just said that prices mattered little within Comecon. What matters, in fact, is not their absolute magnitude as compared with world prices, but the relative prices of goods exchanged within Comecon. These relative prices determine the value of exports and imports, but we should not forget that negotiations on quantities and types of goods exchanged are always conducted prior to price bargaining. Price issues have given rise to hot debate in the past, but this may die down gradually if we move towards long-term stabilisation of world oil prices on a low level (i.e., around $18 per barrel) which would also influence the price of other fuels. Should this occur, the debate about applying the current world price or a formula of the type currently in use (possibly with amendments shortening from five to three years the period over which the average is calculated) would become largely irrelevant. The main concern of Eastern European countries would remain the procuring of guaranteed long-term supplies, and this would determine the future level of Comecon trade, Eastern Europe supplying the USSR just up to the level of its purchases. Was then the subsidy debate totally irrelevant?

Why *should* the Soviet Union, to begin with, have been willing to grant its partners indirect transfers from the oil-price boom in 1973 and up until 1985? The reality of such transfers was gradually acknowledged by Western commentators who, up to the beginning of the seventies, were contending that the USSR exploited its partners, as it logically should, due to its sheer dimension and its political power. The very heated controversy which the work by Marrese and Vanous gave rise to in the USA bears witness to this. These authors provided a non-economic explanation for the subsidies granted. They referred to the non-commercial ('unconventional') Soviet gains from trade with Comecon. These include political allegiance, military integration, and ideological unity. The USSR, so to speak, 'paid' for the advantages it received through a continuous deterioration of its terms of trade (until 1974) and by indirect transfers through the price system, since 1974.

Marrese and Vanous's theses were objected to from varying points of view. In numerous articles Jozef van Brabant sought to demonstrate exactly how the intra-CMEA prices were set, thus partly and indirectly challenging the basis of Marrese and Vanous's calculations. Franklyn Holzman (1986, 1987), Padma Desai (1986) and Josef Brada (1985, 1988), without questioning the calculations themselves, offered an explanation based on the theory of customs unions. Comecon is seen as a trade diverting customs union with trade quotas replacing the external tariff, or even as a 'club' providing its members with political and economic public goods (this last thesis being advanced by Brada, 1988). Alternatively, Dietz (1986) questions the very amount of the subsidies and offers an explanation in terms of 'foregone gains' for the Soviet Union (i.e., the gains the USSR would have derived from Comecon trade *if* Comecon prices had not lagged behind world prices) rather than in terms of subsidies. Poznanski (1988) questions the hypothesis of too high prices, as compared with Western prices charged to the USSR for Eastern machinery.

We should agree rather with the 'East European' thesis as first offered by Köves (1983) and analysed by Brada (1988) as the 'dynamic losses theory' (i.e., the East has had imposed on it the growth strategy and planning management system of the USSR and therefore has been prevented from developing in an efficient way). The rationale behind political relations between the USSR and its Warsaw Pact allies does not seem to us to be based on economic bargaining. Firstly, the USSR has no 'need' to pay for its political domination which is based on specific and varying fundamentals. Furthermore, it is quite obvious that conflicts develop between the USSR and its allies which have nothing to do with the scale of the aid granted. Some have tried to see some link between Romania's increasing alignment with the USSR's political positions and supplies of Soviet oil to Romania which got underway in 1979. A puzzling point is then why Romania paid the lowest price for oil supplied by the USSR to Comecon countries in 1986, while openly challenging Soviet views about the development of Comecon. It would then be more appropriate to look for political explanations of political attitudes. The GDR has, according to Marrese and Vanous, benefited from the greatest price subsidies, and this was still the case in 1986 and 1987, while the position of the GDR in external policy (relations with the FRG) and domestic economic developments (resistance to *perestroika*) have been quite opposed to those of the USSR.

In the US highly politicised climate as regards relations with the USSR, at the beginning of the eighties, Marrese and Vanous had probably to use a political explanation – the 'unconventional' gains which the USSR obtains in trading with Eastern Europe while losing in 'conventional' terms – so as to make acceptable their theses, and not be suspected of complacency towards the USSR. Their theses were indeed transcribed by political scientists in terms of 'costs of the Empire' (Wolf, 1985). But the main argument against the idea of political bargaining can be found in the very cause of the increase in subsidies, i.e., the oil price decided on by OPEC. The USSR benefited from this in its relations with the West. There are no grounds to suppose that it deliberately influenced this decision or later OPEC policy moves, even if it supported them in some cases: in 1986, 1987 and 1989 (see below p. 268–9). OPEC policy, the supply-demand relations on the world energy market, and the traditional intra-Comecon price-fixing mechanism, taken all together, in a way 'trapped' the USSR, and later on, after 1985, its East European partners, in a system of prices without any rationality and with adverse effects on both sides; the USSR and the Six. This is also why the customs union theory is unsatisfactory: not that Comecon should not be understood in such terms, but because it cannot explain the fluctuations which we have witnessed.

This is not to say that *once* a given price pattern had emerged, its consequences were not put to use for other purposes. My own thesis (Lavigne, 1983, commented upon critically by van Brabant, 1984) is that the USSR used the automatic price subsidising system as a means of later accelerating socialist integration in the energy field.*

INTEGRATION AND ENERGY

Already in 1971, the Comecon integration programme, among the objectives of its plan coordination, had included the development of Soviet resources through the pooled efforts of member states. The world energy crisis was to concentrate all Comecon efforts on the solving of the crucial problems facing the socialist community, namely energy supplies. Two new structures were introduced as institutional frameworks, the 'concerted plan for multilateral integration measures' and the 'target long-term cooperation programmes' (see chapter 3).

Cooperation in the energy sector was first based on gas, with the construction of the gas pipeline from Orenburg in the Southern Urals to the Western frontier of the USSR (see Hannigan and McMillan, 1981). This involved linking the Orenburg deposit with the transit gas pipeline which crossed Czechoslovakia, the objective being to supply gas to the USSR's six partners. Each partner-state undertook to supply the USSR with equipment on credit, most of which was bought in hard currency from Western companies, and to construct an approximately 500 km stretch of pipeline using its own manpower. In return, the USSR undertook to reimburse this credit through natural gas deliveries, which were to continue after reimbursement at normal commercial conditions in agreed upon quantities (15.5 billion cm in total annually from an overall capacity of 28 billion cm). The USSR remained the sole owner of the pipeline.

Was this a mutually advantageous and fair deal? To answer this we must compare the gains of the USSR and the costs occurred by its partners.

The USSR gained: (1) The development of its gas pipeline network (by 4 per cent of its length approximately). (2) Western equipment for which no hard currency payment was needed from the USSR. (3) Expert manpower working in difficult conditions. Here, it would appear that the USSR was unable to get the full 13,000 workers promised on the pipeline site due to labour shortages and great reluctance on the part of its partners. Romania had from the outset declined to provide such manpower, and only delivered equipment for the de-sulphurisation of the extracted gas, hence it was entitled to get only 1.5 billion cm of gas per year while the other five were to get 2.8 billion cm each per year. In fact only the Bulgarians and the East Germans met their obligations in manpower. The other countries replaced these by deliveries of consumer goods. (4) The building of the pipeline 'trained' the Soviet Union for its next project in the same field, the construction of the Urengoi gas pipeline (see below p. 259).

For *Eastern European countries*, the main advantage lay in the guaranteed access to gas supplies. As for costs, these were relatively high.

1 The USSR's partners had to incur hard currency debts in order to procure the equipment required for the pipeline. It is true that the costs of the operation were reduced to a minimum. Purchases were carried out by Mashinoimport, the powerful Soviet import agency, so that prices agreed upon were most certainly the lowest. Moreover, the necessary loans were secured though borrowing on the Euromarket by Comecon's International Investment Bank (IIB). As it enjoyed excellent creditworthiness, the IIB again most certainly got the lowest interest rates. The IIB then reloaned the Eastern European countries the sums corresponding to their contribution to the project. So, on the one hand, Eastern Europe ran up a hard currency debt at the Euromarket rate plus the IIB margin. On the other hand, the East European countries were lending to the USSR in transferable roubles at the usual rate of 2–3 per cent for long-term, intra-Comecon loans.

2 In terms of national resources taken from domestic capacities, the cost incurred by each country accounted for between 2.4 per cent and 4 per cent of productive investments.

3 The price of gas supplied by way of reimbursement and thereafter through 'normal' trade channels was the usual price calculated in keeping with the 1975 methods. Some countries had demanded more favourable prices as a consideration for the investments made by them; their requests were rejected. In fact, the deadline for reimbursement was unilaterally brought forward by the USSR, which in 1978 repaid its debt by cancelling part of the commercial trade surplus on its current trade with the Six.

4 Finally, in keeping with the terms of the arrangement between the Six and the USSR, the Six had no right over ownership or management of the gas pipeline. There followed great discussion as to the expediency of undertaking the operation as a joint venture on Soviet territory. However, at the time there was no legislation in the USSR authorising such a move. Legislation on joint ventures with socialist countries on Soviet territory was to be adopted only in 1987. It is doubtful that such a law would have been applied to a venture of this type, looking at the very limited (as in 1989) instances of implementation of the 1987 law.

Was the whole operation worth it? Hannigan and McMillan (1981: 285) think that if we consider the costs Eastern European countries would have incurred to procure equivalent quantities of fuel at world prices, the internal rate of return on this investment would compare favourably both with the average profit rate from joint intra-Comecon investments and the rate of return on similar projects in the West.

However, this kind of cooperation was shelved from 1980 onwards (as we have already seen in chapter 3). The second 'Concerted plan' for 1981–85 saw the ushering in of a new strategy. It contained fewer major projects and was based more on a specialisation pattern which was meant to concentrate the big energy-consuming projects in the USSR.

Joint investments nevertheless resumed after 1985. Already in 1984, it was decided to build a new gas pipeline from the USSR to Eastern Europe, which would be called 'Progress' and would supply 20 to 22 billion cm annually. Few details have been given on this project, for which the general agreement was signed in 1985 (see Merkin, 1988), with bilateral agreements following. The pipeline runs from Yamburg in North-Western Siberia (north of the Urengoi field which has been developed for supplying Western Europe), and covers about 4,600 km. The Eastern European countries do not all take part directly in the realisation of the project. Bulgaria, Czechoslovakia, Hungary and the GDR have actually sent manpower to build, with their own equipment, parts of the pipeline located in European Russia. On account of the same project and so as to be entitled to the gas supplies of the USSR, the Eastern European countries also take part in other oil and gas projects in different parts of the USSR. The total amount of the contribution asked from the partner countries is slightly under 5 billion transferable roubles, of which only a small share (less than 10 per cent) is supposed to be in hard currency (Arakelian, 1987; Merkin, 1988).

However, it is above all in the electricity sector that multilateral cooperation has developed in the eighties.

The energy and raw materials Long-term Target Programme, one of the five Target Programmes to run to 1990, was largely based on nuclear energy and the transport of electrical power. Although the Target Programmes are hardly mentioned any more, and despite the Chernobyl accident, this cooperation is still on the agenda.

Intra-Comecon nuclear cooperation goes back to 1955–56 when it was bilaterally developed by the USSR and some countries (Czechoslovakia, the GDR and Hungary). The nuclear energy field became more multilateral with the Target Programme of 1978 and the specialisation and cooperation agreement signed in 1979 which assigns to member states the manufacture of specific types of equipment for the construction of nuclear power stations. The Complex Programme for Scientific and Technological Progress signed in 1985 named nuclear energy as one of the five priority areas of cooperation. In November 1986, a special agreement was concluded to expand the nuclear-power capacities of the member countries up to the year 2000.

We have seen that the share of electricity is very low in the overall energy balance of the East. The share of electricity produced in nuclear stations is much lower than in Western Europe. In 1985, nuclear energy accounted for 13 per cent of total electricity produced (32 per cent in Bulgaria which is very much the testing ground for nuclear power in Eastern Europe, 24 per cent in Hungary, 15 per cent in Czechoslovakia, 12 per cent in the GDR, 10 per cent in the USSR, none in Romania and Poland, Sobell, 1988). (For the same year, nuclear energy generated 30 per cent of the electricity produced in Western Europe, 70 per cent of it in France.) In 1990, for the whole region, the percentage of nuclear-origin electricity should rise to 20 per cent. In 2000, the region is aiming at having an installed capacity of 50,000 MW as compared with 7,100 MW in 1986. Along with the USSR, Czechoslovakia, which has become Comecon's nuclear workshop, has the key role in the production of equipment for the VVER-400 and VVER-1000 Soviet models (VVER=Russian acronym for pressurised-water reactor; the numbers refer to the MW of installed capacity). These models are quite different from the type of reactor used in the Chernobyl power plant, which accounted in 1986 for over 50 per cent of the nuclear-origin electricity produced in the USSR.

The Target Programme provided for the construction of two 4,000 MW nuclear power stations on Soviet territory with the help of Eastern European countries. Unlike in the case of the Orenburg pipeline, each country contributes through the providing of equipment produced in that country. Each is to receive electricity supplies commensurate with its contribution, for the period 1984–2003 at fixed prices.

The growing environmental concerns emerging in the USSR and Eastern Europe and, in some countries such as the USSR, Poland, and Hungary, the liberalisation of public life leading to the open voicing of anti-nuclear protests is not likely to affect this programme. There will be

lags due to the usual delays in the investment process. The actual completion of the projects is running three to five years behind schedule.*

The construction of high-voltage transmission lines completes the
nuclear programme. This is one area where the USSR is the incontestable
world leader. An initial 750 Kv line linked Hungary and the Ukraine.
Transmission lines of the same voltage are to link up new power stations
with Poland and Bulgaria. These operations reinforce the already existing
link-up of the national grids of Comecon countries through the Mir
system, one of the oldest specialised economic organisations of the socialist community founded in 1962.

Multilateral cooperation overlaps with research and development.
There have been two 'international business associations', i.e., bodies
which may be considered as 'socialist multinationals' (see chapter 4),
functioning since 1972–74 in this field. Interatominstrument covers the
use of nuclear power in biological and medical research and has managed
to develop a service activity in several countries; Interatomenergo coordinates multilateral research on nuclear equipment.

Energy as the motor of East–West relations

Between 1973 and 1982, the percentage of energy in the East's exports to
the West rose from 20 per cent to 50 per cent. For the USSR this figure
went from 34 per cent to 80 per cent. These shares are of course calculated from totals expressed in current prices. From 1983 they began to
drop, and in 1986 amounted to 45 per cent (total) and 70 per cent
(USSR) of exports to the West. In volume, energy sales experienced
fluctuations with a downward trend between 1977 and 1982. The
stabilisation, then the drop, in world energy prices led to a recovery of
the volume of sales which bears witness to the strategic nature of energy
products, especially oil, as a hard currency source for the USSR. This is
also true for the smaller Eastern European nations, though to a lesser
extent.

The role played by energy in East–West relations gave rise in the early
eighties to several politically important questions:

(i)   Would Soviet energy supplies to Western Europe entail the risk of
      dependence on the USSR?
(ii) Should the USSR be assisted in developing its energy resources

through Western technology upon which it relies in crucial areas of energy exploration, recovery, and transportation?

(iii)   Would it be possible to correct the growing imbalance between the USSR and the rest of Eastern Europe in trade with the West, where the USSR accounted for 40 per cent of this trade in 1970 and 65 per cent of it in 1983? Would it not be lasting inasmuch as the West, especially Western Europe and Japan, will always be energy purchasers while their markets are increasingly protecting themselves against manufactures offered by Eastern Europe?

The last question hardly seemed relevant as early as 1988. The USSR and Eastern Europe accounted each for 50 per cent of their total trade with the West, as a result of the drop in oil prices which depressed the value of Soviet trade more than that of Eastern Europe. However this does not answer the basic question of the future trends in East–West trade: should the Soviet Union really try to disengage itself from a primarily fuel-based trade, both in the line of its domestic reform and in consideration of long-term trends in world prices?

Though the political debate in the West on Soviet energy trade was centred on the issue of gas, oil in fact still accounts for the main hard currency revenues from energy sales. In 1987, oil sales, including refined products, still accounted for 80 per cent of total energy sales to the West. Oil sales however are spread over many European clients, and the percentage of oil purchases from the USSR in total Western oil imports never went above 6 per cent. Here it is worth pointing to the lessons of history. In 1932, a record year for pre-war Soviet oil exports, the USSR provided 20 per cent of Europe's import needs, 68 per cent of the needs of Italy, 30 per cent in the case of Sweden, 35 per cent for Belgium and 26 per cent for Denmark! (Hannigan and McMillan, 1984). Gas, on the other hand, is only sold to a small number of European countries (Austria, FRG, Italy, France, and Finland). These countries depend greatly on the USSR: almost 100 per cent for Austria and Finland, 35 per cent for France, 39 per cent for Italy and 40 per cent for the FRG (in 1986, when the effect of the 1981–82 gas contracts signed with the USSR was already being felt).

The state of the hydrocarbon fuels market has been increasingly unfavourable to the sellers since 1982. The USSR reacted in the short term by increasing the volume of its oil sales and by playing the spot market. In the long term, the USSR is counting on gas, which will probably still have a surplus market for some years to come, and might again become a sellers' market in the mid-nineties according to many forecasts. Indeed, it is probable that, after 1990, Europe will have to seek supplies. From the Soviet point of view, the costs of developing gas extraction and even transport are lower than for oil or coal. (Moe and Bergesen, 1987). The shift towards gas in domestic consumption means that investment in gas extraction and transport is first geared to domestic needs. Exports of gas account for slightly over 10 per cent of production. Calculations in the Soviet Union have shown that it would be possible to save 150 billion cm of gas per year (i.e. 20 per cent of the 1988 production), including 50 billion in the gas industry alone. Such savings are equal to 1.7 times the volume of Soviet exports in 1987. They would require massive investment, lower, however, than the investment needed to expand production (*Ekonomicheskaia Gazeta*, April 1989, no. 16).

SOME LESSONS FROM THE EURO-SIBERIAN GAS PIPELINE CASE

The first edition of this book (1985) devoted large space to the analysis of the 'gas pipeline case'. It does not seem relevant to expand on this case several years later, when so much has been written on this topic (see Jentleson, 1986; Maull, 1981; Stern, 1987, among many others). This remains interesting as a textbook case because it contains all the conflicts and contradictions of East–West trade. Let us here sum up this case with its background and main issues, and also assess what may be derived from this case in terms of lessons for policy makers.

The background

When the pipeline case became publicly known in 1981–82, it was felt that the Soviet Union was just beginning to expand its gas industry and transportation, and could not do without Western assistance.

In fact, the Soviet Union had already begun to develop its gas resources at the end of the fifties. Although production increased very rapidly, the USSR was still a net importer in the early seventies. These imports came from Afghanistan and Iran on the basis of long-term agreements concluded in 1963 and 1966. Their aim was to supply gas to the USSR's southern and Central Asian regions so as to allow the USSR to export gas to Europe. Iranian gas was transported through a pipeline called IGAT I (Iranian Gas Trunkline) which had been partly constructed by the USSR. The plans for a second IGAT which were envisaged in 1975 were never finalised because of the Islamic revolution. The uncertain future of Iran–Soviet relations (which have improved since 1986) and of Afghanistan–Soviet cooperation after the pull-out of Soviet troops in 1989 makes hypothetical even the revamping of the existing pipelines.

In the seventies the Soviet Union sought initially to expand its gas sales to Eastern Europe, and built the Orenburg pipeline in cooperation with the Comecon countries (see above p. 253). Slightly less than half the capacity of the Orenburg pipeline could be used for exports to Western Europe, but this was not enough to fulfil the contracts already signed with several Western countries for gas deliveries.

Thus, several other projects were explored in the mid-seventies for the construction of a third major gas pipeline. Finally the choice was made for a pipeline linking the Urengoi deposits in North-Western Siberia to Uzhgorod on the Soviet–Czechoslovak border. The contracts with suppliers of equipment were finalised in September 1981, after the invasion of Afghanistan (December 1979) but before martial law was established in Poland (December 1981). The pipeline was to add 4,500 km to a network of 144,000 km of existing pipelines, most of them built without Western equipment.

The pipeline case is a set of intertwined dependencies in different areas, involving all the partners in the case (see Table 15).

The technological dependence of the USSR

Why did technological dependence emerge in the case of the Urengoi pipeline? The answer is that it was the most powerful construction of its kind undertaken in the USSR, starting in a permafrost region where the laying of pipes is particularly difficult, requiring large-diameter pipes. Alone, the USSR could only build pipelines with less capacity, which would have meant constructing two pipelines using less reliable technology. The Soviet Union turned to Western Europe and Japan; for the core of the technology required, Europe depends almost entirely on American technology.

The financial dependence of the USSR

In the long term, the USSR wanted to obtain a guaranteed source of hard currency through gas sales. In the short term, it had to get credits for

Table 15a. *The gas pipeline case: a summary of the issues (A) the technological dependence of the USSR*

Soviet needs	Western suppliers
Pipes of 56 inches in diameter	Mannesmann (FRG): 1,200,000 t Nippon Steel (Japan): 800,000 t Nuovo Pignone (Italy) Tubes de la Meuse (Belgium) Voest Alpine (Austria) Bos Kalis Westminster (Netherlands)
Pipe layers	Caterpillar (USA) Komatsu (Japan)
Welding (here Soviet technology is good but anti-corrosion protection is not mastered)	Anti-corrosion technologies: import of licences
Refrigeration stations (the pipeline must be refrigerated even in permafrost conditions otherwise the heat given off by the gas would cause the permafrost to melt)	Creusot-Loire Entreprises (France) (Japan)
Monitoring equipment	Thomson (France)
Radio-telecommunication equipment	Nokia Electronics (Finland)

Sources: Various press reports.

buying the equipment needed. The Soviet system of foreign trade and foreign exchange monopoly served Soviet strategy, which consisted in linking the financial negotiations, the negotiations on equipment supplies, and the agreements on gas purchases by the Western buyers. Thus the Soviet Union turned its financial dependence on future hard currency earnings into a set of trade dependencies of its partners.

The foreign trade dependence of the Western manufacturers

All the Western suppliers were big companies with which the USSR traditionally traded. Some of them were in financial difficulties which the 'deal of the century' was bound to alleviate (such as the British company John Brown, the German AEG Kanis, or the French Creusot-Loire which eventually indeed went bankrupt). All of them lobbied their governments and/or exerted pressure on their banks to help the USSR to get the interest rate which was required. The Soviet Union adamantly insisted on a rate of 7.8 per cent which was the consensus rate of 1978, already revised upwards since then as the interest rates were rising on the Western monetary market. The Soviet Union was and remains the only

Table 15b. *The gas pipeline case: a summary of the issues (B) dependence of the West in energy and of the USSR in hard currency resources*

Western buyers	Date of contract	Duration of deliveries (years)	Deliveries started (date)	Annual quantity (billion cubic metres)	Negotiated price (dollars per 10 BTU)*	Level of dependence (% deliveries from USSR in total imports of gas) %	years	Soviet revenues from the sale of natural gas years	amounts (million dollars)	quantities (BCM)
FRG (Ruhrgas)	1970	20	1973	2.6		17–19	1980	1982	1,456	10.3
	1972	20	1975	3.4		20	1982	1983	1,349	11.1
	1974	23	1978	2.6		28–30	1990 (planned)	1984	3,827	13.5
	1981	25	1984	10.5	4.7–4.8			1985	3,900	13.5
(BP, Thyssengas, Salzgitter)	1983	23	1985	0.7 (a)	3.8 (c)	40	1987 (actual)	1986	1,810	15.3
								1987	1,313	17.3
								1988	1,100	15.4
France (Gaz de France)	1972	20	1976	2.5		13–14	1980	1982	537	4.1
	1974	20	1980	1.5		25–27	1990 (planned)	1983	499	4.1
	1982	25	1984	8.0	4.4–4.5	33	1987 (actual)	1984	622	6.0
								1985	837	7.4
								1986	810	9.3
								1987	557	8.8
								1988	523	8.7
Italy (SNAM)	1969	20	1974	5.5		27	1982	1982	1,220	9.3
	1975	23	1978	0.9		30–33	1990 (planned)	1983	1,018	8.5
	1982–84	25	1984	4–8	3.6 to 3.8 (d)	33.4	1987 (actual)	1984	1,074	7.7
								1985	745	8.3
								1986	578	7.9
								1987	526	8.6
								1988	609	10.5

Country								Year	amount	share
Austria (OMV)	1968	1968	23	1.5		1982	80	1982	434	3.1
	1974	1975	26	0.5		1987	97.2	1983	306	4.3
	1975	1978	23	0.5				1984	487	4.0
	1982	1984	25	1.5				1985	561	4.5
								1986	423	4.0
								1987	323	3.9
								1988	296	3.8
Finland (Neste)	1971	1974	20	1.4	1987	100				
	1984	1986	25	1.1						
Switzerland (Swissgaz)	1982	19 88	25	0.36 (b)						
Turkey	1984	1987	25	6.0						
Greece	1987	1992	25	2.4						

	Total gas exports to the West:	
	share in overall exports to West (in %)	amount in million $
1982	14.5	3,757
1983	12.3	3,267
1984	14.6	3,827
1985	17.5	3,900
1986	19.9	3,724
1987	12.6	2,831
1988	10.9	2,649

Notes: (*a*) special contract for West Berlin; (*b*) the contract with Switzerland is to be implemented by taking the required quantities on the FRG quota; (*c*) price fixed during the renegotiation of the contract in 1984; (*d*) price negotiated in 1984.
1 million BTU (British Thermic Unit) = 31 cm (cubic meters) of gas (as 1 BTU = 252 calories and 1 cm of Siberian gaz = 8,190 Kcal). Inversely, 1,000 cm = 32.26 BTU.

Sources: Alois Fischer 'Die Erdgasexportvertrage der UdSSR mit westeuropäische Ländern', *Osteuropa Wirtschaft*, 1983, no. 4: 311–14; Arild Moe and Helge Ole Bergesen (1988) (see bibliography); Jan Stankovsky, 'East–West Trade 1987–89: Slight improvement in sight (Developments in 1987 and Prospects for 1988/89)', *WiiW Forschungsberichte*, no. 150, October 1988, table 36; Anita Tiraspolsky, 'Nouvel éclairage sur le commerce extérieur de l'URSS', *Le Courrier des Pays de l'Est*, no. 331, July–August 1988: 42; Anita Tiraspolsky, 'Le Commerce extérieur de l'URSS en 1988 et 1989: le blocage', *Le Courrier des Pays de l'Est*, no. 343, October 1989: 36 (the data on quantities sold in 1988 are estimates).

large world market for pipeline equipment and especially for large-diameter tubes – and the state of the Western steel industry explains why such consideration is so important.

The energy dependence of Western Europe

Any gas transaction involves interdependence of the buyer and the seller. Buyers and sellers are in limited number over the world. For gas delivered by pipe, European countries are the main clients. Outside Europe, Japan is an importer, but of LNG (liquefied natural gas), and so are marginal importers such as Korea or Taiwan. Latin America is not yet a prospective market, and is out of reach of the USSR. The United States might become a market and were so considered by the USSR in the mid-seventies. Apart from political reasons which would hamper Soviet sales, the huge costs of investing in LNG industry and transporting the liquefied gas lead to the dismissal of such prospects. Suppliers are also limited in number, especially those with large reserves. In Europe, with Dutch reserves running out, Norway remains the only prospective supplier. Outside Europe, the main competitor is Algeria. The importers have little choice. Once they have geared their industry to the use of gas in any significant proportion, they may want to diversify their suppliers, but in doing so will inevitably need to give each supplier a large share of the market. With such a pattern, price-fixing is always a bilateral affair, and there is no such thing as a 'spot' market for gas (although one has sometimes used the words to qualify short-term deliveries of gas over quotas specified in contracts). Usually a compromise is reached in such negotiations, with an advantage to the seller when the demand is strong and *vice versa*.

None of these features seem to have been understood by the United States at the time when passions flared up during the 'pipeline case'. It was inevitable that the Soviet Union should have a large share of the market of Western European buyers, without making those buyers critically and unilaterally dependent on the Soviet Union. Later on, when passions had subsided and market trends were reversed, the Soviet Union was to renegotiate its deals with all its buyers (Poisson, 1988, for the French contract) who were doing the same with all their suppliers, resulting in the emergence of a new standard model. In these revised contracts, the quantities specified are more flexible, upwards or downwards; the reference price has been lowered so as to keep gas competitive with other forms of fuel; the selling price is indexed on the prices of a basket of petroleum products or on the 'netback' value of several types of crude, each buyer having in view the competition with other domestic or imported sources of energy; thus, in French contracts the basket contains an electricity index due to the high domestic consumption of nuclear-origin electricity (Percebois, 1988). In these negotiations, as far as is known, the USSR did not behave differently from other sellers.

The US obsession about excessive dependence entailing possible political pressure from the USSR on its Western partners is unfounded. It is not in the interests of the USSR to undermine its image as a reliable supplier, which even the threat of turning the tap off would immediately entail (see Moe and Bergesten, 1987). In general, the gas market is much more stable and less affected by political influences just because it is narrow and because huge development costs are involved on both sides. The only open political disputes in this market were provoked by Algeria in its relations with the United States, Spain and, in particular, France. In this last case, Algeria claimed and obtained from France an overpricing of its gas as a form of development assistance. This is turn no doubt influenced France as to the share of the Franch market to allot to the USSR. The price paid for Soviet gas is much lower, but official French foreign trade statistics are issued in uniform average prices for gas so as to conceal this discrepancy. Quantities not being manipulated, this inflates the value of French imports from the USSR, and hence the French bilateral deficit which indeed became a political issue between the two countries in 1986 and entailed a six-month suspension of oil imports from the USSR!

Power economics: the US action

The United States tried to stop the pipeline construction at different stages. They first attempted to block the credits, then to stop deliveries of equipment, and finally, to prevent the gas purchase deals. All this created a crisis within the Western Alliance in 1982, and in due course (November 1982) the US had to back down so as to avoid the break-up of the Alliance.

The Soviet gains

For a cost in dollars in the range of 10 billion (and, of course, domestic investment costs several times higher), the USSR gained the capacity to supply the West with gas earning hard currency revenues of $2 to 3 billion annually (taking into account the post-1986 drop in prices and in quantities). This is not a bad deal by any standards.

For the future, the Soviet Union is certainly counting on higher gas sales in the nineties, both to its traditional buyers and to new buyers such as Greece or Turkey. There are two other options in the energy field.

1 Increased sales of oil: this short-term adjustment to the 1986 price cut in world oil prices is not sustainable in the long run without (i) substantial economies in domestic use or (ii) massive investments with the cooperation of Western firms in new oil deposits such as Tenghiz in Kazakhstan or in the recovery of oil in the Tiumen (Siberia) region. Exploration of offshore oil in the Barents Sea as well as in the Okhotsk Sea is still more arduous and risky and will not bring results in a near future.

2 The liquefying of coal from the world's richest open-cast mines in Kansk-Achinsk in Siberia: a very ambitious project, which became very controversial because of its high costs and detrimental environmental effects, and which has been scaled down from the over-ambitious format envisaged in 1984 (Warner and Kaiser, 1987).

The growing pressure in the USSR to develop exports alternative to energy sales is not bound to produce substantial effects before the end of the century. Energy remains thus the main hard currency earner. Oil is the dominant and more flexible source of revenues; gas is the most promising in the long run.

ENERGY SALES BY EASTERN EUROPE

The Six are also exporters on the Western energy market. Traditionally, coal has been very important in Poland's sales to the West. The contrast with the USSR is striking. Although it is a major producer, the USSR exports very little of its coal, which accounts for only about 2 per cent of its fuel sales to OECD countries, while for Poland the shares were 15 per cent in 1970, 25 per cent in 1979, 18 per cent in 1986. The Polish crisis strongly affected coal production and sales though there has been some recovery since 1982.

Export of oil and especially oil products accounted for 4 per cent of the Eastern European countries' hard currency revenues in 1973, 20 per cent in 1981, and 22 per cent in 1986. This trade is artificial and fragile being based as it is on oil imports from the USSR or OPEC. This makes the problem of diversifying exports still more crucial for Eastern Europe than for the USSR.

East–South energy trade

Energy occupies an important place in East–South trade. In the field of economic cooperation, the dam designed to provide hydro-electricity and irrigation was the first symbol of Soviet operations in the Third World (the Aswan dam in Egypt, and dams on the Euphrates in Syria and Iraq). To this should be added thermal power stations in India, Iran, Turkey, etc. The other Eastern European countries are also undertaking energy installations, but less major ones (medium-sized thermal power stations, installation of transmission lines, etc.). Cooperation also involves geo-logical prospecting for gas and oil deposits, the construction of pipes and, less frequently, the construction of refineries. Sometimes cooperation works in the other direction. Libya and Kuwait financed the construction of the Adria oil pipeline, from Krk island in Yugoslavia to Czechoslovakia and Hungary. This oil pipeline, though completed in 1979, has not been used owing to falling oil demands by these two countries.

The most striking developments in East–South energy relations con-cern the oil trade (and the gas trade, in the case of the USSR).

For the USSR, the second largest export item in its trade with the South, excluding the 'residual' (see chapter 8) and following machinery exports, is fuels (mainly oil; gas is to be supplied to Turkey by the end of the eighties). Its share has been growing since 1974 and was over 33 per cent of Soviet identified exports in 1980–83, falling to under 30 per cent after 1984. Fuels represent over 50 per cent of sales to Asia (outside the Middle East), and 60 to 70 per cent of sales to Latin America. The reorientation of Soviet exports following the drop in oil prices in 1986 should also affect trade with the Third World. Adjustments have been realised in India–Soviet trade (through an agreement in 1986 committing the USSR to sell more manufactured goods) but still in 1987 exports to this country consisted of oil and oil products for 47 per cent of their total amount.

Fuels account for the larger share of East European imports from the South (56 per cent in 1983, 51 per cent in 1986). For the USSR the share of oil imports is less than half this amount. It is remarkable that the socialist countries did not adjust to the drop in oil prices in the same manner as the developed market economies. The share of fuels, for the countries of the 'North', declined in their purchases from the South from 54 per cent to about 30 per cent between 1985 and 1986. For all the socialist countries, on the contrary, oil purchases increased in quantity from the beginning of the decline in world oil prices in 1983, and this trend accelerated in 1986.

Of all the CMEA countries, Romania is the only one interested in the oil industry of pro-Western nations, such as Kuwait, and the United Arab Emirates, or of geographically distant ones, such as Gabon or Ecuador.

Most of these imports are made for reexport, in crude or refined form. Is this pattern of 'import for reexport' to last? Carl McMillan (1985: 380) considers it as quite temporary because 'it is dictated by special circumstances, in particular the severe hard-currency balance-of-payments difficulties faced by most of the CMEA countries'. The fall in oil prices in 1986 may affect the future oil trade of the Six in several ways. Starting from the fact that all the Eastern European countries (except Romania) have strived for and achieved surpluses in their trade with Middle East oil exporters, they may find it more difficult to maintain such surpluses as the OPEC countries are bound to decrease their imports from the East in a general policy of curbing non-priority imports.

They are also confronted with shrinking gains in reexports to the West, which may prompt them to concentrate on refined oil products rather than on reexport of oil in a crude form. For some countries, such as Romania, the reexport of refined products is the only way to utilise very large domestic refining capacities which could not rely on domestic or Soviet oil. In any case, oil imports have overall decreased in value but increased in quantity during the year 1986; compensation deals have developed here as was generally the case in worldwide oil trade. But, whereas some countries (Bulgaria, Romania) sharply increased their oil imports, others stabilised (Poland) or even decreased them (Hungary).

In the case of the USSR and due to the non-negligible share of this country on the world oil market (about 6 per cent of the Western market), the question arises of a possible conflict of interests between the Soviet Union and the OPEC countries, especially at a time when OPEC strategy consists in reducing sales so as to prevent oil prices from falling. At the end of 1986, the USSR committed itself to cut its exports by 10 per cent in 1987, so as to support the efforts of OPEC. This support was reassessed at the beginning of 1987. However, Soviet sales of crude to the West expanded by over 15 per cent in 1987, which might suggest that the cuts were referring to a given period, and indeed the Soviet oil sales always decline in the first quarter of each year by comparison with the previous quarter. Beginning in 1989, the USSR again pledged itself to reduce its sales. This time the cuts were announced as an absolute figure of 100,000 barrels a day (about 3 million tons, according to Soviet declarations) during six months, which would amount to approximately 4 per cent of the yearly sales of 1988. The move was explicitly announced, for the first time, as a form of cooperation with OPEC. This might indicate that the Soviet Union has a definite strategy as to the desirable level of international oil prices, and the ways to reach it.

CHAPTER 7

———————— · ————————

AGRICULTURE

The agriculture of the East is generally considered by Western public opinion to be one of short supply, unlike the surplus production of Western and North American agriculture. The East absorbed 8.7 per cent of world food exports in 1970, 10.4 per cent in 1980, and 10.1 per cent in 1985. The USSR alone absorbed 22 per cent of world grain exports in 1981. However, Eastern Europe does have considerable output potential capable of making it self-sufficient. It is true that agriculture in the East has not so far managed to meet the food requirements of its population. The cause of this failure, however, lies outside the agricultural sector iself. Policies introduced in the Eastern countries, especially in the USSR, aim at improving conditions which affect output, transport and distribution. Should these objectives be achieved, the East's agricultural trade would be subject to far-reaching structural changes.

The agricultural potential of the East

In the mid-seventies, the East accounted for over 20 per cent of world agricultural output, 33 per cent of world wheat production, 20 per cent of meat output, and over 50 per cent of potatoes and sugar-beet (Beaucourt, 1984: 153). In 1987 the same countries only accounted for 23 per cent of world wheat production, 45 per cent of the world output of potatoes, and 41 per cent of sugar-beet.

The overall agricultural deficit of the East with the non-socialist world stood at $0.5 billion in 1970, sharply increased as from 1975 due mainly to Soviet food imports. This deficit reached $9.4 billion in 1980 (the USSR accounting for 7.7 billion) and slowed down to 4.6 billion in 1985 (the USSR: 3.8 billion) (UN data, *Monthly Bulletin of Statistics*; trade among socialist countries exluded). However, if we match agricultural and agro-alimentary imports to the size of the population, Romania comes last with $92 of agricultural imports per capita for the period 1981–85, followed by Czechoslovakia and Hungary ($120 each), then by the USSR and Bulgaria ($130). Poland stands at $160 and the GDR has a large lead at $330 (data taking into account imports from the West only; for the GDR, including imports from the FRG; ECE/UN, 1988: p. 56). This situation can be put down to a number of causes.

1   *Climatic influences* have been extremely variable and generally unfavourable over the 1974–83 decade (droughts, floods). Between 1979 and 1985, the USSR regularly suffered poor weather conditions at harvest time. This should be added to a more permanent feature: the USSR, and Eastern Europe generally, possess mediocre soils for agricultural exploitation, with two important exceptions, namely, the Hungarian plains and the Soviet black earth (*chernoziom*) region (Ukraine).

2   *The food situation has improved considerably* since 1970 (see Table 16) except for Romania. This country is starved because of the policy of giving priority to the reimbursement of the external debt. All exportable food is sold against hard currency. Statistics on the levels of food consumption in Romania are no longer published since the mid-eighties. As for the other countries, one may notice, among other foods, the rapid increase in meat consumption. The result has been a great rise in grain requirements as cattle fodder requirements have been added to human consumption needs, this being mainly due to underproduction of green fodder and concentrated protein feeds. In the USSR this shortage accounts for the high level of grain imports. Over 50 per cent of domestic production goes into cattle fodder, 20–2 per cent going to human consumption. The greater part of grain imports is earmarked for cattle fodder. The small East European meat exporting countries are also forced into this situation. Their meat sales provide a precious supply of foreign currency not only from industrialised countries but also from the USSR (over the 1974–85 period Hungary has been exporting meat to the Soviet Union in return for hard currency and this has allowed it to regain a hard currency surplus overall since 1980), and from the developing world. The Third World is a large outlet for Bulgarian agricultural exports; mutton, lamb meat, and live lamb to go the Middle East countries.

3   The share of *agricultural workers* in total manpower is tending to fall, while the rate of increase in the total working population is declin-

Table 16. *Agricultural performance of the USSR and the Six*

	Bulgaria			Czechoslovakia			The GDR		
	1976–80 (yearly average)	1981–85 (yearly average)	1987	1976–80 (yearly average)	1981–85 (yearly average)	1987	1976–80 (yearly average)	1981–85 (yearly average)	1987
Grain production (thousand t)	7,849	8,169	7,326	10,043	10,893	11,600	9,037	10,393	11,224
Meat production (thousand t)	745	826	872	1,423	1,501	1,575	1,821	1,954	2,145
	1970	1980	1987	1970	1980	1987	1970	1980	1987
Agricultural population as % of total working population	35.8	24.5	20.0	18.5	14.2	12.2	13.0	10.5	10.6
Investments in agriculture as % of total investments	15.7	12.4	5.8	10.7	10.7	13.8	12.8	9.7	7.7
Per capita consumption:									
meat (kg)	43.7	64.9	77.0	71.9	85.6	87.4	66.1	89.5	99.4
milk/m. products (kg)	161	234	278	196	228	251	n.d.	n.d.	n.d.
bread and related goods, flour content (kg)	174	160	144	113	107	112	97	95	99
vegetables (kg)	118	126	146	76	66	77	85	94	102
	average 1971–75	1980	1987	average 1971–75	1980	1987	average 1971–75	1980	1987
Net grain trade (thousand t)	94	–41	–710	–1,487	–1,924	–254	–3,424	–4,025	–1,495
Net meat trade (thousand t)	53	112	110	17	23		22	91	

	Hungary			Poland			Romania			The Six			The USSR		
	1976–80 (yearly average)	1981–85 (yearly average)	1987	1976–80 (yearly average)	1981–85 (yearly average)	1987	1976–80 (yearly average)	1981–85 (yearly average)	1987	1976–80 (yearly average)	1981–85 (yearly average)	1987	1976–80 (yearly average)	1981–85 (yearly average)	1987
	12,633	14,423	13,814	19,495	22,224	25,030	19,383	21,701	18,624	78,440	87,803	87,618	205,027	180,311	211,365
	1,472	1,726	1,730	3,064	2,587	2,965	1,623	1,741	1,845	10,148	11,132		14,843	16,226	18,940
	1970	1980	1987	1970	1980	1987	1970	1980	1987	1970	1980	1987	1970	1980	1987
	26.4	22.0	20.9	34.6	26.3	28.4	49.3	29.8	28.7				25.4	20.2	19.0
	21.7	14.6	16.7	16.3	16.9	15.9	16.4	13.3	18.1 (1985)				17.5	19.9	16.8
	75.5	93.6	101.5	61.2	82.1	74.4	31.2	60.0	55.0**				48.0	57.0	64.1
	110	166	190	413	451	423	n.d.	n.d.	n.d.				307	314	341
	128	115	112	131	127	118	173	180	175				149	138	132
	83	80	75	111	101	116	87	140	170				82	97	100
average				average			average			average			average		
	1971–75	1980	1987	1971–75	1980	1987	1971–75	1980	1987	1971–75	1980	1987	1971–75	1980	1987
	601	779	754	−3,327	−7,805	−2,952	142	−342	842	−7,401	−16,310	−3,815	−7,120	−28,950	−28,600
	164	331	453	145	110	138	82	101	266	449	768	967	−249	−821	−858

Sources: OECD (1983), Beaucourt (1984), USDA (1988), Cochrane and Lambert (1988); *The USSR and Foreign Countries* (in Russian), Statistical Compendium, 1988; *Statistical Yearbook of the member countries of the CMEA* (in Russian), 1988; 'Agricultural Country Profiles for Eastern Europe and the Soviet Union, 1981–1985', *Economic Survey of Europe in 1987–1988*, ECE/UN, New York, 1988: 203–30.

ing. The agricultural working force is aging. The growing share of the urban population in total population has the result of reducing the level of own (non-market) consumption. The incentives offered to the private sector, which in all these countries is an important additional supplier of agricultural produce for the market and farmers' own needs, have not proved sufficient to curb the fall in its contribution to total consumption and production. Even in Poland, where private production remains the norm (80 per cent of cultivated land) the level of farmers' own consumption is falling. It is forecast that this drop in the active agricultural population will continue. The effects of this may be offset by an increase in labour productivity.

4   *The growth of productivity* is the priority objective of domestic agricultural policies. It does however involve major investment. For all that, with the exception of the USSR, the share of total investment earmarked for agriculture is tending to fall. In the USSR, the Food Programme adopted in May 1982 – the last major programme of the Brezhnev era – provided that one-third of total economic investment in this period would go into agriculture and the agro-industrial complex. Imports of agricultural produce were meant to drop steadily with an initial increase of imports of agricultural equipment, chemical products, refrigeration, storage, processing and packaging equipment.

5   The *agricultural shortages* of Eastern Europe and the USSR may, to a very large extent, also be put down to losses and wastage owing to poor agricultural management and the pricing system. In the USSR, wastage in the production process, from harvesting right up to the processing of agricultural produce, is particularly high. For grain, the wastage level stands at 13 per cent according to conservative estimates (Kostecki, 1984: 203; USDA, 1988, puts the losses at 20 to 30 per cent of total use) which means that, were these losses to be avoided, two-thirds of imports since 1979 would be unnecessary! Several reasons lie behind this wastage: an inadequate system of getting agricultural equipment to cultivated land in the light of the limited time (three weeks on average during which harvesting is possible); a shortage of spare parts and skilled personnel (this, while the USSR's tractor production in 1986, was six times greater than that of the United States, and the production of agricultural combines, more than ten times greater! But at least one out of three tractors is just a 'reserve' of spare parts); and inadequate transport and silo facilities. As far as fruit and vegetables are concerned, these same factors give even more catastrophic results, with a large proportion of the harvest rotting in the fields. Storage facilities near the main cities are

overburdened and old. Indeed, Soviet daily life abounds with outrageous tales related by city workers called out to Moscow sorting depots on communist Saturdays (*subotniki*) to fight a losing battle against foul-smelling carrots and cabbages.

The smaller Eastern European countries suffer less from such losses, which are compounded by the sheer size of the Soviet territory. However, in all these countries, the policy of supporting retail food prices has led to distortions even if it has most definitely made for improvements in living standards. To-day, in no more than two countries are retail food prices supported as a matter of principle. These are the USSR and the GDR where subsidies equalling 10 per cent to 20 per cent of the state budget are in force. In all the other countries, food prices rose sharply in 1981–82, from 35 per cent (Romania) to 120 per cent (Poland). In the USSR this maintaining of price stability has been called into question after Gorbachev's access to power as the nominal price of bread, which has not been altered since *1954*, is inducing livestock owners to feed it to their animals as fodder, which leads to an even greater demand for grain. It should be noted that human grain consumption in the USSR was estimated at 142kg per inhabitant in the end of the seventies; while in the EEC this figure was 82kg (Beaucourt, 1984: 161).*

The reasons for the East's need to import agriculture produce are various and cannot simply be put down to the inefficiency of planned agriculture.

It would no doubt be unrealistic to aim at complete self-sufficiency through the elimination of these causes. Studies do however agree that we may see a reduction in imports. One OECD study (OECD, 1982) estimates that minimum Soviet grain imports in 1990 will be 10 million tonnes. For Eastern Europe, an American study estimates that by 1990–91 net grain imports might stand at 6 million tonnes (Cook *et al.*, 1984: 26).*

Can these developments be affected by intra-Comecon cooperation? Eastern European agricultural integration is surprisingly poor. In this respect, the EEC and Comecon may be compared, the former being characterised by the importance given to its Common Agricultural Policy and the latter by the stress it puts on a common energy policy.

Trade and agricultural cooperation between socialist countries

It would seem that, given the poor state of agriculture, Comecon countries would do well to develop cooperation in this area. Yet, there is no equivalent of a Common Agricultural Policy, either structural or commercial, between Começon countries. The 'Target Programme' for agriculture and the food industry adopted in 1978 was limited to the exchange of information and joint research projects (in the field of genetics, breeding, chemical crop protection, and the improvement of fodder production technologies). No national production specialisation has been provided for in Eastern Europe. Moreover, the programme specifically laid down that the solving of Comecon's agricultural problems lay first and foremost, in stepping up each country's national production. The only specialisation set out in the programme, on the basis of a multilateral international specialisation agreement signed in 1971 and extended to 1981, concerned seed.

On the other hand, the Long-term Target Programme does envisage more global and active cooperation with underdeveloped Comecon countries, in particular, Cuba. Two multilateral agreements were signed in 1981 to formalise this move. One dealt with sugar (providing for an increase of 45 per cent in Eastern Europe's purchases from Cuba between 1980 and 1990, as well as a set of measures helping Cuba's sugar industry). The second measure concerned the industrial processing of citrus fruit, for which exports to Eastern Europe were to increase nine-fold over the same period.

The agro-industrial and agro-food branches were also catered for by the Target Programme, with the same limitations (research and development in agricultural equipment and technologies, and the development of efficient methods in the fields of preservation, refrigeration, and packaging and bottling). This aspect of the programme was enhanced in 1983 by the adoption of forty-seven 'complex cooperation measures for improving member countries' supplies in foodstuffs'. These measures all tend to develop technology and equipment in cultivation, protection, harvesting, transport and stocking.

Agriculture and the agro-food industry account for a very small proportion of credits granted by the International Investment Bank (2 per cent in the period 1970 to 1988). The Bank has financed a few operations, mainly outside Europe (these include the development of tobacco growing and processing in Bulgaria, citrus fruit growing in Cuba, and wool processing in Mongolia).

The agro-food industry is likewise absent from other forms of joint activity. Among intra-Comecon joint organisations or ventures, one may quote Agromach, an international organisation for the development of agricultural equipment set up in 1964 between Hungary and Bulgaria, which was subsequently joined by the USSR and the GDR.

Is it at least possible to speak of Comecon's superior efficiency in cases of emergency? The Polish crisis showed that, even in a crisis situation, bilateral cooperation and assistance won out over multilateral aid. Three countries, namely the USSR, the GDR and Czechoslovakia, provided the bulk of food aid, mainly through reexporting grain purchased on the world market.

What accounts for this cooperation, which is clearly inadequate, whether we compare it to the powerful means mobilised by Comecon countries in the field of energy, or the EEC's Common Agricultural Policy?

Comparison with the energy situation provides part of the answer. Here, the USSR is the leading supplier and sometimes, as in the case of gas, the sole supplier. Cooperation is based on a few major though limited projects designed to guarantee supplies. When it comes to agriculture, however, all the countries are producers and have shortages in at least one area (crops or livestock). Each country's domestic policy is aimed at self-sufficiency and cooperation is very difficult to implement. Furthermore, plan coordination is practically impossible due to the great differences in internal planning methods, in agricultural structures and the inadequacies and errors in forecasting which beset each nations's agricultural planning.

Why then do they not resort to market instruments following the example of the EEC's Common Agricultural Policy which is based on price support? Such a policy would also fit in with domestic trends in regulation, in which direct planning of agricultural production by command from above has almost everywhere (with the exception of Romania and the GDR) been replaced by economic incentives, such as prices, bonuses, etc.?

When compared to the position agriculture holds in the East's trade with the West or the South, intra-Comecon agricultural trade is not very great (it accounted for 7 per cent of overall trade in 1975, dropping to 4 per cent in 1985, with a steady declining trend). Comecon has never entertained the idea of applying CAP-type measures to exports from its member states. However, since the sixties, there have been calls for a system which would ensure that intra-Comecon agricultural pricing is exempt from the rules governing international socialist price-setting, and would thus escape the long-term trends of the world market, so as to fall into line with intra-EEC prices. This obviously gave rise to conflict between net importers and exporters on the Comecon market. The importers (the USSR, Poland, the GDR, and Czechoslovakia) have always defended reference to the world prices, arguing that these prices reflect international production costs on the world market. The exporters: (Bulgaria, with 34 per cent of the intra-Comecon market in 1980, Hungary, 30 per cent, and Romania, 14 per cent, these sales directed for more than one-half toward the USSR) stress than one could with equal objectivity justify reasons for referring to intra-CEE prices, since climatic and geological conditions are not fundamentally different in Eastern and Western Europe. Two complementary arguments were put forward. These were, firstly, that world prices are partly determined by production conditions in developing countries with a cheap labour force. And secondly, that non-European developed countries exporting to the world market subsidise these exports greatly, which puts the world prices of food products approximately 15 to 20 per cent below the real costs.

As it is, the influence of intra-Comecon net importers is too great for the net exporters to gain the ascendancy in this matter. A more likely assumption is that the net exporters managed to secure some concessions in price bargaining. During many years, over the period 1974–85, Hungary was paid in hard currency for a part of its agricultural exports to the USSR. This is no longer the case since 1986, but Hungary and, probably, also Romania, have negotiated deals with the USSR involving energy supplies in return for food.

It is likely that the future development of the intra-Comecon market for food and agricultural produce will be shaped largely by the state of the energy market. The greater the demand by the Six for energy from the USSR, the more the Soviets will seek concessions on food supplies. As can be seen in the USSR's own food programme, the way to achieve greater independence from foreign suppliers is through the intensification of purchases from 'brother' countries.

Possibilities for more intense cooperation are undermined by the already mentioned difference existing between the various Eastern European agricultural systems. These differences are considerable, ranging from smallholding privatised agriculture in Poland to livestock factories in the GDR, from Bulgaria's agro-industrial complexes to Hungary's multi-activity cooperatives. Of these, only one country has proved able to set up an efficient and prosperous agricultural system, one which provides good living standards for farmers, meets the needs of consumer requirements and secures surpluses for export. This country is Hungary, although it is true that it enjoys natural resource endowments excellently suited to agriculture. The 'Hungarian model', a combination of market incentives and reliance on the most up-to-date technologies and techniques, has been acknowledged as the example to follow. This was particularly the case in the period when Andropov was in power in the USSR, and again after Gorbachev's ascent to power. For all that, the conditions of the Hungarian experience are not too easy to share with the other countries.

Trade with industrialised nations

In East–West agricultural and food trade, the small Eastern European countries account for a smaller share than is the case in East–West trade overall and this share is likely to drop still further especially as far as imports are concerned. The main characteristics of their trade may be presented as follows.

1 Imports are geared to the requirements of livestock farming, either for export (Hungary, Bulgaria) or for domestic consumption (Poland, Czechoslovakia). The GDR, which is a net importer of agricultural products, is actually an exporter of meat to the FRG (West Berlin in particular).

2 Principle exports are meat and poultry. Hungary is the Comecon recordholder here, especially for poultry. One in ten fowls exported on the world market is Hungarian! Poland and Czecholsovakia are the main sugar exporters.

The USSR's agricultural trade is first and foremost marked by the concentration on grain (accounting for 55 to 65 per cent of its food and agricultural imports in the eighties). The USSR has topped Japan as the main world grain importer in the eighties. It is the world's third greatest grain producer after the USA and China. The USA is the world's leading grain exporter (accounting for slightly under 40 per cent of world grain sales). Given these factors, the Soviet Union's grain trade with the United States was bound from the outset to take on the political and strategic character which still marks it. The USSR is also able to call on other suppliers within the EEC, in particular, France. The appearance of politics in these relations has been the most significant factor of the eighties.

AGRICULTURAL TRADE BETWEEN THE USSR AND THE USA

Soviet–American agricultural relations are characterised by the conflict within the United States which pits the economic expediency of selling grain to the Soviets against the political desire to restrain trade relations with this country. During the period 1972–74, the 'golden age' of Soviet–American relations, economic expendiency and political desire coincided, though this was an exceptional situation. This conflict explains the extremely paradoxical nature of agricultural relations between the two countries. Seen from the Soviet point of view, the situation is in no way straightforward. The USSR needs the USA – but only up to a point. It is easier for the USSR to diversify its grain suppliers than it is for the USA to increase its markets outside the USSR. The readiness the USSR has shown to reduce trade with the USA, among others, is a reaction against embargo-sanctions which has been particularly marked since 1981. However, the undeniable tendency of the Soviet authorities and foreign trade officials is to seek the privileged expansion of trade with the USA.

Since 1954, US agricultural policy has been based on the PL 480 Law, a permanent aid programme which takes the form of loans to foreign governments. A new system initiated in 1985, the Export Enhancement Programme, uses surplus stocks managed by the Commodity Credit Corporation to reimburse exporters to targeted markets. The bonus is equal to the difference between the exporter's price and the world market price; it is issued in the form of certificates allowing the purchase of commodities from the CCC. Since the beginning of the programme, the USSR has had the largest share in it, about 33 per cent (USDA, 1988: 40).

The first massive Soviet grain purchases date back to 1963. The USA did not benefit from them, as Canada was almost the sole supplier to the USSR. In October 1963, the US government authorised grain sales to the USSR with commercial credits on 180 days. Up until this time, in keeping with the 1934 Johnson Act, the USSR had no access to private financing, which was forbidden with states which had failed to settle all debts with the United States. This was aimed at pre-revolutionary debts subsequently cancelled by the Soviet authorities. Along with this, in order to win over the transporters as well as the farmers, the US government introduced the '50 per cent clause' which stated that at least 50 per cent of the grain should be transported by US ships. Following these measures, some imports were undertaken by the Soviet Union in 1964 (1.8 million t.).

It was only in 1972 that the USSR started importing on massive scale from the USA. It purchased 19 million tonnes for $1.2 billion, half of which was to be settled in cash, the remaining half on credit over three years. The USSR was asked a very low price owing to very discreet negotiations. The grain prices then doubled within a few months, once Soviet purchase became general knowledge. The '50 per cent clause' which had been lifted in 1971, was reintroduced in 1972 but scaled down to 33 per cent of the transported volume.

The 1972 episode, which has been called the 'Great Grain Robbery' (Goldman, 1975), made the Americans seek to introduce some elements of planning in these relations. This gave rise to the first Soviet–American grain agreement in 1975 and the setting up in the same year of satellite surveillance of Soviet harvests through the LACIE system (Large Area Crop Inventory Experiment) (Morgan, 1979; thriller writers were inspired by this, see Tanous and Rubinstein, *The Wheat Killing*, Arrow Books, 1981). Such observations makes it possible to determine the general harvest prospects as early as March or April and are the basis of evaluations made by the US Department of Agriculture.

The 1975 agreement committed the USSR to the puchase of between 6 and 8 million tonnes of grain annually over the period 1976–80. This quantity was in fact always surpassed except for the agricultural year 1976–77 following the good harvest of 1976 (Table 17).

In the autumn of 1979, the USSR negotiated the purchase of 25 million tonnes of grain up to September 1980. A little over 4 million tonnes of this were delivered before the end of December. The invasion of Afghanistan led the then president of the United States, Jimmy Carter, to impose an embargo on grain sales in January 1980. So as to avoid a breach of contract, the minimal quantities of grain (6 million tonnes over the agricultural year ending in September 1980) were allowed to be delivered. The EEC agreed not to jeopardise the embargo while not actually joining it. Thus, it limited its exports to the USSR to the average quantities sold to that country. In return, the USA agreed not to increase their sales in traditional markets of the EEC (North Africa).

The embargo was to entail a loss of at least $5 billion for the US economy (compensating the farmers, buying back grain held by exporting companies, supporting the reduction of sown areas), while the USSR incurred the additional cost of 1 billion dollars in converting to other suppliers, through an increase in transport costs.

Failure was in fact immediate. Argentina was the first to dissociate

Table 17. *Soviet grain production, imports and exports*

Years	Production	Imports total	Imports from the US	Exports
1971	181	3.5	0.5	9.6
1972	168	15.5	7.2	5.1
1973	222	23.9	14.3	5.8
1974	196	7.1	3.8	8.4
1975	140	15.9	7.5	4.4
1976	224	20.6	12.0	2.4
1975–1976		26.1		
1976–1977		11.0	6.1	
1977 (77–78)	196	18.9	14.8	4.7
1978 (78–79)	238	15.6	15.5	2.5
1979 (79–80)	179	30.5	8.0	3.9
1980 (80–81)	189	29.4[b] 34.5	9.5	1.7[b]
1981 (81–82)	158	47.3	13.9	2.8
1982 (82–83)	187	34.3	6.2	3.0
1983 (83–84)	192	32.5	14.1	2.5
1984 (84–85)	173	55.5	18.6	1.8
1985 (85–86)	192	45.6[b] 29.9	7.0	1.8[b]
1986 (86–87)	210	26.8[b] 27.5	8.2	1.5[b]
1987 (87–88)	211	30.4[b] 32.5	13.2	1.8[b]
1988 (88–89)	195	35.0[b] 39.0[a]	24.0[a]	1.8[b]

[a] Estimates.
[b] Soviet data from the statistical compendium 'The USSR and Foreign Countries, 1987' (in Russian).

Column 1: the calendar years refer to production; the data (col. 2) are from Soviet sources. From 1975 (year of the first US–Soviet agreement on grain trade, Soviet imports are referred to for the 'agricultural year' (October/September).

Column 2: the Soviet data refer to calendar years.

Column 3: beginning from 1975–76 the imports refer to the 'agricultural year'; the same for imports (col. 4) except for the Soviet data shown by [b].

Sources: Soviet official statistics (for production; up to 1976 for exports and imports, and also for X/M data noted by [b]).

US Department of Agriculture sources for foreign trade past 1976, and for US exports. Press reports.

itself from the embargo. In July 1980, it signed with the USSR a five-year agreement for yearly deliveries of 4.5 tonnes of grain. In actual fact, 7.6 tonnes were sold in 1980 and 15.7 sold in 1981 which made Argentina the USSR's main grain supplier for that year and also its leading partner in the Third World.

The embargo was lifted in April 1981, in keeping with the electoral promises made to the farmers by the new president Ronald Reagan, and, at a time when it was already being forecast that the US harvest of 1981 would beat all records so far. In the same month (April 1981) Argentina signed a five year agreement for the supply of 60,000 to 100,000 tonnes of meat per year to the USSR. In May 1981, Canada and the USSR concluded an agreement for the delivery of 25 million tonnes of grain between August 1981 and July 1986.

In the final analysis, during the period in which it ran, the embargo was strictly respected only by the EEC, and this affected France first and foremost as the principle grain exporter. France was forbidden to deliver 60,000 tonnes of wheat to the USSR just a few weeks prior to the lifting of the embargo. As for the USA itself, it is likely that grain multinationals were able to carry out indirect sales to the USSR. In any case, from June 1980, the grain multinationals received authorisation to sell grain not produced in the USA.

Subsequent to the lifting of the embargo, the 1975–80 grain agreement was twice extended by the USA until September 1983. The USSR could therefore purchase at least 6 to 8 million tonnes and, at most, as much as 23 million tonnes of grain annually. However, it chose not to give back to United States their former position of principal supplier and thus protect itself against possible future embargoes. Interestingly, no embargo was introduced after martial law was imposed in Poland in December 1981. Actual grain deliveries fell short of potential orders by some 14 million tonnes. A new five-year agreement was finally signed in August 1983, and this committed the USSR to purchase at least 9 million tonnes annually (and at most 12 million tonnes, anything over this quantity would require prior negotiation) and stated that the US government 'will take no discretionary measure through the American legislation' to reduce grain deliveries. This anti-embargo clause was soon to be put to the test. The 'KAL-707 affair', in which a South Korean Boeing flying over Soviet territory on 1 September was shot down by Soviet fighter planes did not jeopardise this agreement. Quite the contrary, in fact. That same month, the Soviets signed contracts for almost 4 million tonnes of grain.

The long-term agreement which expired in September 1988 was extended for twenty-seven months (ending end-1990) for identical quantities (at least 9 million tons of which 4 of wheat, 4 of corn and 1 of wheat, corn, or soyabeans; at most – without prior negotiation – 12 million tons, the additional 3 being unspecified). The USSR obviously did not want to commit itself for a longer period, for at least two reasons. First, in 1988, following the US drought which reduced the harvest and depleted the stocks of grain, world prices of grain began to increase after a decreasing trend of several years. Second, the Uruguay round of Gatt multilateral negotiations has agriculture on its agenda with the aim of 'liberalising' agricultural trade through the cut in subventions. Added to these, the Soviet Union might after all expect to reap the benefits of the agricultural reform, in the form of reduced imports.*

In any case, the United States has lost its position of quasi-monopoly on the Soviet market which it had in 1979, with 70 per cent of the Soviet market, and is not likely to regain it, whatever the circumstances. The consequences of the grain embargo for the USA were not only economic (i.e., additional costs, and the drop in its share of the market). The embargo also gave rise to political conflict with Western European allies who were all too aware that in terms of profit lost they were bearing the brunt of restrictions on technological sales to the USSR. While these restrictions steadily increased from 1980 onwards, Europeans felt that when US interests were seriously jeopardised, foreign policy considerations were overruled by the interests of domestic policy.

These splits within the Western alliance were surely only to be welcomed in the USSR. From the economic standpoint, there was now proof that grain embargoes were not feasible. Why then should the Soviet Union not further step up its dependence on grain imports?

The question was put in this challenging way by the US economist Jan Vanous. According to him, we have here an exemplary case of comparative advantage. One tonne of oil at world prices is roughly equal to 1.6 of grain (in 1983, 1 tonne of oil cost $213, 1 tonne of grain (wheat+corn) $130). In Soviet prices, 1 tonne of oil equalled 0.3 tonnes of grain. For gas, the comparative advantage was even greater: the gas equivalent of 1 tonne of oil was 1.2 tonnes of grain at world prices and 0.139 tonnes at domestic Soviet prices. Thus, it would be far more profitable for the USSR to invest more in their energy sector and reduce agricultural investment (Vanous, 1982; see also Holzman, 1974). The argument remains valid for a later period. With declining oil prices and increasing grain prices (as in 1988), one tonne of oil still amounts to more grain on the world market than in the USSR.

Soviet officials should not be swayed by this kind of argument. Firstly, it is based on a comparison of relative prices, which is due to yield misleading results because of the irrationality of the Soviet domestic prices, undervaluing energy carriers in particular. The price reform of 1991 should at least double the domestic price for oil, hence its purchasing power of grain. Secondly, there is a political risk of dependency, even with the firmest anti-embargo clauses specified in agreements. Thirdly, transport and storage facilities are constraining factors. Beyond 40 million tonnes a year of grain imports, Soviet port capacities are almost saturated, and this generates delays and losses.

The Soviets are, rather, asking whether one might reduce imports by cutting losses. We have already seen how large were the losses in domestic production. One has to add that a part of the imported grain is lost too, for the same reasons as for domestic production and also because there is a very weak coordination between the importer (the traditional FTO Exportkhleb) and the Gosagroprom representing the end-user. Finally, the production of fodder would strongly reduce import needs. In a broader view, the measures taken in the USSR to increase the incentives offered to peasants might also have an impact on imports in the long term. In August 1989, it was decided to pay the farmers in foreign currency for all wheat sold in excess of the average annual production obtained between 1981 and 1985. The prices would be well under the world prices for grain but still providing an incentive as the farmers would be able to use hard currency for imports for their own use.

As it is, the USSR has still to import a minimum quantity of grain every year. From the long-term agreements signed between 1980 and 1983, one might infer that this amount was of 30 million tonnes. Most of the agreements have been renewed. Up to 1990 the USSR will be able to import 24.5 million tonnes (Argentina, 4.5 million tonnes; Canada, 5; France, 3; USA, 12). Beyond this quantity, the USSR can of course meet its need on the open market. Fears of a diminishing world grain supply emerged at the end of 1988 due to climatic changes. Should this be the case, the USSR would still be able to get preferential supplies from the world exporters; less creditworthy Third World countries would find it more difficult.

AGRICULTURAL RELATIONS BETWEEN THE EEC AND THE USSR

US and EEC interests in this field are both opposed and competing. The USA is the world's leading exporter and the second largest importer of agricultural produce; the EEC is in exactly the reverse position (with a very different commodity composition of agricultural trade). When compared to the running disputes which pit these two partners against each other over reciprocal agricultural trade (the Uruguay Round GATT negotiations are a significant example), conflicts over sales to the USSR rather pale into insignificance. We have already seen how, when it came to it, the EEC actually complied with the US grain embargo without officially declaring it. Another periodically recurrent problem is butter.

The EEC's considerable butter surplus is exported at world prices with subsidies. Sales to the USSR usually give rise to political debates on the theme 'The EEC housewife is paying for the Soviet consumer's butter.' Intra-community confrontation sees France pitted against Great Britain and West Germany.

After the invasion of Afghanistan, export subsidies on butter to the USSR were done away with but a compromise was found in 1981 in the sale of 100,000 tonnes to New Zealand (the world's leading butter exporter), which could then 'possibly' sell its butter to the Soviets! Direct butter sales to the USSR were only resumed in June 1983. Between the end of 1980 and this date, stocks had increased twenty-fold and were reaching the level of 600,000 tonnes; they reached a record level of 1.5 billion tonnes in 1986. Sales to the USSR helped to deplete the stocks and reduce the storage costs. In 1987–88, deals for over 620,000 tonnes were concluded; the last deal, in July 1988, implied a huge subsidy as the price paid by the Soviet Union was 1/15 of the Community price.

Food supplies from the Third World

We should point out here that 'Third World' is used as defined by the East and therefore does not include Cuba. This Comecon country does however play a special role in supplying sugar to the East. Since 1975 the European Comecon nations have been purchasing around 60 per cent of Cuba's sugar exports, the bulk of which goes to the USSR. The first Soviet–Cuban sugar agreement dates from 1964. In 1976, a new agreement was signed, according to which the USSR did not merely commit itself to pay Cuba prices above the world level as it had done in the past. It also guaranteed terms of trade with sugar prices indexed to the prices of imported basic products, particularly oil. In addition to this 25 per cent of the sugar purchases were to be settled in hard currency. Between 1975 and 1980, 90–100 per cent of the USSR's imports of raw sugar came from Cuba, and the proportion was still 85 per cent in 1985. Imports here are as much a form of assistance as a source of supply.

In Comecon purchases from the Third World, food products have a large place. Until 1974, food products accounted for around one-third of these purchases, both in the purchases of the USSR and of the Six. Since then, the proportion of food imported by the Six has been steadily falling, down to under 20 per cent in the mid-eighties. USSR food imports peaked in 1981 with a share of 61 per cent in total imports from the Third World. The share decreased in the following years remaining in the range of 25 per cent.

Underlying these percentage figures, there are two very different situations.

1 In the USSR's food trade, the major importance is given to grain. The 1981 'explosion' of food purchases can be explained by wheat and maize from Argentina following the US embargo on grain sales. Argentina became, in 1981, the leading Third World trading partner of the USSR, even overtaking India which usually holds this position. In 1987, the second year of a good harvest in the USSR, it had dropped to fourth place, despite the long-term agreement between the two countries. There are thus strong fluctuations in Soviet grain imports from the Third World, due to the pattern of Soviet harvests. Similar fluctuations affect imports of tropical foodstuffs (cocoa, coffee and tea) (see Lavigne, 1987), which the Soviet Union buys mainly from direct suppliers and not from traders, unlike the Six. Here, fluctuations are explained by price considerations and also by domestic policy. When imports are to be cut, as was the case in 1986 as a consequence of the drop in Soviet earnings in hard currency, import of consumer goods suffers first.

2 For food, the Six are much less import-dependent than the USSR. One group of imported items consists of 'non-priority' goods (rice, tea, coffee, cocoa, tropical foodstuffs or citruses). The policy of the Six has been to curb these imports, or to shift them to Western traders so as to get better terms. The other important item is fodder. It is a critical item for the animal husbandry of the Six, and particularly for the meat exporters (Hungary, Romania, Bulgaria). There is still a long way to self-sufficiency in this field, although the strategy of the concerned countries is to increase the crops of such cereals as soya or maize.

The USSR does not supply food products. The main sellers among the Six are Southern countries (Romania, Bulgaria, Hungary); the main buyers are Middle East countries, for meat and fresh produce.

PART III

——————— · ———————

FINANCE AND RISK

Centrally planned economies are not monetary economies. Planning mens, first and foremost, real decisions fixing output and inputs in physical units. Indirect market-type regulation methods which were introduced in the course of the economic reforms did not fundamentally alter the nature of the planning decisions. Even when the planner uses exchange or interest rates to influence economic activities, should he fail to get the adequate response, he may always rely on direct methods. The shift toward a 'market socialism' is indeed understood now as a shift toward a greater monetisation of the domestic economy.

In their international economic relations, the socialist countries have had to enter a world governed by money, at least in the geo-political zones where they have had no other alternative. Their mutual trade and, to a large extent, their trade with the Third World remains based on real arrangements. Trade and settlements are managed in kind. On the other hand, trade with developed capitalist economies involves resorting to monetary procedures and international credit. The socialist countries were quick to learn the rules of the game, without it having an impact on the monetisation of their domestic economies or of their intra-system relations.

The East's convertible hard currency debt came about over the 1970–80 decade, as a result of an import-led growth and of a positive attitude on the part of Western lenders. Some of the socialist countries had to undergo rescheduling procedures, while all had to introduce domestic economic adjustments. At the end of the eighties, their debt is mounting again. It remains to be seen whether these nations have become fully fledged members of the international economic system.

CHAPTER 8

——————— · ———————

FROM CLEARING TO THE DOLLAR

Finance is as much compartmentalised as the socialist economies' external relations, according to the geo-political lines of trade. Among Comecon countries trade is settled in one unit of account, the 'transferable rouble', some settlements however being made in hard currency. In relations with non-socialist nations, convertible hard currency settlements are the usual practice. Clearing does still exist to a limited extent with some developing nations.

The socialist world has a basically dual view of foreign financing. On the one hand, there are settlements made in units of account (the transferable rouble or clearing units). In this kind of trade, the debtor is not at a disadvantage, though the perpetuation of the status of debtor is dependent on the tolerance of the creditor who may seek to restore the balance by demanding an increase in purchases, a reduction in sales, or both. On the other hand, there are those deals which are settled in hard currency. Here the debtor is indeed in a disadvantageous, even catastrophic situation if the size of debt leads to the cessation of repayments and to rescheduling.

Western lenders to socialist countries tend to overlook the first aspect of their socialist partner's foreign financing. They only give thought to the net situation of their partners *vis-à-vis* the West (understood as Western governments and banks). This in particular is the basis for risk assessing.

This is an error on two counts. First, each country is seeking to settle its sales to its Comecon and Third World partners in hard currencies. Some have been quite skilled at this. Between 1976 and 1985 Hungary managed to run up a transferable rouble debt with the USSR at the same time as having a hard currency surplus with that country. It also managed to have a hard currency surplus with the developing world while having a deficit in clearing currencies. Such financial techniques helped Hungary to recover its balance of payments with industrialised market economies subsequent to 1980.

Secondly, the very notion of 'foreign financing' is relative when it comes to the East. In a planned economy, monetary settlements are seen as second to real trade. This principle applies to the operation of domestic economies, where inputs are allocated on the basis of planned commands rather than really 'sold' on a market. It also applies to a very large extent to intra-Comecon trade based on bilateral bargaining as to the types and quantities of goods exchanged. To assess the situation of a given socialist country, one must evaluate this bargaining power, rather than the balances in non-convertible units of account.

We should not jump to the conclusion that the East is financially underdeveloped. There is a dual approach, monetary and non-monetary, depending on the type of partners. The East's foreign finance officials are highly skilled in Western finance. Some Eastern bankers are internationally recognised for their competence. However, no matter how important trade in convertible currency may be for these countries, the larger part of their trade is carried out in a sphere in which money has no power.

The rouble zone: trade without money

The title of this section is provocative. There does indeed exist a collective currency, which since 1964 has been known as the transferable rouble (t.r.). There are joint banks within the Comecon system. There is even a (claimed) desire to promote monetary integration. So why 'trade without money'?

Let us recall the standard conditions for monetary integration among market economy countries. Monetary integration supposes the existence of a common market with its ingredients (free movement of goods and services, common external tariff, free movement of factors) and in addition, as a minimum, two conditions:

full convertibility of national currencies, with fixed exchange rates between member state currencies; there might also be a union currency, and/or a pooling of reserves;
a coordination of economic policies.

Should we start with such assumptions when looking at the monetary integration within Comecon, we might just stop here. To begin with, there is no (common or even domestic) market, no free movement of goods or factors. The commitment to make national currencies convertible within the area was taken only recently (July 1988) and it is supposed to take a long time. There is something called 'concertation of economic policies', but when one looks closely at the definitions it is a misleading concept, to be identified rather with what we would call 'industrial policy'. The 'concertation' implies that Comecon might interfere with the growth strategy of individual countries, the selection of priority branches, etc. This is precisely the reason why the concept is quite controversial and has never really been applied in practice since its emergence in the early eighties.

The absence of a 'coordination of economic policies' in the market economy sense is indeed quite logical as there is no 'economic policy' strictly speaking within the domestic economies. There is a combination of central planning and 'market regulation'. The latter has to assist the implementation of the central plan. But how can the market regulators really bring about a due response if the scope of central planning is so large as to exclude (or, in any case, strongly limit) the possibility of manoeuvre of the economic units? Economic policy is then replaced by bargaining supplementing central planning.

One has then to approach 'socialist monetary integration' with quite specific standards.

THE SETTLEMENTS IN TRANSFERABLE ROUBLES: A VARIETY OF CATEGORIES

Western opinion on the transferable rouble (hereafter t.r.), the 'collective socialist currency', displays a contradiction. The most widely spread view holds that this currency has no role at all. Since *perestroika* the same views may be found in the USSR itself. The Soviet economist N. Shmelev wrote in 1987 that the t.r. was 'a stillborn child' (Shmelev, 1987). But it is simultaneously said that the very term points to a certain power or domination of the USSR over its partners. This view is no doubt arrived at by analogy with US domination and the might of the dollar.

The first of these statements is more accurate than the second. The workings of intra-CMEA trade are enlightening here. Let us recall some facts. Each country's foreign trade is planned domestically. Bilateral negotiations between countries establish the nature and quantities of goods traded. This process involves bargaining in which each nation seeks to obtain the greatest quantity of 'hard' goods and offer as little as possible of them, while trying to get rid of 'soft' goods.

Prices used in such trade are in principle based on world prices. As we know, according to the current regulation which dates from 1975, prices are renegotiated each year on the basis of the average world price of the five preceding years for a given commodity. We have already seen just how difficult it is to isolate a 'world price'. In actual practice, this method is only applied in the case of basic products (raw materials, fuels, food products). For manufacturers the prices are in fact negotiated in bilateral bargaining. The fiction of a 'world price' however remains as each partner tries to 'document' the price he is asking for or willing to pay through reference to 'capitalist' prices, using catalogues, invoices, etc.

Whether real or fictitious, world prices may all be expressed in dollars. Immediately after the war, trade between the USSR and most people's democracies was actually denominated in dollar units of account. Subsequent to the setting up of Comecon, the decision was taken to use the clearing rouble as a unit of account. This was the equivalent of the 'devisa rouble' used to calculate Soviet foreign trade figures. In order to convert prices expressed in dollars into clearing rouble values, the official rouble/dollar exchange rate was used (1r.=$0.25 from 1950 to 1961; $1.11 afterwards, up to 1971). This clearing was bilateral. Trade between two countries had to remain balanced and if there was any imbalance, the debtor country would be called upon to make up for this debt in goods the following year.

In 1963, the Comecon countries decided to multilateralise their settlements. This was in principle straightforward since all bilateral trade was settled in the same unit of account. On this basis, the transferable rouble was introduced in 1964.

At present, this is the currency used to express all transactions between member states. Such transactions are not, however, all of the same kind. Three groups emerge:

1   *Trade of goods* at international socialist prices. These are based on 'world' prices converted to t.r.s. using the official exchange rate. The official exchange rate of the t.r. was until 1974 based on the gold parity of the rouble and of the dollar (or of any major capitalist currency in which the 'world price' was expressed). When all 'capitalist' exchange rates became floating, the exchange rate of the t.r. was established, as it

still is now, on a monthly basis, from a basket of about thirteen convertible currencies (the composition and weights of the currency basket are revised every year; any currency which is used for more than 1 per cent of the total settlements of the Comecon countries in convertible currencies is included in the basket).

2 *Trade in services* (transport, tourism, settlements linked with the small manpower movements between Comecon countries). Here national currencies are converted into t.r.s. at rates which differ from official ones and are called 'non-commercial'. These rates basically correspond to purchasing power parity derived from consumer prices, for all the services which are valued in domestic prices. At the end of each year the bilateral balances in t.r.s. are added to the balances resulting from trade in goods. This procedure is particularly obscure, first because the amount of trade in services between Comecon countries is unknown, and certainly one of the best kept secrets within Comecon, and second because the non-commercial rates may be altered by bilateral arrangements which are said to have been spreading since the beginning of the eighties (Achkasov, Preksin, 1988).

When 'non-commercial operations' are small in scope they may be managed in such a way. But the quick expansion of intra-Comecon tourism at the end of the eighties, due mainly to the liberalisation of regulations in the Soviet Union, led to serious problems. This is exemplified by the 'customs war' between Czechoslovakia and some of its neighbours, which was 'declared' in September 1988 and regulated in November. In Soviet–Czechoslovak relations, the tension began to mount when Soviet tourists flocked into Czechoslovakia with large amounts of money in roubles (400 per person, almost two months average wage) which were exchanged at the tourist rate between the two countries and spent on purchases of goods in short supply in the USSR (sheepskin coats, pantyhose, shoes, household appliances, crystal goods, etc.). According to intra-Comecon rules, the Czechoslovak foreign trade bank may convert such roubles (in cash or travellers cheques) in t.r.s, at the non-commercial rate which is less advantageous than the commercial rate. This increases the assets of Czechoslovakia in t.r.s which it cannot readily spend for purchases of goods, even in the Soviet Union, because these t.r.s are not generated by commodity trade operations provided for in intergovernmental agreements. The Czechoslovak government reacted by prohibiting or strongly taxing the 'tourists' exports.

3 *Trade involving joint operations.* Joint investments and the few

joint ventures as exist within Comecon do actually present exchange rate problems. When there is joint investment, it is possible to calculate the goods trade this gives rise to (equipment, intermediate goods). This is not so straightforward when it comes to assessing costs in national currencies (civil engineering, local transport, use of local energy, telephone expenses, overheads, etc.). The solution is to apply coefficients *ad hoc*. For one single joint venture, several dozen of these may be required, as was for instance the case for the first one, the Polish–Hungarian Haldex company founded in 1959. There has been a call for a gradual unification of rates in this field. An agreement of 19 October 1973, for the management of joint investments, was signed in Karl Marx Stadt and established a rate between each domestic currency and the t.r. The introduction of a periodical readjustment of the rates in a concerted way was also suggested. But who should monitor the concertation? By which rules? The 'Karl Marx Stadt rates' were in fact used only as a reference.

In addition to the joint investments and joint ventures, a new form of joint operation began to emerge after 1984. The 1985 Programme for Scientific and Technical Progress stressed the role of 'direct links' between Comecon enterprises. Its chapter 3 devoted to the 'means of implementation' advocated 'a large development, on a contractual basis, of direct links between organisations and enterprises', and names a whole range of joint entities to be formed for the needs of R and D, production and training. A little more than a year later, the USSR issued a decree on joint ventures between Soviet and CMEA enterprises, the same day (13 January 1987) as the decree on joint ventures with the participation of Western enterprises. Just before, during the 42nd Session of the CMEA in November 1986, all the CMEA countries except Romania signed bilateral agreements with the USSR to develop inter-enterprise links. A first move to solve exchange rate problems arising from this new format was made beginning March 1988 when the Soviet Union and Czechoslovakia decided to settle all payments stemming from 'direct links' and 'joint ventures' between Soviet and Czech enterprises in crowns or roubles using a special rate of exchange (10.5 crowns to 1 rouble, which meant a slight devaluation of the crown by comparison with the official rate, which was then 8 crowns to 1 rouble). This is more symbolic than effective due to the very few cases to which such settlements might apply. Identical agreements were later on reached with Bulgaria, Poland, and Mongolia.

HOW TO 'ACTIVATE' THE TRANSFERABLE ROUBLE

Would it be possible to unify all these various exchange rates, so as to prepare convertibility? This is hindered by the extreme differences in relative prices between the various Comecon countries. In all the discussions on convertibility, it is assumed that a 'realistic' exchange rate may be found between a given domestic currency and foreign currencies. In fact, at present, there exists in many countries (Czechoslovakia up to 1989, Bulgaria, the GDR, the USSR) a great number of coefficients linking domestic and convertible (or non-convertible) currencies, varying according to the products exchanged. When there is a single commercial exchange rate (as in the case of Hungary, Poland, Romania) the cross-rates rouble/dollar are very divergent, and there is no rational way of making them compatible. The divergences stem precisely from the way these 'commercial rates' are computed, as the average cost in domestic prices for earning a unit in exports to a given country or area. The differences in relative prices, as well as in the commodity composition of exports, explain the differences in the cross rates. It is thus difficult to figure how, for a given socialist currency, a single rate for the t.r. or for each of the other currencies might emerge, and how the fluctuations of these rates might be centrally monitored within Comecon.

The t.r. is not convertible; nor is it transferable, despite its name. Intra-Comecon settlements are basically related to an exchange of goods and are almost without exception bilateral. Only in very few cases (amounting to 1 per cent of the total flows at most) has the mulilateral settlement system proved effective. A multilateral system would imply that any country (A) which has a trade surplus with a partner (B) could use this to settle its deficit with a creditor nation (C). This is impossible given the conditions of bilateral planning of trade in kind. The creditor nation (C) has no interest in getting t.r.s – it wants goods. It does not suit (C) for (B) to become its debtor; (C) is already carrying on *ex-ante* balanced trade with (B) and may not want to buy more from it. Should (C) want to get additional goods from (B), the country (B) would find no advantage in such a transfer of liability. (B) has delivered to (A) less than it has obtained from it. (B) therefore does its best to postpone the settlement for as long as possible with its direct partner.

The multilateralisation of settlements would only become feasible if credit balances in transferable roubles could be freely spent on purchases

not already covered by quotas, in any member country. This 'real convertibility' condition has never been met, and even became increasingly
difficult to fulfil. Alternatively, this might be so if credit balances could be
converted into hard currencies. Neither of the two possible solutions was
implemented.

Since 1975, the overall imbalance between the USSR and the Six has
led the USSR to make its energy deliveries increasingly conditional on
larger quantities and improved quality of the goods supplied by its
partners. This 'naturalisation' or 'demonetisation' of trade also affects
trade between the Six. The (real or potential) constraint of having to
export more to the Soviet market has induced the East European
countries to limit their offer on the (non-USSR) intra-Comecon market to
the level of what they can obtain from their partners. But since 1987–88,
with the beginning of a decrease in intra-Comecon energy prices, the
USSR is sliding into the position of a debtor. There is no parallel with the
former situation: while the USSR has agreed for more than ten years to
remain a creditor in TRs, it partners are not ready to turn into creditors
of the USSR, and this will certainly entail a lasting decrease in the overall
intra-CMEA trade.

Between the Six themselves, there is in fact a better balance in trade
than with the USSR. Since 1975, however, one structural creditor has
emerged, namely, the GDR, whose surplus with the Five accounts for
almost 7 per cent of exports to this zone. Bulgaria and Czechoslovakia
are permanent debtors (for 3 per cent of their imports from the Five).
Romania has a virtually nil balance for the period 1975–87, while Hungary went into deficit at the end of the period, and Poland shifted from the
position of a permanent debtor up to 1984 to that of a creditor,
obviously beginning to repay its debts.

The 'real' inconvertibility of the t.r., i.e., the fact that this currency may
not be used for the free purchase of products within Comecon, has two
consequences. Firstly, it leads to a bilateral balancing of trade and, subsequently, brings trade into line with the capacity to offer 'hard' goods
(which, by definition, are in short supply). Secondly, when this balance is
upset, the creditor country is at a disadvantage since it must grant free
credit to its debtor partner(s). Since 1975 the USSR has played precisely
this role of structural creditor *vis-à-vis* the Five (the Six less Romania,
which began to import Soviet oil only in 1979 and then paid for it in hard
currency). The GDR has occupied this position *vis-à-vis* the Five. It is as
if the GDR, 'benefiting' from the largest deficit with the Soviet Union up

until 1980 (when Poland took its place), had to take the responsibility of providing the rest of the 'support' granted by the USSR to the other Eastern European countries.

Is there any way in which the collective currency within Comecon can be 'activated'? The answer to this question is straightforward. The t.r. will never be a true instrument of settlement unless it is made 'convertible' into goods or into convertible money. It is impossible to conceive of free circulation of goods within Comecon without relaxing the planning mechanisms of each nation. Trade between enterprises within each country must also be granted greater freedom and be less strictly administered.

These conditions are not yet fulfilled in most countries. Even in Hungary which is the closest to a 'free' market between enterprises, shortages (in particular of imported production goods) and domestic monopolies hinder the operation of a market. Everywhere else, the allocation of goods remains regulated by state bodies. In the USSR, *perestroika* is supposed to bring about a 'wholesale trade of means of production', but is still far from it.

In the USSR, already in 1987 and 1988, some enterprises (see chapter 4) have been granted, along with a number of industrial ministries and administrations, the right to trade on their own, bypassing the FTOs (foreign trade organisations). Although the incentives provided have proved inadequate, and the rights of the enterprises were often violated by the bureaucracy, the enterprises managed to accumulate earnings both in hard currency and in t.r.s. Having exported in these currencies, the enterprises in principle had the right to retain a share of these revenues for their own use. The t.r. earnings amounted to about t.r. 2 billion for the first eighteen months. In principle, the Soviet enterprises were entitled to use them for direct 'shopping' in the CMEA countries for this amount. But they could not materialise this right as their Eastern partners would not accept t.r.s in payment for transactions which by definition were not included in the bilateral inter-government agreements. An *ad hoc* solution was found: 'fairs' in t.r.s. The first one was held in Moscow in November 1988. The fair was supposed to bring together Soviet and Eastern European enterprises, for direct trade in transferable roubles. In fact, to allow Soviet enterprises to buy goods from Eastern European firms, the 'direct' transactions were actually included in an inter-governmental framework, through the Soviet Gossnab (the administration responsible for allocating production goods to the Soviet enterprises).

Transactions concluded during the fair were thus re-included into the commitments stemming from the trade agreements. This is very far indeed from direct trade.

Should one try and achieve a market at once among all Comecon members? Some economists, especially Hungarian, have come up with the following scheme: relations between the Soviet Union and the Six (as far as organisation is concerned) would remain as they are, while a common market would be set up between the willing Eastern European countries (which would obviously also exclude the GDR and Romania). But the political conditions for such a scheme could hardly be implemented.

Technical solutions have also been put forward. In order to discourage a country from remaining a debtor, interest rates paid by the debtor were raised (in 1970) to the maximum rate of 5 per cent. However, raising interest rates only succeed in increasing the debt and does nothing to transform it into goods. Added to this is the fact that since 1975, the t.r. has been steadily depreciating, this being linked to intra-Comecon price rises. The real interest rate on rouble credits is therefore close to nil if not negative.

Following the same line, a 1968 Polish proposal, based upon the mechanism which allowed postwar European currencies to become convertible once again, led to a 1973 agreement between five Comecon countries according to which 10 per cent of the passive balance should be paid in hard currency. The European Payments Union had already applied this method, with a yearly increase in the amount of the balance to be paid back in convertible currency. In 1958 it achieved full convertibility (a model of an international organisation as it disappeared having successfully completed its task!). As for Comecon, the agreement lasted for one year only.

Another proposal relates to the creation of a third CMEA bank for managing such settlements related to 'direct links', for making them more effective.

Finally, we should address the question of whether the introduction of currency settlements for certain transactions involving the delivery of hard goods (above-quota oil, foodstuffs) should be seen as a step towards convertibility. Such hard currency settlements were introduced in the early seventies and by the end of that decade they probably affected between 8 and 10 per cent of total Comecon trade (between 15 and 20 per cent for Hungary, the first country to publish statistics on this, followed in the eighties by Poland). Hungary managed to secure large surpluses in its meat and grain hard currency trade with the USSR, which helped it to offset its deficits with the West in the early eighties. The USSR decided to stop this hard currency trade in 1986. What we have here is an implicit acknowledgement of a dual system of payments, with one zone where settlements are in non-convertible currency and where trade is based on the bilateral coordination of foreign trade, and another, fringe zone where settlements are in dollars and where market factors come into play, with 'capitalist' prices being applied.*

THE COMECON BANKS

Such a dichotomy is a feature of Comecon operations, and is to be found also in the two Comecon banks. The International Bank for Economic Cooperation (IBEC) was set up in 1963 (becoming operational in 1964) to handle all settlements in t.r.s. Almost from the very outset, it also handled short-term hard currency operations on the euromarket, and derived big profits from it. Along with the International Investment Bank (IIB) set up in 1970, the next decade saw it undertaking medium and long-term borrowing for intra-Comecon investments, with the implicit guarantee of Soviet creditworthiness. The 'umbrella theory', which proved wrong for the individual borrowing of Eastern European counties, was indeed right here. Unlike the IBEC, which carries out most of its operations in t.r.s, the IIB has made very little use of this currency for its loans. These loans are meant for helping the Comecon members to purchase equipment for investments that are supposed to benefit all or most of the other member countries. It very soon emerged that t.r.s could not be used to purchase equipment from Comecon members. Such purchases were over and above the normal foreign trade flows and hence, no supplier would accept a settlement in t.r.s which he could not subsequently get rid of. This explains why IIB credits were largely made in hard currency, for equipment imports from the West. From 1980 onwards, the IIB reduced its involvement in the Euromarket. Its operations reached their ceiling in fact at that date. From the end of 1974 to the end of 1979, the cumulated total of hard currency loans granted by the IIB went from t.r. 250 million to t.r. 2.5 billion equivalent. Overall, from the beginning of its operation up to the end of 1987, the Bank is supposed to have financed 111 projects for which it extended an amount of t.r. 5 billion in hard currency or in roubles. Since 1985, the Bank is supposed to help the implementation of the Complex STP Programme and thus to finance joint research and development.

The absence of a transferability and of a goods convertibility of the t.r. also explains why the IIB and the IBEC never succeeded in involving non-Comecon members in their activity. A 'Special Fund' of r. 1 billion was supposedly set up in 1973 by the IIB to ensure a multilateral mechanism for helping the Third World; it seems that it was never operational. As we know, it is impossible to use a loan extended in t.r.s if it is not 'pegged' to a bilateral relation between a CMEA country and a developing country, as this currency is not really 'transferable' even between CMEA members, not to speak of its convertibility. This is also why no developing country was able to take advantage of a proposal made some time later (in 1976) in the framework of the IBEC to extend to the developing countries the ability to settle transactions with their CMEA partners in t.r.s.

The rouble zone may therefore be said to be a trading zone, but definitely not a currency zone. Attempts to open up to Western banks the possibility of making deposits or loans in roubles, an idea raised in 1974–76, ended in total failure. Certain countries or certain operators did show interest, but soon realised that they would never manage to use their balances in t.r.s.

Given these conditions, the socialist countries can hardly resist the pull towards the dollar zone. Since very recently, the Soviet Union seems to want to introduce a reorientation towards the ECU, growing increasingly interested in the workings of the European monetary system. Given that they cannot set up their own currency zone, the socialist countries may contribute to the consolidation of currency multipolarisation, still in embryonic stage in the Western world.

East–South trade: with what money?

Most of intra-Comecon trade is settled in non-convertible currency. This is close to a settlement in form of bilateral clearing. East–West settlements are made in convertible currencies as a rule, except in the case of Finland. In East–South trade, settlements offer a mixed picture.

The crucial question is: do the socialist countries derive hard currency revenues from their trade with the South, which allows them to pay for part of their debt to the West? The answer matters first for their Western creditors. East–South relations have to be taken into account for the risk rating of socialist countries. It also matters from a more general point of view. Is it proper for the developed socialist countries, given the political principles which have been asserted as the basis for East–South relations, to earn hard money in the South so as to pay for their purchases in the West?

The matter is very complex indeed. The socialist countries have overall a surplus with the Third World, but are in deficit with certain regions. The settlements are not homogeneous. They are increasingly made in convertible currencies, but settlement in clearing remains in trade with certain countries or for certain kinds of transactions. In consequence, it is very difficult to assess the actual hard currency gains, if any, of the East in East–South trade.

THE OVERALL SURPLUSES OF THE EAST IN EAST–SOUTH TRADE

Table 4 (Appendix) shows the magnitude of these surpluses for selected years during the period 1970–87. While the overall picture shows a persistent surplus, one has to treat the Soviet case differently from the East European–South balances.

The *Soviet Union* has a permanent and very large surplus in its overall trade with the developing world. It is always (with only two exceptions since 1970, that is, in 1978 and 1979) in deficit with its identified partners in the Third World. This is due to the large residual in its exports. This residual is the difference between the overall exports to the Third World as stated in the USSR *Foreign Trade Yearbook*, and the sales to identified countries of the Third World. Up to the mid-eighties the residual remained in the range of 50 per cent of Soviet exports, and since then has increased up to almost 60 per cent in 1988. On the import side, the residual is very small, in the range of 2 to 3 per cent.

This residual is an enigma. The usual approach is to consider these sales as arms exports. This is not totally satisfactory, not to speak of the fact that according to the official stance of the Soviet Union, military trade is not included in foreign trade statistics. The arms deliveries of the Soviet Union, when estimated directly by such agencies as SIPRI in Stockholm, or the CIA (see Despres, 1988) are much higher than the residual. They should be indeed, as they include free of charge deliveries to politically privileged clients. But, on the other hand, the residual cannot consist solely of arms sales. It must include the sales to the fifty countries or so with which the USSR trades, and which are not mentioned in the

Foreign Trade Yearbook, such as all the Oceania partners, several Asian countries (Korea, Taiwan, Hong Kong, the United Arab Emirates, Oman) and many African countries such as Benin, Gabon, Mauritania, Niger, Senegal, Togo, Uganda, Zaire, Zambia, to mention only these. Undisclosed Soviet exports may also include other strategic goods such as diamonds, and nuclear energy goods. However, even if we may assume that the residual indeed gives some indication of the trends in arms trade, there remains the question of how to allocate it among the Third World partners of the USSR.

Here again, one has to proceed by guesstimates. The usual approach is to allocate the largest share of the 'residual' (75 to 80 per cent) to the main clients of the USSR for arms deliveries, which may be identified through other sources, i.e. the Middle East countries (Iraq, Syria, Libya) and to India. But such guesstimates are really too harzardous to allow for a recalculation of Soviet balances with these countries. In addition, as Laure Després has shown, deliveries made to a given country are often paid for by another. Libya has often in the past paid for arms deliveries to amed organisations such as the PLO, and to other countries. Saudi Arabia, Kuwait have also footed the bill for other nations.

Finally, what part of these 'residual' sales is paid in hard currency? Some of it is probably not paid at all; some is made on commercial credit conditions, or on a long-term cooperation credit basis, and in both cases does not produce hard currency earnings in the year the sales are made. Some are made on barter conditions, especially since the drop in oil prices and the oil glut. If the barter is in oil, then it may be considered as payment in hard currency, because the USSR resells oil to the West. What is the final balance? It was assumed, at the time when the Middle East oil exporters and arms buyers were themselves deriving large earnings from their oil sales, that the USSR was getting paid in hard currency for 60 to 90 per cent of its arms sales to these countries. Since 1985–86, this figure may have decreased to 50 per cent – or even less. One has thus to be very careful as to statements of the type: 'In (any) year, the Soviet Union earned (x) billion dollars in arms sales to the Third World.' That the USSR *is* actually earning something in hard currency is indisputable. Stating in July 1989 that the USSR had r. 22 billion worth of assets in convertible currencies (slightly over $36 billion), the Soviet officials presumably alluded to credits extended to developing countries and which were to be repaid.

The case of the *Eastern European countries* is simpler. Eastern Europe also has a traditional surplus with the South. This surplus remained small up to 1980, then increased considerably for all countries but Romania, whose deficit since 1978 is due to large oil imports from the Middle East countries. The East European countries then embarked on a policy of expanding exports towards those of their Third World partners who were able to pay in hard currency, and strongly cutting imports. The surpluses with the Third World, which have been growing up to 1985 inclusively, were curtailed in 1986, still remaining positive except for Romania as usual. In 1987 the trend was again on the increase, while the trade balance deteriorated with the West.

EASTERN GAINS FROM TRADE WITH THE SOUTH

We still have to estimate the corrections to be introduced in the analysis due to the fact that some settlements are made in clearing. This is not an easy assessment.

From various sources and in particular the IMF *Yearbook on exchange restrictions*, it is in principle possible to derive the share of total trade conducted in clearing with the Third World (see Table 18). In the mid-eighties, 40 per cent of Soviet trade with the developing countries was under the regime of clearing agreements. For the Eastern European countries, this share is still high but decreasing: it amounted to 24 per cent of the total exports of Eastern Europe to the South in 1983, 20 per cent in 1986, and the corresponding figures for imports were 37 and 30 per cent.

The net balances in clearing are generally positive in the case of the USSR, and negative for Eastern Europe except for Poland (and Czechoslovakia, in 1983 only).

For all the other East European countries, the negative sign of the clearing balances amounts to a gain: a negative balance in clearing has to be 'cleared' in hard currency only after a grace period, which may be rather long. Conversely, in the case of the USSR it may be seen as a form of aid to the countries allowed to keep a clearing deficit with the Soviet Union. But such statistical conclusions may largely be misleading.

First, even when there is a clearing agreement between a centrally planning country and a developing country, this does not mean that all settlements are cleared in that way; there may well be some transactions settled in hard currency. Second, one cannot know when the clearing balances are finally settled, as they should be, in hard currency, and not

Table 18. *Clearing agreements between the East and the Third World (in force in 1988)*

	Bulgaria	Czechoslovakia	GDR	Hungary	Poland	Romania	USSR
Afghanistan		×	×				×
Bangladesh	×	×	×	×	×	×	×
Brazil	×		×	×			
Colombia	×			×	×	×	
Ecuador*a*			×	×	×		
Egypt							×
Ghana	×		×			×	
India		×	×		×	×	×
Iran	×	×	×	×	×	×	×
Lebanon*b*					×		
Mali							×
Mozambique			×				
Nepal	×	×			×		×
Pakistan	×	×		×	×		×
Sao Tome			×				
Somalia							×
Syria							×
Turkey		×			×	×	×

Note:
*a*For most settlements.
*b*For some settlements only.
Source: IMF, *Annual Reports on exchange arrangements and exchange restrictions*, 1987, 1988 and 1989.

even whether they are actually settled at all. Third, even between countries which have not concluded a clearing agreement, some settlements may be made on barter or compensation terms.

All these developments boil down to a conclusion: the prospects for earning hard currency from trade with the South are becoming dimmer for all the socialist countries. Even excluding the countries with a socialist orientation, which were never supposed to provide hard currency gains to their partners, a growing number of outstanding balances with the Third World, even denominated and in principle settled in hard currency, consist of soft loans which are hardly likely to be repaid.

East–West: trade with credit

The settlement of East–West trade transactions is not achieved entirely by the use of credit. This is not even true of the majority of transactions, which are simply paid for in cash. However, a vast amount of Western writings insist on the problems of East–West credit financing. This has to be related to the very nature of the transactions being financed. Credit covers equipment sales which are often concluded on the basis of contracts for huge sums, which are of great consequence for the firms involved as well as for their governments. Bank credits are used to finance current account deficits, the growth of which may send signals of financial crisis.

We will first examine the mechanisms of export credits which usually go hand in hand with state support (in the form of guarantees and possibly improved interest terms). In the mid-seventies, the extremes to which Western governments went to help their exporters clinch big contracts with the East, have in turn led to a 'consensus' agreement aimed at limiting this type of competition. Only a very blurred line separates export credit from bank credit not linked to specific commercial operations. The lenders have gradually moved towards a complex system of combined credits far less open to scrutiny than the traditional forms of finance.

One should however state that the socialist countries remain 'traditional' borrowers in the sense that they have not been included in the movement toward the use of 'financial innovations' which soared along with the Third World financial crisis in the eighties. The 'securitisation' of international borrowing left the socialist world behind. The internationalisation of transactions in shares and equity-linked securities is typically a 'systemic' capitalist phenomenon. It relies on domestically developed capital markets or, in the case of the Third World, on large opportunities offered to foreign capital for controlling domestic capital. The socialist countries have an embryonic capital market, even if some countries (Hungary, Poland, the USSR) announce the opening of stock and bond markets. Although allowing joint ventures on their territory, they do not carry the process of domestic privatisation far enough to turn these ventures into sources of financial liquidity. This may indeed, in the long run, increase their reliability as borrowers if the international securities market is to experience new financial shocks as in October 1987.

EXPORT CREDITS

As the term suggests, these credits are granted to facilitate exports from companies located in the country granting credit. They are often, though not always, officially supported when governments assist the granting of such credits through interest subsidies or insurance guarantees. Export credits became widespread practice in East–West trade between 1966 and 1970, and up until 1975–76 remained the main source of loans obtained by the socialist world. Since then, they have lost ground to bank credits. In the eighties, export credits accounted for a quarter to a third of the East's total debt. The USSR and Poland have been resorting to export credits more than the socialist bloc overall, proportionally speaking, while Hungary has used it least.

There are two forms of export credits, namely supplier credit granted to the exporter by its bank so that the exporter may extend a loan to its client, and buyer credit offered by one or several banks to the purchaser's bank. In the case of the socialist countries, the debtor bank is either the national bank, or the foreign trade bank. The banking diversification going on in several socialist countries (Hungary, Poland, the USSR) has brought about the setting up of 'commercial banks' as from 1986–88 but has not yet altered the foreign exchange monopoly of the state. Should there be a devolution of this monopoly to a number of decentralised banks the procedures of buyer credits would change. This is, however, not likely to happen in the short run because it might increase the risk of lending.*

Buyer's credit is slightly more costly in fees, although it has the advantage of freeing the supplier of any loan management. It has developed greatly to become the prevailing option used in major equipment contracts. In the eighties, supplier's credit made a come-back for reasons difficult to admit. Being, to all intents and purposes, a domestic loan (from a national bank to a client in the same country) it is easier to conceal from the scrutiny of international organisations (see chapter 9). It also easier to manipulate the interest rate in the case of a supplier's credit, and thus to evade the consensus rules described in the following section, as the supplier and the buyer may decide on arrangements whereby a part of the interest rate might be included in the price of the equipment sold.

Initially, export credits were always extended in the currency of the exporter. It is logical as the credit is intended to finance an export from the lending country; usually the national rules define a share of the financed export deal which might include a foreign component. This is the case when the equipment goods exported include parts which have to be supplied by manufacturers from countries other than the lender's. Even in this case, export credits were for a long time granted in national currencies. The diverging trends in the rates of interest and in the exchange rates of Western currencies have led to the development of export credits in foreign currencies. Great Britain initiated this in 1977 and most Western countries followed. This is particularly appealing to lending countries with weak currencies and (relatively) high interest rates. In such cases (for example, for France or Italy) the loan expressed in a foreign currency (very often the German Mark) may carry an interest rate which would be unsustainable for the lender in its own national currency. For the same reasons, loans in ECU, the European Currency Unit, appeared in the mid-eighties (Nême, 1985).

Government support may imply a variety of 'grant' elements, by comparison with the normal domestic conditions. These may be the period for which it is extended (if government supports helps to increase this period beyond the normal terms), the grace period during which no repayment is due, the definition of the instalment, the share of cash payments as a percentage of the export contract value, the total amount of the credit lines, the support for financing of local costs, etc. However, government support mainly appears in two forms.

The first is a subsidy to the interest rate. The difference between the domestic monetary market rate and the export credit rate is taken care of by the budget, by various procedures (see OECD, 1987). Obviously such subsidies are vital to stimulate exports in such countries (France, Italy, Great Britain) where domestic interest rates are high. When this is not the case (Japan, the FRG or Switzerland) subsidies are not necessary when the borrower accepts the market rate. In France the deregulation of the banking system conducted since 1985 led to a strong reduction in interest rate subsidies, meaning that the banks themselves had to provide the conditions asked for by the borrower if the market rate happened to be higher.

Even in this last case, there remains a public support if the government, or a public institution, guarantees reimbursement through insurance underwritten by a state body. The institutions providing insurance may be a ministry (the MITI or Ministry of Trade and Industry in Japan), a government agency Compagnie Française d'Assurance pour le Commerce Extérieur (COFACE) in France, Office National du Ducroire in Belgium, Sezione Speciale per l'Assicurazione del Credito All'Esportazione (SACE) in Italy, Export Credit Guarantee Department (ECGD in Great Britain), or a private institution operating under an agreement with the government (the Nederlansche Credietverzekering Maatschappij in the Netherlands). There are two particular cases worth pointing out in this connexion. In West Germany, export credit insurance and guarantees are taken care of by a private company, Hermesversicherung AG. This is largely a fictious outfit which allows the Federal Republic to disclaim the public nature of the guarantee provided though the fact still remains that the federal budget is committed to grant cover within an exposure limit. Claims are paid from the budget and premium payments are credited to the budget. To this one may also add that there is a special body for guaranteeing credits to the GDR, Treuarbeit AG, which is definitely a public agency – but inner-German trade, as we know, is not considered as export trade. In the United States, Eximbank both finances and guarantees government loans. Since 1975, it has had no dealings with the USSR, and very few with other Eastern European countries. The United States is the only country which denies export credit to non-market-economy countries on other than financial grounds. The present restrictions originate from the Jackson–Vanik Amendment to the Trade Act of 1974 specifying that a non-market economy may be denied US government export credits if it denies its citizens the right to emigrate.

Thus official support may include interest rate subsidies and guarantees, or just the latter. In this second case, the official support is said to be of 'pure cover'.

Since 1975–76, export credits have come under attack, with different arguments being put forward. It is not an easy business to clarify. Motives, some of them not entirely disinterested, underlie the fine principles of transparency and equal treatment actually expressed. For what reasons may one justify limitation placed on credits for exports to socialist countries? There are three of them.

1 The first reason is a general one and applies to all types of credit. It was first mentioned during 1974–75 when some fears appeared at the suddenly growing indebtedness of the East toward the West. The creditworthiness of the East was not, however, immediately affected. The so-called 'umbrella theory' reassured the lenders. The Western banking community firmly believed that the USSR would not allow a Comecon nation to default on its financial obligations and would come to its aid as a last resort borrower. Furthermore, the East European countries were all good debtors, meeting all their obligations on time. The Polish financial crisis really made governments aware of the risk involved in lending to the East. Although all the Eastern European countries except Poland managed to control their financial situation in 1982–84, the very increase

of rescheduling on a world level in the eighties now makes all the prospective lenders cautious. But so also are the borrowers, who have learnt the lessons of the past.

2 Approximately at the same time, in the mid-seventies, a second consideration gave rise to a coordination among lenders when establishing credit condition. This may be expressed as a moralising argument: 'to provide the institutional framework for an orderly export credit market and thus to prevent an export race in which exporting countries compete on the basis of who grants the most favourable financing terms rather than on the basis of who provides the highest quality and the best service' (OECD, 1987: 7). In other words, financial competition is viewed as unhealthy and damaging whereas 'real' competition is favoured. The argument runs as follows. The aim of export credits is to help sell national equipment. The sellers are facing 'monopoly' state trading purchasers who are perfectly aware of the different conditions each exporter offers. There is no point in subjecting oneself to fierce competition which leads to a downward equalisation of the advantages granted. It is far better to control loan operations and ensure that there is an upward equalisation at the highest level compatible with market conditions. This is the rationale which inspired the 'consensus'.

The 'consensus' regulates, but does not suppress, all aspects of government support. It applies whenever there is government support. This means that when export credits are financed and guaranteed by banks on their own account, the advantages granted to the borrower are only limited by market competition and conditions. However, even in this case, it has been claimed that lending to the East should be restricted by a sort of voluntary restraint.

3 Beginning in 1980 a political argument was added to those propounding the East's reduced creditworthiness and the need to bring Western financial competition under control. The US administration sought to associate the Allies in the restrictive practices which had been applying in the credit field almost continuously since the Second World War. It was actually the Soviet invasion of Afghanistan (December 1979) and the introduction of martial law in Poland (13 December 1981) which made the US government advance the political sanction argument, which sought to limit credits to Eastern Europe and, in particular, the Soviet Union. This argument may run directly counter to the first argument outlined in 1, when it affects the country whose credit-rating is the highest among the socialist countries. In 1982 the US government made

an attempt to influence not only the Western governments providing official support to export credits, but also Western banks providing such credits without support, or even granting purely 'financial' credits not linked to export deals. This was the 'credit squeeze' (see below p. 319) which succeeded only partially but deeply impressed the Eastern European countries, shaping their borrowing policies from then onwards.

New appeals to refrain from 'subsidising the Soviets' were heard from US politicians in 1988 (see Senator Bradley, 'Perestroika, without Western subsidies', *The New York Times*, 3 January 1989). The political argument is different here. The idea of a sanction is no longer present, but rather the feeling that the West need not 'help Gorbachev' to avoid a difficult choice between 'guns and butter', and that credits extended to the USSR are not available for the developing world. But is the USSR still taking credits from the West on subsidised terms? The evolution of the consensus provides an answer.

THE CONSENSUS

Attempts to harmonise export credit conditions go back to the pre–war period and the setting up of the Berne Union in 1934 in the context of world recession. The aim then was to protect credit insurance companies from borrowers' insolvency.

The present day consensus is the result of coordination implemented within the framework of the OECD. After several partial and experimental arrangements, in 1972, 1974, and 1976, the OECD countries, with the exception of Iceland and Turkey, agreed to adhere to the 'consensus' which came into being in April 1978 ('Arrangement on Guidelines for Officially Supported Export Credits'). The guiding spirit of this agreement was the wish to avoid disorderly and wasteful competition among lenders. This concerns all export credits to all countries likely to benefit from them, listed accordingly to their per capita GNP as 'relatively rich', 'intermediate' and 'relatively poor'. It established minimum interest rates to be applied according to the category of borrower and the term of the credit, the maximum repayment term of the loans, and the minimum share of the contract to be paid in cash (see Table 19). All new agreements or protocols with an Eastern European country or with the USSR have to be notified, and the signatory states are likewise to inform their partners of any derogations and deviations, as well as to promote com-

Table 19. *The consensus on export credits*

| Date of decision | Minimum interest rates | | | |
| | Relatively rich countries[a] | | Intermediate countries[b] | |
	2–5 years	5–8.5 years	2–5 years	5–8.5 years
July 1976	7.75	8.0	7.25	7.75
July 1980	8.5	8.75	8.0	8.5
November 1981	11.0	11.25	10.5	11.0
July 1982	12.15	12.4	10.85	11.35
October 1983	12.15	12.4	10.35	10.7
July 1984	13.35	13.6	11.55	11.9
January 1985	12.0	12.25	10.7	11.2
January 1986	10.95	11.2	9.65	10.15
July 1986	9.55	9.8	8.25	8.75
July 1987	10.15	10.4	8.85	9.35
July 1988	market rates[c]		9.15	9.65

Notes:
[a] Czechoslovakia, GDR, USSR, since 1982.
[b] All the Eastern European countries up to July 1982; since then, Bulgaria, Hungary, Poland, Romania.
[c] Since July 1988 rich countries may only get loans at proxies for market rates (CIRRs), or guarantees of commercial loans ('pure cover' credits)
Sources: OECD (1987); press reports.

mon attitudes. Additional information and consultation procedures were provided for by decisions of the Council of the European Communities (1973 and 1976), but in fact not implemented. In 1988 and 1989, it seemed however that the EC Commission was heading towards new proposals for a greater coordination in this field.

Let us make clear that the consensus is not a device designed on purpose for lending to the East. The share of the East has steadily declined in the total of outstanding export credits supported by Western governments, and was in 1988 11 per cent on average of this total. Another very important field is that of credits to developing countries. The consensus allows credits wholly or partly (in this case, they are called 'mixed') financed from public funds for development and tied to purchases in the granting country. The United States have strongly opposed this and pleaded for a gradual elimination of mixed credits so as to draw a clear line between assistance to developing nations and aid to national exporters. As for the credits to the East, they are politically the most sensitive, even though their economic impact may be significant in terms of export promotion.

As has already been mentioned, the consensus only applies to loans with official support. Companies and banks are completely free to offer more favourable terms as such loans do not receive more advantageous interest rates through official subsidisation and either have no guarantee or are guaranteed by private firms (the second case being that of West German export credits). Since 1983, lending at rates below the minimum rates fixed by the consensus is allowed, even with official support, in the case where the loan is denominated in a currency for which the domestic market rate is under that minimum level. In this case any country may provide such support as long as the interest rate is not less than the 'commercial interest reference rate' (CIRR) for that currency. The CIRRs are based on the government borrowing costs in long-term, fixed-rate bonds, to which a margin of about 100 points is added. This rule had to be adopted because, following the sharp increase in market interest rates at the beginning of the eighties, a decreasing trend brought these rates into line with consensus rates, and several countries had still lower rates (e.g. Japan, the FRG, and even the UK).

In the beginning, the consensus was renewed at irregular intervals. In 1978 it was agreed to renew it yearly. In 1983, it was decided to adjust the minimum rates of interest semi-annually according to an automatic method based upon changes in the rates of interest of the SDR (special drawing rights), and the first application of this automatic reference system occurred on 15 July 1984.

The history of the consensus has been marked by conflicts and disputes over the conditions of loans to Eastern Europe and the USSR.

The United States were the first to oppose their Western partners. Since they were not extending government supported loans to the East (although, ironically enough, the Exim Bank had been created in 1934 for the purpose of granting loans to the Soviet Union!), and since their interest rates were above the limit set by the consensus, the consensus was unfavourable to them.

Initially the United States sought to get the rates of interest increased in return for an extension of the repayment period, but were unsuccessful. In 1980 again, they sought to increase interest rates and, in addition, to alter the classification of countries by placing the GDR, Czechoslovakia and the USSR in the 'relatively rich' category while ruling out credits of more than five years duration to this category as well as forbidding all credit lines and derogations to the consensus rules. The change of classification was accepted only in 1982, in the midst of the 'credit squeeze' and the 'pipeline affair'. The three above-mentioned countries were indeed classified as 'rich' nations (i.e. nations with over $4,000 per capita GNP in 1979). Since the July 1988 revision, countries of category I cannot get any government subsidised interest rates for their credits; only the market rates, i.e. their proxies mentioned above, the CIRRs, may apply.

What is the present significance of the consensus? It has been drawn up in line with a world monetary situation where domestic inflation rates, interest rate levels and exchanges rates tend to vary without great divergence from country to country. Already, since the beginning of the eighties, this was no longer the case. The philosophy of the consensus is also one of direct government intervention, which is supposed to be kept under common control. The move toward deregulation and privatisation does not mean the end of subsidies and support. It means that subsidies, if any, are bound to be granted in a more hidden way. The consensus is clearly not adjusted to such conditions.

In the East, the bargaining power of countries is different. While those Eastern European countries which resorted to officially supported credits usually accepted the consensus rates without much discussion, the USSR has always succeeded in imposing its will when very large deals were at stake. It also cleverly differentiated among partners. While accepting from Italy non-lira loans (mostly in DM) at low interest rates, it has consistently requested from France loans in French francs at the initial consensus rate for intermediate countries, and never departed from that, the result being that the financial protocols with France have not contained any explicit interest rate since 1981. Also, though lines of credit are in principle forbidden, the USSR had no trouble in obtaining credit lines from various Western European countries and Japan for a total amount of about $9 billion in 1988. This was strongly criticised by the United States. However, the USSR finally took about a quarter of this total amount in actual loans, as if it had mainly wished to test the good will of its prospective lenders.

FINANCIAL CREDITS

These credits may be divided into bank credits in euro-currencies and money raised in the form of the issuing of euro-bonds. Bond offerings are mainly a speciality of Hungary – on the modest scale. The USSR made a first offering in 1984 through its bank in Great Britain, the Moscow

Narodny Bank, for $50 million. Much more dramatic was the first issue of the Bank for Foreign Economic Affairs (BFEA) in January 1988, for Swiss Francs 100 million worth of 10-year bonds carrying 5 per cent interest – which was called the first bond issue since the ill-fated 'Russian loans' were repudiated by the Soviet government in 1917. Since then the Soviet Union has issued bonds in Germany, in 1988 and 1989.

Bank credits are in principle independent of commercial operations. The may however be combined with commercial export credits (especially if it allows a manipulation of interest rates so as to bend the rules of the consensus). They may also accompany export credits, so as to provide financing for the share of the total contract which cannot be covered by such credits and which amounts to 15 per cent according to the consensus, or to cover local costs on major equipment deals. Finally, many export credits are now granted in foreign currency, as bank credits, which makes the distinction even more difficult. True, export credits usually have a fixed interest rate while bank credits have a variable interest rate, but in some cases export credits may also carry revisable interest rates.

'Bank' credits are extended by banks, as are, by the way, commercial (export) credits. This designation only means that such credits are part of the financial activity of the banks. Often they are extended by consortia of banks, under the aegis of a leading bank. Socialist banks operating in the West usually participate in such deals with discretion (especially true of Soviet-owned banks, for which they are appreciated by Western bankers).

Interest rates are not subsidised. They refer to the LIBOR (London inter-bank offered rate) plus a margin or *spread* reflecting the general condition of the monetary market at the time the loan is being made and the reputation of the lender. The rates granted at the time the loan is made are not fixed. They are generally subject to six-monthly revison. Eastern Europe and the USSR have generally enjoyed favourable conditions except for some periods and some countries. Before 1974 these countries borrowed with a spread of less than $\frac{3}{4}$ above LIBOR. In 1977 the average spread just passed one point. Rates subsequently fell and then rose from 1980 onward, in some cases above $1\frac{1}{2}$ points. Eastern borrowing dropped sharply during the period of the credit squeeze following the Polish and Romanian suspensions of payments (1981) and the political crisis of 1981–82 already mentioned. Borrowing resumed only in 1984, reached a peak in 1985, then again stabilised. The ability of most of the

Eastern countries to manage their financial difficulties in the early eighties soon entailed a decrease in the spreads down. While in 1983 the average spread was still of $1\frac{1}{6}$, it dropped to less than one in 1984 and decreased to $\frac{1}{4}$ in 1986–87. The smallest spreads are obtained by the USSR and Czechoslovakia who were able to borrow in 1987 at $\frac{1}{8}$ over the LIBOR.*

Gradually the Eastern European countries and the USSR resorted to new techniques of borrowing, even though they did not take part in the movement of 'financial innovations' after 1982. Here we put aside the opportunities used by those countries belonging to the IMF and the World Bank, which will be mentioned in the next chapter and concern only Romania, Hungary and (since 1986 only) Poland.

Among these other techniques, one may mention the *à forfait* (i.e. without recourse) market. This market is managed by specialised institutions (mainly Swiss), which buy medium-term promissory notes sold at a discount by the importers – here, the Eastern European countries, including the USSR. These countries meet the requirements as good borrowers on such a market; most of them are considered as low or medium risk, the forfeiting operations are guaranteed by the state (i.e. the foreign trade bank, usually). In 1987 the East accounted for 35–40 per cent of forfeiting activities (OECD, *Financial Market Trends*, March 1988: 32).

Hungary is the most imaginative among the Eastern countries and uses different financial techniques, such as floating rate notes, currency swaps, multicurrency facilities, and eurobonds. In May 1984 Hungary was the first socialist country to get a banker acceptance back-up facility for three years under the conduct of an American bank (this is a sort of private drawing right on commercial banks for six months at most for each drawing). Hungary signed its first note issuance facility (NIF) in 1985, for $100 million and a seven-year maturity.

The East and especially the USSR are also increasingly resorting to bank-to-bank short-term credits. After the financial crisis of 1981–83, several countries, in particularly the GDR and Hungary, sought to improve the maturity structure of their debt and increased their borrowing so as to extend the share of medium and long-term loans. At the same time, there was an increase of direct short-term banking arrangements, whose terms, and often amounts, are not disclosed. This helps to gain confidentiality in view of the international statistical coverage of external indebtedness, but certainly raises questions as to the real level of the debt and consequently the creditworthiness of the countries concerned.

Finally, among the financing techniques open to countries which otherwise would hardly be able to get new money, leasing may be used in specific deals, namely aircraft or ship imports. Thus Poland engaged in a leasing deal for three Boeing jets beginning in 1989. This was the country's first large long-term borrowing since 1981. The loan allows an offshore subsidiary company of the state Polish airline LOT to buy the aircraft so as to lease it to LOT. A repossession insurance guarantees the lenders against non-payment. Such complex financing schemes are however limited in scope as they usually apply to bulky transport equipment which may be repossessed outside the territory of the borrowing country.

Should one also range joint ventures among the financial techniques open to the East for obtaining hard currency on credit, exactly as one could name compensation deals among the possible ways to get cash (or to avoid disbursing it)? The Eastern countries certainly regard joint ventures on their territory as a financial technique, in so far as it helps to obtain equipment without having to pay for it immediately. In the case where a share of the Western partner's equity is in hard currency, then the financing device is still more obvious. Two arguments go against such a treatment. Firstly, in standard Western analyses, direct foreign investment is treated differently from financial capital flows, precisely because of its illiquidity. Secondly, should we nevertheless consider it meaningful to add this source of finance as such, it would yield a very small amount of finance in any case. The issue has to be mentioned, but its relevancy here is questionable.

IS A NEW 'CREDIT SQUEEZE' STILL POSSIBLE?

Politics are a permanent feature of East-West relations, not only in commodity trade as we have seen for technology, energy and agricultural trade, but also in financial relations. The political events of the early eighties, the Afghanistan invasion by Soviet troops and martial law in Poland, triggered a response from the West: a credit squeeze in 1982, which we have already mentioned. The rumours of a sudden surge of massive borrowings by the Soviet Union in 1988, although not confirmed subsequently, were immediately followed by the same recommendations from the United States.

In relation with this, one has to answer three questions: was the credit squeeze a reality?; how was it motivated? how was it conducted?

1 Was the credit squeeze a reality?

Apparently it was. The new financial credits granted to the East gradually fell off, from $4.7 billion in 1979, to 2.6 billion in 1980, 1.5 in 1981 and 0.7 in 1982. New borrowing reached $1.1 billion in 1983 (almost exclusively from Hungary and the GDR, motivated by the restructuring of the debt maturity). In 1984–87 the level of new borrowing remained between $3.4 and 3.9 billion, except in 1985 when it peaked at $5.3 billion.

Should we conclude from this that there actually has been a credit squeeze in 1982.

For the year 1982, all Eastern countries quoted the financial boycott of the United States to explain the fall in their borrowings. It is actually true that the US government sought to make its Western partners limit all kinds of credits to the East, and this effort on the part of the US reached its apogee at the June 1982 Versailles Summit. The US government wished to persuade the other Western governments not only to stiffen conditions on officially supported export credits, but also to limit the overall volume of credits. This was done in exchange for a more flexible US stance on the 'pipeline deal' (see chapter 6). In fact the US did not gain the explicit support of its allies, and was finally compelled also to soften its demands in the pipeline case.

Why then did the credits decrease, in fact? The East actually did attempt to reduce its debt in order to improve its external financial situation. Like Bulgaria and Czechoslovakia, the Soviet Union withdrew from the international monetary market from 1980. True, the USSR did not need financial credits as, at the same time, in 1981 and 1982, it was getting huge commercial credits in relation to the major contracts for the gas pipeline. From 1981 onwards, Poland and Romania had to reschedule their debt and were not in position to take new loans. This leaves us with Hungary and the GDR. These two countries did indeed experience difficulty getting the finance they sought, and both bitterly complained of the harmful publicity which an organised smear campaign had on their financial situation. In any case, it seems clear that Hungary was the victim of credit restrictions born of political considerations and that at the start of 1982, European and American banks – to which one also has to add, as has been suggested, the Soviet banks – suddenly withdrew their short-term deposits in the National Bank of Hungary, amounting to almost $1 billion. Even the exchange activities of the banks of Comecon countries with Western banks dropped in the first six months of 1982, with their usual dealers having greatly reduced the number of operations.

As for the Western bankers, they do not have the same perception. They stress the fact that compared to the bank's attitudes in the Latin American financial crisis, there was not a rapid exit by most of the lending banks: 'for the most part, banks maintained their levels of credit exposure, but avoided any increases' (Brainard, 1986: 187). If the political climate had an influence, it was through 'increasing perceptions of uncertainty on the part of banks' senior management' (Eichler, 1986: 195). CIA analysts, on the other hand, consider that the bankers' response was much more negative toward Eastern Europe than toward the Third World: 'the credit squeeze on Eastern Europe was comparatively more severe than on the developing countries' (CIA, 1986: 155), but also stress that political factors acted primarily as a factor of increased risk. *Détente* gave the bankers a green light in the seventies; conversely, the invasion of Afghanistan and the Polish crisis acted as risk warnings.

2 How was the credit squeeze motivated?

There is undoubtedly a parallel here with the reasons motivating a limitation of export credits to the East. There was certainly pressure from the US government wanting to sanction the Eastern European countries and the USSR for the behaviour of the Soviet Union and Poland. But there was also a perception by the banks of an increased financial risk after the Polish and Romanian insolvency. Other reasons may be put forward: an awareness that the 'umbrella theory' was no longer valid, the mounting economic difficulties of the East.

As no single reason emerges, one may ask how such a policy could be implemented. It had to be conducted by the banks; it was undoubtedly influenced by governments' attitudes.

3 How was the credit squeeze conducted?

When it comes to government supported export credits, it is not hard to imagine that negotiations do take place between governments, and in this respect, the conflicts which pitted the USA against their European and Japanese allies over consensus are a perfect illustration. How though does the US government actually exercise an influence over the world banking system? Firstly, US business and banking circles are definitely more sensitive than their Western European counterparts to governmental pressure exercised in the name of national interest. Secondly, the international banking network is very much an interconnected affair. US banks have branches in Europe. As a corollary to this, all the major Europen banks have deposits and branches in the United States. US banking and tax laws are well known for their complexity and great penalties ensue when the slightest management or accounting errors are made. This puts effective pressure on partners who may not spontaneously have the national interests at heart. Thirdly, quite apart from any external pressure, American banks were affected more than European banks by the financial crisis in Poland and Romania due to their exposure in these countries. After 1982, once the period of great tension was over, they remained distrustful, refusing to step up operations with the East, perhaps using the political argument as a pretext. As for the USSR, the exposure of the US banks is very low. The Johnson Act of 1934 prohibits private US banks from granting general purpose loans (i.e. financial loans) to any country which has defaulted on its repayments of obligations to the US government, which is the case for the Soviet Union cancelling the Tsarist debts in 1917.

At the end of 1988 and beginning 1989, the situation was in some sense reversed. While some US and European authorities were still warning against an increase of loans to the USSR, the Soviet Union itself was deciding to take less credits than it was offered. The very idea of 'a New Marshall Plan for the East' which emerged in various political meetings at the same period is at its core a scheme for larger credits to help the East in its modernisation and reform drive. The dramatic changes in Polish political life in 1989 induced the United States, and then the industrialised countries along with the EEC, to set up a scheme for Poland, which is definitely not meant to offer 'unsound credits'. One should however remember that when offered, credits never seem unsound to the creditors. This is not to say that the East should not be granted financial support, but that political reasons for granting it or not are always subjective in the light of economic rationality.*

CHAPTER 9

DEBT AND RESCHEDULINGS

The East's debt which reached a first peak in 1981 then began to increase again in 1985, has become something akin to a myth. Western public opinion, strongly influenced by the Polish debt, tends to exaggerate the risk involved in credits to the East. Poland and Romania had to go through rescheduling procedures a year before the Latin American financial crisis. Since then, the share of the East in total world indebtedness has strongly declined. The East's debt amounted to 20 per cent of that of the Third World at the end of 1974, less than 10 per cent at the end of 1988.

Three questions emerge here. First, is the Soviet and Eastern European debt really excessive and should it worry Western lenders, apart from the political considerations evoked in chapter 8? An assessment of these countries' liabilities and assets, as well as of the past trends in their indebtedness, should provide some answers. Secondly, all the Eastern countries had to implement stabilisation and adjustment programmes, for some countries under the surveillance of the IMF. The quality of debt management thus is, in addition to the figures on debt, an indicator of the financial reliability of the East. Thirdly, if the socialist countries appear as partners of good standing in this qualitative sense, what should prevent them from being more involved in the international monetary system? This in turn raises the question of a greater participation of the East in Western international monetary organisations such as the IMF and the World Bank.

Debts and assets

The total or gross debt of a given country is the sum of all its liabilities for all its borrowings, whatever their nature. Net debt is equal to gross debt less assets held in Western banks. It may be useful to take into account other assets such as gold reserves, and here the exact amount of the Soviet reserves is a crucial question.

The figures of the Eastern debt have been since the very beginning shrouded in mystery as the East did not for a long time provide any data. On the basis of the figures available, one may explain why the East has run into debt and whether it represents a greater risk than other borrowers.

THE FIGURES

The East's debt is difficult to assess, though not much more so than that of the Third World or even of the developed nations. One has only to recall the astonishment of the financial world when Mexico announced its financial crisis in 1982, or the 'revelations' on the unexpected amount of France's foreign debt in 1983. True, the Eastern countries do not publicise data on their balance of payments, except for the few who have joined the IMF. Even in this last case, membership in the IMF is not always matched with statistical openness (Romania joined the IMF in 1972 and until its 1982 rescheduling kept the financial statistics on a confidential basis, data were available to the Fund but not published). However, it is misleading to single out the East's statistical secrecy and pretend that other countries are completely open in this matter. In the West, state financial documents do not show everything and the 'overseas' departments of central banks are hardly the most accessible of places.

In the eighties, there has been definite progress when it comes to information. No longer is it necessary to go in search of whatever figures one can glean from lenders, as was the case in the seventies. In particular, the statistical coverage and methodology have considerably improved (see *External Debt*, 1988). The international institutions which regularly publish debt statistics, i.e. the BIS (Bank for International Settlements), the International Monetary Fund, the World Bank and the OECD, have set up a working group to provide a central definition of the external debt and a better understanding of the collecting and statistical methods of each institution. This is not tantamount to a harmonisation as each institution has different aims in establishing debt statistics.

For our purposes, an essential development was the joint publication of external debt data by the BIS and the OECD, starting in 1984 (with

Table 20. *The net debt of the USSR and Eastern European countries (in convertible currencies; billion dollars; end-year figures)*

	1970	1971	1972	1973	1974	1975	1976	1977	1978	1979	1980	1981	1982	1983	1984	1985	1986	1987	1988
Bulgaria	0.3	0.7	0.9	1.0	1.4	2.3	2.9	3.3	3.8	3.9	2.9	2.4	1.9	1.2	0.7	1.4	3.5	5.1	6.6
Czecho-slovakia	0.0	0.1	0.1	0.2	0.6	0.7	1.3	1.9	2.3	2.8	3.3	3.0	3.0	2.6	2.1	2.3	2.7	3.5	3.4
GDR	0.9	1.2	1.2	1.9	2.6	3.6	5.2	6.6	8.0	9.2	11.6	12.3	10.7	8.7	7.1	7.1	8.6	10.1	10.2
Hungary	0.8	0.8	1.0	1.1	1.5	2.2	2.8	4.1	6.7	7.1	7.7	7.8	7.0	6.9	7.3	9.5	12.9	16.2	16.1
Poland	0.9	0.7	0.8	2.0	4.7	7.7	11.3	14.5	17.7	22.6	23.5	25.2	24.9	25.1	25.4	28.1	31.8	36.2	35.3
Romania	1.0	1.2	1.2	1.5	2.4	1.4	2.4	3.4	4.8	6.9	9.3	9.9	9.5	8.4	6.6	6.3	5.8	4.3	1.3
The Six	4.2	4.8	5.3	7.7	13.2	17.9	26.0	33.9	43.4	52.3	58.2	60.6	56.9	52.9	49.0	54.6	65.3	75.5	73.0
The USSR	0.6	1.4	2.3	3.4	4.6	12.2	16.1	18.3	18.3	17.3	16.6	20.5	18.4	16.0	14.2	18.3	22.5	26.2	25.6
The Seven	4.8	6.2	7.7	11.1	17.8	30.2	42.1	52.2	61.7	69.6	74.8	81.1	75.3	68.8	63.3	72.9	87.8	101.6	98.6

Sources: As mentioned in the text there are a variety of sources on the Soviet and East European debt. But for figures from 1981 on the most authoritative source (in any case the most quoted) is the statistical set published jointly by the OECD and the BIS, to which one may add the figures provided by the OECD alone (in a special issue of *Financial Market Trends* or in the special volumes of *External debt statistics: the debt and other external liabilities of developing, CMEA and certain other countries and territories.*)

Other agencies provide their own estimates: the CIA, in various non-classified reports; Wharton Econometric Forecasting Associates in *Centrally Planned Economies, Current Analysis*; PlanEcon, in *PlanEcon Report*; the Wiener Institut für internationale Wirtschaftsvergleiche in Vienna (WiiW), in special reports; the Deutsche Institut für Wirtschaftsforshung (DIW) in Berlin.

The main source of divergence between these estimates lies in the evaluation of what is not covered by the OECD–BIS report: on the liabilities side, the claims from developing countries, and some non-identified claims from reporting countries to the BIS; on the assets side, the loans to developing countries. This induces large discrepancies as far as the USSR is concerned.

For this table, the main source used was the ECE/UN (*Economic Survey of Europe in 1988–89*, pre-publication text, Appendix Table C.11). The ECE/UN basically refers to the BIS/OECD sources, and also to national statistics for Hungary, Poland and Romania. Its figures are slightly higher than the OECD/BIS, especially for the USSR. One should remember that the ECE/UN report is presented for approval by the ECE Secretariat to the member countries, which include the European CMEA countries.

The figures for the USSR include the debt of the CMEA banks, which is a fairly constant figure since the end of the seventies, in the range of $3.5– 4 billion.

coverage going back to December 1982). Initially, in the seventies, the BIS collected data on the positions of reporting banks in all countries outside the reporting area. The reporting banks' data are collected through the central banks of the reporting countries. These countries comprise the 'Group of Ten' countries (Belgium–Luxembourg, Canada, the FRG, France, Italy, Japan, Netherlands, Sweden, United Kingdom, USA, including the off-shore US banks), plus Austria, Denmark, Finland, Ireland, Norway, Spain, Switzerland; the financial centres of the Bahamas, Bahrain, Cayman Islands, Hong Kong, the Netherlands, Antilles, and Singapore are also included. These data only include bank credits. When the OECD joined the BIS to issue a common statistical report every six months, both the geographical and the functional coverage were extended. In addition to the countries covered by the BIS, the OECD data are also collected in Australia, Greece, New Zealand, Portugal. These OECD data refer to external bank claims, and non-bank trade-related credits. External bank claims are added to data collected by the BIS, after elimination of double counting; what the OECD collects is all the export credits granted by government agencies as well as the buyers' or suppliers' credits which are guaranteed or insured by public agencies. Some of these loans (suppliers' and buyers' credits), but not all, are also included in the BIS coverage, hence the need for eliminating double counting. The great advantage of the new presentation is to include export credits with official support, which up to then were ignored by the BIS as long as they were suppliers' credits, i.e., loans formally extended to a resident firm, and not to a non-resident borrower. But some information is still missing, including the following items:

credits granted by international agencies (e.g. the IMF, the World Bank); these can easily be retrieved from the publications of such agencies, for the Comecon countries which are members;

non officially supported bank credits granted by banks of OECD countries which do not report to the BIS (see above), and all bank credits granted by banks of non-BIS-reporting countries (e.g. credits from Arab banks to the East);

non-guaranteed suppliers' credits, as these credits are extended by a domestic bank to a client of the same country without official support and do not appear as external claims;

non-bank non-trade related loans (here we find the very broad category of security offerings: this is the case when a non-bank operator

buys bonds issued by a borrowing country). This is certainly a case
for statistical distortion, but much more for the developing countries
than for the Comecon countries, as the latter are much less involved
in the international 'financial innovations', and only marginally
appear on the euro-bond market, as shown in chapter 8);

    credits extended by the FRG to the GDR, due to the special relations
between the two countries (see chapter 2); these credits are however
well publicised in the FRG;

and the errors and omissions according to usual practice.

Special statistical issues occasionally published by the OECD supply
some of the missing data (*External Debt Statistics: The Debt and Other
External Liabilities of Developing, CMEA and Certain Other Countries
and Territories*, vols. 1987 and 1988). What is it possible to derive from
these figures?

A first problem relates to the consideration of gross/net indebtedness.
The joint OECD/BIS report only gives gross indebtedness, which includes
at a given date the amounts of all liabilities of borrowers for loans
extended, committing the borrowers to the repayment of the loan (with
or without interest payments) or to the payment of interests (with or
without repayment of the principal). The quarterly statistics of the BIS
also provide the assets of the borrowing countries' banks in the form of
loans or deposits held in the banks situated in the reporting countries.
This allows the amount of the *net* debt of the Eastern countries towards
the Western banks to be calculated. In view of the difficulties which arise
in connection with the concept of 'net debt', the joint OECD/BIS report
as well as the International Working Group on External Debt Statistics
has decided to retain only the notion of gross debt. First the deposits
made by the Eastern countries in Western banks are probably in a large
part very short-term cash deposits and should not be identified with
assets. Second, should we seek a definition of the Eastern countries' hard
currency net debt, for each country we should include the following
items: (i) the net indebtedness of each country in hard currency toward
other Eastern countries; (ii) the net claims in hard currency on the Third
World. This second item is very controversial, especially for the Soviet
Union. We have already discussed this in chapter 8. Formally almost all
countries of the Eastern bloc have a claim in hard currency on the Third
World, resulting from trade surpluses covered by loans, and development
loans. But even when expressed in hard currency and not included in

clearing agreements, most of these loans are not collectable. In the case of the USSR, should the overall hard currency claims of this country on the Third World be taken into consideration, the USSR would appear as a net lender to the rest of the world. This would however be quite misleading because only a small share of these claims (amounting to several dozens of billion dollars) is bound to be repaid.*

A second question which became crucial in the eighties is the *foreign-exchange rate valuation effect*. This is due to the sharp fluctuations of the exchange rate of the dollar since 1980. The debt statistics are expressed in dollars. When the value of the dollar expressed in other currencies is growing, the debt in these currencies is automatically reduced when converted into dollars. When the value of the dollar is falling, the non-dollar debt increases once converted into dollars without any variation in the actual debt figures in DM, pounds, sterling, etc. Though all reports on debt data always point to this, this is not readily perceived by the general public.

Finally the indebtedness analyses usually rely on *ratios* derived from figures in absolute numbers.

The ratio usually considered as the most telling is the *debt service ratio*. It is the ratio of the yearly interest payments, plus the amortisation on medium and long-term debt due for the same year, to the total exports of a given year. Between 1981 and 1987 (OECD 1988: 27) this ratio has always remained under 25 per cent for the USSR (with a high of 24 in 1981 and a low of 14 in 1983), and has decreased from 67 per cent in 1981 to 41 per cent in 1987 for the 'Six'. The average for the Six relates to very different situations. Bulgaria and Czechoslovakia have displayed ratios in line with those of the USSR, even lower in the case of Czechoslovakia. Romania has joined these two countries at the end of the period. The GDR and Hungary were closer to the average, with an increasing trend in the case of Hungary and a decreasing one for the GDR. Poland's ratio, though initially very high (169 per cent in 1981, 180 per cent in 1982) dropped fastest, amounting still to 67 per cent in 1987.

The problem with this ratio is that its meaning is controversial. The time is past when, in the seventies, one could state that a ratio of 25 per cent or 30 per cent was a 'sound' one. A general objection to the use of this ratio for any country is that the ratio is significant only if we know the maturities of the debt and the interest rates applied for the various credits. International publications only provide incomplete or scattered information, especially as far as non-bank claims are concerned. This concerns the numerator of the ratio. As for the denominator, there are specific problems for the Eastern countries. The data on exports have to include all hard currency exports, which is not tantamount to exports to the West. From these, we must subtract the earnings in clearing currencies, and this applies in particular to Soviet–Finnish transactions. On the other hand, we must add hard currency earnings from exports to the East and to the Third World. Hard currency earnings with the East are not disclosed by all countries; they are available for Hungary and since 1982 for Poland. With the Third World, we already know that we should not consider as hard currency exports all sales made to countries with which there are no bilateral clearing agreements. Even when there is a clearing agreement, some settlements may be made in hard currency. Conversely, even when there is no commercial clearing, significant flows, especially those born of cooperation agreements, are covered by barter deals. Finally, a large share of sales in hard currency, as has already been said, is never paid for. All estimates of 'receipts in hard currency' are necessarily the result of 'guesstimates'.

The debt service ratio is increasingly complemented by the *ratio of net interest payments to exports*. The standard debt service ratio introduces a bias of estimates when a group of countries includes rescheduling countries along with others, as the rescheduling countries do not repay the principal of their rescheduled debt. In this case it is more significant to look at the interest-exports ratio (see *Economic Bulletin for Europe*, 1988, vol. 40, table 2.17, for the period 1981–88). The same trend as for the debt service ratio is to be observed. The USSR is never above a 5 per cent ratio. For Eastern Europe, the ratio drops from 23 per cent in 1981 to 14 per cent in 1988. As expected, Poland's ratio is highest, however, dropping from 53 per cent in 1981 to 38 in 1988.

Other ratios sometimes used include (i) the *ratio of net debt to exports*; (ii) the *net debt per capita*. The first of these two ratios indicates the total burden of debt on a country. A ratio of 100 per cent or less is considered as a 'light debt burden', and a ratio of above 200 per cent a 'heavy debt burden' (OECD, 1988: 23). The USSR and Czechoslovakia are undoubtedly in the first category throughout the 1981–87 period, as well as the GDR and Romania after 1984 and Bulgaria until 1985. The Polish ratio is almost constantly over 400 per cent. Hungary goes above the 200 per cent in 1985. The net debt per capita yields an impressively high ratio for Hungary. It should not be considered as significant as the burden of the debt is less linked to the population of a country than to its export/GNP ratio.

The OECD uses a 'vulnerability ratio' which compares the country's liquid assets (reserves, unused credit commitments) which potential claims on these assets (the current account balance, plus short and long-term maturities). If the difference between the two numbers is negative the country is said to be vulnerable as its requirements in hard currency are greater than its resources. As the OECD report in 1988 states, this ratio is significant if one assumes that the countries are to meet growing difficulties in borrowing. In addition, 'at two extremes no discussion is needed: countries which are illiquid and countries which are invulnerable' (OECD, 1988: 26); Poland is an example of the first case, the USSR and the GDR of the second. We should consider such an indicator either as redundant (the Polish case is significant enough) or as strongly misleading. First, there are huge statistical difficulties in establishing the ratio. We lack national or international (IMF) current accounts sources for all countries other than Hungary, Romania and Poland. The 'reserves' may increase for different reasons: purely foreign exchange valuation effects, reconstitution of reserves in view of securing a 'war chest' (typically the GDR policy), rebuilding of reserve positions in a policy of restructuring the maturity of debt, etc. The presence of undisbursed credit commitments may also provide misleading information. If the country has sought to obtain credit lines not to use them but just to prove that it could get them (as was the Soviet policy in 1988), then the country appears invulnerable – just because it *is* invulnerable!

The ECE/UN and the OECD also use a less sophisticated index which is the ratio of reserves to hard currency imports. It may be read in a more straightforward way, as it shows how many months a country may live on its reserves while still meeting cash requirements for imports. The overall figures show that the Seven Eastern countries have gradually improved this index, from about three months in 1981 to six months in 1987 and 1988. Here again the significance of this index may be misleading. Over the whole period 1981–87 Romania had a very low index. This is linked with this country's pre-payment of debt policy, which in turn implies cutting down on imports and forcibly promoting exports, and does not require the building up of reserves.

All this amply shows the difficulty of using the right ratios to demonstrate various conclusions. We shall revert to this question when discussing risk analysis. Instead of giving all these figures, we limit ourselves to the figures on the amounts of the debt (gross and net). Table 19 has selected the data given by the UN Economic Commission for Europe. The differences from one source to another were large in the seventies; they tend to be smaller now due to better coordination among the institutions providing data. In any case the trend emerges clearly. After a sharp increase in 1974–75, the debt rose more slowly in the second part in the seventies and reached a peak at the end of 1981. After this first peak there was a decrease up to the end of 1984, followed by a new increasing trend. How are these changes to be interpreted?

WHY THE EAST IS IN DEBT

The reasons for the East's indebtedness have varied over time. Several stages may be identified.

In the initial stage (1970–74), two factors explain the rise of the debt, on the demand side and on the supply side. This period was also the 'golden age' of East–West relations. The Eastern European countries and the USSR were all engaged in a policy of industrial modernisation – what they called the strategy of shifting from extensive to intensive growth. The modernisation drive necessitated imports of equipment from the West, which had to be financed by credit. The supply of governmemt backed credits was high and intensified subsequent to the onset of the crisis in 1973. The debtor countries reckoned on being able to pay off this debt by the export surpluses which they could achieve through new production capacities.

In the second stage (1975–81) the Eastern European countries went into large deficits with the West. The shrinking of the markets due to Western recession meant that it was no longer possible to develop the export of manufactures to planned levels. Only the USSR benefited from the crisis as there was a rise in the value of its energy sales. At the same time, the initial purchases of equipment from the West in the previous period led to major purchases on intermediary goods necessary to ensure the proper functioning of equipment already bought. While the demand for further equipment and, therefore, the demand for new export credit was slowing down, there was a rise in demand for bank credits to finance trade deficits and to service the past debt. The flow of 'petrodollars' from OPEC countries allowed banks to offer loans at increasingly low interest rates. Only at the end of the period did the interest rates display an ascending trend.

During the third stage (end of 1981 to 1983) there was a simultaneous contraction of demand for credit and of supply. There was a drop in demand for several reasons: a deceleration of growth in the East, particularly in investments; import cuts intended to reduce or stabilise the debt in connection with adjustment policies; reaction to the interest rates rise as from 1980 particularly affecting the demand for bank credits. The supply of Western credits was also to drop owing to several factors. There was a general contraction of banking liquidity as oil exporting nations were seeing their surplus fall. The financial crisis of Poland and Romania frightened the bankers. From 1982, there was the influence of political considerations, with the USA seeking, and partly succeeding, in stopping the East's access to further credits.

The fourth stage (beginning in 1984) saw the return of the East on the financial markets and the resumption of export credits. This cannot however be identified with the beginning of a new cycle similar to the previous one in three stages, for many reasons which are mostly to be found on the demand side. This means that while the lenders were ready to expand credit, as the international monetary and financial markets were liquid and as most of the Eastern countries enjoyed good rating (especially by comparison with the Third World), in an improving political climate, the borrowers remained very reserved.

There are greater differences in the situation of individual countries than in the seventies. Poland and Romania have to be set apart from the outset. Poland is still in the process of rescheduling (see below) and until 1989 could not get new money, while claiming that a resumption in lending would allow it to increase exports and meet its financial commitments. Romania has achieved large trade surpluses and sizeable current account surpluses with the West since 1982, and claimed at the beginning of 1989 to have achieved its aim of totally eliminating its debt. It has also pledged an end to foreign borrowing in the future.

All the other countries have increased their borrowing. The latest have been Bulgaria and Czechoslovakia (as from 1985). In all cases there has been simultaneously a deterioration of the trade balance with the West, but still remaining well under control, unlike in the seventies.

Why does the East borrow in this last stage?

First, it borrows to service the existing debt. Secondly, the borrowing is also meant to finance imports, but in a spirit very different from the early seventies. True, imports of machinery are given priority, and are meant to generate exports, but credits are no longer geared to large imports of turn-key plants, and domestic restructuring of industrial production rather than import is meant to lead to growth. Thirdly, the economic reforms (and here this is true even of the GDR where industrial combines are getting more foreign trade rights) entail a decentralisation of foreign trade which makes the future prospects difficult to predict. On the one hand, enterprises may now, more or less extensively according to countries, acceed to foreign trade. On the other hand, they have a very limited access to foreign currency, as internal convertibility is still embryonic, and made of piecemeal measures (retention of a share in the hard currency earnings, hard currency auctions, limited rights to borrow hard currency from the central bank or the bank for foreign trade). This leads to a dissociation between trade and finance which has no precedent so far in centrally planned economies. While foreign trade increasingly becomes an area of micro-economic decisions, external finance remains regulated on the macro level. This very dichotomy introduces an uncertainty in the macro-economic borrowing policy: why should the central authorities borrow? Nowhere is this uncertainty felt more than in the USSR. In 1988 and 1989, a debate arose in Soviet journals as to why the country should need hard currency: to finance major import deals for centrally planned large investments in heavy industry? to help the enterprises with the modest equipment imports in the consumer goods industry? to import consumer goods so as to persuade the people that *perestroika* has an impact on everyday life? Such a debate is likely to expand with the reforms themselves. This new setting is also bound to react on the risk-rating of the East.*

IS LENDING TO THE EAST RISKY?

This question is to be carefully separated from the political question of the desirability of Western lending. Sometimes a 'linkage' is introduced between both issues: one should not lend to the East and besides, it is risky. Is it actually?

In the seventies, as already noted, the 'umbrella theory' dispensed with any serious risk analysis. After the Latin American financial crisis erupted in 1982, risk analysis was developed also for the Eastern countries, although it was felt that for most of them the risk was much smaller than for most of the developing countries.

Standard risk indicators, such as various debt ratios, the commodity composition of foreign trade, the GNP level and the growth potential through the rates of growth of GNP, of its main sectors of origin and of investment, are certainly valid. Financial analysts should also lend importance to specific aspects of external and domestic economics of the socialist countries, something which is overlooked by the automatic extrapolation of methods applied to developing nations.

When it comes to evaluating the healthiness of the domestic economy, inflation and unemployment indicators are often difficult to assess, and not easy to interpret. The Hungarian inflation rates going from 7 per cent to 10 per cent at the close of the seventies pointed not to any lessening of control, but rather to a very deliberate attempt to improve price-fixing through market regulation. The Polish inflation in 1982 (which saw prices double) was in no way comparable with the galloping inflation of an underdeveloped nation, but meant an adjustment postponed for fifteen years. In so far as one is able to evaluate domestic price movements in socialist countries, one must examine their causes and mechanisms to determine whether they actually constitute a controlled and rational restructuring, through the repercussions, of foreign prices, the adjusting of prices to costs and the removal of subsidies, or whether they aim at short-term results such as cuts in consumption. Shortage indicators such as the amount of household savings, the delays in getting durable goods (cars or housing), the value of non-installed equipment, are good proxies of inflation indicators. Instead of unemployment indicators, which in any case do not exist, one has to analyse the trends and levels of the productivity of labour and capital.

In the foreign trade area, standard risk analysis usually only retain ratios or figures concerning trade with the West. Transactions within the Comecon are treated as a shadowy area and basically as a constraint for the East. Any rise in non-Comecon trade is readily seen as a sign of the East opening up. The opposite, i.e. an increase of Comecon's role in trade, is seen as an autarkical inward-turning attitude. This approach is obviously oversimplified. In 1982, when the solvency of the GDR and of Hungary was questioned, this aspect was overlooked. In fact, the GDR, since 1975, had 'benefited' from its deficit with the USSR, the greatest of all the Eastern European countries, which in real terms was tantamount to a transfer of resources available for export to the West (resources which the GDR would otherwise have had to sell to the USSR to cover its deficit). Furthermore, the GDR was able to capitalise on raw materials, oil in particular, which it had acquired from the USSR in transferable roubles, exporting them to the West. Bulgaria's position was comparable in this respect. Hungary, from its part, could then procure hard currency from its exports to the USSR. Though all these advantages are recognised as such, they are not adequately taken into account. One could thus say that, starting from 1986, the dwindling of Hungarian hard currency sales to the USSR could be taken as an increasing risk factor. The same might be said for the fact that, starting from 1988, most of the Eastern countries began to show surpluses with the USSR. Even if the exports granting these surpluses could not for the greatest part have been redirected towards the West due to the low quality or inadequate commodity composition of the relevant goods, the very emergence of surpluses signals that the Eastern European countries are no longer getting from the USSR the goods they might expect.*

Advantages stemming from trade with the Third World are still harder to assess. As most of the hard currency surpluses of the East on the developing countries may be treated as soft loans, the usual practice is just to ignore all these surpluses for a risk evaluation. This should be treated in a more differentiated way. Some surpluses are actually matched by hard currency inflows (according to the partners in the Third World). Trade with Opec countries may lead to hard currency revenues through reexport of oil obtained on a compensation or clearing basis (see chapter 6 on energy).

We have to close this section with a special mention of Soviet gold, as it is currently said that Soviet gold reserves are a significant asset improving the rating of the USSR.

The USSR, whose gold production is said to be rising moderately, is the world's second greatest gold producer after South Africa where extraction figures are falling. Production figures are not published by the Soviet authorities and have to be reconstructed mainly by the CIA in the United States and by companies specialising in gold transactions in Great Britain (the British professor Michael Kaser who until the early eighties was consultant for such a company, has regularly published his findings). Table 21 provides estimates which show large discrepancies, especially on Soviet gold reserves as we have no idea of domestic gold consumption and possible transactions between the USSR and its socialist partners. On the other hand, Soviet gold sales on the Western market are much more obvious, particularly from figures supplied by operators on the gold market (London and Zurich) and international financial institutions

Table 21. *Soviet gold production and sales*

Years	Annual production (tonnes)			Annual sales		
	(1)	(2)	(3)	Tonnes	Receipts million $	Ratio of gold sales to hard currency receipts (%)
1950	125	89		0	0	0.0
1960	159	128		178–80	200	14.8
1965	194	166		488–500	555	21.2
1970	264	218	202	0	0	0
1971	271	223		20	26	0.1
1972	285	240		150–90	317	9.8
1973	298	249		275–80	868	19.3
1974	301	262		220	1124	13.6
1975	309	258		141–50	755	8.7
1976	322	276		300–26	1283	13.4
1977	325	286		340–400	1642	13.6
1978	331	296		410–30	2375	18.9
1979	336	307		200–50	2200	11.5
1980	345	318	311	50–90	1377	5.6
1981	348	327		280–300	4290	17.9
1982		300		168–200	2400	9.2
1983		332		80–100	1160	4.4
1984			300	200	2315	8.8
1985			271	236–50	2450	11.0
1986				303–50	3845	20.6
1987	320–30			300	4300	19.2
1988				260	3650	15.1

Sources:
Production:
Column 1: Estimates by M. Kaser (1984a and b); 1987 figure, estimate by Wharton 'Soviet Foreign Trade in 1987 and First Half of 1988', *Centrally Planned Economies Service*, December 1988;
Column 2: CIA estimates (*Handbook of Economic Statistics*, various issues); same source as Schoppe (1978);
Column 3: Soviet figures supplied in 1988 when the Soviet Union made its first bond offering in Zürich, *Neue Züricher Zeitung*, 16 January 1988.

Sales:
Amounts in tonnes: from various sources (press information, often the *Financial Times*; BIS annual report; ECE/UN, etc. There is a large amount of guess in these estimates as the USSR uses different channels to sell its gold. However the guesses are fairly convergent as may be seen from the table.

Receipts: conversion in dollars of the average quantity sold using the average gold price for each given year. This may yield quite erroneous results as the quantities sold are estimates, and because the price of gold has been rather widely fluctuating in the eighties within each year. In addition the USSR does not sell its gold against dollars only, and this may be an additional source of distortion.

Ratio to hard currency receipts: the ratio has been calculated on the earnings from sales to the West only, using Soviet statistics. No account has been taken of hard currency sales to the South.

(especially the BIS). We should note however that since 1981, Swiss customs no longer publish data on monthly gold movements, which hinders evaluations. The USSR occasionally seemed to move towards more openness on this matter. Its first large eurobond offering in Swiss francs in 1988 went together with the release of information on gold and non-ferrous metals production. The publication of such data did not become customary, however, even though occasional details were released on the management of gold sales (P. Stephens: 'Moscow reveals nuggets on gold trade', *Financial Times*, 16 September 1988).

According to widespread opinion, the USSR sells gold when it requires large amounts of cash, in particular, to buy grain. According to sales statistics over a long period (see Schoppe, 1978), the USSR reappeared on the gold market in the mid-fifties after the Second World War and carried out massive sales (500 tonnes a year) in 1963–65, a time of poor Soviet harvests. Between 1966 and 1971 gold sales were negligible but picked up in 1972, a year in which the Soviets made major grain purchases from the United States. Subsequently, the pattern is not so clear. In 1980, gold sales were few, a fact doubly surprising in that it was the year when gold prices reached in all-time record ($850 per ounce at the start of the year) and the USSR had to make large grain purchases after the poor harvest in 1979. However, this was also the year which followed the second oil shock, and the USSR made good profits from the doubling of oil prices on the world market. This same factor may also explain the earlier drop in gold sales in 1974 and 1975. It would appear that the Soviet Union is managing its gold stocks with great care, only risking its third source of hard currency when the first (oil) and the second (arms) fail to provide it with sufficient earnings. As a hard currency earner, gold comes far behind oil and arms. Since 1972 it has been providing between 6 per cent and 21 per cent of the visible hard currency revenue, according to the year (see Table 21).

Does the USSR speculate on the international gold market? This question has inspired several novels, including one in 1973 by the talented Paul Erdman called *A Billion Dollar Killing*, (a figure which to-day hardly impresses!) Speculation is kept alive by rumours every now and then that the Soviets are selling their gold off with the help of certain of their socialist partners (especially Bulgaria) or the Middle East countries and even Japan. There are also calculations made which suggest there is discrete collusion with South Africa. This idea is by no means improbable since such collusion does indeed exist for the sale of Soviet diamonds undertaken by the Central Selling Organisation of the de Beers company.

On the other hand, it is also true that planners do not go in for speculation and generally seek to maintain and increase gold reserves. The USSR is aware that its interventions on the gold market can have a destabilising effect. It is in its own interest to avoid a fall in prices which would result from massive sales. In any case, unlike South Africa, for the USSR, gold is only a contributory source of export earnings. It has profited in the past decade from gold price rises. If the gold prices remain in the range of $350 to 450 per ounce, the Soviet gold strategy should go on unchanged.

The Eastern European countries are not gold producers with the exception of Romania which extracts around 6 tonnes of gold a year (data supplied by Romania to the IMF).

Individual countries: reschedulings and adjustments

We have already mentioned the differences among the Eastern countries as to their debt management. On the whole, this management was satisfactory as most of these countries avoided rescheduling, and have since 1981 restored their creditworthiness, which strongly contrasts with the situation of the Third World. Does this reveal a particular feature of centrally planned economies? One has to review the adjustments country by country. Let us however begin with a general statement from a 1988 OECD report:

> It is well to recall that due to fears that Eastern Europe would be engulfed in the international debt crisis in 1982–83, the East Europeans were almost completely driven out of the publicised medium-term markets; and the private international finance community made a determined effort to reduce exposure in the region. After 1983 the CMEA countries so impressed the markets with their subsequent adjustment that private creditors were eventually persuaded to reassess the region and to resume lending on a significant scale ...' (OECD, 1988: 38)

Any given country may experience difficulties over debt service. Three solutions are possible in theory.

1 The country may opt to cease payments of interest and the amortisation of capital. It may then be declared in default by its creditors, but this is a seldom resorted to solution, first because there is no longer a chance for any part of the debt to be paid, second because it forces the lending banks into write-offs.

2 The country may ask for a refinancing (a new credit which would ensure the payments due as service of the previous debt) or, more often, for a rescheduling, whereby the interests and/or the principal falling due at a given date are to be paid later, at dates and conditions agreed with the lenders.

3 The country may finally seek to ensure debt service at all costs, by cutting imports and mobilising all availble sources of finance.

No Eastern European country was declared in default, although the Polish case was much discussed in this light in the United States during 1981–82. Poland and Romania underwent rescheduling procedures. Hungary and the GDR seemed to be near to it in 1982 but managed to avoid rescheduling. Bulgaria, Czechoslovakia and the USSR were never in a critical position but nevertheless took measures to control debt increases.

THE RESCHEDULED COUNTRIES

We will only review the cases of Poland and Romania. In a more comprehensive approach we should add a non-European Comecon nation, Cuba, which went into rescheduling in 1983, and a non-Comecon European socialist country, Yugoslavia, whose financial difficulties are treated, both domestically and on the international level, as a case of a developing country.

Initially the Polish and the Romanian case had much in common. Both countries were indebted to governments (for officially supported export credits, which were automatically transferred to the state through the guarantee procedure) and to banks (for commercial non-guaranteed credits, and for financial credits). In both countries, domestic adjustment programmes were implemented. Romania being a member of the IMF, the stabilisation programme was put to work under IMF control and as a condition for IMF loans. Poland sought IMF membership in November 1981. Subsequently, when martial law was adopted in December 1981, the US government vetoed Polish membership. The adjustment programme was thus negotiated with the authorities which managed the rescheduling, the 'Paris Club' for governments and the banks' steering committee, as a set of policy measures with which the debtor nation had to comply.

The rescheduling of the Polish debt

From 1980, Poland informed its Western creditors that it was having increasing difficulty with debt service. At the same time, in 1980, Poland was borrowing on the euromarket, managing to secure a major loan of $325 million, while also bilaterally negotiating facilities with Western states, which could actually be seen as a kind of refinancing.

Multilateral negotiations however did not get underway until 1981. At the start of that year, the financial situation in Poland was as follows. It owed over $26 billion of which $10.4 billion were guaranteed export credits and $16.2 billion bank credits. In addition Poland owed the USSR some $700 million in hard currency.

After 26 March 1981, when the Polish government notified its creditors that it was no longer able to service its debt, the initial negotiations saw the participation of fifteen governments (out of the seventeen creditor states) and took place in the 'Paris Club'. This led to an agreement of 27 April 1981, which laid down rescheduling conditions for 90 per cent of the debt maturing in 1981 and not yet repaid, and of the interest due (i.e. $2.5 billion). These conditions established the reimbursement period, the grace period, the commitments of the debtor to reduce the deficit in its balance of payments (see Table 21). In due course bilateral negotiations with each creditor state followed.

At the same time, Western banks had started discussions with the Handlowy Bank (the Polish Foreign Trade Bank) to secure an agreement which was only to be signed after credit renegotiation with governments. The 501 creditor banks set up a consortium, or task force, of 21 banks which reached agreement in principle after painstaking debates, on 30 September 1981. It was the first major rescheduling for the banks; this experience was to prove quite useful when the Mexican crisis occurred in 1982. The renegotiation of bank debts can actually be seen to possess two particular traits which distinguish it from those procedures undertaken by governments. First, deferral should guarantee payment of interest. The interest payments, written under the banks' assets, help to maintain the fiction that the principal is still due even if in many instances it is indeed lost for the bank. This is really the difference between rescheduling and defaulting on payments, both for creditor and debtor. Secondly, rescheduling has to be granted by unanimous decision of the creditors so as to ensue perfect equality among them. No one should be granted privileged repayment conditions over the others.

Table 22. Conditions of the Polish and Romanian rescheduling agreements

Poland	Debt due to governments (date of agreement)			Debt due to banks (date of agreement)				
	27 Apr. 1981	November 1985 (tentative)	16 Dec. 1987 (tentative)	6 Apr. 1982	3 Nov. 1982	3 Nov. 1983	13 July 1984	20 July 1988
Period when rescheduled debt was falling due	May–Dec. 1981	1982–85	1986–88	26 March–Dec. 81	1982	1983	1984–87	1988–93
Share of total debt rescheduled (%)	90% interest and principal	100%	100%	95% of principal	95% of principal	95% of principal	95% of principal	95% of principal
Amount of debt relief (billion $)	2.2	9.0	8.8	2.3	2.3	1.2	1.6	9.4
Grace period	4 years	6 years	5 years	$4\frac{1}{2}$ years	$4\frac{1}{2}$ years	$4\frac{1}{2}$ years	5 years	none
Maturity of rescheduled debt	8 years	11 years	10 years	8 years	8 years	$9\frac{1}{2}$ years	10 years	15 years
Repayment period	1986–89			1985–88	1985–89	1988–92	1989–93	1988–2002
Terms of payment				7 equal semesters	7 equal semesters	8 semesters progressive payments	8 semesters progressive payments	8 semesters progressive payments
Bank fees				1%	1%	1%	1%	1%
Interest rate (spread over LIBOR)				$1\frac{3}{4}$	$1\frac{3}{4}$	$1\frac{7}{8}$	$1\frac{1}{4}$	$\frac{13}{16}$
Amount of interests due (in parentheses: share of interests 'relend' in revolving credits)				0.450	1.1 (50%)	1.1 (65%)		

Romania	Debt due to governments (date of agreements)		Debt due to banks (date of agreement)		
	28 July 1982	18 May 1983	7 Dec. 1982	23 June 1983	1986–87 (agreements changing terms of 1982–83 reschedulings)
Period when rescheduled debt was falling due	1982	1983	1981 (arrears) and 1982	1983	
Share of total debt rescheduled (%)	80% interest and principal	60% principal	80% of principal (including short-term)	70% of total debt	
Amount of debt relief (billion $)	0.234	0.195	1.6	0.6	
Grace period	3 years	3½ years	3 years	1½ to 3½ years	
Maturity of rescheduled debt	6½ years	6 years	6½ years	1½ to 6½	
Repayment period	1985–88	1986–89	1985–88	10% due in 1984, 60% in 1987–89	
Bank fees			1%	1%	
Interest rate (spread over LIBOR)			$1\frac{3}{4}$	$1\frac{3}{4}$	$1\frac{1}{3}$ to $1\frac{7}{8}$

Sources: Various press reports; CIA (1986); OECD (1988); *Financial Market Trends*, no. 39.

Difficulties arose over these two points. On the one hand, it was not obvious that Poland would be able to pay off the interest on the debt due (Poland was actually to seek further loans to cover this at the end of the year). On the other hand, the American banks were for some time playing an individual game in setting additional terms and seeking in particular to obtain assurances as to the exact amount and maintainance of Soviet aid to Poland.

The agreement in principle signed in September had therefore to be confirmed by a final agreement before the end of the year once Poland would have paid off the interest due and provided fuller information on its economic situation and financial relations with the other Comecon countries.

The proclamation of martial law in December 1981 introduced a new factor.

From the point of view of the banks, as was expressed privately by people in the profession, this was likely to improve things as bankers viewed developments in the Polish social crisis with some awe and were rather satisfied to see that a strong government might make Poles go back to work. The Paris Club adopted a much more political stance. In January 1982 it decided to suspend all renegotiation of guaranteed debt until martial law was lifted, also stopping all government backed loans except humanitarian aid in credits for food (the USA also banned any credits for food purchases). The suspension of negotiations with governments, a measure only lifted in 1984, had a paradoxical outcome. Though conceived as a sanction, it actually granted Poland legal dispensation from all payments on guaranteed debt for almost three years. Only in January 1985 was a pre-agreement concluded for the 1982–84 debt.

Banks could not afford to take such a strict view for fear of ruining all chances of ever seeing interest paid off. Once again, political pressure brought to bear by the US government almost succeeded in creating further difficulties. The then Secretary of Defence Caspar Weinberger attempted to make US banks declare Poland in default. If this were the case, US banks could then seize Polish assets throughout the world which would lead to other banks following suit in a chain reaction. A final financial crisis would then ensue. Congress was to reject this plan, as did the White House, for fear of risking serious disagreement with the US's European Allies.

The way was then paved for the confirmation of the initial debt rescheduling (May 1982), followed by a succession of further negotiations for the 1982 debt (an agreement was signed in November 1982), and the 1983 debt (November 1983). In both these agreements, Poland obtained a quasi-rescheduling of the interest due as well, as it was granted a revolving credit equal to 50 per cent of the interest due in 1982 and 65 per cent of that due in 1983. The credit itself was to be paid back after a three-year period of grace. Having, so to speak, been 're-lent' part of its interest payments, Poland was to be able to cover its priority imports (foodstuffs and semi-products). The following agreement of July 1984 reflects a development in the attitudes within the world banking community and takes us beyond the isolated case of Poland. As in any case it appeared that further reschedulings would be necessary if a declaration of default was to be avoided, it seemed logical to arrange rescheduling for a number of consecutive years, so as to give the indebted nation greater opportunities to manage its debt and its stabilisation programme. A kind of normalisation of relations between the debtor and its creditors is thus established, both of them involved in long-term mutual dependence.

The following period saw a further progression in rescheduling, especially on the side of the Western governments, with a new impetus when following a relaxation in the US political attitude, Poland was admitted, in 1986, to the IMF and the World Bank. A November 1985 agreement with the Club of Paris provided for the rescheduling of the entire amount of the government-owned debt, on condition that Poland eliminate all its arrears due in 1981. A following agreement was devised in December 1987 on the rescheduling of 1986–88 maturities but never finalised as Poland insisted on lower interest rates and did not reimburse all of the arrears due. In July 1988, an agreement was reached with the creditor banks on the model of the one signed in 1984.

Further reschedulings are to be expected, in the wake of the agreement with the Club of Paris reached in February 1990 following the package of relief and aid measures offered by the US administration and the EC. Poland complains of not been treated as favourably as Third World debtors. Being a member of the IMF, Poland has to implement a stabilisation programme and, as Third World countries, it warns of political and social risks should the strain on the population be excessive. The country tentatively launched the idea of debt-for-equity swaps under which Western creditors might get shares in Polish companies in exchange for writing off part of the debt. The proposal, made in 1987, did not meet with enthusiasm from potential buyers. It might develop in association with the joint ventures format, or along various arrangements such as 'debt-for-environment swap' – a part of the debt to neighbour countries being written off against Polish investments in cleaning the Baltic sea – or 'debt-for-culture swap' – where part of the debt to Federal Germany might be offset by Polish government expenditures in zlotys to promote German culture in Poland.

In launching an appeal for partial debt relief in March 1989, Poland has joined the numerous group of Third World countries which no longer accept carrying on the debt burden for years. This is a political decision, entirely opposed to the Romanian path.*

The rescheduling of the Romanian debt

Romania's situation in September 1981, when it was about to submit its first unofficial demand for the refinancing of its short-term debt by post-poning the payment date, differed from the Polish situation in several respects. Romania's debt was lower ($10 billion end-1980). The country was a member of the IMF and of the World Bank. Politically, it was looked on with more favour, its disagreements over foreign policy with the USSR serving rather to win it US sympathy (despite a continuing dispute with the USA over emigration conditions for Romanian Jews). However, Romania lost the sympathies of the banks having attempted in 1981 to avoid rescheduling by using money derived from foreign exchange trading transactions – a highly condemnable action in bank practice.

The rescheduling procedure, once Romania made an official request early in 1982, followed a similar course to that of Poland. Results were more forthcoming because Romania could count on the participation of the IMF along with bank and government lenders, and also because it adopted a line of stringent domestic austerity.

In 1981, the IMF extended a standby credit of $1,265 million to be drawn over three years (equivalent to three times the share of the country's SDR quota in the IMF) for the implementing of a stablisation programme involving consumption and investment cuts, currency devaluation and a price system reform. All drawings on the loan were suspended in November 1981 owing to the inadequate implementation of this programme. On Romania's request, drawing was once again permitted in June 1982 following new austerity measures taken by the authorities and the providing of more complete information on the financial state of the country.

This IMF decision to reauthorise drawings determined the ending of negotiations with lending governments. The agreement was reached in July 1982, on terms slightly less favourable than those obtained by Poland. The IMF decision was also crucial for the agreement with the fourteen most important lending banks concluded in December 1982, despite difficult problems arising from Romanian demands (i.e. to include suppliers credits as well as short-term debts in the rescheduling of medium and long-term bank credits). The details of the two reschedulings of 1983, in February with banks and in May with governments, were quickly finalised. Moreover, having succeeded in restoring its external current account balance and in gaining a surplus in hard currency, Romania decided not to seek further rescheduling in 1984, and to cancel the last part of its stand-by credit. It has however to enter new rescheduling agreements with the banks due to difficulties in debt servicing in 1985 and 1986. Nevertheless the goal of repaying (even prepaying) all of the outstanding debt by 1990 was stated, and apparently reached as soon as March 1989.

Romania's performance may be seen as brillant, and indeed it satisfied IMF experts. For all that, this result was achieved at the cost of drastic economic measures which spelt food shortages for the entire country and which considerably lowered the living standards of the population as a whole. The decision taken in 1989 not to take new credits altogether means a further estrangement from the world financial community.*

COUNTRIES WHICH HAVE AVOIDED RESCHEDULING

The Hungarian debt

The good renown of Hungarian bankers and that country's opening up to the West since 1968 after introducing its 'New Economic Mechanism', were very important factors in the increased confidence it enjoyed. Since 1977 Hungary has been providing data on its balance of payments in convertible currency, the first country to do so. In November 1981, Hungary officially submitted a request for IMF membership. For all these reasons, despite a relatively high debt ($7.5 billion according to official sources at the end of 1981) the country reckoned itself safe from serious financial problems, especially since its balance of payments had shown signs of recovery as early as 1980.

Paradoxically, Hungary was the most affected by the largely political credit restrictions (see above p. 319) which hit Eastern Europe in 1982. The initial months of 1982 saw a race against time to find short-term credits for debt service. Hungary was able to get some bank-to-bank facilities and a short-term loan of $210 million from central banks relayed by the BIS in April 1982. This was really in anticipation of the country's imminent IMF membership which actually went through in May. In June, Hungary was to go as far as to pledge some of its gold with Swiss banks against a short-term loan. In August, Hungary obtained the first loan in euro-currency extended to any Eastern country since the start of martial law. This was a loan of $260 million over three years, followed soon after by a further bridging loan from the BIS which in turn was taken over by an IMF loan of $500 in December. From that point onwards, the situation was no longer critical and in 1983 Hungary was to return several times to the euro-currency market. It was even the object of an unprecedented financial transaction, receiving a $200 million loan (August 1983) guaranteed with the participation of the World Bank, which therefore meant that it had a kind of in-built guarantee against non-payment. The ultimate sign of Hungary's status of full 'normalisation' came in May 1984 when under, the aegis of a US bank, the country was granted a three-year acceptance facility, the first loan of this type ever offered to Eastern Europe. Another stand-by arrangement was extended by the IMF the same year for slightly over $400. In 1984–88 Hungary returned every year on the euromarket, raising loans for an amount comprised between $1.2 and 1.9 billion a year. In 1987, the country launched a stabilisation programme for 1988–90, with a commitment to stop the increase in debt by 1991. This allowed Hungary to obtain a new stand-by arrangement in 1988, for $350 million. The last instalment was halted by the IMF in May 1989 pending new austerity measures which were eventually voted by the Hungarian parliament in June 1989. The country was then the most heavily indebted in terms of debt per capita among East European countries.

Hungary was accepted to the World Bank as well in 1982 and also received development aid loans, based on its per capital GNP of $2,100 in 1981, no doubt a very conservative figure and one which gave rise to great controversy (Marer, 1985). Since Hungary got its first credit in 1983, up to mid-1988, sixteen project loans have been agreed, for a total amount of $1.5 billion, for various sectors such as food processing, energy saving, transport, and industrial restructuring.

In 1989, Hungary, like Poland, was selected for emergency assistance from the developed nations, according to decisions taken at the Paris Summit of the Seven most industrialised countries, and on the basis of a programme coordinated by the EEC. Hungary itself formulated its needs in July 1989. Though asking for new credits, the Hungarian government mainly insisted on financial support in the form of an aid to the inflow of private investment into the country, and to the strengthening of the market orientation. The government also linked this assistance with a better access to Western markets through commercial measures on the side of the EEC and the other partners of Hungary, very cleverly taking this opportunity of promised financial aid to further push trade concessions already negotiated with the EEC in 1988.*

The GDR's debt

Like Hungary, at the start of 1982 the GDR found itself in a difficult situation with its capacity to service its debt being questioned. Debt reached $9.6 billion at the end of 1981. Furthermore, it could not manage to borrow on the euro-currency market which was closed to Eastern Europe. Unlike Hungary, the GDR never publishes information on its debt and even denies the very notion of indebtedness as, according to the GDR bankers, one can speak about indebtedness only when the debtor fails to pay what is owed when due.

The GDR had one advantage over Hungary, i.e. the existence of a financial arrangement between the two Germanies going back to 1951 and including interest-free credit, known as *swing credit*. The advantage of this should not however be exaggerated. Since 1976 this credit has been equal to 850 million DM units of account. Under a 1982 agreement, this was to be gradually reduced to 600 million by 1985. The GDR does not use the totality of this amount. According to West German estimates, the GDR drew on 95–70 per cent of the maximum authorised amount from 1970 to 1980, with this percentage tending to drop steadily down to 50 per cent in the late eighties. Swing credit can only be resorted to for German products purchased in Germany and for certain specific categories of goods. In particular, swing credit may not be used for interest payments, which means its share in the GDR–FRG capital accounts balance is not great and is being still further reduced (30 per cent in 1976, 15 per cent in 1982). Politically, however, the very availability of this credit, symbolising as it does a continuing special relationship between the two Germanies, is indeed important. The six-month extension of the

swing agreement due to expire at the end of 1981 was actually granted in
the capital of the GDR four days after martial law was imposed in
Poland. Eventually the agreement was renewed, the last renewal to-date
being in 1985. This bears witness to the continuity of specific inter-
German relations.

In 1983, for the first time in the history of the two Germanies, West
Germany extended a billion dollar DM credit (some $400 million) to the
GDR, to help it pay off the interest on its foreign debt. A further credit of
950 million DM ($327 million) was granted in 1984 in return for politi-
cal concessions from the GDR. In addition there are private transfers
from the FRG to the GDR, for an amount unknown but supposed large,
some estimates putting it at 2.5 billion DM annually in the first half of
the eighties (Leptin, 1989: 288). The rules on these transfers were relaxed
in a 1988 agreement between the two countries. These included emigration rights of its citizens to the West and for certain categories of visitors
to the GDR a reduction on the amount of currency which must be
changed at the border. The GDR again borrowed heavily on the euromarket in 1985 but seems since then to prefer bank-to-bank credit and
the use of the à forfait market. What is the most remarkable feature of
the German behaviour is the building up of very large reserves held in
Western banks. The ratio reserves/imports is the highest of all the socialist bloc, and was over 1 in 1985–88 (the reserves could cover a whole
year of imports). At the end of 1988, the amount of these reserves was
over $9 billion in Western banks, and accounted for more than half of
the total Eastern European countries' assets. Either the GDR has been
very shocked by the difficult situation it was in during 1982, or it wants
to accumulate for the future. These reserves are seemingly not held to
increase imports.

The new GDR government is bound to face increased financial needs
in relation with a new economic policy more open to the West, and with
steps taken toward the convertibility of the mark. These needs are more
likely to be satisfied by a recourse to West financing than by a reintegration in the international monetary system.*

COUNTRIES WHICH ARE A GOOD RISK

Czechoslovakia was quicker than any other Eastern European country to
stop the growth of its foreign debt, which levelled off in 1979. The
country only marginally resumed borrowing after 1984, although it

would be able to get excellent terms. The cautious debt policy reflects an uncertain growth strategy and the weak competitiveness of Czechoslovak exports.

Bulgaria, as Czechoslovakia, returned very late on the euro-currency market, in 1985 only. It succeeded in getting large surpluses in hard currency from some Third World countries (oil exporters) through its agricultural trade. After the drop in oil prices which hit its clients, Bulgaria resumed borrowing and has had a fast rising indebtedness.

The USSR was considered by the international banking community as an excellent risk, at least up to 1989, but for political reasons any Soviet move is closely watched, especially when it is meant to be dramatic as in October 1988 when in a few weeks the USSR discussed the opening of credit lines for more than $9 billion (see p. 315). The country still satisfies any criterion of creditworthiness. Although its assets in the Third World are mostly soft, i.e. not easily recoverable, they nevertheless contribute to increase its total assets in hard currency. Paradoxically the USSR itself began to shake the Western creditors' confidence by publicising in 1989 much higher figures for its debt than was until then computed by Western institutions such as the OECD and the BIS. These official statements about the external debt added to the acknowledgement of a domestic financial crisis, with a huge budget deficit, a growing deficit, and a 'monetary overhang' due to the fact that the population could not spend its very large cash holdings on purchases of goods in an acute shortage situation. For any other country such a picture would entail a serious loss of creditworthiness. However, by mid-1989 the USSR had not made use of all the credit lines available from Western European governments. The fears expressed by the Soviet government as to the amount of the hard currency debt may well be an excuse for resisting suggestions to borrow so as to import consumption goods (this is proposed by 'radical' Soviet economists). These fears may also help to justify the implementation of drastic adjustment programmes. Ultimately the growing openness about debt issues might support Soviet moves toward IMF membership.*

The Eastern countries and the IMF

The economic difficulties of some East Europan countries at the start of the eighties came at a time when these countries were seeking to increase participation in the international monetary system. Romania joined the

IMF in 1972 and was followed by Hungary in 1982. Poland was admitted only in 1986 after the lifting of sanctions following the 1981 martial law. Three major issues are to be raised here:

(1) Why did these countries want to become members of the IMF?
(2) Are IMF adjustment requirements conditional on financial assistance from the Fund compatible with centrally planned systems?
(3) Can we envisage a general participation by socialist countries in the IMF? This last question is tantamount to the issue of Soviet participation.

REASONS FOR IMF MEMBERSHIP: CENTRIFUGAL TENDENCIES OR ECONOMIC PRAGMATISM?

Initially, there was no barrier between the socialist world and the international monetary system born of Bretton Woods. In fact the Bretton Woods agreements were adopted in July 1944 by the delegations of the USSR, Poland (its government in exile in London) and Czechoslovakia, among others. The Soviet Union played more than a nominal role here, standing as a great power set on playing a part on the postwar international scene. It advanced the articles safeguarding the interests of those nations having suffered most the effects of the war and the specific features of centrally planned economies (the USSR was the sole representative of the last category). However, the USSR was never to ratify these agreements. In 1945 the advent of the Cold War cut off such bridges as had been built, with the result that this chapter of Soviet economic history has been studiously ignored in the USSR. On the other hand, Poland and Czechoslovakia did ratify the agreement, but Poland withdrew from the IMF in 1950 and Czechoslovakia was expelled in 1954 for failing to respect the Articles of Agreement – in fact, due to political incompatiblity.

Poland's withdrawal and Czechoslovakia's expulsion added weight to the idea that any attempt by the socialist countries to rejoin the IMF would necessarily suggest political confrontation within Comecon, or the setting up of centrifugal tendencies. It was with this idea in mind that, in 1972, Romania was duly granted membership; it was seen as a sign of independence or even rebellion against Soviet views. Things were therefore made easy for Romania which was allowed to keep its financial figures secret (they were provided only to the Fund's bodies themselves by a dispensation from the usual rule) and provisionally maintain the non-convertibility of the national currency, the leu. It is probable that Romania was motivated by essentially political considerations. Romania made moderate use of its borrowing rights until 1980, it was only in 1981, just before its interruption of payments, that it requested and was granted a major loan from the IMF (a stand-by credit of $1.3 billion over three years).

In November 1981, within only a few days of each other, both Hungary and Poland requested membership. Their immediate motivation was strictly economic (i.e. to obtain financial support and at the same time some credibility *vis-à-vis* their lenders). In Hungary's case, there was also the attendant consideration of winning 'international respectability'. Just as Hungary had sought to become a GATT member under conditions geared to market economies, it was showing its desire to join the IMF on the same basis. To this end it had outdone Romania in meeting the prerequisites of membership. From 1980, the domestic price mechanism was closely linked to external prices and measures were put forward for convertibility of the forint – which is still to come.

As for Poland, its need for financing was urgent at a time when it had undertaken the first rescheduling of its debt. Moreover, its lenders were as anxious as Poland itself was to see the IMF take over part of the financial burden linked with rescheduling.

In these different cases economic considerations became gradually dominant. But were the expectations met on both sides?

ECONOMIC COMPATIBILITY BETWEEN THE ADJUSTMENTS RECOMMENDED BY THE IMF AND PLANNED MECHANISMS

Are the mechanisms for taking action recommended by the IMF actually efficient in a planned economy? Are they acceptable to such a system?

The first of these questions was raised by the Fund itself in a confidential study carried out in 1982. The answer was positive. The reason given in the study was that centrally planned economies have characteristics similar to those of the Third World, where IMF policies had so far proved applicable, i.e., multiple exchange rates, administered prices, foreign exchange restrictions, and a large public sector. In fact, the Fund behaved 'as if' it believed that policy instruments such as exchange rates or interest rates might prove operational for influencing consumption, investment and foreign trade in centrally planned economies.

In fact, the adjustments were quite effective in Hungary and Romania, in a very short time-span as compared to what happened in Third World countries. But: (a) similar adjustments were conducted in other Eastern European countries without any intervention of the Fund, in particular, in Czechoslovakia (Dyba and Kupka, 1987); in Hungary, an adjustment programme had been launched even before that country's membership (Asseto, 1988: 172); (b) the use of indirect policy instruments to achieve these results was strictly nil in Romania and hardly actual in Hungary; direct state intervention allowed for the necessary adjustments.

What did this experience bring about in terms of greater integration in the international economic system? An increased statistical *glasnost*, but mostly from Hungary which would probably in any case have opened its statistics earlier than other CPEs; a more 'real' exchange rate (again, this holds true mostly for Hungary) and a link between domestic and foreign prices (quite cosmetic in the case of Romania). It is not at all obvious that such developments (which also applied to Poland after 1986) are linked with IMF membership.

Poland immediately applied for an IMF stand-by loan when it joined the organisation in 1986, and even before the admission had implemented a stabilisation programme, with several devaluations of the zloty, price increases, and elimination of subsidies. At the beginning of 1989 new regulations extending the private sector were introduced, and the convertible zloty declared a target by 1991–93. Poland is also the first Eastern European country to have legalised private transactions in hard currency in March 1989. However, the country is still waiting for its World Bank loans, which are meant to help in developing the agricultural private sector along with projects in energy, telecommunications and transport sectors. At the beginning of 1989 an arrangement had not yet been reached with the IMF either.

IS A GENERAL INCLUSION OF THE SOCIALIST SYSTEM IN THE IMF AT ALL CONCEIVABLE?

Membership would pose a great problem for the Soviet Union. Whereas the smaller East European countries may maintain exchange restrictions even for a long period, behaving like the vast majority of the IMF members, the Soviet Union could not join on the basis of Article XIV and should obviously make its money convertible. Other obligations would follow, such as providing statistics on balance of payments, foreign exchange reserves, the production and export of gold – *glasnost* should help here – and more active participation in international financial assistance. Should the USSR experience financial difficulties and need the Fund's help, it would have to comply with the conditionality requirements, Unlike Romania, Hungary and Poland, the USSR could obviously not benefit from World Bank development loans.

A most debated question is that of the Soviet quota in the Fund. According to some estimates, the USSR might be assigned a quota amounting to 6 per cent of the voting power, well short of the 15 per cent veto minority. However, such a quota would allow the Soviet Union to qualify for the right to appoint an executive director and thus entail the displacing of one of the five appointed directors, which would fall on either France or Great Britain, unless other arrangements were made (Feinberg, 1989).

One may ask why should the USSR want to join a system whose imminent decline it has always heralded. Even if history is now written differently, the present system is widely reckoned – on the Western side – as needing revamping. But would a 'new Bretton Woods' with active Soviet participation be acceptable to either the USSR or the USA – apart from the fact that there are no really feasible blueprints for that. For the time being, the USSR has no need of the IMF either for guaranteeing its financial credibility or providing extra resources.

Thus, while participation in the IMF might of course mean, as in the case of GATT, increased international respectability for the USSR, the issues are not at all parallel. Neither the international monetary system nor the USSR are ready yet for Soviet membership in the IMF.*

CONCLUSION

What place do the socialist economies occupy in the world economy today, and what place will (should) they occupy tomorrow?

In this book, we have partly answered the first question, with data as to the share of the socialist countries in world production and trade, and with analyses of these countries' behaviour in international trade or financial markets. We now have to answer the second question.

To begin with, less than ever, the socialist system can be considered as a bloc. This is not just because not all Eastern European countries have agreed to engage in reforms as the Soviet Union does now. This is also because the notion of socialism itself is becoming increasingly fuzzy.

Seen from a 'capitalist' point of view, the 'reformed socialist economy' is certainly a puzzling object, to which the classical, or standard, centrally planned economy might be preferred. On the micro level, reforms have as a first consequence a disorganising effect. Instead of trading (exceptionally cooperating) with state trading entities (the well-known FTOs, foreign trade organisations), the businessman has now to find his way among all sorts of potential partners who themselves know little about their own rights and about foreign trade in general. On the macro level, the governments of the reform-ed (or-ing) socialist economies ask to be treated according to the usual practice applying to market economies, and the past (and future) negotiations between the EC Commission and the Eastern European countries are a demonstration of this. When shifting from the strictly economic to the political perspective, there is a feeling that the West 'should' help the East (How? To achieve what?) so as to be logical with a past policy promising more flexibility on the part of the West if only the 'collectivist' regimes were to abandon the principles of directive planning and the overwhelming domination of state ownership, in line with a single party political system.

It is generally felt that the reforms should induce a higher rate of participation in the world economy. But how? And with what consequences? There are three possible approaches.

1 The *relational*, or *participative* approach. This suggests that there is a 'world international system' to which the socialist countries did not belong up to now, or did belong only marginally. The basic problem is then to include them in the world economy. This in turn raises a number of questions:

(i)   How are we to *measure* this process?
(ii) What *conditions* might be required for that?
(iii) What *advantages* would derive from such an involvement?
(iv) Is it possible to expect a greater participation of socialist countries in *international economic organisations*?

2 The *comparative approach*. This leads to a discussion of the convergence issue. By the way, we should not speak of convergence, because there is no sign of it in the 'capitalist' world. On the contrary, when comparing the present situation with the one existing at the time when Jan Tinbergen launched the concept, we see that market economy regimes are consistently removing what still remains of planning or state regulation. Neither should one speak of 'submergence' as did Grossman debating with Tinbergen. Presently the reformed economies are not 'converging' along with capitalist economies towards something common, nor are they submerged by capitalism. They are rather verging on a new system which they call market socialism without having yet defined it.

3 The *feedback approach*. This looks like a paradox. We have always (in the West) assumed that the changes occurring in the socialist economies were bound to affect them more or less strongly, without affecting the West. This applies to the developing as well as to the developed economies. But is it really so? If successful, the changes which occur in the socialist 'reformed' world might have some impact on the West as well.

The second and third approaches would be proper for a book on comparative economic systems and largely exceeds the scope of this book. In a broader perspective, they should not be omitted. The socialist countries claim their willingness to open to the world economy. What should be achieved first, a domestic 'socialist market' (or 'market socialism', both wording being far from identical) or the opening up which would facilitate domestic reforms? In this process, how far can one go without renouncing socialism? If the very essence of socialism can no longer be defined, where is now the socialist model? In the past, the official Marxist doctrine in the East rejected the social-democrat model (rather, set of 'models') as a-socialist and often anti-socialist in Marxist terms. Now Soviet authors plead for the social democrat type of capitalism (Sheinis, 1988). It follows then that the very concept of 'socialist orientation' as applied to some Third World countries has to be reviewed as well. Formerly, when this concept was (very cautiously) questioned, it was because the countries with a socialist orientation were not always very constant in their choice and had to be re-classified. Now the essential question is: a socialist orientation, towards *which* socialism? (Maksimenko, 1988).

This is only a sketch of the problems to be addressed. In an international perspective, what are the issues?

This book began with stating the commonplace approach: the standard centrally planned economy behaves in an autarkic way. The 'classics' in this field (Pryor, 1963; Wiles, 1968; Holzman, 1968, 1974, 1976; see chapter 1) have demonstrated and analysed that behaviour (for the most recent treatment, see Wolf, 1988). This means that, due to the very characteristics of their system, the CPEs tend both to insulate their economy from the outside world and, as a regional grouping, to achieve 'trade destruction' in addition to trade diversion.

Having during quite a long time strongly opposed this description of their 'system-autarkic' economies, the economists of the socialist countries now insist on the need to 'open up' to trade and cooperation with the outside world.

1 How to analyse this 'openness', or 'opening up'?

The 'system-determined' *statistical problems*, as Wolf (1988) calls them are not so easy to solve. The *participation ratio* measuring the share of foreign trade in national income (product) is certainly better approached in a reformed economy (hence after RE) than in a traditional CPE when there is a significant exchange rate and better national account statistics. But new discrepancies emerge because the various REs apply different methods – and because there remain 'non-REs'! As for the measure of the 'block autarky' (or, if preferred, of the centrifugal/centripetal trends within Comecon) nothing has improved; on the contrary. When all Comecon members were standard CPEs there was a coherent cross-rate rouble:dollar for all the currencies. This might occur again if and when Comecon becomes a real 'unified market'. For the time being, nobody can answer the question: what is the share of trade conducted within Comecon in the total trade of the socialist countries.

These are not only technicalities. The difficulties mentioned have an impact on the measurement of Eastern competitiveness, a standard, if any, type of indicator in foreign trade theory. Bienkowski (1988) discusses Western measurement methods for assessing competitiveness and sorts out the 'methods to be used without, or with only small, modifications' (such as the 'constant market share' indicator), from methods which require great caution or are misleading if not outright inadequate.

We are thus left with very simplified indicators which do not show much. Are the REs more open than the standard CPEs? Yes, they have to be just because they are REs, which means that they have a more 'realistic' rate of exchange which immediately makes them *look* more open. Are they competitive? No, they are not: the only meaningful measures revolve around indicators which show that the Eastern European countries are losing ground to the NIEs (newly industrialising economies) in the Western developed markets.

This leaves us with few conclusions about the ways to increase openness, or to improve competitiveness. Moreover, it amounts to considering only part of the international activities of the REs, as openness, in these approaches, makes sense only towards the West, and competitiveness is measured only on the Western market. True, it is probably impossible to do more, because the REs, as well as the 'non-REs' (a group in which we should include both GDR and Romania, although for quite different arguments), belong to a 'non-RE' integration grouping. But then it is really disturbing to leave such a large field aside: could one imagine discussing how the EEC countries participate in the world economy while leaving the EEC itself aside?

2 What are the conditions to be met by the REs in order to be considered as fully-fledged members of the international economic system?

Most of the conditions have already been set by the various bodies which were entitled to express them. For instance:
1 Indicative planning at most, autonomy of decision of firms at the lower level, meaningful prices linked with world prices, meaningful rates of

exchange: these are the conditions which Hungary has (successfully) met in negotiating with GATT (1973) and the EEC (1988). (As we know, these conditions were not exactly met in 1973 but the admission to GATT was also a political move; as for the negotiation with the EEC, it was very difficult for Hungary to get rid of the 'reciprocity' argument, according to which a state-trading country has to make 'reciprocal', and not just 'equivalent' concessions in trade negotiations).

2 Same as above, plus a meaningful domestic interest rate, allowing the standard package of adjustment measures recommended by the IMF as a condition for loans to work effectively. These were the conditions asked from Romania (1981), Hungary (1982), later on Poland. The conditions were 'met' in the sense that the adjustment measures were effective (in the case of Romania and Hungary) – but not because market instruments were used; because the central planning methods were put to work, and we know how harshly in the case of Romania.

Moving to a much more political field, what about the Cocom restrictions on exports to the 'communist' countries? What conditions are to be met so that they will be eliminated? Should these countries cease to be 'communist', and might this trend be identified with moves towards a multiparty system? What if some of them move in this direction, and the others do not? If Cocom restrictions are justified by the need to reduce the military potential, or to limit the military build-up of these countries, what will happen if disarmament – not to speak of the possible neutralisation of some countries – goes on?

The human rights question should also be addressed here. For many years the socialist countries were accused of not allowing their citizens the freedom to emigrate or to travel abroad. Some of them still apply such restrictions. The countries which have lifted them partially or totally are not always exempted from the sanctions their former record entailed (for instance in the case of Poland and the USSR). At the same time, the human and economic consequences of this liberalisation already begin to appear harmful from the point of view of the West. The country most confronted by this evolution in the West, the Federal Republic of Germany, is already devising restrictive measures to stop the flow of non-German Eastern European citizens.

3 What are the advantages from a growing involvement in the world economy?

The REs' governments, who believe in competition, expect greater efficiency in their domestic enterprises from the competition with the external world, and also a 'learning' effect which is particularly sought through the operation of joint ventures, special economic zones, etc. They are beginning to understand that competition from outside is only beneficial and effective when there is competition within. In actual fact, the reforms did not bring competition within. There are now, operating side-by-side, the traditional monopolies or oligopolies (i.e. the state enterprises) and a host of mini-monopolies of a 'primitive capitalist' type, in the form of cooperatives or private enterprises, which derive huge rents from the general shortage. On the international scene, the socialist countries have also to get better acquainted with all the non-trade, non-commodity aspects in the operation of the international economic system, and with the ways of non-price competition.

By 'non-trade' aspects or restrictions (which is quite different from the protectionist restrictions in trade) is meant in particular the operation of the multinational enterprises. Should the movement of joint ventures expand, the REs would become more familiar with these practices, which they do not know and which will not be readily disclosed to them by their partners.

By 'non-commodity' aspects is meant the operation of the world financial markets. The socialist countries are not ready to enter that world. The 'financial innovations' now practised (auctions, capital markets, etc.) are fascinating in their developments, but have little to do with what we witness in the real 'capitalist' world. A standard CPE, with a monobank system and clever, well-trained people having a monopoly access to the foreign currency reserves of their country, has probably greater opportunities to take advantage of the capitalist financial markets than have the half-decentralised REs. The socialist countries are not, and it is difficult to imagine how they might be, involved in the restructuring of the financial instruments which was induced by the soaring of Third World debt.

One may ask, in this connexion, whether the reforms are going to have an impact on the management of external debt. They should not add to the creditworthiness of these economies; they might affect it negatively if it felt that borrowing is going out of control by the central authorities.

Not a single RE has reached such a degree of decentralisation. As seen from the case of the USSR, the reform process allows a discussion on the amounts and aims of borrowing to develop, which may worry the lenders. If such discussions lead to more rational choices as to objects which should be financed by foreign borrowing, this might be seen as a positive outcome, not yet to be observed.

What about the West? The Western businessmen look first for markets, and second for profits. They see a contradiction between their drive for markets and the East's desire to increase exports, and they fear the solution lies only in increased compensation deals. This might be avoided by increased and more successful industrial cooperation (which would also generate profits, if only by reduced transport costs by comparison with Third World ventures). Again we are brought to the joint ventures, not so successful up to now.

4 Would the reforms allow the REs to play a more active role in international organisations?

This is a point very much discussed in the press. It has been analysed in this book. When it comes to participation in GATT or the IMF, then it is clearly a political issue, to be discussed between the USA and the USSR – or else among Western countries.

The issue of the 'European common home' is reluctantly approached in the West. The much more practical issue of whether a given socialist country (first and foremost Hungary) might be associated to the EC, even become a member, is far more disturbing. It is dismissed as fantasy. Should it become a reality, Comecon would sooner or later dissolve. But what then about the European Communities? Would they stand the shock? Political, economic, human consequences would follow. This is a much more far-reaching question than just asking how the Western market might be protected.

In any case, few hopes may be put in Comecon. The scepticism which the *perestroika* of Comecon arouses when mentioned, the powerful centrifugal tendencies expressed in almost all the European members – with different reasons – may well impair a successful openness. There are formidable obstacles to a real change within Comecon, be it from the point of view of trade arrangements, of price-fixing, of currency mechanisms. But the West should not be so happy to witness these centrifugal tendencies. A strong and market-oriented Eastern European community would serve the interests of the West more than an ineffective plan-regulated integration falling to pieces.

What happens in the socialist world – including the Chinese developments – has implications for the West. A world socialist economy cannot stand as an alternative to a world capitalist economy. In consequence, the standard UN three-term division into developed market economies, developing market economies and centrally planned economies is hardly relevant any more. The standard Comecon classification of international relations of the socialist countries according to three 'poles' is also outdated. In intra-Comecon relations, conflicts of interest are mounting, up to the point of preventing trade and setting up new barriers, as exemplified by the 'customs war' between Czechoslovakia and its neighbours, when that country decided in November 1988 to stop the haemorrhage of consumer goods bought by foreign 'brother' tourists. East–South relations, wrongly considered in the West as duplicating the pattern of North–South relations, are increasingly 'South–South' relations of a specific type. This in turn points to East–West relations as a South–North pattern, where the socialist countries of Europe feature as inefficient NIEs. The West begins to perceive this, mostly with jubilation. Is there room for jubilation? For a long time the West feared the military threat from the East – seen as the Soviet Union with its satellites. One should rejoice at witnessing earnest moves towards a peace-minded orientation, not at seeing economically well-endowed countries getting into structural recession. What was understood by the United States after the Second World War – that one should help one's partners to recover for one's own benefit – should be understood in the nineties. History does not repeat itself, and it is meaningless to think in terms of a 'new Marshall plan'. What the USSR and Eastern Europe need most is expertise and cooperation. The West also needs it for its own growth.

POSTSCRIPT 1990

The title of this book, *International Political Economy and Socialism*, was meant to convey two ideas. First, in order to understand the specific mechanisms of international trade relations in the centrally planned economies, one has to apply a political economy approach, more institutional and pluridisciplinary than the standard tools of economic analysis. Secondly, this book refers to a comparative economic systems perspective: there are two different systems in the world, capitalism and socialism, and the systemic features determine the way the economy operates.

In the present (1990) conditions, a political economy approach seems more relevant than ever. Institutional, political and sociological factors are essential in shaping the transition underway in the Soviet Union and Eastern (which we should now rather call Central) Europe. The systemic approach becomes highly questionable for the future: are there still different systems? It remains valid for the past.

In the following pages, I am updating the information given in this book, and these additional facts may be soon outdated themselves. What we are observing in the East is unprecedented, and not only as regards new trends emerging. Everybody now senses that we are witnessing the birth of a new world. What is less often stressed is that the assessment of the past is changing as well. A case in point is economic statistics. We were accustomed to work with incomplete or biased information, but the experts in the field had grown used to that and had developed a fairly wide consensus about the credibility and the interpretation of the data. In the course of this book I have given several instances of such an approach, for instance about the treatment of the incomplete Soviet foreign trade data in USSR–Third World trade, or the figures on Eastern indebtedness. Now all this is challenged as well. It is claimed in the East that we were grossly misled and overall too optimistic: debt figures are now dramatically increased, official growth rates are said to have been inflated to a point which even the most cautious Western analysts did not suspect. This assessment seems to be evidenced by the facts about the poor shape of the Eastern economies, well beyond any educated estimates formerly suggested in the least optimistic Western studies. For instance, we used to speak about the 'success story' of the East German economy: what is now revealed is a terrible deterioration. It is too early to offer definitive figures and assessments – and will not perhaps be possible until a long period has lapsed. The figures quoted in this book have to be accepted with caution.

As mentioned in the Preface, I have used asterisks to signal that a specific update is to be found in these pages. However, I have not mentioned each time some recurring points for which an update would be necessary, in particular as regards the qualification of individual countries. At the time of writing, Hungary and Poland were the only countries obviously on the way to a market-oriented reform. The Soviet Union was implementing a reform – the *perestroika* – the orientation of which was, and still is, undecided. Bulgaria was groping for change, and not much new has yet emerged. Romania, the GDR and Czechoslovakia are repeatedly mentioned in the book as 'non-reforming' countries. Following the November 1989 'velvet revolution', Czechoslovakia has joined the group of the most 'market-oriented' countries even if the actual steps toward restructuring are slow. Romania got rid of the Ceaucescu rule in December 1989 and has shed some of its most salient features in international trade and economic relations, such as the insistence on maintaining a hard currency surplus at the expense of drastic sacrifices exacted from the population, but has yet to implement positive measures. As for the GDR, it is now slipping out of the concern of the experts on Eastern European economics, as it is going to be absorbed into the West German economy through the unification process beginning in July 1990. All this has to be borne in mind when these countries are mentioned in the text.

Chapter 1

This chapter has a definite historic approach which ends in 1985, just before the Soviet *perestroika*, although for some points, such as the trends in the exchange rate policy, more recent developments are mentioned. It shows mainly how traditional centrally planned economies have a specific approach to international trade which makes them less open, all things being equal, than market economies. Some questions raised in this chapter may now be seen in a new light. This is the case for the theory of international trade to be applied to socialism. We may now answer that the question is no longer relevant. There cannot be a *specific* theory of international division of labour under socialism, nor of international *socialist* division of labour, as these systemic categories have proved non-viable.

Another point to make in this connection relates to international monetary economics. I may certainly be blamed for having dwelled so little on the convertibility issue, which is now a major one in the discussion of the transition. But from the point of view of a centrally planned economy convertibility is hardly relevant. In international trade, exchanges are conducted in foreign currencies, convertible or not. The main point here is that domestic currencies are largely non-convertible into goods. Only when these countries have completed the marketisation process does international convertibility make sense. Until then, what only matters is how to allow decentralised economic agents, enterprises or individuals, to get access to foreign currency. This is why I have focussed on a different question: how to devise a significant exchange rate in non-market conditions, pp. 29ff.

p. 36. A new section would open here beginning from 1989. In the transition economies, devaluation becomes a standard instrument of economic policy, and Poland has led the way in the new policy of the non-Communist government set up in 1989, which brought the exchange rate of the zloty down to its market value, through twenty-one devaluations. One of the first moves of the new Romanian government was to devalue the leu and to introduce a single exchange rate in February 1990, of 21 lei for 1 dollar. We have to remember though that even in the transition economy, devaluation does not automatically trigger responses comparable to its consequences in a market economy, due to the still imperfect link between external and internal prices. In all these countries and especially in the USSR, the price reforms are still underway. Frequent adjustments of the exchange rate are thus to be expected. Finally, the case of the GDR will be solved here, as in other matters, by a merger with the West German currency in July 1990. The East German Mark will be exchanged for Deutschmarks at different rates depending on the nature of the assets (or liabilities) in Marks and on the economic agents (individuals, coporations, state agencies) detaining them. The fixing of the rate has been decided upon on the basis of largely non-economic, political considerations, with a compromise between a 'realistic' rate of 2 Ost Marks for 1 DM suggested by the West German *Bundesbank*, and a 'grant' rate of 1 to 1 aiming at safeguarding an acceptable living standard for the East Germans (especially pensioners and families with children), and at preventing a large emigration wave.

p 49. In 1990, we can no longer speak of socialism. In the middle of

1989, the concepts of market socialism, or socialist market, though questioned, were still on the agenda. A year later, the picture has shifted. Where, as in Romania or Bulgaria, some governments still cling to ideological concepts, this seems a rearguard action. Even in the Soviet Union, in May 1990, the most 'conservative' programme, i.e., in the peculiar meaning of political categories which has emerged in these countries, the closest to the old communist ideas, refers to a 'regulated market' and drops the reference to socialism. And politically, as elections in Poland, Hungary and Czechoslovakia have shown, what seems most appealing to the population in these countries is not a variant of a Western European Social Democrat ideology, but one definitely more conservative in its values – true, with provisions for a social 'safety net' which would protect the people from the most undesirable consequences of the transition such as unemployment and a drastic reduction in the standard of living.

We now refer to these countries as economies in transition, or post-socialist. The concept of transition itself is far from clear. Should we say 'back to capitalism'? This would not be appropriate as this would suggest going back to an old-fashioned, grassroots economic and social system which no longer exists anywhere. The word capitalism itself is not adequate as it only made sense as long as it could be opposed to socialism. What should we call the global economic system now emerging? The safest answer is a market system, but then how does one account for the growing sphere of non-market relations which develops in our own economies and will have to develop there as well?

It is now increasingly believed in the West that the transition process must be as quick as possible. The new 'model' is the Polish one, which is applied since January 1990, with two features. First, the whole package of institutional reforms and short-term adjustment measures has been implemented at once, as opposed to the 'step-by-step' approach still favoured in most of the other countries. Secondly, the new government which came to power after democratic elections in 1989 had enough popular support to embark upon a 'shock therapy', meaning a sharp decline in living standards and rising unemployment. This approach seemed to pay off in Poland during its first months of testing. Inflation went down; demand and supply were more balanced on the consumer markets. However, it was felt that, despite its merits, such a plan was very dependent on favourable political conditions, and could be jeopardised by public protest if austerity went too far.

Do the present developments in Eastern Europe, and particularly in Poland, mean that the Western experience is universal? The advice sought by Eastern governments and economic managers, and offered by Western international organisations, government or private experts, often results in economic policy or business management packages which merely transpose Western economic recipes for the use of the East, without accounting for the specifics of the (ex-)socialist economies. The violent rejection of communism in most of the Eastern countries, the deep desire to move to a point of no return back to central planning, may explain this hasty endorsement of capitalist lessons. We may, however, safely say that the transition is going to take many years, with possible backfire, no matter how quickly the stage is set for the new system. Both in the domestic and in the international sphere, the specifics of the (ex-)socialist countries cannot be ignored, even if in the competition between private capitalism and socialism the former is to win, contrary to Lenin's views quoted above (p. 48).

Chapter 2

*p. 54. The 'three-way polarisation' which has shaped the international economic relations of the Eastern block since the war is apparently finished with. Intra-Comecon trade fell in 1989 by some 10 per cent and might decrease in the nineties to half its present share in the total trade of its members. The institutional framework of the organisation might disappear to give way to a very loose structure, if any. The commitments toward the Third World are no longer felt as binding. The East had become in the seventies and the eighties a competitor of the South for Western markets; since 1989 it is increasingly a competitor for Western aid. The East is now striving to become a part of the West, and this is particularly felt. The questions to ask now are the following: how long will it take to achieve the desired integration into the Western (basically European) economy? Can the former links with other areas be discarded?

* p. 56. Though much less discussed than the East European revolution, similar processes happen in the Third World. The question asked in the text is certainly not relevant in its form. The socialist-oriented countries are moving away from this orientation. The events in the East certainly triggered political changes in the South in 1990, such as the reunification of the two Yemen states in May, the gradual shift away from Marxism in Ethiopia and Benin, the Nicaraguan election of April. In these and other socialist-oriented countries, economic changes such as the commitment to privatisation, an opening up to foreign capital, were provoked by several causes. The feeling that aid from the socialist countries (above all from the USSR) would be decreasing was compounded with the conditio-

nality attached to the aid granted by international organisations such as the IMF or the World Bank.

p. 60. The restructuring of the East is no longer to happen along the line of a shift from 'extensive' to 'intensive' growth. The very wording belongs to the past. The tasks of restructuring are also seen as much more daunting than they appeared previously. The two most striking cases are those of the GDR and Czechoslovakia, two countries which in Western views were credited with a more advanced industrial policy than the others. It is now acknowledged that a number of plants in the heavy industry sector have to be scrapped altogether, and that the seemingly more advanced machine-building sector, including high technology factories, is to be revamped, its main merit lying in the skills of the workers. The restructuring is indeed going to rely on market mechanisms, but will require far more capital than has ever been envisaged by the old regime in power, and will be achieved with a large involvement of Western investment. In the case of the GDR, these changes take the form of an economic merger, which according to the treaty signed between the two German governments on 18 May 1990, is aiming at a 'social market economy' – certainly not a socialist one.

It follows of course that the STP Programme of 1985 is to be considered as obsolete before having begun to function. In the East Central European space, i.e. among the European members of Comecon, inter-firm relations in advanced technology branches are surely to be expected. Such links will not be fostered by the present governments who are eager to connect their firms to their Western counterparts. Rather, the Western multinationals investing in the East will gradually build a network of business contacts, cross-country mergers, and industrial cooperation of the type existing in the Western business world. Such a pattern is already appearing in some industries such as the automobile sector.

p. 61. At this point in our developments we were forecasting a future for Comecon, as well as assessing in retrospect how it could be qualified.

A short answer to both questions would be to say that whatever the institutional arrangements still in force in 1990, Comecon is dead if not yet buried, and that anyhow it hardly ever existed. Such a statement may sound provocative, but is in fact implied in many comments.

The idea of a single socialist market is certainly a stillborn concept. The working committee which was to detail the measures to be taken to this effect has been disbanded. The 45th session of the Comecon council was convened in January 1990, after having been postponed several times. It merely decided to shift to trade at 'world market prices' and in convertible currencies, beginning in 1991. The future of the organisation was to be discussed later, but it was already clear that if Comecon was to be maintained, it would be in the form of a joint information body, without any operational power.

Could there possibly be a new economic grouping uniting some of the (ex-)Comecon members? This idea is not popular in the East. The Soviet Union is not pressing for it. The East Central European countries do not want an association with the Soviet Union. This country is no longer looked upon as a superpower dominating or exploiting the bloc, but as an unstable country, not really engaged to the reform. Thus, it would be harmful to associate with it in the transition period. Within East Central Europe, interests are diverging. The case of the GDR is to be disjoined due to the economic union with West Germany. The union will maintain the commitments resulting from already signed bilateral trade and cooperation agreements, but on a strictly bilateral basis. The future of the Romanian and Bulgarian regimes, during the first part of 1990, was felt as too uncertain to make any involvement in a new grouping likely. The Central European area – Poland, Czechoslovakia, Hungary – could be seen as more ready for a new association, but the aim common to these three countries is really more to join the EEC than to institutionalise their mutual relations, even if non-Comecon members such as Austria, Italy or Yugoslavia could join such an organisation (see p. 78).

Perhaps the greatest failure of Comecon is to have lacked in the past any of the features of an economic union. As we have seen earlier in this book, plan coordination was never introduced, specialisation was very limited, and there were definitely no market relations at all among the member states. What did exist was a network of bilateral agreements centred on the USSR, and a set of rules for pricing and currency arrangements which left all the members with the feeling that they were losing from these relations, unavoidable as they were (see pp. 62–3). This certainly explains why it is so difficult, for Eastern Europe, to sense the benefits they might expect from a resumption of such links, even in a deeply modified form.

As to the non-European members of Comecon, their future is still dimmer. Only the Soviet Union remains committed to assistance to them, and probably not for long as foreign aid is increasingly questioned in the new democratic institutions of the country. A shift towards the market is well underway in Vietnam and has begun in Mongolia. If and when political changes follow in these countries as well as in Cuba, then these countries would be on the agenda for Western assistance, Mongolia only remaining in the Soviet orbit due to its geographic situation. But the reintegration of Vietnam into the South Asian economic space and of Cuba into the Central American economic space would also have a political dimension well beyond its economic consquences.

* p. 68. The large amount of international aid and of foreign investment to be channelled to Eastern Europe gives a new dimension to this debate (see comments to p. 321).

* p. 72. The whole issue of assistance to the East will be discussed as a comment to p. 321.

* p. 79. The future of the institutions of Comecon cannot be foreseen in 1990. Bilateral links and institutions are to be maintained or dissolved on the same, bilateral basis. As for the bodies and agencies created on a multilateral basis, one has to distinguish between the 'technical' agencies (such as 'Mir', see p. 76, or the managing agencies of the oil and gas pipelines) which remain necessary, and the 'policy' agencies such as the committees and standing commissions, which are likely to be suppressed. The minimum framework would thus be a small permanent secretariat, which would organise the meetings of the representative of the members, on an inter-government level to be defined.

* p. 81. It was again renewed in January 1990 in a similar way.

* p. 85. The relations between the EC and the Comecon European countries have to be distinguished from EC's role as the coordinator of Western aid to the area. Three significant developments have occurred since the end of 1989 in these relations.

First, though the EC–Comecon 'Joint Declaration' of 1988 on mutual recognition has not been repudiated, and though some technical meetings were still going on in 1990, any prospect of closer relations depends on the future of the Comecon itself.

Secondly, the particular framework of GDR–FRG relations is disappearing along with the economic union in force on 1 July 1990. However, during an interim period, until the political union is completed, the inner-German border becomes a customs barrier between the Community and the third countries, so as to avoid the entry of third-country goods freely into the EC. At the same time, a *de facto* customs union is set up between the EC and East Germany, which gives free access of East German goods into the EC (as was the case previously between the GDR and the FRG) and exempts EC goods from duties in East Germany. The particular format of GDR–FRG relations disappears as such, but might be used in relations between East Germany and its (ex-)Comecon partners, to manage the bilateral trade and cooperation relations, especially with the USSR. The *swing* clearing arrangements between the two Germanys are not however to be revived between the USSR and East Germany.

Thirdly, the bilateral agreements reached by the EC between 1988 and 1990 with all the European CMEA countries, including the GDR, paradoxically as it may seem (the last one to be initialled was with Romania in June 1990), were to be renegotiated for political and economic reasons. Politically there is a willingness to offer Central and East Europe some prospects for an integration within the EC in a future which is felt as distant but without barring this outcome. Thus a 'second generation' of trade and cooperation agreements was on the agenda in mid-1990, which would provide for an association status evolving ultimately into membership. As a side effect this would also end the special status of Yugoslavia, which has benefited from such an association since 1963. Economically the first agreements signed with Hungary, Czechoslovakia (1988) and Poland (1989) had to be modified so as to embody some aid elements. Agreements with Hungary and Poland were amended so as to accelerate the lifting of the discriminatory quotas on imports from these countries as early as from 1 January 1990. The agreement with Czechoslovakia, which was initially signed as a trade agreement, was renegotiated in 1990 so as to include a cooperation component. These three countries have additionally signed in June 1990 agreements with EFTA with a view to establishing free trade areas betwen EFTA and each of them. But while EFTA means to assist Eastern Europe on the road to reform, there is a clear propensity in each of the three countries to regard such arrangements as a stepping-stone into the EC, which may certainly be seen as wishful thinking at this stage. Some of the EFTA countries, and first among them Austria, have interests of their own as far as membership in the EC is concerned.

*p. 86. All these agreements are probably obsolete in 1990.

Chapter 3

*p. 95. The future of intra-Comecon specialisation is mixed. Multilateral arrangements are likely to be abandoned, but there were few of them. Some specialisation schemes are to be maintained through bilateral agreements on the enterprise level, and most likely through the action of Western companies. For instance, in the automobile sector, major companies of Western Europe (Fiat having the lead), Japan (Toyota) and South Korea were preparing investment projects involving a global strategy of expanding in low-cost countries, which would obviously initiate cooperation between enterprises of East European, South European and developing countries.

*p. 125. New Soviet figures on its Third World aid were released in 1990, in a move to provide more openness about Soviet indebtedness and consequently assets. Outstanding loans to the Third World were reported at over $66 billion by the end of 1989, of which countries with a socialist orientation (Afghanistan, Angola, Ethiopia, Mozambique, Nicaragua, South Yemen and Cambodia) accounted for over 18 billion, Sub-Saharan African countries for almost 12 billion, and Middle East countries for almost 22 billion. The largest individual debtor country was India with $14 billion. To these figures one has to add the debt in transferable roubles of the socialist Third World countries, amounting to 37 billion, i.e. 58 billion equivalent dollars (*Izvestia*, 1 March 1990). Most of the socialist Third World debt is likely not to be repaid, and in any case not in convertible currencies. There is also little hope for the USSR to recover the debt owed by the countries with a socialist orientation, and by the least developed countries, most of them African. The Middle East countries may be repaid for the most part, and so might be, in a more distant future, India's debt.

Another Soviet source (*Ekonomika i Zhizn*, March 1990, no. 12) disclosed the amounts of aid extended in 1989 (12.5 billion roubles, amounting to almost 20 billion in dollars) and planned for 1990 (9.7 billion roubles, i.e. over 15 billion dollars). This suggests, as confirmed by Western sources (*PlanEcon Report*, 21 March 1990) that Soviet aid increased since Gorbachev's access to power, though the Western estimates are again much lower than the Soviet ones: *PlanEcon* suggests an average of $8.5 billion annually during 1986–9. The Soviet source rejoices in the tendency for lending to diminish. It also cautions against the figures it quotes, and which are provided by the Soviet Ministry of Foreign Affairs, recalling that according to the ministry, this assistance amounts to 1.4 per cent of the Soviet GNP, and criticising this percentage along the same lines as I do myself on p. 123.

Chapter 4

* *p. 142.* Most of the information given on pp. 129 to 142 now belongs to the history of state trading. This is not to say that the old structures have not left their legacies.

In Hungary, Poland, Czechoslovakia, and also in East Germany, the access of the enterprises to foreign markets is going to be shaped by the transition to private or corporate ownership. In the first three countries, agencies for conducting privatisation have been set, as will be the case in East Germany after economic union with West Germany (July 1990). A new generation of company laws is to be approved by the parliaments. The foreign trade companies, in most cases, are likely to be turned into merchant houses or to disappear altogether. However, this does not mean that a radical change in foreign trade behaviour should be expected. The state sector is bound to remain large, if only because of the lack of private (foreign or domestic) investors and the lack of a capital market. We would forecast that at least 50 per cent of the industrial assets will remain the property of the state or of state institutional investors (special agencies, banks, insurance companies). Most of the foreign trade will be conducted by state entities. Even if the management of these entities follows the rules of the market, the specific habits of the past will not disappear before long.

The situtation is different in Romania and Bulgaria, where the previous institutional framework has not been substantially modified. In the Soviet Union, the foreign trade reform did not go any further after December 1988, even though the number of enterprises being granted foreign trade rights is steadily increasing. None of the constraints which we mentioned, pp. 140–1, has been substantially lifted.

*p. 143. While the zloty has become fully convertible for residents (private persons and enterprises) since January 1990, the Hungarian government has promised in May 1990 to make the forint convertible by the middle of 1992. The internal convertibility of the Czechoslovak crown is scheduled for January 1991.

*p. 147. The deadline set in 1988 for abolishing the differentiated currency coefficients by January 1990 has not been met. At the beginning of 1990 still 1,000 to 2,000 coefficients were used. The main reason for this is the non-implementation of the price reform, which has been delayed several times. It was anticipated in 1990 that once the price reform would be achieved, it would be possible to introduce a new, unified rate of exchange, with foreign currency exchanges to be set up in 1991.

*p. 149. The worst indeed happened, and it seems that in many cases the new regulation on the 10 per cent of foreign currency revenues of the enterprises to be allotted to the workers' collectives for buying consumer goods abroad is simply by-passed by the management of the enterprises, who see it as a 'luxury' (*Ekonomika i Zhizn*, no. 14, April 1990).

*p. 151. As is logical, in Poland the foreign currency auctions were stopped in 1990, due to the introduction of the internal convertibility of the zloty. In the Soviet Union, the auctions held in 1990 displayed the same pattern as the first one in 1989. The government did not inject hard currency funds into the auctions. The amount of hard currency traded did not exceed 16 million dollars each time. The depreciation of the rouble went on, closely following the black market rate: at the third auction in February the average rate was already over 13 roubles for 1 dollar.

*p. 170. The joint venture issue has become in 1990 one of the most important in the East European transition to the market. At the same time, the significance of the process has changed. What was still at stake in 1989 was penetration of Soviet and East European markets, and the joint venture was seen as an alternative to other ways of financing trade, such as compensation deals. Even the liberalised legislations of Hungary and Poland, though providing for fully foreign-owned companies, did not create proper conditions for foreign direct investment as understood in Western practice. The joint ventures remained enclaves in a centrally planned or at least centrally regulated environment.

However, as mentioned pp. 164–5, a new pattern emerged in 1989 for Poland and Hungary, and has developed in Czechoslovakia and East Germany in 1990. Foreign investment in these countries is seen as an instrument of privatisation of the former state enterprises, a means of developing new sectors (services, high technology industries) and of modernising the hard core of the previous state sector. The process is bound to be significantly assisted by international organisations (the World Bank, the IMF, the new European Bank for Reconstruction and Development set up in May 1990), by individual Western governments (in particular, the FRG for East Germany) or private funds. According to very global estimates in these three countries (not including the GDR) the value of assets available already in 1990 for sale to Western investors amounts at least to 100 billion dollars, a figure to be compared with a cumulative foreign investment in existing joint ventures of less than half a billion dollars as of the end of 1989. The profile of the investors is bound to change dramatically. While up to 1989, with some exceptions, the Western partners were mainly small and medium enterprises, especially in Poland, the biggest Western multinational companies are exploring the new opportunities, especially in the automobile industry and other consumer-related industries and services. But these new prospects will not become real if the domestic reforms are not implemented quickly, and if the investors do not get firm commitments as to the guarantees of their investments and as to the repatriation of profits, especially at a time when the financial risks are perceived as high in these countries.

The cases of Bulgaria, Romania and the USSR are different. Romania adopted in March 1990 a decree-law on foreign capital investments, which allows for fully owned foreign enterprises but is still restrictive in terms of profits repatriation and not very attractive as to the tax regime. The rules have not been modified in Bulgaria and in the USSR, but there has been some relaxation in their application. The main stumbling block remains the requirement of earning hard currency to repatriate profits. Following the US example (see p. 166), French companies created to this effect a 'consortium' regrouping some ten enterprises engaged in joint ventures, among which were some hard currency earners, such as the oil company Total, and other hard currency users, so as to set up a currency pool for the repatriation of profits. In March 1990, this consortium formed in turn a joint venture with a Soviet consortium. The new venture, called 'Interconsortium', should manage a kind of rouble-hard currency swap for an amount of about 700 million dollars per year.

Another disincentive is the lack of guarantees for investments. Though such guarantees have been negotiated bilaterally with some countries (such as France and Germany in 1989) they do not really provide sufficient protection, and keep prospective partners from investing. In the case of France, the Coface (see p. 309) had in 1990 to agree to insure small and medium-size French companies against the political risk of nationalisation of their assets. In addition, the deteriorating financial situation of the USSR in 1990 delayed the creation of joint ventures, which slowed down from 1989.

Nevertheless, the Soviet Union might ultimately emerge as the most likely country for foreign investment, in a quite different way from East Central Europe. The USSR announced in April 1990 that it would enact a new law on foreign direct investment, so as to complete the set of new laws already enacted (such as the law on ownership adopted in March 1990, the new law on enterprise and the law on joint stock companies in June 1990. What the Soviet leadership has in mind is not to assist a privatisation process which has not yet begun, but to take advantage of the huge natural resources of the country, allowing foreign businessmen to exploit them. The first such agreement, reminiscent of the 'concessions' of the NEP period (see p. 155), was signed in May 1990 with a French firm, Elf Aquitaine, and allowed the oil company to develop an oil field north of the Caspian sea on its own account.

Foreign investors now move towards East Europe and the USSR as they would do into developing countries. The area is near especially to Western Europe. Eastern Europe offers advantages similar to industrialising economies, with skilled manpower and low wages (but also with a greater risk of social unrest). The USSR is attractive because of its natural resources, especially to very large companies.

The following data were available on the number of joint ventures set up in the USSR and the East Europe by 1 March 1990:

USSR: 1,400 (with an amount of foreign capital invested of $1.9 billion)
Bulgaria: 30
Czechoslovakia: 60
GDR: 1,145 (end-April)
Hungary: 1,000
Poland: 1,000
Romania: 5
Sources: Scott, Norman, 'East–West Trade on the threshold of the 1990s: current state and prospects', paper presented at the NATO Colloquium 1990; 'The Central and East European economies in the 1990s: prospects and constraints'; UN/ECE, *East–West Joint Ventures News*, no. 4, April 1990; 'Soviet joint ventures: developments through the first quarter of 1990', *PlanEcon Report*, vol. no. 17, 27 April 1990; *The Financial Times*, 22 May 1990.

p. 173. The currency agreements for the 'direct links' have been repudiated in 1990 by Czechoslovakia and Hungary. The fate of the 'socialist multinationals' is unclear. Those which had purely coordinating functions are probably being dissolved in 1990. The bilateral or multilateral joint enterprises actually conducting production or service activities should continue to operate until the restructuring of their partners.

More generally, joint ventures between Eastern European enterprises or between them and Soviet enterprises may have attractive prospects in the future after the completion of market-type reforms. Any modernisation of business activities implies the set-up of ventures with foreign partners. Most such ventures will probably be with Western partners in the beginning. But the Western companies themselves will be eager to take advantage of international specialisation for their own sake, and should rather soon set in motion joint ventures between their own subsidiaries in the East, probably with some reluctance from the East Central European countries.

p. 180. As in the case of Poland mentioned further on this page, the quantitative restrictions which were lifted for Hungary concerned *discriminatory* quotas (specific to the Eastern European countries). The non-discriminatory quantitative restrictions which apply to all third countries remained in force, as also did the restrictions stemming from voluntary arrangements (for steel and textiles). Agricultural trade was not affected either, except for some Hungarian and Polish agricultural products. (UN/ECE, *Economic Survey of Europe in 1989–90*, Geneva–New York, 1990).

Although Czechoslovakia signed in 1990 a new trade and cooperation agreement with the EC (see addition to p. 86), quantitative restrictions are to be lifted in this case only in 1992. In the case of Bulgaria and Romania (agreements initialled in May and June 1990), as earlier (1989) in the treaty signed with the USSR, the deadline is 1995.

p. 181. The Soviet tariff code was still to be submitted to the Supreme Soviet by the middle of 1990. The tariff itself was in the process of elaboration, and could not possibly be ready before the domestic price reform on the agenda for 1991.

*p. 183. Poland and Hungary obtained the benefit of the General System of Preferences regime from the EC as from January 1990, as part of the aid package granted to them. This means a lifting of tariffs applied to a range of industrial goods imported from these countries.

*p. 185. On 3 June 1990, during the Bush–Gorbachev Summit, a trade pact was signed between the USA and the USSR. However, this does not mean an automatic granting of the MFN clause. The USSR had still to enact an emigration law so as to deserve a waiver of the Jackson–Vanik amendment.

Chapter 5

*p. 222. In June 1990, at a meeting of the ministerial committee of the Cocom, it was decided to reduce the list of embargoed products by about 30 per cent by the end of the year, this including in particular most sensitive items such as powerful computers, precision machine-tools and telecommunication equipment. But the 'foreign policy' approach is still present, through the discrimination in favour of Poland, Hungary and Czechoslovakia who will be granted preferential treatment in exchange for pledges not to re-export sensitive equipment to the USSR. This discrimination against the USSR will mainly affect sales of high technology telecommunication exchanges, and just before the meeting the USA had blocked the construction of an optic fibre cable across Siberia. The discrimination may be relaxed if the Soviet Union shows more flexibility in the Baltic question and accepts Lithuania's independence. The concept of sanction thus remains in force in Cocom's operation, and is supplemented by a positive concept of 'reward' for achieving democratisation and liberalisation in the case of the three countries which are granted preferential treatment. There is a definite contradiction between such a policy and the recognised need for accelerating Western investment in the East. One of the main bottlenecks in the modernisation process is the backwardness of the telephone system, which blocks, among others, the computerisation of these economies. To deprive the Soviet Union of access to modern telephone links may greatly hamper the development of joint ventures and foreign investment.

Chapter 6

*p. 241. The Soviet production of oil declined again in 1989 by almost 3 per cent. To the shortcomings of the oil sector mentioned on p. 240 one has now to add the impact of political unrest and strikes which have disorganised production in the Siberian fields in 1989. The Soviet authorities seemed willing in 1990 to cut domestic investment in the oil sector, but at the same time to encourage foreign investment in the new form of concessions of exploration and development rights to foreign companies. The first such contract was concluded with a French firm (see addition to p. 170) and a feasibility agreement for a similar venture was signed in June 1990 with the US firm Chevron.

*p. 252. The subsidy debate seems closed since January 1990. At the 45th Comecon meeting, it was agreed to shift from 1991 to settlements in world prices and in hard currencies between the USSR and its partners. At that time, the picture was similar to that described on p. 249. The intra-Comecon price for oil, at the official rate of the transferable rouble, was above the world price (it amounted to 24 dollars for a barrel in 1989), though it had decreased by 10 per cent in 1989. The Soviet Union was in deficit with its European Comecon partners for TR 4 billion in 1989, an increase of two-thirds over 1988. The decision reached in 1990 was mainly motivated by the unwillingness of the Six to maintain this surplus position in a non-convertible currency.

However, the calculations on the impact of the new system made it clear that the Soviet Union would benefit from it. They showed that with this system the USSR would be in *surplus, by* altogether 11 billion dollars in 1991 (*The Wall Street Journal*, 22 January 1990). We do not know exactly how the calculations about the gains derived by the USSR from the new system have been made. They have probably taken into account the average world price of oil (with assumptions as to its evolution). They have also included estimates of the value of Eastern European manufactured goods usually sold to the Soviet Union, should the Soviet Union have to pay for these goods not at the inflated TR price but at a realistic price reflecting their low competitiveness on the Western market. Have these calculations included volume effects as well? Soviet supplies of oil are not likely to pick up due to the difficulties in domestic production. A further decrease in Soviet deliveries was publicised at the beginning of 1990. The USSR announced a decrease in its supplies of fuel to Poland (by one-third for the first three months of the year), Czechoslovakia (by 20 per cent in January) and Bulgaria (by an undisclosed amount in January. See *The Financial Times*, 14 February 1990). Additional large cuts were announced for the second half of 1990. Overall the decrease in oil supplies might reach 20 per cent in 1990. As for the Soviet imports, the forecast is ambiguous. On the one hand, the Soviet Union might want to buy the same amount of Eastern European goods with a large discount, as these goods (especially the machinery) fit into the obsolete Soviet production system which cannot be revamped with Western machinery at short notice. On the other hand, the Soviet Union might use its surpluses in hard currency accruing from the East to import more from the West, and in this case the volume of trade would shrink on the import side.

The overall conclusion to derive from the impact of the changes decided in 1990 may be that in fact the Soviet oil price had never ceased to be lower than the world price, once a proper exchange rate was applied to the transferable rouble, and this is the position of Vanous (*PlanEcon Report*, vol. 6, no. 9–10, 7 March 1990). Following the Gulf crisis in August 1990, the higher world market price for oil will increase the Soviet gains in trade both with the East and the West.

*p. 257. The future of the energy trade and cooperation between the Six and the USSR is ambiguous. In the present state of the East Central European economies, with their high level of energy consumption as compared with the West, the dependence on the Soviet Union is high. Alternative energy suppliers do exist for oil (the Middle East exporters), natural gas (Algeria and Norway), electricity (France). The shift to such suppliers requires hard currency: in theory this would no longer matter as purchases from the USSR are to be paid in hard currency, but we shall see (addition to p. 301) that Soviet–East European arrangements may in fact result in an intermediate regime of payments which would delay actual hard currency settlements. In addition, such a shift would require large investments in pipeline construction and electricity grid linkups.

The environmental issue is also crucial here. Because the Six are willing to get rid of their reliance on the Soviet Union, and because of their hard currency constraints, they may be tempted to maintain their traditional energy balance where coal is the dominant fuel. The damage to the environment, which has been assessed in 1990 at a much higher level than was thought before is a threat to all of Western Europe. This might in turn induce the West to suggest that the East should indeed strengthen its Soviet link and import growing quantities of Soviet gas, which is a cleaner fuel. In this case, assistance to the Soviet Union would be needed to help the country to expand its pipeline network. Another issue is the future of the nuclear industry. The new governments of Eastern Europe are under pressure from their public opinion to close down the Soviet-built nuclear power stations. This policy will be implemented as soon as 1990 for East

Germany. Though environmental concerns may plead for an increase of the share of cleaner (as compared to coal) nuclear energy in the energy balance, the political feelings against Soviet nuclear domination in the Comecon area will be difficult to resist.

Chapter 7

*p. 257a. An increase in the price of bread by 1 July 1990 was again opposed by the deputies to the Supreme Soviet in June 1990.

*p. 257b. Such estimates are obviously obsolete. The prospects for food imports by East Central Europe depend on the restructuring of the agricultural sector which should increase production in the medium term, and on a policy of satisfying the needs of the population which has already led in 1989 to an increase of imports, along with the granting of emergency food aid to Poland. Concerning the USSR, and though Soviet grain imports increased since 1987, reaching 35 million tons in 1988 and 37 in 1989 (Soviet sources, *Ekonomika i Zhizn*, no. 15, April 1990), Western analysts still expect them to decrease in the 1990s if a proper policy is applied in the agricultural sector. But the very fact that the USSR has renewed grain agreements in 1990 (with France and the USA) suggests that the USSR is expecting stable levels of imports throughout the decade (USDA, *USSR, Agriculture and Trade Report*, May 1990).

*p. 284. A new agreement was signed in March 1990 for five years. It increases to 10 million tons the minimum quantities which the Soviet Union is to buy annually, of which at least four of wheat and four of corn, the balance being filled with purchases of feed-grains in addition to wheat and corn. The amount of grain which may be bought without previous consultation is also raised, to 14 million tons.

Chapter 8

*p. 301. The transferable rouble and all the Comecon system of settlements seemed to be definitively discarded in January 1990, when the 45th Comecon meeting agreed to shift, beginning in 1991, to settlements in hard currency. However, this shift is not going to occur immediately and for all transactions. After the decision was made and due to its unfavourable impact on the Six (see addition to p. 252), a committee was set up to study the possible arrangements, and bilateral agreements have been negotiated between the USSR and its partners. The general idea was that the USSR's partners were entitled to get a partial payment in hard currency of the cumulated Soviet transferable rouble debt, and that the transition to hard currency payments as from 1991 should be gradual. The agreements reached by the end of May 1990 were the following:

1. A Bulgarian–Soviet agreement in January 1990 provides for cuts of about 15 per cent in mutual trade for that year, along with a gradual introduction of hard currency settlements beginning in 1991; for three years both the TR and the dollar would be used in the transactions, according to the goods traded.

2. In March, a Polish–Soviet agreement was reached on the volume of trade for 1990, and on the principle of settlements *accounted* in hard currency beginning in 1991. The case of Poland is specific as it is the only country still indebted to the USSR, both in TR (over 5 billion) and in dollars (1.5 billion), both rescheduled. Poland is now arguing that in fact it has repaid its debt ot the USSR, through its past contributions to joint CMEA investments on the Soviet territory.

3. The *Soviet–Hungarian* agreement was reached in March after Hungary had suspended, in January 1990, the export licences granted to the Hungarian enterprises to sell to the USSR, then renewed them on a case-by-case basis, so as to 'divert' as few goods as possible to the CMEA market and to prevent the export to the USSR of goods saleable to the West. Overall, trade with the USSR should decrease by one-third in 1990, on account both of the Hungarian machinery sales and of the Soviet oil deliveries. What is remarkable in this agreement is that it provides for a settlement in dollars of the TR Soviet debt. Beginning in 1991, this debt will be reimbursed at a rate of 0.92 dollar to 1 rouble. Should the Hungarian cross-rate rouble/dollar be applied, Hungary would have got only 0.40 dollar for each rouble of the Soviet debt; should the official TR/dollar rate be retained, it would have yielded 1.52 dollar for one TR. It thus appears that both parties have struck a fifty/fifty deal – deriving a rate of exchange just the average of the two cross-rates. As for the future, the significance of the settlements in dollars remains obscure; the Hungarian comments seem to suggest that this might be rather a clearing in dollars than an actual settlement in dollars, and this may also appply to the relations of the USSR with other East European countries.

The end of the transferable rouble system has been widely approved of in the West. Surpluses in non-convertible trade have a negative impact on the domestic economy as they increase inflationary pressures. This was of particular concern to the IMF in its negotiations with Hungary and Poland. In both cases, the mechanisms of clearing in transferable roubles implied that the exporting enterprises were not paid by the Soviet importer but by the Central Bank (Hungary) or the Foreign Trade Bank (Poland) in domestic currency. As exports were higher than imports a net creation of money occurred, while fighting inflation was considered as one of the most pressing aims in domestic economic policy.

The Economic Commission for Europe of the United Nations is the only significant Western institution to have expressed some views about the suitability of a new scheme comparable to the post-war European Payments Union ('Lessons from history: a new EPU as a bridge-gap', ECE/UN, *Economic Survey of Europe in 1989–1990*, p. 3-74 to 3-76). The quoted source proposes a new EPU-scheme for the 'reforming' countries only (Poland, Hungary, Czechoslovakia), as a transition to a full-fledged reform of the domestic economy and to a new pattern of international economic relations. The system could be monitored by the BIS and the heart of it might be the ECU, which would clearly designate the scheme for assistance provided by Western Europe (or the Group of Twenty-Four).

While agreeing upon the need for a transitional arrangement among the (ex-)Comecon members, I would personally recommend a scheme which would give the national currencies a greater role. A feasible scheme would be a multilateral monetary arrangement providing for settlements in the domestic currencies, with a commitment to make these currencies gradually fully convertible (for residents and non-residents) within the area and outside the area. Such a monetary arrangement would have to be part of a trade arrangement (free trade area or, better, customs union). It would include provisions for monitoring the exchange rates of the domestic currencies, which would help to reduce the differences in the cross-rates mentioned above (p. 297).

A main obstacle would be the lack of political good will. This is why the impulse should come from outside. The monetary arrangement should be granted some support from the West, for example in the form of an Exchange Reserve Fund in hard currency managed by a Central European organisation but with some control by a Western institution (for instance by the new European Bank for Reconstruction and Development). The latter choice would allow for the financial involvement of the Soviet Union, which would be the price to pay for the country not being marginalised in the new European architecture.

Where would the West's interests lie? They would wish to assist the economic reconstruction of Eastern Europe, while ensuring an organised transition to increased links with the West. It would also allow for many questions pertaining to relations with the Community to be solved not just on a case-by-case basis, but in a multilateral way.

p. 308. The foreign exchange monopoly has been abolished in Poland and Hungary, where since January 1990 authorized commercial banks are allowed to conduct convertible currency transactions.

*p. 317. In 1989, due to the mounting indebtedness of the East and to uncertainties about the economic reforms, the borrowing terms hardened again, and the average spread was over 1/2 over the Libor, more than twice that in 1986–87 (OECD, *Financial Market Trends*, February 1990).

*p. 321. International support for Eastern economic reforms has developed in a multitude of initiatives since mid-1989. It would require a whole book by itself, which could not be written anyhow before some time had elapsed. New information appeared every day in 1990 in the general and specialised press. We refer the reader to a publication by the Economic Commission for Europe (UN/ECE, 'International initiative in support of Eastern reforms', *Economic Survey of Europe in 1989–1990*, Geneva–New York, 1990, section 4.4), which is the most comprehensive to-date (mid-1990) and is to be updated. Let us here summarise the main developments and tendencies in five points:

  1 *The supporting countries.* The core of the aid package is the PHARE (French acronym, Pologne, Hongrie, Assistance à la Restructuration Economique) programme, coordinated by the Commission of the European Communities following a decision taken at the July 1989 Paris Summit of the seven richest nations. It involves twenty-four Western countries (Group of 24 or G-24). Other international institutions than the EC are participating inasmuch as they advise and finance the Eastern countries, which is the case for the IMF and the World Bank. Individual governments also set up packages of their own, in particular the United States and Japan. European governments are selectively involved in helping individual countries. West Germany is devoting a very large amount of assistance to East Germany, which, after July 1990, may also be likened to support granted by any given country to its less developed parts. France has been actively supporting Romania since the December 1989 revolution.

  2 *The recipients.* Initially the international initiative was meant to support the transition to democracy and the market in Poland and Hungary. In 1990, these countries still remain the main beneficiaries. Later on, Czechoslovakia, East Germany, Bulgaria and Romania submitted requests for assistance. Their formal inclusion in the PHARE programme (which would be renamed) was decided upon in June 1990. The USSR is not included. The Soviet authorities have repeatedly said in 1989 and 1990 that the only 'aid' they needed was technical assistance in management, though since May 1990 various Soviet officials suggested that the USSR would need help from the West if the economic reform was to be completed. Should this aid be extended, it would probably be done on a bilateral basis rather than in the framework set up for Eastern Europe.

3 *The purpose.* From the beginning it was said that the Western initiative was linked with the political and economic reform movement. Conditions are thus attached: aid is a reward, and may be stopped as a sanction in the case of non-democratic political trends or failure to move towards a market system. Aid is also meant to meet the interest of the West, namely to ease trade (through better access of the East to Western markets which is expected to induce a greater opening of the East to Western goods), to improve financial relations (through assistance to convertibility), and to facilitate Western investment in Eastern Europe.

4 *The instruments.* There have been a number of measures, and some of them are only indirectly linked with the core program. We have already mentioned the trade policy measures (additions to p. 85, 180 and 185), and the relaxation of the Cocom rules (addition to p. 222). The specific measures already implemented are:

emergency food shipments to Poland and Romania;

technical assistance to Poland and Hungary;

financial commitments in the form of loans and credit guarantees mainly channelled through bilateral lines of credit or through IMF, World Bank or European Investment Bank loans to Poland and Hungary.

One may mention two specific initiatives, a $1 billion stabilisation fund for supporting the convertibility of the zloty, to which twelve countries contributed, but which Poland did not use as the rate of exchange of the zloty remained stable; a loan of 1 billion ECU to Hungary for five years to support the country's restructuring.

There is a considerable confusion in the press about the exact amount of money involved. While big figures are mentioned in regard to Eastern European needs, up to $25 billion per year, the actual grant package to Hungary and Poland totals less than $1 billion for 1990, in the form of technical aid, environmental protection and (for Poland) food aid. Most of the other commitments, which totalled about $11 billion by May 1990, are in form of loans and have only partly given way to actual disbursements. These loans will ultimately increase the debt service burden. They are supposed to increase the export potential of the beneficiaries, but this is a long-term process.

5 *The institutions.* A single specific institution has been created, the European Bank for Reconstruction and Development (EBRD), whose name reminds one of the International Bank for Reconstruction and Development created in 1944 and now better known as the World Bank. The agreement was signed in May 1990. The Bank, located in London, has forty members of which the EC states detain 53.7 per cent of the capital, the US 10 per cent, Japan 8.5 per cent. All Eastern European countries

participate, including the USSR with a share of 6 per cent, and all are eligible to draw from the Bank's funds with some restrictions for the USSR. The Bank has a capital of 10 billion ECU ($12 billion) and will operate from January 1991. The Bank is meant to assist privatisation: at most 40 per cent of its loans will be available to the public sector of the recipient countries. The resources of the Bank will mainly be devoted to promote Western productive investment in the East, the creation of financial markets, and environment protection.

Chapter 9

* p. 327. In 1990, new figures were disclosed by the Eastern countries on the amount of their debt. The figures of the net debt for 1989 are significantly higher than the amounts for the end of 1988, both because indebtedness has actually increased and because of the new data released, which suggest that the figures for the past years might also be higher than had been estimated earlier in the West. Here is the amount of the net debt at the end of 1989 (UN/ECE, *Economic Survey of Europe in 1989–1990*, pp. 4–23), in billion dollars: Bulgaria: 9.3; Czechoslovakia: 5.8; GDR: 11.0; Hungary: 19.5; Poland: 36.5; Romania: −0.1; USSR, including the CMEA banks: 44.3. See also the addition to p. 125.

* p. 332. This risk is already perceived as very high, especially in the case of the Soviet Union. In the first months of 1990 Western suppliers of the USSR had increasing difficulties in getting paid, and this shattered the traditional creditworthiness of the country. The Soviet VEB (Bank for foreign economic activities) argued that Soviet enterprises allowed to trade on their own engaged in imports without having the necessary hard currency funds. Between March and May 1990, in a series of negotiations with the creditors, the VEB and the State Bank committed themselves to obtain the arrears, amounting to a total of $2 billion, to be settled by the end of the year at the latest, with special priority for the small and medium enterprises. The explanations of the VEB have been well accepted in the West. It is felt that in the Soviet Union (and in East Europe as well) the banking system is not yet developed enough to provide well-founded guarantees of borrowings by individual enterprises, and that until such a system is set up a centralised system of guarantees is to be preferred. But, in the Soviet case, it seems that the VEB has deliberately blocked the enterprises' access to their own currency funds, on which they could legitimately count when signing import contracts, with the sole affect of making it clear that centralisation was indeed required.

*p. 334. This has triggered the shift towards payments in hard currencies starting in 1991. See addition to p. 301.

*p. 344. Poland reached a rescheduling agreement in February 1990 with the Club of Paris, whose members held at the end of 1989 about $27 billion of the $40 billion country's gross debt; $9.4 billion of principal and interest will be rescheduled over fourteen years; this is the largest sum yet rescheduled in the history of the Club of Paris. Poland will have no payments to make until February 1991.

*p. 345. By the end of 1989 Romania was a net creditor. Following the change of government in December 1989, it was expected that the country would again borrow on Western financial markets.

*p. 347. See addition to p. 321.

*p. 348. The foreign debt of the GDR is to be taken over by West Germany, which from July 1990 assumes responsibility for East Germany's monetary policies.

*p. 349. The creditworthiness of the three countries mentioned has deteriorated in 1990. The least affected is Czechoslovakia despite the increase in its debt figures (see addition to p. 327). Bulgaria has asked a moratorium on its debt service in March 1990. The Soviet Union experienced a liquidity crisis in the beginning of 1990 (see addition to p. 332).

*p. 353. Czechoslovakia and Bulgaria have applied to the IMF and the World Bank and may be admitted into these institutions in 1990 or 1991. The prospects for the USSR are more remote, mainly for political reasons. The generalised involvement of the Bretton Woods institutions in East Central Europe will then be increasingly geared to the restructuring of these economies, and no longer to macro-economic stabilisation as was the case in the early eighties and again, for Poland and Hungary, in 1989–90, hand-in-hand with the 'G-24' assistance package.

*p. 354. I was bold enough to offer a conclusion to this book in 1989. Now, the time has not yet come for a conclusion. I leave it to the reader to try and build his/her own conclusion in this transition phase which is bound to last.

APPENDIX: DOMESTIC GROWTH AND FOREIGN TRADE OF THE USSR AND EASTERN EUROPE

Table 1. *Indicators of growth (1970–1988) (annual % change)*

	Bulgaria	Czecho-slovakia	GDR	Hungary	Poland	Romania	USSR
National income (net material product)							
1971–75	7.9	5.7	5.4	6.3	9.7	11.3	5.1
1976–80	6.1	3.7	4.1	2.8	1.2	7.2	3.7
1981–85	3.7	1.8	4.5	1.4	−0.8	4.4	3.2
1986	5.3	2.6	4.3	0.9	4.9	7.3	3.6
1987	5.1	2.2	3.6	3.6	1.7	4.8	2.3
1988	6.2	2.5	3.0	0.5	4.5	3.2	4.4
Industrial output							
1971–75	9.1	6.6	6.5	6.3	10.4	12.9	7.4
1976–80	6.2	4.6	4.9	3.4	4.7	9.5	4.4
1981–85	4.3	2.7	4.1	2.0	0.4	4.0	3.7
1986	4.0	3.2	3.8	1.9	4.7	7.7	4.8
1987	4.2	2.5	3.2	3.5	3.4	4.5	3.8
1988	5.2	2.0	3.7	0.0	5.4	3.6	3.9
*Agricultural output**							
1971–75	2.9	2.2	2.7	4.5	3.7	6.5	0.8
1976–80	0.9	1.9	1.3	2.5	−1.7	4.2	1.6
1981–85	−0.6	1.8	2.5	0.5	2.1	3.5	2.1
1986	11.7	0.6	0.0	2.4	5.0	12.9	5.4
1987	−5.1	0.9	−0.7	−2.0	−2.3	2.3	−0.9
1988	−0.1	2.2	−4.0	4.5	0.6	2.9	2.7

*Growth rates for quinquennial periods are calculated as average annualised percentage change as compared with the average output in the previous five-year period.
Source: National statistics of the countries.

Table 2. *Indicators of economic efficiency (1976–1988) (annual % change)*

	Bulgaria	Czecho-slovakia	GDR	Hungary	Poland	Romania	USSR
Labour productivity							
1976–80	6.1	3.3	3.7	4.1	1.7	6.7	3.2
1981–85	3.5	1.3	4.3	2.1	0.1	4.2	3.0
1986	5.1	2.5	4.5	2.3	4.6	6.8	3.6
1987	5.2	1.6	3.6	5.5	1.9	4.3	2.6
1988	6.5	2.2	3.0	1.0[a]	6.4	2.9[a]	5.1
Gross investment							
1976–80	6.1	2.8	3.3	2.4	−3.0	8.5	3.3
1981–85	4.6	−1.1	−1.0	−3.1	−7.5	−1.3	3.5
1986	8.0[b]	1.4	5.3	6.5	5.1	1.2[b]	8.3
1987	7.2[b]	4.4	8.0	9.8	4.2	0.9[b]	5.7
1988	6.0[b]	4.5	5.0	−7.7	6.0	−1.3[b]	4.8
Capital productivity							
1976–80	−1.9	−2.4	−1.5	−3.2	−6.9	1.1	−3.0
1981–85	−2.9	−3.4	0.2	−2.2	−3.4	4.2	−2.7
1986	0.2	−2.3	0.1	−2.7	2.7	−0.3	−1.1
1987	−2.6	−2.5	−0.9	1.1	−1.1	−2.7[a]	−2.7
1988[a]	−0.7	−2.0	—	−2.5	1.0	−2.7	−0.2

Note:
[a] Estimate.
[b] In current prices.
Labour productivity is calculated as the net material product per employee in the material sector.
  Capital productivity is calculated as the net material product per unit of fixed assets in the material sphere.
Sources: National statistics of the countries. ECE/UN, Economic Survey of Europe, 1981 and 1988–89.

Table 3. Trends in foreign trade (1965–1987) (annual variation, in %, from values in current prices converted into $).

	1966–1970		1971–1975		1976–1980		1981–1985		1986		1987	
	X	M	X	M	X	M	X	M	X	M	X	M
The Six: trade with												
World	9.0	9.7	19.9	22.5	12.2	10.9	1.7	-1.5	8.8	14.4	8.6	5.4
Socialist countries	8.3	9.0	19.1	19.7	10.2	10.5	2.7	2.4	12.9	16.2	8.5	4.8
Comecon–Euroep	8.0	10.3	19.1	19.5	10.0	10.3	2.5	1.6	13.7	16.5	9.9	4.5
Developed ME	11.4	12.8	20.0	28.1	14.8	8.1	-0.7	-3.0	6.6	16.0	12.2	9.8
Developing ME	8.5	4.3	25.6	24.6	16.9	24.7	1.4	-4.5	-10.4	-5.3	0.0	-4.4
The USSR: trade with												
World	9.4	7.8	21.1	25.8	18.7	13.3	2.8	4.9	11.8	7.2	10.6	8.0
Socialist countries	8.5	6.4	19.3	20.4	15.4	13.5	5.1	6.9	22.1	17.1	7.7	12.0
Comecon–Europe	8.2	7.8	19.6	18.2	14.4	13.4	6.0	5.9	25.6	19.7	6.4	14.6
Developed ME	9.8	11.6	28.9	36.6	23.5	12.5	-2.2	-0.9	-15.9	-2.3	20.1	-3.5
Developing ME	12.7	9.3	17.6	26.7	18.2	13.5	1.6	3.2	18.1	-23.9	13.7	7.9
The Six+the USSR: trade with												
World	9.1	9.0	20.4	23.8	14.8	11.9	2.6	4.1	10.3	10.8	9.8	6.6
Socialist countries	8.4	8.0	19.2	19.9	12.4	11.7	3.8	4.1	17.4	16.6	8.1	8.2
Comecon–Europe	8.2		19.2		9.4		3.7		17.8		27.9	
Developed ME	10.8	12.4	23.5	31.5	19.0	10.1	-1.3	-2.2	-4.7	6.2	15.7	3.7
Developing ME	11.0	7.4	20.9	25.7	17.6	18.7	1.4	1.1	5.4	-15.9	8.2	1.9

Notes:
X=Exports; M=imports; ME=market economies.
The Six: Bulgaria, Czechoslovakia, the GDR, Hungary, Poland, Romania.
Comecon–Europe: the Six+the USSR.
Socialist countries: Comecon (the Six, the USSR; Vietnam, Cuba, Mongolia); Albania, Yugoslavia, China, North Korea, Laos after 1978.
Source: ECE, General Economic Analysis Division, data file based upon national statistics.

Table 4. Regional distribution of foreign trade (1965–1987) (in % of total trade; from values in current prices converted into $).

LR1	1965 X	1965 M	1970 X	1970 M	1975 X	1975 M	1980 X	1980 M	1985 X	1985 M	1987 X	1987 M
The Six: trade with												
World	100.0	100.0	100.0	100.0	100.0	100.0	100.0	100.0	100.0	100.0	100.0	100.0
Socialist countries	71.5	70.0	69.2	67.6	66.9	60.1	60.7	58.5	64.0	67.4	66.4	68.1
The Six	27.2	27.3	27.5	26.6	27.2	24.1	22.4	20.9	20.8	22.2	22.9	23.3
The USSR	40.0	38.3	36.5	36.8	34.7	32.1	33.0	33.1	38.0	40.1	38.6	39.8
Developed ME	21.4	23.5	23.9	27.0	24.0	33.8	28.5	31.0	25.4	24.3	25.7	25.7
Developing ME	7.2	6.5	7.0	5.4	8.8	5.9	10.8	10.5	0.5	8.3	7.9	6.2
The USSR: Trade with												
World	100.0	100.0	100.0	100.0	100.0	100.0	100.0	100.0	100.0	100.0	100.0	100.0
Socialist countries	68.0	69.6	65.4	65.1	60.7	52.4	54.2	53.2	61.2	61.2	64.9	69.4
Comecon–Europe	55.7	58.0	52.8	58.0	49.4	42.4	42.1	42.9	46.8	47.6	50.4	56.5
Developed ME	18.3	20.2	18.7	24.0	25.5	36.4	32.0	35.4	25.6	27.8	20.8	22.8
Developing ME	13.7	10.1	15.9	10.8	13.6	11.2	13.8	11.5	13.2	11.0	14.3	7.8
The Six+the USSR: trade with												
World	100.0	100.0	100.0	100.0	100.0	100.0	100.0	100.0	100.0	100.0	100.0	100.0
Socialist countries	70.1	69.8	67.6	66.7	64.3	56.9	57.6	56.2	62.2	64.3	65.6	68.7
Comecon–Europe	62.2	62.3	59.4	60.8	56.7	50.4	49.1	49.2	52.8	54.9	55.1	59.9
Developed ME	20.1	22.2	21.7	25.8	24.7	34.9	30.2	32.9	25.5	26.1	23.2	24.3
Developing ME	9.8	8.0	10.7	7.5	10.9	8.1	12.3	10.9	11.9	9.7	11.2	7.0

Notes:

X=Exports; M=imports; ME=market economies.

The Six: Bulgaria, Czechoslovakia, the GDR, Hungary, Poland, Romania.

Comecon–Europe: the Six+the USSR.

Socialist countries: Comecon (the Six, the USSR; Vietnam, Cuba, Mongolia); Albania, Yugoslavia, China, North Korea, Laos after 1978.

Source: ECE, General Economic Analysis Division, data file based upon national statistics.

Table 5. *Commodity composition of foreign trade (1970–1987)*

| SITC sections | East–East trade | | | | | | | | East–West trade | | |
| | among the Six | | | | the USSR with the Six | | | | the Six with the West | | |
	1970	1975	1980	1987	1970	1975	1980	1987	1970	1975	1980
Exports											
0+1	8	7	9	7	6	3	0	0	23	17	12
2+4	4	2	2	2	17	15	9	6	13	10	8
3	6	6	3	2	15	26	41	53	10	18	20
5	6	6	6	7	2	2	2	3	7	8	9
7	50	53	54	56	21	23	21	15	11	16	14
6+8	25	25	22	24	29	24	10	7	35	31	34
Residue	1	1	3	3	10	7	17	16	1	0	3
Total (0 to 9)	100	100	100	100	100	100	100	100	100	100	100
Imports											
0+1					11	11	10	8	12	9	17
2+4					3	2	2	1	10	7	8
3					3	4	2	1	2	1	2
5					7	7	6	7	13	14	16
7					47	50	55	56	31	35	27
6+8					24	22	23	25	32	33	28
Residue					5	4	3	2	0	1	1
Total (0 to 9)	100	100	100	100	100	100	100	100	100	100	100

Note: SITC (Standard International Trade Classification):
0+1, Food, beverages and tobacco
2+4, Crude materials (excluding fuels), oils, fats
3, Mineral fuels and related materials
5, Chemicals
7, Machinery and transport equipment
6+8, Other manufactured goods
9, Commodities and transactions not classified elsewhere..
Here the 'East' means the USSR and the Six, the 'West' means developed market economies, the 'South' means deve
market (non-socialist) developing nations. The data for 1987 are not totally comparable with the data for the previous ye
in 1985 Yugoslavia was reclassified as a developing market economy.
Exports and imports are those of groups (the Six) or countries (the USSR) with their partners. Among the Six, total impo
equal to total exports by definition, and the commodity composition of trade is given under Exports.
Commodity composition is calculated as a percentage of total values at current prices in dollars.

				East–South Trade							
the USSR with the West				the Six with the South				the USSR with the South			
1970	1975	1980	1987	1970	1975	1980	1987	1970	1975	1980	1987
5	2	1	2	10	13	13	12	4	5	4	3
26	22	9	8	3	3	4	7	4	5	13	13
28	54	71	65	3	4	2	4	4	11	18	21
3	4	2	3	8	12	12	15	1	3	3	2
5	6	3	3	43	41	40	33	33	24	21	21
27	10	2	2	30	28	27	26	10	6	7	5
6	2	12	17	3	0	1	2	44	46	34	36
100	100	100	100	100	100	100	100	100	100	100	100
8	16	22	134	36	24	25	19	34	39	46	20
7	4	4	5	41	28	20	14	38	21	20	17
0	0	1	1	5	34	44	27	3	19	13	9
10	8	12	14	2	1	1	6	22	3	3	5
39	36	26	28	0	1	0	11	0	1	1	20
35	36	35	37	16	11	9	22	23	17	16	29
1	0	1	2	0	1	0	0	0	0	1	1
100	100	100	100	100	100	100	100	100	100	100	100

Table 6. *Foreign trade balances (1970–1988)*

Reporting countries	Partner countries or groupings	1970	1974	1975	1976	1977	1
Bulgaria	the USSR	111	32	−132	−108	−163	−
	other Five	53	−109	−28	81	94	
	developed ME	−65	−526	−843	−475	−388	−
	developing ME	44	154	282	246	373	
Czecho-slovakia	the USSR	12	33	−111	−67	−176	−
	other Five	80	−130	−158	−18	−78	−
	developed ME	−133	−393	−581	−773	−732	−
	developing ME	116	58	215	174	109	−
GDR	the USSR	−183	−41	−340	−388	−661	−
	other Five	125	187	153	8	−72	−
	delevoped ME	−293	−901	−1,018	−1,428	−1,308	−1,
	developing ME	3	−175	48	126	151	
Hungary	the USSR	−38	36	−94	−36	−31	−.
	other Five	−70	122	−161	−56	62	
	developed ME	−45	−593	−642	−487	−720	−1,
	developing ME	−45	−109	−129	−118	−153	−
Poland	the USSR	−99	13	49	−150	−272	−
	other Five	−96	−24	228	187	78	−
	developed ME	77	−2,310	−2,943	−3,258	−2,498	−2,
	developing ME	71	163	270	326	342	
Romania	the USSR	25	49	105	38	5	
	other Five	−42	38	−48	−100	−4	
	developed ME	−171	−456	−425	−80	−476	−
	developing ME	44	86	293	77	429	−
the USSR	the Six (Soviet data)	112	105	555	880	1414	
	the Six (partner data)	172	−122	523	711	1,298	1,4
	developed ME	−429	146	−4,936	−3,965	−1,504	−3,
	developing ME (total)	767	629	431	1,240	3,179	4,2
	developing ME (identified)	0	−668	−1,439	−1,046	−642	
Hungary	non-rouble trade balance with CMEA countries, expressed: in dollars in roubles						

Sources: The same as for Table 3. In addition, the Soviet foreign trade Yearbook (for figures ab identified Third World countries).

Symbols: the same as for Table 3. For each country, 'the Five' refers to the Six minus the country itsel

The Romanian data must be considered as estimates beginning from 1986, when Romania stopp publishing figures by partner country.

The data for 1988 are estimates.

The deficit of the country considered is shown by the minus sign.

Values are expressed in millions of transferable roubles (TR) for intra-CMEA trade (the first two ro for each country), and in millions of dollars for trade with non-socialist countries.

	979	1980	1981	1982	1983	1984	1985	1986	1987	1988
	243	−230	−525	−399	−256	−269	−94	44	293	1220
	−29	−24	−52	−191	−147	−61	−77	−52	−149	−142
	−43	−22	−718	−619	−445	−587	−943	−1,362	−1,397	−1,469
	701	1,012	1,370	1,260	824	1,176	865	268	967	267
	236	−109	−182	−272	−519	−453	−380	−481	−121	644
	236	−138	46	−35	53	−352	−315	−266	−106	−259
	803	−452	−322	−146	−29	197	66	−266	−427	−440
	319	459	639	630	808	599	565	561	381	321
	−10	−389	−386	−461	150	257	227	−443	−162	143
	372	234	104	410	530	404	236	364	551	419
	,855	−1,578	−443	818	876	910	876	145	−125	−383
	78	−12	566	721	441	246	245	218	417	362
	358	−27	376	499	535	423	734	231	569	802
	143	56	69	−95	−203	51	5	−103	−347	−112
	745	−707	−1,067	−580	−75	121	−583	−746	−603	−33
	63	33	276	237	24	43	360	157	215	196
	172	−708	−1,625	−621	−384	−622	−828	−1,122	107	1,276
	7	−105	−20	44	−166	−64	219	119	126	359
	,605	−843	−568	495	704	923	488	391	767	491
	−79	−141	593	949	732	643	445	781	447	565
	30	112	22	188	64	199	504	−318	−84	65
	−169	17	−106	−30	76	40	−157	−53	56	79
	−387	−146	245	1,369	2,197	2,486	2,259	2,235	2,896	3,767
	−692	−1,757	−34	96	132	294	−133	−238	−465	−552
	,058	1,824	3,149	1,972	1,624	1,883	945	2,638	61	−2,401
	645	1,351	2,320	1,066	410	465	−163	2,089	−602	−4,150
	,131	217	−1,202	−60	1,257	2,170	−851	−3,858	494	−2,727
	,732	2,740	1,240	4,788	4,508	4,161	2,355	6,610	7,914	6,949
	436	−1,881	−3,607	−1,549	−2,237	−2,625	−2,675	−957	−267	−1,549
		559	704	779	583	445	282	94	75	314
		656	900	1,098	957	823	530	155	130	609

or the USSR the balance of trade with the Six is shown (first line) according to the Soviet figures and (second line) ording to the figures of its partners.

A special problem is posed by the Hungarian trade with the CMEA countries (in fact, mainly with the USSR) in lars. The balances for this trade are given separately, in dollars and in roubles. To have a clear picture of the ngarian situation, the dollar balances are to be *added* to the balances with the developed market economies. The ne balances in roubles are to be *subtracted* from the transferable rouble balances of Hungary, and probably almost otality from the balances with the USSR.

or trade figures between the USSR and the Third World, see chapter 8, section on East–South trade, to account for distinction between the overall balance with the Third World countries and the balance with identified countries.

REFERENCES

Achkasov, A. I., and Preksin, O. M., 1988, *International Monetary and Credit Relations: Two Ways of Development* (in Russian), Moscow, Finansy i Statistika.

Altmann, F. L., and Clement, H., 1979, *Die Kompensation als Instrument in Ost–West Handel*, Munich, Osteuropa Institut.

Amann, Ronald, and Cooper, Julian, eds., 1982, *Industrial Innovation in the Soviet Union*, New Haven, Yale University Press.

1986, *Technical Progress and Soviet Economic Development*, Oxford, Basil Blackwell.

Amann, Ronald, Cooper, Julian, and Davies, Robert W., eds., 1977, *The Technological Level of Soviet Industry*, London and New Haven, Yale University Press.

An Analysis of Export Control of US Technology: A DoD Perspective, 1976, Washington, DC, US Department of Defense.

Arakelian, G., 1987, 'Joint construction of gas industry projects', *Foreign Trade* (in Russian) no. 1, pp. 14–15.

An Assessment of the Afghanistan Sanctions: Implications for Trade and Diplomacy in the 1980s, 1981, Washington, DC, Congressional Research Service.

Antonov, E., 1988, 'The DCCs: present and future', *Foreign Trade* (English version of *Vneshniaia Torgovlia*), vol. 12, pp. 46–50.

Assetto, Valerie J., 1987, *The Soviet Bloc in the IMF and the IBRD*, Boulder, Westview Press, Praeger Publishers.

Ausch, Sandor, 1972, *Theory and Practice of CMEA Cooperation*, Budapest, Akademiai Kiado.

Bach, Quintin V. S., 1987, *Soviet Economic Assistance to the Less Developed Countries: A Statistical Analysis*, Oxford, Clarendon Press.

1985, 'A note on Soviet statistics on their economic aid', *Soviet Studies*, vol. 37, no. 2, April 1985, pp. 269–75.

Bahri, S., 1986, 'Les relations économiques entre les pays socialistes européens et les pays de l'OPEP', PhD Dissertation, University of Paris I.

Balassa, Bela, and Tyson, Laura, 1985, 'Policy responses to external shocks in Hungary and Yugoslavia: 1974–76 and 1979–81', in *East European*

Economies: Slow Growth in the 1980s, vol. 1, *Economic Performance and Policy*, Washington, Joint Economic Committee, Congress of the United States, US GPO, pp. 57–80.

Balsam-Herzog, E., 1984, 'Les Échanges en compensation dans le commerce Est–Ouest', *Le Courrier des pays de l'Est*, no. 284, May, pp. 4–30.

Beaucourt, Chantal, 1984, 'L'Offre et la demande de produits agricoles en URSS et en Europe de l'Est à moyen et long terme', *Agriculture et agroindustrie dans les relations franco-soviétiques*, M. Lavigne, ed., Paris, Université de Paris I, pp. 153–68.

Becker, Abraham S., 1983, *East–West Economic Relations: Conflict and Concord In Western Policy Choices*, Santa Monica, The Rand Corporation, December.

ed., 1983, *Economic Relations with the USSR, Issues for the Western Alliance*, Lexington, D. C. Heath.

Bergson, Abram, 1983, 'Technological progress', in Bergson and Levine, eds., pp. 34–78.

Bergson, Abram, and Levine, Herbert, eds., 1983, *The Soviet Economy: Toward the Year 2000*, London, George Allen and Unwin.

Berliner, Joseph, 1976, *The Innovation Decision in Soviet Industry*, Cambridge, MIT Press.

Bertsch, Gary K., ed., 1988, *Controlling East–West Trade and Technology Transfer, Power, Politics and Policies*, Durham, Duke University Press.

Bertsch, Gary K., and McIntyre, John R., eds., 1983, *National Security and Technological Transfer: the Strategic Dimensions of East–West Trade*, Boulder, Westview Press.

Bethkenhagen, Jochen, 1987, 'Energy in the USSR: a new course? Coal and nuclear power not yet a substitute for oil', in NATO Colloquium.

Bethkenhagen, Jochen, and Machowski, Heinrich, 1986, 'Oil price collapse causes problems for Soviet foreign trade', *Economic Bulletin, DIW*, vol. 23, no. 5, July, pp. 1–4.

Bienkowski, Wojciech, 1988, 'The applicability of Western measurement methods to assess East European competitiveness', *Comparative Economic Studies*, vol. 30, no. 3, Autumn, pp. 33–50.

Birman, Igor, 1981, *Secret Incomes of the Soviet State Budget*, The Hague, Martinus Nijhoff Publishers.

Blaha, Jaroslav, 1987, 'Un projet "Eureka" pour les pays socialistes', *Le Courrier des Pays de l'Est*, December, no. 324, pp. 21–37.

Blaho, Andras, 1978, 'Socialist countries and the multinationals' (in Russian), *Acta Oeconomica*, vol. 20, no. 4, pp. 413–33.

Bogomolov, O. T., 1989, *Socialisme et compétitivité, les pays socialistes dans l'économie mondiale*, trans. from the Russian, Paris, Presses de la Fondation Nationale des Sciences Politiques.

1980, *The Socialist Countries in the International Division of Labour*, Moscow, Nauka; 2nd edn, 1986.

ed., 1982, *The World Socialist Economy: Questions of Political Economy*, Moscow, Ekonomika (in Russian); new editions in 1984 and 1988.

Bogomolov, O. T., and Bykov, A. N. 1986, *The CMEA Countries in the World Technology Trade* (in Russian), Moscow, 'International Relations'.

Borin, Vadim, 1988, 'La Coopération compensatoire', *Commerce Extérieur (URSS)*, no. 2, pp. 30–35.

Bornstein, Morris, 1985, *East–West Technology Transfer, The Transfer of Western Technology to the USSR*, Paris, OECD.

Brada, Josef C., 1985, 'Soviet subsidization of Eastern Europe: the primacy of economics over politics?', *Journal of Comparative Economics*, vol. 9, no. 1, March, pp. 80–92 (review article).

1988, 'Interpreting the Soviet subsidization of Eastern Europe', *International Organisation*, vol. 42, no. 4, Autumn, pp. 639–58.

Brada, Josef C., Hewett, Ed A., Wolf, Thomas A., eds., 1988, *Economic Adjustment and Reform in Eastern Europe and the Soviet Union*, Essays in Honor of Franklyn D. Holzman, Durham and London, Duke University Press.

Brada, Josef C., and Hoffman, Dennis L., 1985, 'The productivity differential between Soviet and Western capital and the benefits of technology imports to the Soviet economy', *Quarterly Review of Economics and Business*, vol. 25, no. 1, Spring, pp. 6–18.

Brainard, Lawrence, 1986, 'Trade and Payment Problems in Eastern Europe: The Debt Crisis Forces Policy Changes', in JEC, pp. 186–91.

Bubnov, Boris, 1987, *Foreign Trade with the USSR: A Manager's Guide to Recent Reforms*, Oxford, Pergamon Press.

Caillot, Jean, 1971, *Le CAEM, aspects juridiques et formes de coopération économique entre les Pays socialistes*, Paris, LGDJ.

Chadwick, Margaret, Long, David, and Nissanke, Machiko, 1987, *Soviet Oil Exports, Trade Adjustments, Refining Constraints and Market Behaviour*, Oxford Institute for Energy Studies, Oxford University Press.

Clark, Susan L., ed., 1989, *Gorbachev's Agenda: Changes in Soviet Domestic and Foreign Policy*, Boulder, Co, Westview Press.

Clement, Hermann, 1988–89, 'Changes in the Soviet foreign trade system', *Soviet and Eastern European Foreign Trade*, vol. 24, no. 4, Winter, special issue.

Cochrane, Nancy J., and Lambert, Miles J., 1988, *Agricultural Performance in Eastern Europe, 1987*, USDA, Economic Research Service, December.

Cook, E., Cummings, R., and Vankai, T. A., 1984, *Eastern Europe Agricultural Production and Trade Prospects Through 1990*, USDA, Foreign Agricultural Report no. 195, February.

Cooper, Julian, 1986, 'The civilian production of the Soviet defence industry', in Amann and Cooper, 1986.

Copelman, Serge, 1987, 'Le Secteur pétrolier de l'URSS', NATO, pp. 127–51.

Desai, Padma, 1976, 'The production function and technical change in the post-war Soviet industry', *American Economic Review*, vol. 66, no. 3, June, pp. 372–81.

1986, 'Is the Soviet Union subsidizing Eastern Europe?', *European Economic Review*, vol. 30, no. 1, pp. 107–16.

Després, Laure, 1988, 'Third World arms trade of the Soviet Union and Eastern Europe', in Lavigne, ed. (1988), pp. 51–63.

Dienes, Leslie, 1987, 'The Soviet oil industry in the twelfth five-year plan', *Soviet Geography*, vol. 28, no. 9, November, pp. 617–55.

Dienes, Leslie, and Merkin, Victor, 1985, 'Energy policy and conservation in Eastern Europe', in *Eastern European Economies: Slow Growth in the 1980s*, vol. 1, Joint Economic Committee, Congress of the United States, Sates, Washington, USGPO, pp. 332–55.

Dietz, Raimund, 1986, 'Soviet foregone gains in trade with the CMEA Six: a reappraisal', *Comparative Economic Studies*, vol. 28, no. 2, Summer, pp. 69–96.

1986, 'Advantages and disadvantages in Soviet trade with Eastern Europe: the pricing dimension', *East European Economies, Slow Growth in the 1980s*, vol. 2, Joint Economic Committee, Congress of the United States, Washington, USGPO, pp. 264–301.

Doronin, Igor, 1988, 'The problems of the improvement of the monetary and financial instruments', *Foreign Trade*, no. 4, pp. 33–36, and no. 6, pp. 24–27.

Drabek, Zdenek, 1988, 'The East European response to the debt crisis: a trade diversion or a statistical aberration?', *Comparative Economic Studies*, vol. 30, no. 1, Spring, pp. 29–58.

Dyba, Karel, and Kupka, Vaclav, 1987, 'Accommodating the Czechoslovak economy to external blows (a macroeconomic analysis for 1973–81)', *Soviet and Eastern European Foreign Trade*, vol. 23, no. 1, Spring, pp. 6–28.

ECE–UN, 1973, *Analytical Report on Industrial Cooperation Among the Countries of the ECE Region*, Geneva.

1982a, 'Reciprocal trading arrangements in East–West trade', *Economic Bulletin for Europe*, special issue, vol. 34, no. 2, June.

1982b, 'The relative performance of South European exports of manufactures to OECD countries in the 1970s: an analysis of demand factors and competitiveness', *Economic Bulletin for Europe*, vol. 34, no. 4, ch. 3.

1983, 'Exports of manufactures from Eastern Europe and the Soviet Union to the developed market economies, 1965–1981', *Economic Bulletin for Europe*, vol. 35, no. 4, 1983, ch. 3.

1986, 'Investments goods trade of the East European countries and the Soviet Union, 1975–83', *Economic Survey of Europe in 1985–86*, New York, ECE–UN, ch. 4.

1988b, *East–West Joint Ventures*, Geneva. This is the most comprehensive survey on joint ventures to date, with detailed analyses of the legislation and of the practice of Western firms involved in this activity. A permanent review is provided by ECE–UN, *East–West Joint Ventures*, a Quarterly Newsletter, as from the beginning of 1989.

1988a, 'East–West agricultural and food trade: development and prospects', *Economic Bulletin for Europe*, no. 40, pp. 49–86.

1989, 'The effects of Western European integration on imports of manufactures from Eastern and Southern Europe', *Economic Survey of Europe in 1988–1989*, New York, United Nations, prepublication text, ch. 2.5.

Economic Bulletin for Europe, 1981, vol. 33, no. 4; 1988, vol. 40.

Energie internationale 1987–1988, Rapport annuel sur les évolutions énergétiques mondiales, 1987, Institut d'Économie et de politique de l'Énergie, Grenoble; Paris, Economica.

Eichler, Gabriel, 1986, 'The debt crisis: a schematic view of rescheduling in Eastern Europe', in *JEC*, vol. 00.

Ekonomicheskaia Gazeto, 1988, 1989.

External Debt: Definition, Statistical Coverage and Methodology, 1988, Report of the International Working Group on External Debt Statistics, published for the World Bank, the Bank for International Settlements, the IMF and the OECD, Paris, OECD publications.

Fallenbuchl, Zbigniew, 1983, *East–West Technology Transfer: Study of Poland (1971–1980)*, Paris, OECD.

1986, 'The economic crisis in Poland and prospects for recovery', in *East European Economies: Slow Growth in the 1980s*, vol. 3, *Country Studies on Eastern Europe and Yugoslavia*, Washington, Joint Economic Committee, Congress of the United States, USGPO, pp. 359–98.

Fallenbuchl, Zbigniew, and McMillan, Carl, eds., 1980, *Partners in East–West Relations, The Determinants of Choice*, New York, Pergamon Press.

Feinberg, Richard E., 1989, 'The Soviet Union and the Bretton Wood institutions', Discussion Paper, Institute for East–West Security Studies, East–West Task Force on Seeking Security in the 1990s.

Fink, Gerhard, and Mauler, Kurt, 1988, 'Hard currency position of CMEA countries and Yugoslavia', Vienna Institute for Comparative Economic Studies, November 1988, Die Erste österreichische Spar-Casse-Bank, *Reprint-Serie*, no. 115, January 1989.

Fox, Lesley, 1982, 'Soviet policy in the development of nuclear power in Eastern Europe', in *Soviet Economy in the 1980s. Problems and Prospects*, Joint Economic Committee, Congress of the United States, Washington: USGPO, pp. 457–508.

Gabrisch, Hubert, and Stankovsky, Jan, 1989, *Special Forms of East–West Trade*, Part I–II, special issue of *Soviet and Eastern European Foreign Trade*, Spring, vol. 25, no. 1; Part III, *ibid.*, Summer, vol. 325, no. 2.

Gicquiau, Hervé, 1988, 'Situation et perspectives des industries soviétiques dites mécaniques. Productions et technologies', *Le Courrier des Pays de l'Est*, no. 332, September, pp. 3–37.

Gilbert, Jean-Paul, 1984, 'Un cas de coopération économique Pologne–RDA: la filature de coton polono-allemande de Zawiercie', *Economies et Sociétés*, vol. 18, no. 2, série G, 'Economie planifiée', no. 40, pp. 45–77.

Goldman, Marshall, 1975, *Détente and Dollars, Doing Business with the Soviets*, New York, Basic Books.

1980, *The Enigma of Soviet Petroleum: Half-Empty or Half-Full?*, London, Allen and Unwin.

Golt, Sidney, 1988, *The Gatt Negotiations 1986–90: Origins, Issues & Prospects*, London, British–North American Committee.

Gomulka, Stanislaw, Nove, Alec, and Holliday, George D., 1984, *East–West Technology Transfer*, I. *Contribution to Eastern Growth: An Econometric Evaluation* (Gomulka and Nove); II. *Survey of Sectoral Case Studies* (Holliday), Paris, OECD.

Gorski, V., Chebotareva, E., 1988, 'The single internal market of the European communities: problems for third countries', *Foreign Trade* (USSR), 12, pp. 35–9.

Graziani, Giovanni, 1987, 'The Non-European members of the CMEA: a model for developing countries?', in Kanet, ed., pp. 163–80.

Guide To Joint Ventures in the USSR, 1988, Laws, Regulations, Model Documents and Practical Information, Paris, International Chamber of Commerce.

Gustafson, Thane, 1981, *Selling the Russians the Rope? Soviet Technology Policy and US Export Controls*, Santa Monica, The Rand Corporation.

1985, *Soviet Negotiating Strategy, The East–West Gas Pipeline Deal, 1980–1984*, Santa Monica, Rand Corporation.

Gutman, Patrick, 1981, 'Tripartite industrial cooperation and East Europe', *East European Economic Assessment*, Part II *Regional Assessments*, Joint Economic Committee, Congress of the United States, Washington, USGPO, pp. 823–71.

Haegel, Françoise, 1983, 'Les Restrictions aux exportations de haute technologie vers les pays de l'Est', Ph.D. dissertation, University of Paris I.

Haendcke–Hoppe, Maria, ed., 1988, *Aussenwirtschaftssysteme und Aussenwirtschaftsreformen sozialistischer Lander, ein intrasystemarer Vergleich*, Berlin, Duncker und Humblot.

Hamilton, G., ed., 1986, *Red Multinationals or Red Herrings*, London, Frances Pinter.

Hamori, J., and Inotai, Andras, eds., 1987, *Hungary and the European Communities, Trends in World Economy*, vol. 57, Budapest, Hungarian Scientific Council for World Economy.

Hannigan, John B., and McMillan, Carl H., 1983, *East European Responses to the Energy Crisis*, East–West Commercial Relations Series, Ottawa, Carleton University, Institute of Soviet and East European Studies.

1981, 'Joint investment in resource development: sectoral approaches', *Joint Economic Committee, East European Economic Assessment*, Washington, USGPO, pp. 259–95.

Hanson, Philip, 1981, *Trade and Technology in Soviet–Western Relations*, New York, Columbia University Press.

1987, *Soviet Industrial Espionage: Some New Information*, London, The Royal Institute of International Affairs, Discussion Paper no. 1.

1988, *Western Economic Statecraft in East–West Relations. Embargoes, Sanctions, Linkage, Economic Warfare and Detente*, London, Chatham House Papers, no. 40, Royal Institute of International Affairs, London, Routledge and Kegan Paul.

1982, 'The end of import-led growth? Some observations on Soviet, Polish and Hungarian experience in the 1970s', *Journal of Comparative Economics*, vol. 6, no. 2, pp. 130–47.

Hewett, Ed A., 1974, *Foreign Trade Prices in the Council for Mutual Economic Assistance*, Cambridge University Press.

1984, *Energy Economics and Foreign Policy in the Soviet Union*, Washington, The Brookings Institution.

1987, 'Soviet oil', in Robert Mabro, ed., *The 1986 Oil Price Crisis, Economic Effects and Policy Responses*, Oxford, Oxford Institute for Energy Studies, pp. 129–31.

1988, *Reforming the Soviet Economy, Equality versus Efficiency*, Washington, The Brookings Institution.

Hill, Malcolm R., 1983, *East–West Trade, Industrial Cooperation and Technology Transfer: the British Experience*, Aldershot, Gower House.

Holzman, Franklyn, D., 1974, *Foreign Trade under Central Planning*, Cambridge, Mass., Harvard University Press.

1976, *International Trade under Communism, Politics and Economics*, New York, Basic Books.

1987a, *The Economics of Soviet Bloc Trade and Finance*, Boulder, Westview Press, Praeger Publishers.

1986, 'The significance of Soviet subsidies to Eastern Europe', *Comparative Economic Studies*, vol. 28, no. 1, pp. 54–65.

1987b, 'Dumping by centrally planned economies: the Polish golf cart case', in Holzman, 1987a, pp. 121–36.

1987c, 'Further thoughts on the significance of Soviet subsidies to Eastern Europe', *Comparative Economic Studies*, vol. 28, no. 3, pp. 59–64.

Inotai, Andras, 1982, *Auswirkungen weltwirtschaftlicher Veränderung aus den Westhandel der RGW-Länder*, Forschungsinstitut für internationale Politik und Sicherheit, Stiftung Wissenschaft und Politik, Ebenhausen, October (English text, mimeo).

International Transfer of Technology: An Agenda of National Security Issues, 1978, Washington, DC, Congressional Research Service.

Ivanov, Ivan D., 1987, 'Restructuring the mechanism of foregoing economic relations in the USSR', *Soviet Economy*, vol. 3, no. 3, pp. 192–218.

Jacquemin, Alexis, and Remiche, Bernard, eds., 1988, *Coopération entre entreprises. Entreprises conjointes, stratégies industrielles et pouvoirs publics*, Brussels, Association Internationale de Droit Economique, De Boeck Université.

Jentleson, Bruce W., 1986, *Pipeline politics: The Complex Political Economy of East–West Energy Trade*, Ithaca, NY, Cornell University Press.

Joint Economic Committee (JEC), 1979, *Soviet Economy in a Time of Change*, Part I, a compendium of papers submitted to the JEC, Washington DC, USGPO.

1986, *East European Economies: Slow Growth in the 1980s*, vol. 2, *Foreign Trade and International Finance*, selected papers submitted to JEC, Congress of the United States, Washington.

1987, *Gorbachev's Economic Plans*, study papers submitted to JEC, Congress of the United States, Washington, USGPO, vols. 1 and 2.

Kanet, Roger E., ed., 1987, *The Soviet Union, Eastern Europe and the Third World*, Cambridge University Press.

Kaser, Michael, 1984a, 'External relations of Comecon countries: gold sales and prospects', in Nato, *External Economic Relations of the CMEA Countries*, Brussels, pp. 157–70.

1984b, 'The Soviet impact on world trade in gold and platinum', in M. M. Kostecki, ed., 1984, *The Soviet Impact on Commodity Markets*, London, Macmillan, pp. 156–70.

1988, 'The impact of technological change on East–West economic relations', in Larrabee, ed. (1988), pp. 147–63.

Kelly, Margaret, *et al.*, 1988, *Issues and Developments in International Trade Policy*, Occasional Paper no. 63, Washington, DC, International Monetary Fund, December.

Kelly, William L., Shaffer, Hugh L. and Thompson, Hugh J., 1986, *Energy Research and Development in the USSR: Preparations for the Twenty-First Century*, Durham, NC, Duke University Press.

Kiss, Tibor, 1971, *International Division of Labour in Open Economies, with Special Regard to the CMEA*, Budapest, Akademiai Kiado.

Kornai, Janos, 1980, *Economics of Shortage*, Amsterdam, North–Holland, 2 vols.

Kostecki, M., 1984, 'The Soviet Union in international grain markets', in M. Kostecki, ed., 1984, *The Soviet Impact on Commodity Markets*, London, Macmillan, pp. 194–217.

Köves, Andras, 1983, ' "Implicit subsidies" and some issues of economic relations within the CMEA (remarks on the analyses made by Michael Marrese and Jan Vanous)', *Acta Oeconomica*, vol. 31, no. 1–2, pp. 125–36.

Krasznai, Zoltan, 1982, 'Le Poids des multinationales occidentales dans les échanges Est–Ouest', *Le Courrier des Pays de l'Est*, no. 267, November, pp. 3–18.

Labbé, Marie-Hélène, 1988, 'Controlling East–West trade in France', in Bertsch, ed., (1988), pp. 183–203.

Lachaux, Claude, Lacorne, Denis, and Lamoureux, Christian, avec la participation de M. H. Labbé, 1987, *De l'arme économique*, Paris, Fondation pour les Etudes de Défense Nationale.

Larrabee, F. Stephen, ed., 1988, *Technology and Change in East–West Relations*, New York, Institute for East–West Security Studies, Boulder, Westview Press.

Lavigne, Marie, 1968, 'Coefficient de capital et politique de l'investissement dans l'économie soviétique', *Annuaire de l'URSS 1967*, Paris, CNRS, pp. 267–306; 2, pp. 589–605.

1973, *Le Comecon (Le Programme du Comecon et l'intégration socialiste)*, Paris, Cujas.

1975, 'The problem of the multinational socialist enterprise', *The ACES Bulletin*, Summer, vol. 17, no. 1, pp. 33–61.

1976, 'Les Transferts de technologie entre les pays socialistes européens', *Mondes en Développement*, vol. 15, no. 2, pp. 589–605.

1978, 'The International Monetary Fund and the Soviet Union', in *International Economics – Comparisons and Interdependencies*, Essays in Honor of F. Nemschak, ed. by F. Levcik, Vienna–New York. Springer-Verlag, pp. 367–82.

1983a, *Les Économies socialistes soviétique et européennes*, Paris, Armand Colin, 3rd edn, p. 437. (In English: *The Socialist Economies of the Soviet Union and Europe*, London, Martin Robertson, 1974.)

1983b, 'The Soviet Union inside Comecon', *Soviet Studies*, vol. 35, no. 2, pp. 135–53.

1986, 'Eastern European countries and the IMF', in Béla Csikos-Nagy and David G. Young, eds., *East–West Economic Relations in the Changing Global Environment*, Proceedings of an IEA Conference, London, Macmillan, pp. 287–97.

1987, 'Soviet trade with LDCs', in JEC, vol. 2, pp. 504–31.

ed., 1988a, *East–South Relations in the World Economy*, Boulder, Westview Press (also author of chs. 2, 5, and 6).

1988b, 'Enterprises conjointes et coopération Est–Ouest', in Jacquemin and Remiche, eds., (1988), pp. 175–94.

Lemoine, Françoise, 1982, *Le Comecon*, Paris, PUF (series Que Sais-je?), no. 2032.

Lemoine, Françoise, and Seranne, C., 1976, 'L'Intégration économique à l'Est: le Comecon', Notes et etudes Documentaires, no. 4268.

Lenz, A., and Kravalis, M., 1977, 'An analysis of recent and potential Soviet and East European exports to fifteen industrialized Western countries', *East European Economies post-Helsinki*, Joint Economic Committee, Congress of the United States, Washington, USGPO, pp. 1055–131.

Leptin, Gert, 1989, 'Economic relations between the two German states', in F. Stephen Larrabee, ed., *The Two German States and European Security*, New York, The Institute for East–West Security Studies, London, Macmillan, 1989, pp. 269–92.

Levcik, Friedrich, and Skolka, Jiri, 1984, *East–West Technology Transfer: Study of Czechoslovakia*, Paris, OECD.

Lhomel, Edith, 1987, 'Les Aménagements de l'organisation du commerce extérieur roumain', *Le Courrier des pays de l'Est*, no. 314, January, pp. 64–71.

Liebrenz, Marylin L., 1982, *Transfers of Technology: US Multinationals and Eastern Europe*, New York, Praeger.

Mabro, Robert, ed., 1988, *The 1986 Oil Price Crisis, Economic Effects and Policy Responses*, Oxford University Press.

Maksimenko, V., 1989, 'The Socialist orientation: a *perestroika* in understanding', *MEiMO* (*World economy and international relations*), no. 2, pp. 93–103.

Marer, Paul, 1985, *Dollar GNPs and Growth Rates of the USSR and Eastern*

Europe, Baltimore and London, The Johns Hopkins Press for the World Bank.

1986, *East–West Technology Transfer: Study of Hungary 1968–1984)*, Paris, OECD.

Maresceau, M., ed., 1989, *The Political and Legal Framework of Trade Relations Between the European Community and Eastern Europe*, Dordrecht, Kluwer Academic Publishers.

Marples, David R., 1987, *Chernobyl and Nuclear Power in the USSR*, New York, St Martin's Press.

Marrese, Michael, and Vanous, Jan, 1983, *Soviet Subsidization of Trade With Eastern Europe: A Soviet Perspective*, Berkeley, University of California, Institute of International Studies.

Martens, John A., 1986, 'Quantification of Western exports of high-technology products to communist countries', in Joint Economic Committee, pp. 91–114.

Matejka, Harriet, 1988, 'Export restraint arrangements and the small country: issues raised by evidence on Eastern Europe', in Dobozi, Istavan and Harriet Matejka, eds., *End-Century Small Country Options: Hungarian and Swiss Economic and Political Perspectives, Trends in World Economy*, vol. 60, Budapest, Hungarian Scientific Council for World Economy, pp. 169–85.

1988, 'More joint enterprises within the CMEA?', in John P. Hardt and Carl H. McMillan, eds., *Planned Economies: Confronting the Challenges of the 1980s*, Cambridge University Press, pp. 171–89.

Maull, Hanns W., 1981, *Natural Gas and Economic Security*, Atlantic Papers no. 43, Paris, Atlantic Institute.

McIntyre, John, 1988, 'The distribution of power and the inter-agency politics of licensing East–West high technology trade', in Bertsch, ed., (1988), pp. 97–133.

McMillan, Carl H., 1985, 'Eastern Europe's relations with OPEC suppliers in the 1980s', in Joint Economic Committee, *Eastern European Economies: Slow Growth in the 1980s*, vol. 1, *Economic Performance and Policy*, Washington, USGPO, pp. 368–82.

1986, 'Trends in direct investment and the transfer of technology', in Bela Csikos-Nagy and David G. Young, eds., *East–West Relations in the Changing Global Environment*, London, Macmillan, pp. 260–75.

1987, *Multinationals from the Second World, Growth of Foreign Investment by Soviet and East European Enterprises*, London, Trade Policy Research Center, Macmillan.

McMillan, Carl H., and Kevin G. White, 1989, *The East–West Business Directory, A Listing of Contact Points in the OECD Countries for the Conduct of Business with Eastern Europe and the Soviet Union*, Ottawa, Carleton University, Duncan Publishing.

Merkin, Victor, 1988, 'Intra-Comecon bargaining and world energy prices: a backdoor connection?', *Comparative Economic Studies*, vol. 30, no. 4, Winter, pp. 25–51.

Mesa-Lago, Carmelo, and Gil, Fernando, 1988, 'Vingt ans de relations économiques entre l'URSS et Cuba', *Le Courrier des pays de l'Est*, no. 335, December, pp. 52–73.

Moe, Arild, and Bergesen, Helge Ole, 1987, 'The Soviet gas sector: challenges ahead', in NATO, pp. 153–74.

Morgan, Dan, 1979, *Merchants of Grain*, New York, Viking.

Moreton, Edwina, and Segal, Gerald, eds., 1984, *Soviet Strategy Toward Western Europe*, London, George Allen and Unwin.

Nagels, J., 1986, *Laissez faire, laissez troquer*, Brussels, Editions de l'ULB.

NATO, ed., 1987, *The Soviet Economy: A New Course?*, Nato Colloquium, 1–3 April, Brussels, NATO.

  1988, *The Economies of Eastern Europe Under Gorbachev's Influence*, Nato Colloquium, 23–5 March 1988, Brussels, Nato.

Nau, Henry N., 1988, 'Export controls and free trade: squaring the circle in Cocom', in Bertsch, ed., pp. 390–416.

Nême, Jacques and Colette, 1986, 'L'Avenir de l'ECU dans les relations CEE-pays de l'Est', *Le Courrier des Pays de l'Est*, no. 303, February, pp. 28–36.

Neuberger, Egon, Portes, Richard, and Tyson, Laura d'Andrea, 1981, 'The impact of international economic disturbances on the Soviet Union and Eastern Europe: a survey', in *Eastern European Economic Assessment*, Part 2, Joint Economic Committee, Congress of the United States, Washington, USGPO, pp. 128–47.

Neuberger, Egon, and Tyson, Laura d'Andrea, eds., 1980, *The Impact of International Economic Disturbances on the Soviet Union and Eastern Europe, Transmission and Response*, New York, Pergamon Press.

OECD, 1981, *Les Échanges Est–Ouest, l'évolution récente des échanges compensés*, Paris.

  East–West Technology Transfer Data Basis, Paris, OECD, permanent update.

  1980–86, *East–West Technology Transfer*, a series of surveys and country studies, see Zaleski and Wienert (1980), Gomulka, Nove and Holliday (1984), Fallenbuchl (1983), Levcik and Skolka (1984), Bornstein (1986), Marer (1987), Wienert and Slater (1987), Paris, OECD.

  1981, 1982, *Trends and Prospects of Agricultural Production and Trade in Eastern Europe*, vol. 1, *Poland, GDR, Hungary*, vol. 2, *Bulgaria, Czechoslovakia, Romania*, Paris.

  1983, *Prospects for Soviet Agricultural Production and Trade*, Paris.

  1985, *Countertrade: Developing Country Practices*, Paris.

  1987, *The Export Credit Financing Systems in OECD Member Countries*, Paris.

  1988, *Financial Market Trends*, no. 39.

Office of Technology Assessment (OTA), 1979 (1983), Congress of the United States, *Technology and East–West Trade*, Washington, DC, updated.

  1981, Congress of the United States, *Technology and Soviet Energy Availability*, Washington, DC.

Olechowski, A., and Yeats, A., 1982, *The Influence of Non-Tariff Barriers on*

Exports from Socialist Countries of Eastern Europe, UNCTAD, Discussion Papers, no. 6.

Paszynski, M., 1980, 'The concept of new international economic order and the socialist countries', *Development and Peace*, vol. 1, Autumn, pp. 26–41.

Percebois, Jacques, 1988, 'Le Marché international du gaz naturel: constraintes et stratégies', *Energie internationale 1987/88*, Paris, Economica, pp. 75–87.

Pinder, John, 1988, 'The EC and Eastern Europe: how normal could relations become?', Nato, pp. 266–79.

Pissula, Petra, 1984, 'The IMF and the countries of Eastern Europe', *Intereconomics*, vol. 19, no. 2, 4 March, pp. 65–70.

   1988, 'Das Verhältnis der Sowjetunion zum GATT und zum Internationalen Währungsfonds', *Osteuropa Wirtschaft*, no. 4, pp. 319–41.

PlanEcon, 1988, 'Top commodities in East–West trade: what can be bought and what can be sold', *PlanEcon Report*, vol. 4, no. 12–13, 30 March.

Poisson, Véronique, 1988, 'The renegotiation of the 1982 gas contract between France and the USSR', *Soviet and Eastern European Foreign Trade*, vol. 24, no. 2, Summer, pp. 26–37.

Portes, Richard, 1980, 'Effects of the world economic crisis on the East European economies', *The World Economy*, no. 3, pp. 13–52.

   1983, 'Central planning and monetarism: fellow travellers?', in Padma Desai, ed., *Marxism, Central Planning, and the Soviet Economy*, Essays in Honor of Alexander Ehrlich, Cambridge, MIT Press, pp. 149–65.

Poznanski, Kazimierz, 1986, 'Competition between Eastern Europe and developing countries in the Western market for manufactured goods', in *East European Economies: Slow Growth in the 1980s*, vol. 2, *Foreign Trade and International Finance*, selected papers submitted to the Joint Economic Committee, Congress of the United States, Washington, DC, USGPO, pp. 62–90.

   1988, 'Opportunity cost in Soviet trade with Eastern Europe: discussion of methodology and new evidence', *Soviet Studies*, vol. 40, no. 2, April, pp. 290–307.

Pravitel'strennyi Vestnik (Government Monitor), 1989, no. 4.

Primakov, E., 1980, 'The law of inegality in development and the historical fates of the developing countries', *Mirovaia Ekonomika i Mezhdunarodnye Otnosheniia* (in Russian), no. 12, pp. 28–42.

Pryor, Frederic L., 1963, *The Communist Foreign Trade System*, London, Allen and Unwin.

Rosefielde, Steven, 1973, *Soviet International Trade in Heckscher–Ohlin Perspective*, Lexington, D. C. Heath.

Salgo, Istvan, 1986, 'Economic mechanism and foreign trade organization in Hungary', *Acta Oeconomica*, vol. 36, nos. 3–4, pp. 271–87.

Samson, Ivan, 1984, 'La Cooperation économique entre la RDA et ses partenaires du CAEM: une forme d'insertion dans la DIST?', *Economies et Sociétés*, série G, 'Economie planifiée', vol. 40, pp. 79–114.

Saunders, Christopher, ed., 1981a, *East–West–South Economic Interactions between Three Worlds*, London, Macmillan.

1981b, *Regional Integration in East and West*, London, Macmillan.

Schiavone, Giuseppe, 1981, *The Institutions of Comecon*, London, Macmillan.

1989, 'Export controls: general framework', in Maresceau, ed., (1989), pp. 241–54.

Schoppe, Siegfried, 1978, 'Funktionswandlungen des Goldes im Rahmen der Sowjetischen Aussenhandelsregie seit 1945–1946', *Osteuropa Wirtschaft*, vol. 23, no. 1, pp. 27–45.

Senin, M., 1986, *Socialist Integration*, Moscow.

Shastitko, V. M., ed., 1988, *The Management of Socialist Economic Integration*, in Russian, Moscow, Nauka, 1988.

Shastitko, V., and Simanovski, S., 1983, *The International Socialist Division of Labour in the Conditions of the Scientific–Technical Revolution*, Moscow, Nauka.

Shlaim, Avi, and Yannopoulis, G. N., 1978, *The EEC and Eastern Europe*, Cambridge University Press.

Sheinis, Viktor Leonidovitch, 1988, 'Capitalism, socialism and the economic mechanism of contemporary production', *MEiMO* (*World economy and international relations*), in Russian, pp. 5–23.

Shiriaev, Ju. S., 1977, *The International Socialist Division of Labour (problems of theory)* (in Russian), Moscow, Nauka.

Shmelev, N. P., ed., 1978, *The Comecon Countries in the World Economic Relations* (in Russian), Moscow, Nauka.

Shmelev, N., 1987, 'Avansy i Dolgi' (Assets and liabilities), *Novyi Mir*, vol. 6, pp. 142–58.

Simai, Mihaly, 1984, *International Technology Transfer and Economic Development in the Late 20th Century*, Budapest: Trends in World Economy, no. 48.

Simanovsky, S., 1980, 'Conditions and prospects for licence exchanges of the CMEA countries', *Foreign Trade*, no. 2, pp. 18–21.

1983, 'The development of relations between the East and the developing countries in the field of technology transfer', *Foreign Trade*, no. 3, pp. 28–35.

Sinclair, Craig, ed., 1988, *The Status of Soviet Civil Science*, A Nato Symposium, The Hague, Martinus Nijhoff.

Sobell, Vladimir, 1984, *The Red Market, Industrial Co-operation and Specialisation in Comecon*, Aldershot, Gower.

1986, 'Technology flows within Comecon and channels of communication', in Amann and Cooper, (1986), pp. 135–52 (and the numerous notes of this author in *Radio Free Europe Research* publications.

1988, 'The Cmea's post-Chernobyl nuclear energy program', *RFE/RAD Background Report*, 15 February.

Sobeslavsky, V., and Beazley, P., 1980, *The Transfer of Technology to Socialist Countries: The Case of the Soviet Chemical Industry*, Westmead, Gower.

Sokoloff, Georges, 1983, *L'Économie de la détente: l'URSS et le capital occidental*, Paris, Presses de la Fondation Nationale des Sciences Politiques.

Stern, Jonathan P., 1987a, *Soviet Oil and Gas Exports to the West: Commercial Transaction or Security Threat?*, Aldershot, Gower.

1987b, 'Soviet Oil and Gas Production and Exports to the West, A Framework for Analysing and Forecasting', JEC, pp. 500–13.

Tasky, Kenneth, 1979, 'Soviet Technology Gap and Dependence from the West: The Case of Computers', JEC, Soviet Economy . . ., pp. 510–23.

Thornton, Judith, 1987, 'Soviet Electric Power in the Wake of the Chernobyl Accident', JEC, pp. 514–32.

Tiraspolsky, Anita, 1986, 'Les Choix énergétiques à l'Est', *Le Courrier des Pays de l'Est*, Panorame de l'Europe de l'Est, no. 309, 310, 311, August–September–October, pp. 250–65.

1987, 1988, 'Les Sociétés à capital mixte URSS–Ouest', *Le Courrier des Pays de l'Est*, no. 324, 326, 327, 329, 332 , updated lists of joint ventures in the USSR.

Tiraspolsky, Anita, and Zouheyri, Hafida, 1987, 'Les Sociétés à capital mixte en URSS: projets et réalités, *Le Courrier des Pays de l'Est*, no. 323, November, pp. 27–60.

Treml, Vladimir, and Kostinsky, Barry, 1982, *The Domestic Value of Soviet Foreign Trade*, US Department of Commerce, Washington, USGPO.

Tretyakova, Albina, and Kostinsky, Barry, 1987, 'Fuel use and conservation in the Soviet Union: the transportation sector', in JEC, pp. 545–66.

Trzeciakowski, Witold, 1978, *Indirect Management in a Centrally Planned Economy: System Constructions in Foreign Trade*, Amsterdam, North Holland.

UNCTAD, 1984, *Recent Developments in East–West Cooperation in Third Countries and Tripartite Cooperation*, TD/B/100, Geneva, United Nations, June.

USDA, 1988, *USSR, Agriculture and Trade Report*, Situation and Outlook Series, Economic Research Service, May.

Valkenier, Elizabeth K., 1983, *The Soviet Union and the Third World: an Economic Bind*, New York, Praeger.

Van Brabant, Jozef, 1973, *Bilateralism and Structural Bilateralism*, Rotterdam, Rotterdam University Press.

1980, *Socialist Economic Integration, Aspects of contemporary economic problems in Eastern Europe*, Cambridge University Press.

1984, 'The USSR and socialist economic integration: a comment', *Soviet Studies*, vol. 36, no. 1, January, pp. 127–38.

1985, 'World prices and price-formation in intra-CMEA Trade: selected empirical evidence', *Osteuropa Wirtschaft*, vol. 30, no. 3, September, pp. 163–80.

1985, 'The relationship between world and socialist trade prices – some empirical evidence', *Journal of Comparative Economics*, vol. 9, no. 3, September, pp. 233–51.

1987a, 'Further evidence on the relationship between socialist and world trade prices', *Osteuropa Wirtschaft*, vol. 32, no. 2, June, pp. 122–44.

1987b, 'Socialist and world market prices: an ingrowth?', *Journal of Comparative Economics*, vol. 11, no. 1, January, pp. 21–39.

1987c, *Adjustment, Structural Change, and Economic Efficiency, Aspects of Monetary Cooperation in Eastern Europe*, Cambridge University Press.

1988, 'Production specialization in the CMEA – concepts and empirical evidence', *Journal of Common Market Studies*, vol. 26, no. 3, March, pp. 287–315.

Van Hoof, L., 1983, *La Compensation dans les échanges Est–Ouest – analyse théorique et vérification empirique dans l'UEBL*, Ph.D. dissertation, University of Paris I, and appendices.

Vankai, T., et al., 1984, *Eastern Europe, Outlook and Situation Report*, Washington, USDA, May.

Vanous, Jan, 1982a, 'Dependence of Soviet economy on foreign trade', Wharton Econometric Forecasting Associates, *Centrally Planned Economies, Current Analysis*, 14 July.

1982b, 'Comparative Advantages in Soviet grain and energy trade', *Centrally Planned Economies Current Analysis*, Wharton, 10 September.

1985, 'Macroeconomic adjustment in Eastern Europe in 1981–83: response to Western credit squeeze and deteriorating terms of trade with the Soviet Union', in *East European Economies: Slow Growth in the 1980's*, vol. 1, *Economic Performance and Policy*, Washington, Joint Economic Committee, Congress of the United States, USGPO, pp. 22–56.

ed., 1989, 'Soviet energy trade during 1986–87: quantity statistics are released for the first time since 1976';, *PlanEcon Report*, vol. 4, no. 28, 15 July.

Vine, Richard D., ed., 1987, *Soviet–East European Relations as a Problem for the West*, An Atlantic Institute for International Affairs Research Volume, London, Croom Helm.

Wallace, William V., and Clarke, Roger A., 1986, *Comecon Trade and the West*, New York, St Martin's Press.

Warner, David, and Kaiser, Louis, 1987, 'Development of the USSR's Eastern coal basins', in JEC, pp. 533–44.

Weitzman, Martin L., 1970, 'Soviet Post-War Economic Growth and Capital-Labor Substitution', *American Economic Review*, vol. 60, September, pp. 676–92.

1979, 'Technology transfer to the USSR: an econometric analysis', *Journal of Comparative Economics*, vol. 3, no. 2, pp. 167–77.

Wienert, Helgard, and Slater, John, 1986, *East–West Technology Transfer, The Trade and Economic Aspects*, Paris, OECD.

Wilczynski, J., 1974, *Technology in Comecon*, London, Macmillan.

Wild, Gérald, 1981, 'De la compensation Est–Ouest au retour du bilatéralisme d'Etat', *Economie prospective internationale*, no. 6, April.

Wiles, Peter, 1968, *Communist International Economics*, Oxford, Basil Blackwell.

ed., 1982, *The New Communist Third World*, London, Croom Helm.

Wolf, Charles, 1985, 'The Costs of the Soviet Empire', *Science*, 29 November, vol. 230, no. 4729, pp. 997–1002.

Wolf, Thomas A., 1975, 'Estimating "Foregone Gains" in Soviet–East European foreign trade: a methodological note', *Comparative Economic Studies*, vol. 27, no. 3, Autumn, pp. 83–98.

1987, 'On the conversion of ruble trade flows into dollars', *Journal of Comparative Economics*, vol. 11, no. 4, pp. 558–71.

1988, *Foreign Trade in the Centrally Planned Economy*, International Monetary Fund, Chur, Harwood Academic Publishers.

Zaleski, Eugène, 1980, 'Advanced technology and the choice of partners: the Soviet policy', in Fallenbuchl, McMillan, pp. 343–69.

1981, 'Le Niveau technologique en URSS à travers une récente publication du Congrès américain', *Analyses de la SEDEIS*, no. 21, May, pp. 5–12.

ed., 1969, *Science Policy in the USSR*, Paris, OECD.

Zaleski, Eugène, and Wienert, Helgard, eds., 1980, *Technology Transfer between East and West*, Paris, OECD.

Zloch-Christy, Iliana, 1987, *Debt Problems of Eastern Europe*, Cambridge, Cambridge University Press.

Zverev, Andrei, 1988, 'The monetary instruments of the foreign trade activities of the industries', *Foreign Trade*, no. 7, pp. 37–41.

INDEX